Agency Uncovered

Archaeological perspectives on social agency, power, and being human

Edited by Andrew Gardner

UCL
PRESS

First published in Great Britain 2004 by UCL Press
An imprint of Cavendish Publishing Limited, The Glass House,
Wharton Street, London WC1X 9PX, United Kingdom
Telephone: + 44 (0)20 7278 8000 Facsimile: + 44 (0)20 7278 8080
Email: info@cavendishpublishing.com
Website: www.cavendishpublishing.com

Published in the United States by Cavendish Publishing
c/o International Specialized Book Services,
5824 NE Hassalo Street, Portland,
Oregon 97213-3644, USA

Published in Australia by Cavendish Publishing (Australia) Pty Ltd
45 Beach Street, Coogee, NSW 2034, Australia
Telephone: + 61 (2)9664 0909 Facsimile: + 61 (2)9664 5420
Email: info@cavendishpublishing.com.au
Website: www.cavendishpublishing.com.au

British Library Cataloguing in Publication Data
Agency uncovered: archaeological perspectives on social agency, power and
being human
1 Social archaeology   2 Agent (Philosophy)
I Gardner, Andrew
930.1

Library of Congress Cataloguing in Publication Data
Data available

ISBN 1-84472-038-1

3 5 7 9 10 8 6 4 2

Typeset by Phoenix Photosetting, Chatham, Kent
Printed and bound in Great Britain

Cover illustration: the individual is subordinated to the group in the porphyry statue of
the Tetrarchs (four Roman emperors, late 3rd/early 4th centuries AD),
St Mark's Basilica, Venice. © Andrew Gardner.

Acknowledgments

Many people were involved in the conference that initiated the preparation of this volume, which was held in the Institute of Archaeology, UCL, on 8 November 2001. This event was sponsored by the Institute's Social and Cultural Dynamics Research Group, whose co-ordinator, Ruth Whitehouse, did much to help with the organisation. In addition to the authors of a number of the chapters in this volume, John Barrett and John Robb contributed much to the day's proceedings, and Camilla Briault, Sarah McCarthy and Ash Rennie also lent invaluable assistance with publicising and running the event. Subsequent to the conference, Cyprian Broodbank, Peter Ucko, the anonymous referees, Ruth Massey at UCL Press, and of course the contributors are all owed many thanks for making this volume possible.

Andrew Gardner
May 2004

Contents

COMMENTARY

About the contributors

Andrew Gardner is currently a Lecturer in Roman Archaeology at the University of Leicester, and a Teaching and Learning Co-ordinator in the School of Continuing Education, University of Reading. His research interests include the social dynamics of the Roman empire, understandings of time in past societies, and the development of archaeological theory.

Brad Gravina is a graduate research student in the Department of Archaeology, University of Cambridge. He is currently pursuing his work on the Palaeolithic period with a thesis focused on the Chatelperronian. He has participated in archaeological projects in France, Bulgaria and Great Britain.

Fiona J.L. Handley recently completed her PhD at the Institute of Archaeology, University College London. Her research interests include the presentation of Transatlantic slavery to the public at heritage sites in Europe and the USA, historical archaeology, especially of Louisiana, USA, and the relationship between different perceptions of heritage at local, national and global levels.

Matthew Johnson is Professor in Archaeology at the University of Durham. His interests include archaeological theory, historic landscapes, and buildings. He is currently working on the theoretical and cultural background to English landscape interpretation, and on a new account of vernacular architecture.

Peter Jordan currently holds a Leverhulme Trust Special Research Fellowship at University College London to investigate cultural and linguistic transmission amongst a range of indigenous groups. From March 2005 he will be taking up a Lectureship in Material Culture at the Department of Archaeology, University of Sheffield.

Stephanie Koerner is currently lecturing in the University of Manchester's School of Art History and Archaeology on the archaeology of the pre-Columbian Americas, Latin-American art history and on the history of the philosophy of the human sciences. She is pursuing cross-disciplinary projects in archaeology and areas of overlap between the histories of art, science and the humanities, relating the courses she offers at Manchester and as a Research Associate of the Universities of Pittsburgh and Vienna.

Mark W. Lake is a Lecturer at the Institute of Archaeology, University College London. His major research interests are mechanisms of cultural change, the human use of space, and quantitative methodologies for exploring both of these areas.

Astrid Lindenlauf is Academic Secretary at the German Archaeological Institute in Athens. Her interests include the perception and management of waste and dirt across time within the field of Greek archaeology, the archaeology of value, and biographies of votive offerings. Recent fieldwork includes excavations at the Kerameikos cemetery.

Justin Morris is a curator in the Department of Asia at the British Museum. He recently submitted his PhD thesis which explores the nature of cultural change during the later prehistoric period in the Northwest Frontier Province, Pakistan through lithic technology. His other interests include research into experimental lithic technology and its role in helping us to understand the nature of lithic technologies employed in the past.

Tim Schadla-Hall is Reader in Public Archaeology at the Institute of Archaeology, University College London. His research interests include all aspects of public involvement in archaeology, as well as post-glacial Northwestern Europe.

Stephen Shennan is Director of the AHRB Centre for the Evolutionary Analysis of Cultural Behaviour and Professor of Theoretical Archaeology at the Institute of Archaeology, University College London.

Bill Sillar is a Lecturer at the Institute of Archaeology, University College London. His research has focused on how people make and use material culture to shape the world they live in, with a particular focus on the Andes. He undertook ethnographic fieldwork in Peru and Bolivia to study modern pottery production, exchange and use. More recently Bill has been working at Raqchi, near Cuzco, Peru, with the aim of placing the construction of the Inka site within a longer-term understanding of continuity and change in landscape development.

List of figures

CHAPTER 1

INTRODUCTION: SOCIAL AGENCY, POWER, AND BEING HUMAN

Andrew Gardner

The systematic study of the relationship of the individual to society has, from its very beginning, been marked by acrimonious contention over both its proper procedure and its goal.

Schutz 1967: 3

AN INTERDISCIPLINARY PROBLEM

The problem of agency is, in many respects, the problem of the human condition. It concerns the nature of individual freedom in the face of social constraints, the role of socialisation in the forming of 'persons', and the place of particular ways of doing things in the reproduction of cultures. In short, it is about the relationships between an individual human organism and everyone and everything else that surrounds it. It is no surprise, then, that the literature on the subject across the human sciences is vast – and expanding. Within this context, the present volume represents the continuing engagement of archaeologists with these issues, insofar as they are essential considerations in understanding people in the past and their ways of life, or 'life-worlds' (Schutz and Luckmann 1973: 3). As such, it is also indicative of the widening commitment of practitioners in the discipline to addressing the diversity of human life – past and present – at a profound level.

In part, this book is a response to the call for dialogue on the subject of agency framed by Dobres and Robb (2000: 4), taking up some of the questions posed in their volume, as well as others that have emerged in the ongoing debate upon how archaeologists can best proceed towards understanding the historical constitution of human societies (cf. also Dornan 2002; Ortner 2001). The goal of this volume is to focus attention on three main themes within this debate: the problematic notion of individualism; the connection between agency and power; and the relationship between definitions of agency and of what it is to be 'human'. These are all themes which have arisen in archaeologists' confrontations with past ways of life, but which also bear strikingly upon current discussions across a range of disciplines. My aim in this Introduction is to summarise some of these debates, and in doing so to demonstrate how the chapters included in this volume will help to move them forward.

Although Alfred Schutz's remark which opened this chapter was first published (in German) in 1932, and was part of a commentary on the previous half-century of scholarship, it could be argued that little has changed since then. Disagreement is still commonplace, particularly over the success – or otherwise – of the widely-cited ideas of Anthony Giddens and Pierre Bourdieu, who might both be labelled 'structurationists' (Parker 2000: 5) – that is, theorists who attempt to unite 'the individual' (agency) and 'the social' (structure) within a single analytical framework. Their work, following on from that of some of the leading figures of late 19th and earlier 20th century sociology, philosophy and social psychology (e.g. Marx, Durkheim, Weber, Elias, Parsons, Goffman, Mead, Merleau-Ponty), has been extremely influential, in practical ways, in a wide range of fields, including accountancy, geography, and of course archaeology (Bryant and Jary 2001; Jenkins 1992). At the same time, the theoretical debate has continued around the key concepts developed by Giddens and Bourdieu, such as the duality of structure (Parker 2000) and *habitus* (Crossley 2001), as well as opening up areas of enquiry that they have tended to neglect, like the place of ethics (Barnes 2000), emotion (Archer 2000) or temporality (Emirbayer and Mische 1998) in theories of agency.

All this is in spite of the fact that these two individuals turned to other, albeit related, interests during the 1990s, having published their most influential 'structurationist' works in the 1970s and 1980s. Anthony Giddens has increasingly engaged with practical politics in his recent publications (e.g. 2000), and the same was true for Pierre Bourdieu before his death in 2002 (e.g. 1999). The connection that Giddens and Bourdieu have made, implicitly or explicitly, between academic theory and politics is actually an important issue to pursue at a later stage. For now, we must remain with the 'structuration' debate, and examine it in more detail as the background for the three sections which follow. Although it is Giddens who is primarily associated with the term 'structuration', Bourdieu's work has also been given this label, as their agendas have much in common (Parker 2000: 5). In essence, both scholars attempt to unite the concerns of micro-, actor-centred sociologies and macro-, structure-centred sociologies, by positing a framework which connects both levels in a strongly recursive fashion. Thus, rather than arguing that actors are the fundamental units upon which all else that is 'social' builds, or conversely that individual action is wholly determined by social forces (cf. e.g. Garfinkel for the former view [1984 (1967)]; Parsons for the latter [1951]; Parker 2000: 14–36), Giddens and Bourdieu put forward a mechanism to bring these two approaches firmly together.

For Giddens, this is the duality of structure, a simple equation that makes actors dependent upon the rules and resources of structure, but allows them knowledgable and conscious choice in manipulating these. The latter creates room for change, while the former ensures structural reproduction through more routine actions (Giddens 1993 [1976], 1979, 1984). For Bourdieu, the key concept is *habitus*, which effectively accommodates the duality of structure within a single framework of shared dispositions that simultaneously constrain and enable individual actors (Bourdieu 1977 [1972], 1990 [1980]). Now, it will be left for later sections, and individual chapters within this volume, to discuss in detail the utility or otherwise of these specific accounts of social life. Suffice it to say here that much of the debate in the social sciences more broadly has focused – whether in agreement or disagreement – upon these two sets of approaches (which, interestingly, have rarely been compared by their authors [Parker 2000: 39–40]).

Critics of the structurationist approach include Margaret Archer and Nicos Mouzelis, who have both argued that, while a balance between agency and structure has to be maintained, it is nonetheless necessary to avoid conflating these concepts within a single framework. Rather, an analytical dualism should be kept intact to allow us to see what is particular about actors and what is particular about structures (Archer 1996 [1988], 1995, 2000; Mouzelis 1995; Parker 2000: 69–101). In this vein, Archer has argued for a multi-level understanding of agency (2000), which succeeds in incorporating aspects such as emotionality (see below). This work draws on a number of other inspirations too, such as the writings of Rom Harré, and this reminds us of the obvious fact that there are many other independent traditions dealing with the self/society problem which Bourdieu and Giddens sometimes refer to, and sometimes ignore – traditions as diverse as psychoanalysis, Foucauldian post-structuralism, queer theory, and American pragmatism (cf. Cohen 2000; Elliott 2001; Emirbayer and Mische 1998). Threads from some of these traditions are woven into a number of chapters in this book, and they can certainly help us here in addressing the three main problems which have arisen in both archaeological and broader consideration of the dominant 'structuration' problem: whether agency is confined to individuals (and if so of what kind?); how it relates to power; and what the implications of agency theory are for definitions of humanity and human rights.

AGENCY = INDIVIDUAL?

A major component of the problem of agency is whether this term refers to an essential property of individuals, or whether it lies somehow in the relationships *between* individuals, a possibility which might also afford us a notion of 'collective agency'. In either case, another question is begged: what do we mean by individuals? This kind of issue is addressed in various ways by the first group of chapters in the present volume. As I note in Chapter 3, such a question is very much at the heart of the critical debate over the social theories of Giddens, rather more so than for Bourdieu (cf. Bohman 1999; see next section), in both sociology and archaeology. Giddens has been accused of making his actors too self-oriented, with too much self-reflexivity and potential for self-mastery, and thus as too abstract and disembodied (Elliot 2001: 41; Gregory 1989: 211–13; Moore 1994: 49–53). Within the archaeological literature, this has been echoed in accusations that Giddens' actors embody an ethnocentric and androcentric individualism (Gero 2000: 37–38; MacGregor 1994: 80–85), and that by defining agency as a property of competent, knowledgable and corporeal beings (Giddens 1984: 1–14, 220), Giddens produces a model which may be at odds with alternative kinds of self-understanding that archaeologists could encounter in the past.

That there is more than one way of understanding the individual person is not in doubt, as a number of anthropological studies have confirmed (Burr 2002: 4–10). Marcel Mauss, for example, surveyed a range of these, in contexts as diverse as Zuñi pueblos and ancient China, as well as charting the origins of the Western self in pagan and early Christian Rome (Mauss 1979: 59–94; cf. Carrithers *et al.* (eds.) 1985; Gardner 2003; Morris 1991). But, to be fair to Giddens, not only have his attempts to deal with the problem of individualism through the mechanisms of the duality of structure been less than fully appreciated by some critics (although these mechanisms have also drawn criticism for making actors' lives excessively routinized [Cohen 1994: 21–22; Mouzelis 1995: 119–20] – see the next section), he is also focusing primarily on the conditions of modernity (Cohen 1989: 123, 153; Elliot 2001: 41; cf. Giddens 1984: 180–206). These have long been recognised – by writers such as Marx, Durkheim, Simmel and Weber – as involving a historically-unusual degree of alienation between the individual and society, even if these writers have also tended to essentialise such a division (Burkitt 1991: 8–27).

In addition to the anthropological work noted above which suggests that this division is anything but essential, there is a considerable body of classical and recent literature emphasising the social nature of human persons, and the role of 'others' in the constitution of the 'self', even in modern societies. This includes the 'figurational' approach of Norbert Elias, which embeds people in networks of interdependence (Elias 1978 [1970]; Bauman 1989), and the work of John Macmurray on the 'form of the personal', which argues strongly for a social view of agency (1957; 1961). Perhaps most successful, and enjoying renewed attention in sociology, philosophy and social psychology (e.g. Aboulafia 1999; Burkitt 1991; Joas 1996 [1992]; Emirbayer and Mische 1998), if not yet archaeology (though cf. Richardson 1989; Gardner 2003), is the work of George Herbert Mead and his colleagues in the pragmatist school of American philosophy. Mead's stress on the role of other people – and of physical objects – in the constitution of the self again spreads agency into an intersubjective space (Mead 1934; cf. Crossley 1996; McCarthy 1984), implying that while we cannot conceive of agency without individual human organisms, agency exists only by virtue of the relationships between those organisms. Giddens certainly goes a good way down this road, but there is considerable potential for constructive criticism from these other kinds of sources.

The connections between organic individuals and social persons and groups are addressed in this volume by Stephen Shennan (Chapter 2), from an evolutionary perspective, in ways which highlight the deficiencies of an overly-individualistic view of agency. Ironically, this is a view which Archer, one of Giddens' fiercest critics, has fallen into in arguing for the priority of the 'self' over the 'social'. Archer also tends to equate 'the social' with language, as against 'practice' which is prior but less social (2000: 121–90, 253–82, 306–19). To the contrary, archaeologists are in a good position to demonstrate the social nature of material practices, as illustrated by all the chapters in this section. In this way, we have the potential to provide not only a social account of selfhood, but also an account of how *groups* of people can come to develop their own agentic capabilities (elaborated further in Chapter 3; cf. Archer 2000: 261–305; Giddens 1984: 220–21).

This offers a way through another aspect of the 'individualism' problem, raised by both Justin Morris and Brad Gravina (Chapters 4 and 5), which has to do with the nature of *archaeological* individuals. There has been considerable debate about whether 'digging for agency' simply means looking for the actions of single people (e.g. Barrett 2001; Dobres 2000; Hodder 2000; Johnson 1989). The view of agency outlined above would imply that this is certainly not the case, and may even be taken to suggest that this is not only unnecessary but, on one level, impossible – and not merely because of the obstacles of site formation processes. All agentic processes are social, and thus, as Morris and Gravina ably demonstrate, patterns of practices which inevitably transcend single organisms can still indicate different balances of tradition and transformation.

AGENCY = POWER?

Having outlined the ontological status of agency vis-à-vis different social entities, we can elaborate this by pursuing the question of what kind of relationship agency actually *is*. The key problems here are to do with intentionality, ideology, practice and reflection, and again they beg questions of archaeological visibility. Despite the diversity of current definitions of agency (Dobres and Robb 2000: 8–10), the term usually has something to do with power. 'Power' is itself a notoriously ambiguous concept, at the same time as being one which sits very firmly on the boundary between academic and political debates (Dowding 1996). It is common and useful to distinguish between 'power over' – i.e. the ability to affect what someone else does – and 'power to' – the basic ability to do something oneself (Dowding 1996: 4–5). Considerations of agency have focused on the latter, with the former effectively positioned on the structure side of the agency-structure relationship. This emphasis may not be appropriate, as both senses of power allow us to say that part of the fabric of agentic relationships is a *capacity for action*. However, we need to pin down the kind of action we are talking about if we are to understand the particular character of human life (cf. the next section), and the potential for variation within that category. This requires us to consider two critical problems: choice and intentionality.

When studying any instance of human activity from a perspective of hindsight, as archaeologists are professionally predisposed to do, we tend to think of people's actions from the point of view of causation (Bauman 1990: 107–09). However useful this kind of explanatory approach might be in some circumstances (as in the creation of laws, whether in physics or jurisprudence), it does not fully reflect the human experience of each passing moment, when a range of options is open rather than a single determinate chain of events. Human actors *act* in the sense that they select particular ways of engaging with the world on a moment-by-moment basis, albeit constrained both by past traditions and future goals (Baert 1992; Emirbayer and Mische 1998; Flaherty and Fine 2001; Macmurray 1957: 84–164; Mead 1934: 345; 1938: 616; 2002 [1932]). This in turn requires that creatures which act do so with some degree of self-consciousness with regard to the acting being undertaken, and it is this which differentiates the actions of people from the movements of rocks (Macmurray 1957: 100–03; Mead 1934: 73, 182, 225; Taylor 1985: 15–44).

The importance of choice to an understanding of agency has not gone unrecognised by archaeologists, with much of the *chaîne opératoire* literature focusing on precisely this issue (e.g. Dobres 2000; Lemonnier (ed.) 1993; cf. Chapters 4 and 5, this volume). To broaden this consideration out from studies of particular technical processes, however, we have to overturn our whole way of thinking about the past – as the *past* – and consider the ranges of possibilities open to people in their own time (Barrett 2001; cf. and *contra* Mead 2002 [1932]: 58), and indeed how wide or narrow they considered this range to be (Emirbayer and Mische 1998: 985–92). Investigating past agency is thus partly about investigating the conditions for the kind of social engagement described in the previous section, given that this engagement involves *action* rather than *causation*.

The other key issue in understanding agency in terms of power is intentionality. As we have just seen, some element of reflexive decision-making is a key aspect of agentic actions. But does this mean that all agentic actions must be intentional? One of Giddens' major contributions to the agency/structure debate has been to argue forcefully for the importance of the unintended consequences of actions, particularly those which occur on a routine basis. Indeed, such actions are critical to the reproduction of structures in Giddens' structuration theory, at the same time as reflective (or 'discursive') actions are an important element in the potential for change (1984: 5–28; cf. Mouzelis 1995: 119–20). This approach represents an effective solution to a long-running debate in Western philosophy about the relationship between reflective and habitual action – or theory and practice (Crossley 2001: 8–61; Macmurray 1957: 39–103). It makes clear sense if we accept that habit is open to reflexive monitoring, and if we thus define action not in terms of intentionality *per se*, but rather (as above) in terms of the *capacity* for actors to engage with their world in an open, rather than determined fashion, which allows for varying levels of reflective involvement, depending upon the circumstances of the interaction.

The maintenance of a distinction between habitual and reflective action requires some justification, as a number of authors have rightly stressed the role that habit plays in thinking – even revolutionary scientific ideas, for instance, are often reached by people thinking in their habitual language (Baert 1992: 64–65; Crossley 2001: 135–39; cf. Macmurray 1957: 87–90). However, if habit is over-privileged (as, some critics argue, in Bourdieu's concept of *habitus* [Bohman 1999; Crossley 2001: 109–19]), there is a risk of losing any potential for innovation, either with respect to existing social norms (Mouzelis 1995: 119), or with respect to novel and potentially problematic situations that actors may confront (Emirbayer and Mische 1998: 994–1002; Mead 1934: 347–48).

At the very least, then, and in the spirit of Giddens' emphasis on relating concepts by mechanisms of duality, rather than dualism (1984: 25; cf. Macmurray 1957: 97–98), it seems vital to distinguish practical and reflective action, and at the same time appreciate how intimately they are related. Almost any action has the potential to move between these modalities at any time, although frequently forms of action are initially confronted reflectively, as they are learnt, and then habituated (James 1983 [1890]: 109–31), until such time as their successful performance is interrupted (Mead 1934: 347–78; cf. Baert 1992: 64–68; Heidegger 1962: 102–07), or called into question through an encounter with difference. This requires that actors monitor their performance – i.e. that they are reflexive – and this monitoring (or self-awareness) is always in relation to 'others', of whatever nature (Mead 1934: 253). Such a distinction is also vital to archaeologists, simply by virtue of the fact that they excavate patterns of similarity and difference in past actions (cf. Gardner 2002). These patterns can readily be interpreted in terms of routines, or of innovations and improvisations, and thus in terms of the reproduction or transformation of social norms. In this volume, Peter Jordan (Chapter 7) deals with this relationship between meaningful practices and agency, using both ethnographic and archaeological case studies.

Having established some of the parameters for understanding the 'action' element of the concept of agency (a third modality of 'affective' action will be considered below), we must of course acknowledge that human capabilities with respect to reflexivity are bound up with the nature of the body, and the constraints and affordances thereof (such as, in the latter case, the capacity for language and material engagement provided by the nervous system and vocal and manipulative organs [Macmurray 1957: 107–26; Mead 1934: 236–37]; cf. on constraints Berggren 2000; Meskell 1999: 25–26). They are also very much entwined with the many and inevitable constraints and opportunities which the social nature of agency implies. These have been understood in a wide range of ways in theories of the relationship between agency and structure, and in this volume Fiona Handley and Tim Schadla-Hall (Chapter 8), and Astrid Lindenlauf (Chapter 6), look at how they operate both on and for archaeologists.

To summarise some of the broader literature, Giddens and Bourdieu differ markedly in their approaches to social power. While Giddens defines structure in terms of the 'rules and resources' which actors draw upon, he has been criticised for under-theorising the way in which actors tend to be differentially situated with respect to their abilities to draw upon and shape these, offering only a limited analysis of social roles (Giddens 1984: 16–25; 83–92; Parker 2000: 105–06). Bourdieu's approach is rather more useful in this regard, with an actor's 'capital' (which can itself be multi-faceted: economic, social, cultural or symbolic) positioning them in a particular relational network or social 'field' (Jenkins 1992: 84–85). This gives Bourdieu potentially greater purchase on processes of subordination and domination than Giddens (Parker 2000: 103–08). Another way of conceptualising the opportunities and constraints which actors experience is simply in terms of identities. Along a whole range of different dimensions (gender, age, status, ethnicity etc.), these structure social interactions in ways which can be both flexible and open to improvisation, but also reproductive of reified institutions (Jenkins 1996; Gardner 2002; Goffman 1990 [1959], 1990 [1963]).

These kinds of concepts are crucial in understanding the ways in which specific agentic relationships are structured, and the kinds of actions that are deemed possible and impossible in particular situations. Along with the notion of ideology, as "the ways in which meaning is mobilized in the service of dominant individuals and groups" (Thompson 1990: 73), these are all elements of social relations which have long been preoccupations of archaeologists. In the context of the 'agency debate' as represented in this volume, such concerns are touched upon by many of the chapters, but particularly those in Part 2. Here, all three chapters confront the ways in which actors' practices – whether they be those of

Siberian hunter-gatherers, Greeks in the Classical period, or archaeologists working in Britain – are structured by a range of opportunities and constraints. They also address the symbolic mechanisms (like dirt and cleanliness) through which these structural features are mediated in actors' understandings. The benefit of the 'agency' approach here lies in opening up the potential for seeing these from the perspective of the situated actor (cf. Barrett 2001: 155–62), rather than as causal mechanisms identified in hindsight. This also opens up the possibilities for understanding some of the ethical dimensions of action, and it is to such topics that the chapters in the final section of this volume turn.

AGENCY = HUMANITY?

Ultimately, the reason that the ideas considered in this volume are important is not simply because they are useful – or fashionable – ways of understanding past societies, but because they have a profoundly political dimension that archaeologists would be ill-advised to ignore. As stated at the outset, the problem of defining agency is intimately bound up with the problem of defining humanity, and there is no doubt that this is a question of more than philosophical significance. As Richard Wilson notes in the Introduction to a volume of anthropological perspectives on human rights (1997: 3), one of the key current issues under debate is "what concept of human ontology is to be used, and what rights naturally extend from that view of human nature"? Beyond the similarly important questions surrounding particular *cultural* bases for establishing human rights, then, we have the issue of how 'human-ness' entitles one to rights, and therefore of defining 'human-ness'. This problem is at the heart of the chapters in Part 3 of this volume.

While recent discussions of agency have dealt with issues such as the powers of objects, and of other species (Gell 1998; Ingold 1993a; Latour 2000; Urry 2000: 77–79, 168–72), and archaeologists have considered the possibility of finding different ways of being human in the past (Thomas 2000: 155), the political and ethical implications of these positions have to be carefully considered. Many oppressions and atrocities have been committed in the name of particular definitions of humanity, but abandoning the concept altogether equally leaves us with no basis for distinguishing between the way people treat each other as against other entities. Before addressing this ethical dilemma more fully, we can work towards the problem by considering two of the issues just raised: can artefacts have agency, and can other species be actors? The approaches to agency reviewed so far can help us answer these questions, but can also be developed further in the process.

The literature of Actor-Network Theory (ANT) offers one perspective on the first question (e.g. Law and Hassard (eds.) 1999), but so too does anthropological work in non-Western societies, an example of which is provided here by Bill Sillar (Chapter 9). Put simply, ANT concerns the relationships that people develop with other people and objects, creating networks of actors rather than siting agency in individual entities. The value of a relational approach to agency, rather than one which treats the concept as an essence or property, has already been emphasised, and there is little doubt that the material world is an important element in human interactions. Artefacts are much more than an "extra-somatic means of adaptation" (Binford 1962: 218), but mediate social relations in all kinds of ways (Dant 1999; Miller 1994). More fundamentally, the relationships which people have with, and form through things arguably play an important role in precisely the kind of self-reflexivity that has been suggested above as being a necessary condition for 'action' (Gardner 2003; Ingold 1993b; Mead 1934: 237; McCarthy 1984; Williams and Costall 2000).

Thus artefacts generate both actors and agentic relationships, but are they actors themselves? Sillar addresses this problem in Chapter 9, considering Andean views of the agency of artefacts, ancestors, and deities. This clearly raises issues of cultural relativism, and – as noted above – while a universalising framework could leave no basis for respecting such views or understanding the people who hold them, a truly relativist approach might be equally disempowering (Wilson 1997: 8–10). This issue will be considered further below, but one could argue the view that all cultures (Western and non-Western) anthropomorphise the world around them (cf. Macmurray 1957: 116); the different ways in which people conceive of this process are of profound importance in appreciating their self-understandings, but do not compromise their identity *as people*.

How, though, does this identity differ from those of other animal species – if at all? Archaeology, along with many other disciplines, has long been torn between emphasising the similarities between human and animal 'behaviour' and placing humans in a unique and often privileged position (Shanks and Tilley 1992: 55–56; Thomas 2000: 145; cf. Shennan, Chapter 2, this volume). In trying to find a way between these positions, a question to focus on in the context of agency theory is whether the kind of self-reflexive consciousness that has been associated with human action can be found in other species. Mead argued that this was not the case – that animals do not have a personality (and therefore, strictly speaking, have no rights either), largely because they do not have the linguistic or material means of extending their consciousness through time, and thus of being self-conscious (Mead 1934: 182–83).

More recent research on the self-awareness of animals has, however, shown that some species (for instance chimpanzees) do show signs of being able to recognise themselves (De Waal 2002: 48–50; cf. Strum and Latour 1987). This clearly suggests that there is a scale of difference between humans and other species, rather than a polarity. It also suggests that there may be such a thing as chimpanzee agency – or indeed electronic agency, as discussed by Mark Lake in Chapter 10 – but this need not undermine the distinctiveness of human agency (cf. also Gravina, this volume). The reasons for this distinctiveness, which can still accommodate a range of variation, are not to do with some special human essence (Thomas 2000: 146–48), but rather depend upon the kinds of relationships that humans can engage in, by virtue of their perceptive, manipulative and communicative capabilities. These relationships are also the foundation of an ethical dimension of agency.

Questions of ethics have always shadowed theories of agency, but the 'structuration' debates that have recently been dominant have tended to sublimate such considerations, prompting understandable criticisms (e.g. Archer 2000; Barnes 2000; Gero 2000; Moore 2000). In this volume, Stephanie Koerner (Chapter 11) elaborates this discussion and provides some suggestions for resolving it. In short, and in sympathy with other authors' chapters, she suggests that the social nature of agency is crucial for establishing the ethical dimension of human life, in that self-aware creatures only emerge through contact with others with this quality (cf. Barnes 2000: 64–78; Macmurray 1957: 145; Mead 1934: 379–89; Todorov 2001 [1995]; Vygotsky 1978). This entails a network of rights, responsibilities and respect which become manifest in the actions that actors undertake – both structuring them and enabling them.

This is true for the two modalities of action identified above – habitual and reflective – and perhaps especially for a third category of affective or emotional action (Bauman 1990: 110–11; Archer 2000: 193–305; cf. Chapters 3 and 9, this volume). Ethics thus become bound up with power as the fabric connecting actors, and crucially the open-ness of action discussed above furnishes the capacity for actors to judge each other as being 'right' or 'wrong' (Macmurray 1957: 140–42). It is on this basis that the idea of human agency can underpin, rather than undermine, the concept of human rights, without flattening human cultural diversity. Distinguishing *human* agency only becomes dangerous if this is treated as a property of particular entities, rather than of particular relationships between entities. The character of these relationships may be variable, but it is their very existence – or the denial thereof – which furnish criteria for ethical judgements.

WHITHER AGENCY IN ARCHAEOLOGY NOW?

My aim in this Introduction has been to identify the major trends in recent discussions of agency, the problems these throw up, the solutions they point towards, and the ways in which the chapters in this volume fit into these trajectories. Overall, the importance of an archaeological concern with agency for these broader debates is grounded in the unique potential that archaeologists have to explore such themes in a range of particular contexts, and it is here that the real strength of this volume lies. The multiplicity of hermeneutic spirals in which archaeologists are entwined (Shanks and Tilley 1992: 107–08) make our task challenging but also rewarding, and calls for empirical studies into the 'structuration' problem (Parker 2000: 125) can very readily be answered by archaeologists, through investigations of practices in a range of cultural contexts, including our own. Although many recent studies suggest that the agency/structure dichotomy can be dissolved by viewing agency in terms of relationships, thus offering what might seem to be a prescriptive framework, this is very much open to cultural variation, and herein lies a great opportunity for archaeology.

To summarise, we have seen that agency can be regarded as a relational concept, rather than as a property of individuals, but that it also depends on humans being part of those relationships, because agentic relationships can exist only by virtue of the unique way in which humans engage with the world. These relationships provide a foundation for ethical action. The endowment of humans with rights depends upon their capacity for responsibilities, which in turn depends upon their self-reflexive attitude – a feature which, while perhaps not unique to humans, has nonetheless taken on a particular form through the combined significance of language and material culture. This framework provides grounds for distinguishing human agency, but certainly does not exclude either an ethical concern for other species or even objects (which can be seen, as discussed above, as part of 'actor-networks'), or cultural variation in the ways in which these relationships take shape, which will always entail a degree of contextual sensitivity in addressing ethical issues (Bauman 2001: 140; McDavid 2000; Wilson 1997: 12). Archaeologists, through investigating the construction of social relations in past societies, have the potential to broaden the scope of 'the human', rather than narrow it.

Given this importance of an archaeological contribution to agency theory, what should this look like from an archaeological point of view? If agency is a fundamental feature of human relations, and thus is everywhere we look, what prevents archaeologists from simply taking their existing approaches and 'adding actors and stirring' (Dobres and Robb 2000: 13–14)? The contributions in this volume point towards studies of the conditions and possibilities of action in particular contexts (cf. Barrett 2001; Matthew Johnson, Chapter 12, this volume). How do people act – and perceive of their acting – in different times and places? This brings us back to a problem which has perhaps slipped into the background in the foregoing discussion: the nature of structure. One of the major elements of the criticism levelled against Giddens and Bourdieu by 'analytical dualists' like Archer is that to relate agency and structure too closely is to inhibit meaningful analysis either of actors or of structures, and thus prevent understanding of their specific qualities (Archer 1995; Parker 2000: 102–25). There is certainly a danger that if, as discussed above, 'agency' is identified with the properties of individuals, then social scientists, including archaeologists, will lose sight of the development of institutional structures over time.

However, the concern with social agency, and with relationships of power between actors, which this volume points towards, should ensure that this pitfall is avoided. By taking more factors into account in the definition of the 'structuration' process, it is possible to strengthen our accounts of actors' development in relation to each other, and of the more elaborate forms – institutions – that those relationships can take. Furthermore, the involvement of archaeologists in this project is critical, as already discussed, permitting the examination of social dynamics of variable duration in a range of contexts. These offer the potential to stretch our understandings of the kinds of relationships that people have with each other, and how these are manifested over time in more 'structural' ways – whether as political institutions, religious rituals, or cultural traditions. The work of Giddens, in particular, emerges as a persistently supportive plank in this kind of approach, and begs the question of whether the 'dualist' critique is entirely valid – certainly, it seems to perpetuate some of the individualist problems that have been identified above as a major flaw in many conceptions of agency (e.g. Archer 2000: 305).

Whether or not such issues can be resolved in a definitive fashion, the point this book makes is that archaeologists can contribute to the debate, through theoretically dynamic and empirically diverse studies. This contribution is unique and important. On one level, we are seeking to imagine the *presents* of a very broad range of human societies, and the ways in which people in those societies saw their place in the world. On another, we are drawing upon the *pasts* of contemporary societies, and thus affecting our own conditions of future possibilities, and contributing to the ability of people today to reflect upon themselves. While the concept of agency has been discussed in archaeology for some time, and has attracted criticism for being, at best, abused (Dobres and Robb 2000), or at worst simply useless (Chapman 2003: 65–66), it is hoped that the chapters in this volume demonstrate that more coherent approaches are emerging which, in emphasising the social and material dimensions of agency, offer much food for archaeological thought.

Acknowledgments

Thanks are due to Stephanie Koerner, Kathryn Piquette, Koji Mizoguchi, Bill Sillar, Steve Townend and Peter Whitridge for stimulating discussion on some of the issues addressed in this Introduction.

References

Aboulafia, M. 1999. A (neo) American in Paris: Bourdieu, Mead, and Pragmatism. In R. Shusterman (ed.) *Bourdieu: a critical reader*, 153–74. Oxford: Blackwell.

Archer, M.S. 1995. *Realist Social Theory: the morphogenetic approach*. Cambridge: Cambridge University Press.

Archer, M.S. 1996 [1988]. *Culture and Agency: the place of culture in society*. Cambridge: Cambridge University Press (Revised edition).

Archer, M.S. 2000. *Being Human: the problem of agency*. Cambridge: Cambridge University Press.

Baert, P. 1992. *Time, Self and Social Being*. Aldershot: Avebury (Avebury Series in Philosophy).

Barnes, B. 2000. *Understanding Agency: social theory and responsible action*. London: Sage Publications.

Barrett, J.C. 2001. Agency, the duality of structure, and the problem of the archaeological record. In I. Hodder (ed.) *Archaeological Theory Today*, 141–64. Cambridge: Polity Press.

Bauman, Z. 1989. Hermeneutics and modern social theory. In D. Held and J.B. Thompson (eds.) *Social Theory of Modern Societies: Anthony Giddens and his critics*, 34–55. Cambridge: Cambridge University Press.

Bauman, Z. 1990. *Thinking Sociologically*. Oxford: Blackwell.

Bauman, Z. 2001. *Community: seeking safety in an insecure world*. Cambridge: Polity Press.

Berggren, K. 2000. The knowledge-able agent? On the paradoxes of power (with a comment by B. Chan and T. Georgousopoulou). In C. Holtorf and H. Karlsson (eds.) *Philosophy and Archaeological Practice: perspectives for the 21st century*, 39–51. Göteborg: Bricoleur Press.

Binford, L.R. 1962. Archaeology as Anthropology. *American Antiquity*, 28.2, 217–25.

Bohman, J. 1999. Practical reason and cultural constraint: agency in Bourdieu's theory of practice. In R. Shusterman (ed.) *Bourdieu: a critical reader*, 129–52. Oxford: Blackwell.

Bourdieu, P. 1977 [1972]. *Outline of a Theory of Practice*. Cambridge: Cambridge University Press (Translated by R. Nice).

Bourdieu, P. 1990 [1980]. *The Logic of Practice*. Cambridge: Polity Press (Translated by R. Nice).

Bourdieu, P. 1999. *Acts of Resistance: against the tyranny of the market*. New York: New Press.

Bryant, C.G.A. and Jary, D. 2001. The uses of structuration theory: a typology. In C.G.A. Bryant and D. Jary (eds.) *The Contemporary Giddens: social theory in a globalizing age*, 43–61. Houndmills: Palgrave.

Burkitt, I. 1991. *Social Selves: theories of the social formation of personality*. London: Sage Publications.

Burr, V. 2002. *The Person in Social Psychology*. Hove: Psychology Press.

Carrithers, M., Collins, S. and Lukes, S. (eds.) 1985. *The Category of the Person: anthropology, philosophy, history*. Cambridge: Cambridge University Press.

Chapman, R. 2003. *Archaeologies of Complexity*. London: Routledge.

Cohen, A.P. 1994. *Self Consciousness: an alternative anthropology of identity*. London: Routledge.

Cohen, I.J. 1989. *Structuration Theory: Anthony Giddens and the constitution of social life*. Houndmills: Macmillan.

Cohen, I.J. 2000. Theories of action and praxis. In B.S. Turner (ed.) *The Blackwell Companion to Social Theory*, 73–111. Oxford: Blackwell (2nd edition).

Crossley, N. 1996. *Intersubjectivity: the fabric of social becoming*. London: Sage Publications.

Crossley, N. 2001. *The Social Body: habit, identity and desire*. London: Sage Publications.

Dant, T. 1999. *Material Culture in the Social World*. Buckingham: Open University Press.

De Waal, C. 2002. *On Mead*. Belmont, CA: Wadsworth/Thomas Learning, Inc.

Dobres, M.-A. 2000. *Technology and Social Agency*. Oxford: Blackwell.

Dobres, M.-A. and Robb, J.E. 2000. Agency in archaeology: paradigm or platitude? In M.-A. Dobres and J.E. Robb (eds.) *Agency in Archaeology*, 3–17. London: Routledge.

Dornan, J.L. 2002. Agency and archaeology: past, present and future directions. *Journal of Archaeological Method and Theory*, 9:4, 303–29.

Dowding, K. 1996. *Power*. Buckingham: Open University Press.

Elias, N. 1978 [1970]. *What is Sociology?* New York: Columbia University Press (Translated by S. Mennell and G. Morrissey).

Elliott, A. 2001. *Concepts of the Self*. Cambridge: Polity Press.

Emirbayer, M. and Mische, A. 1998. What is agency? *American Journal of Sociology*, 103:4, 962–1023.

Flaherty, M.G. and Fine, G.A. 2001. Present, past, and future: conjugating George Herbert Mead's perspective on time. *Time and Society*, 10:2/3, 147–61.

Gardner, A. 2002. Social identity and the duality of structure in late Roman-period Britain. *Journal of Social Archaeology*, 2:3, 323–51.

Gardner, A. 2003. Seeking a material turn: the artefactuality of the Roman empire. In G. Carr, E. Swift and J. Weekes (eds.) *TRAC 2002: Proceedings of the 12th Annual Theoretical Roman Archaeology Conference, Canterbury 2002*, 1–13. Oxford: Oxbow Books.

Garfinkel, H. 1984 [1967]. *Studies in Ethnomethodology*. Cambridge: Polity Press.

Gell, A. 1998. *Art and Agency: an anthropological theory*. Oxford: Clarendon Press.

Gero, J.M. 2000. Troubled travels in agency and feminism. In M.-A. Dobres and J.E. Robb (eds.) *Agency in Archaeology*, 34–39. London: Routledge.

Giddens, A. 1979. *Central Problems in Social Theory: action, structure and contradiction in social analysis*. Houndmills: Macmillan.

Giddens, A. 1984. *The Constitution of Society*. Cambridge: Polity Press.

Giddens, A. 1993 [1976]. *New Rules of Sociological Method*. Cambridge: Polity Press (2nd edition).

Giddens, A. 2000. *The Third Way and its Critics*. Cambridge: Polity Press.

Goffman, E. 1990 [1959]. *The Presentation of Self in Everyday Life*. Harmondsworth: Penguin.

Goffman, E. 1990 [1963]. *Stigma: notes on the management of spoiled identity*. Harmondsworth: Penguin.

Gregory, D. 1989. Presences and absences: time-space relations and structuration theory. In D. Held and J.B. Thompson (eds.) *Social Theory of Modern Societies: Anthony Giddens and his critics*, 185–214. Cambridge: Cambridge University Press.

Heidegger, M. 1962. *Being and Time*. Oxford: Blackwell (Translated by J. Macquarrie and E. Robinson).

Hodder, I. 2000. Agency and individuals in long-term processes. In M.-A. Dobres and J.E. Robb (eds.) *Agency in Archaeology*, 21–33. London: Routledge.

Ingold, T. 1993a. The Reindeerman's lasso. In P. Lemonnier (ed.) *Technological Choices: transformation in material cultures since the Neolithic*, 108–25. London: Routledge.

Ingold, T. 1993b. Tool-use, sociality and intelligence. In K.R. Gibson and T. Ingold (eds.) *Tools, Language and Cognition in Human Evolution*, 429–45. Cambridge: Cambridge University Press.

James, W. 1983 [1890]. *The Principles of Psychology*. Cambridge, MA: Harvard University Press (Paperback edition).

Jenkins, R. 1992. *Pierre Bourdieu*. London: Routledge.

Jenkins, R. 1996. *Social Identity*. London: Routledge.

Joas, H. 1996 [1992]. *The Creativity of Action*. Cambridge: Polity Press (Translated by J. Gaines and P. Keast).

Johnson, M.H. 1989. Conceptions of agency in archaeological interpretation. *Journal of Anthropological Archaeology*, 8, 189–211.

Latour, B. 2000. The Berlin key or how to do words with things. In P.M. Graves-Brown (ed.) *Matter, Materiality and Modern Culture*, 10–21. London: Routledge.

Law, J. and Hassard, J. (eds.) 1999. *Actor Network Theory and After*. Oxford: Blackwell.

Lemonnier, P. (ed.) 1993. *Technological Choices: transformation in material cultures since the Neolithic*. London: Routledge.

MacGregor, G. 1994. Post-processual archaeology: the hidden agenda of the secret agent. In I. Mackenzie (ed.) *Archaeological Theory: progress or posture?* 79–91. Aldershot: Avebury (Worldwide Archaeology Series, 11).

Macmurray, J. 1957. *The Self as Agent (Volume I of the Form of the Personal)*. London: Faber and Faber.

Macmurray, J. 1961. *Persons in Relation (Volume II of the Form of the Personal)*. London: Faber and Faber.

Mauss, M. 1979. *Sociology and Psychology: essays*. London: Routledge and Kegan Paul (Translated by B. Brewster).

McCarthy, E.D. 1984. Toward a sociology of the physical world: George Herbert Mead on physical objects. *Studies in Symbolic Interaction*, 5, 105–21.

McDavid, C. 2000. Archaeology as cultural critique. Pragmatism and the archaeology of a Southern United States plantation (with a comment by L. Daniel Mouer). In C. Holtorf and H. Karlsson (eds.) *Philosophy and Archaeological Practice: perspectives for the 21st century*, 221–39. Göteborg: Bricoleur Press.

Mead, G.H. 1934. *Mind, Self and Society, from the standpoint of a social behaviorist*. Chicago, IL: University of Chicago Press (Edited with an Introduction by C.W. Morris).

Mead, G.H. 1938. *The Philosophy of the Act*. Chicago, IL: University of Chicago Press (Edited with an Introduction by C.W. Morris).

Mead, G.H. 2002 [1932]. *The Philosophy of the Present*. Amherst, NY: Prometheus Books.

Meskell, L. 1999. *Archaeologies of Social Life*. Oxford: Blackwell.

Miller, D. 1994. Artefacts and the meaning of things. In T. Ingold (ed.) *Companion Encyclopedia of Anthropology: humanity, culture and social life*, 396–419. London: Routledge.

Moore, H.L. 1994. *A Passion for Difference*. Cambridge: Polity Press.

Moore, H.L. 2000. Ethics and ontology: why agents and agency matter. In M.-A. Dobres and J.E. Robb (eds.) *Agency in Archaeology*, 259–63. London: Routledge.

Morris, B. 1991. *Western Conceptions of the Individual*. Oxford: Berg.

Mouzelis, N. 1995. *Sociological Theory: what went wrong?* London: Routledge.

Ortner, S.B. 2001. Commentary: practice, power and the past. *Journal of Social Archaeology*, 1:2, 271–78.

Parker, J. 2000. *Structuration*. Buckingham: Open University Press.

Parsons, T. 1951. *The Social System*. London: Routledge.

Richardson, M. 1989. The artefact as abbreviated act: a social interpretation of material culture. In I. Hodder (ed.) *The Meanings of Things: material culture and symbolic expression*, 172–77. London: Harper Collins (One World Archaeology 6).

Shanks, M. and Tilley, C. 1992. *Re-Constructing Archaeology: theory and practice*. London: Routledge (2nd edition).

Schutz, A. 1967. *The Phenomenology of the Social World*. Evanston, IL: Northwestern University Press.

Schutz, A. and Luckmann, T. 1973. *The Structures of the Life-World (Volume I)*. Evanston, IL: Northwestern University Press.

Strum, S.S. and Latour, B. 1987. Redefining the social link: from baboons to humans. *Social Science Information*, 26, 783–802.

Taylor, C. 1985. *Human Agency and Language (Philosophical Papers 1)*. Cambridge: Cambridge University Press.

Thomas, J. 2000. Reconfiguring the social, reconfiguring the material. In M.B. Schiffer (ed.) *Social Theory in Archaeology*, 143–55. Salt Lake City, UT: University of Utah Press.

Thompson, J.B. 1990. *Ideology and Modern Culture*. Stanford, CA: University of Stanford Press.

Todorov, T. 2001 [1995]. *Life in Common: an essay in general anthropology*. Lincoln, NE: University of Nebraska Press (Translated by K. Golsan and L. Golsan).

Urry, J. 2000. *Sociology Beyond Societies: mobilities for the twenty-first century*. London: Routledge.

Vygotsky, L.S. 1978. *Mind in Society: the development of higher psychological processes*. Cambridge, MA: Harvard University Press.

Williams, E. and Costall, A. 2000. Taking things more seriously: psychological theories of autism and the material-social divide. In P.M. Graves-Brown (ed.) *Matter, Materiality and Modern Culture*, 97–111. London: Routledge.

Wilson, R.A. 1997. Human rights, culture and context: an introduction. In R.A. Wilson (ed.) *Human Rights, Culture and Context: anthropological perspectives*, 1–27. London: Pluto Press.

PART 1: SOCIAL AGENCY

CHAPTER 2

AN EVOLUTIONARY PERSPECTIVE ON AGENCY IN ARCHAEOLOGY

Stephen Shennan

INTRODUCTION

In a recent review of agency theory in archaeology Dornan (2002) outlines some criticisms of the ideas of the founding fathers of agency theory – Pierre Bourdieu and Anthony Giddens – and identifies three interrelated issues in the field that remain unresolved. The first concerns the proper unit of analysis. If agency theory is concerned with individual action, the power of individuals to act, and the relation between these and social structure, what is the nature of these individuals? How generic or specific are they? If a key aspect of the relation between structure and agency is the internalisation of social norms within individuals, how can we separate out those elements of structure which they have internalised? The second issue concerns the role of rationality, and agency theory's emphasis on the ability of the individual to resist ideological domination. Why should individual resistance to ideological domination ever be an appropriate strategy? The third issue concerns the relationship between intentionality and the consequences of actions. How much do individual intentions matter? Are the unintended consequences of action far more significant?

The object of this chapter (cf. Shennan 1989, 1991) is to argue that very similar issues have arisen in the context of evolutionary studies of animal social behaviour in general and of human social and cultural behaviour in particular. While these approaches have not necessarily provided any general answers to the questions that arise in particular cases – indeed, there are arguably no general answers, only specific ones – they have, nevertheless, produced an important set of general principles and a powerful methodological toolkit with which they can be productively addressed.

RATIONALITY

The key starting point for addressing the issue of evolutionary agency has to be the question of rationality since natural selection provides the basis for exactly the kind of universal logic that Dornan (2002) and other agency theorists criticise. The dominant view among those who practice the behavioural ecological study of humans assumes that "people tend to select behaviours from a range of variants whose net effect is to maximise their individual reproductive or inclusive fitness" (Kelly 1995: 51). This is not to say that people always make conscious choices with this end in view, or that they lack intentionality. Nevertheless, the upshot of the decisions they make, consciously and unconsciously, is that they act in ways that an outside observer can recognise as conducive to their survival and reproductive success – to their fitness, in other words.

The reason for taking this view is that, as with other species, the history of evolution by natural selection has produced in us psychological capacities and propensities, not least our emotions, which predispose us to act in ways which lead to this end. Even though most of the variation we observe in people's behaviour arises through learning, by trial-and-error and from other people, the behavioural ecology expectation is that our inherited propensities will tend to make us 'opt for' fitness-enhancing behaviour.

Optimal foraging theory

Foraging theory provides one area in which the assumption of evolutionary rationality provides a powerful analytical tool whose assumptions are often borne out. Animal studies clearly suggest that foraging strategies are under selective pressure even in circumstances where actual food shortages are not a problem.

We can apply the same sort of optimal foraging principles to understanding human foragers (and indeed to any human economy, but most work has been done with hunter-gatherers). At first sight it might seem obvious that the best way to exploit an environment is to make use of those resources that are most widely available. In fact, this is not the case. What is known as the *diet breadth model* predicts that the resources that will be exploited are not those that are most widely available, but those which provide the best return for a given amount of effort. The effort or cost is divided into two components: the time taken to find the prey item and the handling costs which arise when it has been found, such as the butchery of game or the processes required to make acorns suitable for eating. Search costs will vary with the density of the resource concerned, but also with the technology available for searching, such as the use of the horse in bison hunting. Handling costs will likewise vary depending on the technology available.

When a forager encounters a resource, a decision has to be made about whether to make use of it or pass it by and try to find something better. The diet breadth model predicts that individuals will ignore the resource if they think they can soon find something that gives a better rate of return; otherwise, they will decide to exploit it. Accordingly, if we know something about the resources available, in terms of the average time taken to find them, the amount of time it takes to kill/collect and process them, and the energy return from them, we can predict which resources will be used if the aim is to maximise extractive efficiency. Thus, resources can be ranked in terms of the returns they produce once they have been encountered and we can find out which combination of resources will produce the maximum returns, taking into account the time it takes to locate them. The highest return diet will only include a small number of highest return resources. If the inclusion of a specific resource in the diet mix leads to a decrease in net returns, it is not included. Even if certain resources are plentiful in the environment they will not be included if the handling costs are large and the return rates in terms of calories per unit time are low.

What would lead to change in the optimal diet? One possibility would be a technological innovation which drastically reduced the capture/handling costs of one of the low-ranked resources initially not in the diet and thus made it worth exploiting. Another possibility would be the situation that arises when the highest-rated resources become rarer as a result of exploitation, so that search times increase. In these circumstances the exploitation of resources not originally in the optimal diet might become worthwhile. In fact, where optimal foraging assumptions hold, as environments are increasingly exploited, return rates go down, the diet breadth increases as people have to look to other resources, and they have to do more work to maintain the same levels of production as before, unless the opportunity of migration to less heavily-exploited areas is available.

It appears that the predictions of optimal foraging theory based in evolutionary theory are very often met when we analyse people's subsistence decisions, but in some circumstances they will not account for the patterns we find. For example, Mithen's (1990) analysis of Mesolithic foraging strategies in Denmark led to the conclusion that maximising the rate of calorie capture could not have been the main aim. Nevertheless, optimal foraging theory presents us with a powerful and illuminating predictive framework from which we can learn even when its predictions are not met. In the case of humans, as opposed to other animals, technology and its development play a key role in defining patterns of costs and benefits, but particular technological trajectories cannot be assumed to be inevitable.

THE COMPLICATIONS OF CULTURE

Mention of technology obviously makes the point that humans are far more reliant on culture than other animals. From the evolutionary point of view the key point about culture is that it represents a new mode of inheritance of information that affects fitness. Of course, unlike the genetic system, the mechanism through which it operates is not biological reproduction but social learning. A good description of what is involved is provided by Ruddle (1993: 20):

> A body of knowledge develops over generations to refer to the various activities involved in a given resource system, and takes on a linguistic form. For example, consider fishing:
>
> 1 Vocabularies define species, habitats, weather patterns, sea conditions, seasons, fish behaviour and the like.
>
> 2 A collection of 'recipes' must be learned in order to fish both correctly and with consistent success.
>
> 3 Knowledge is also a channelling and controlling force that underlies fishing institutions.

4 In the persistence and crystallization of fishing institutions, knowledge becomes the objective description of the activity/institution.

5 An objective arena/field/ethnoscience of fishing develops in parallel with the activity of fishing.

This body of knowledge is transmitted to the next generation as an *objective truth* during socialization, and then it is internalized as *subjective reality*.

At this point we have arrived at *dual inheritance theory*. Humans have two systems of inheritance: the genetic system which they share with all living creatures, and a cultural system which, although not unique to humans, is certainly developed to an unprecedented degree among them. What are the processes that affect this second inheritance system, producing stability and change, and how do they relate to agency?

To start with, we need a mechanism that changes the information that is transmitted. If the reproduction of cultural or genetic information were perfect every time then there would be no novelty on which other processes could act. Genetic mutations are 'blind', in that they occur randomly and are unrelated to the processes of selection which act on their outcomes. In contrast, cultural innovations are generally regarded as purposive. However, this need not always be the case. People can, in effect, make copying errors and alter the way they do things quite unwittingly. In the case of genetic mutations, many if not most will disappear very quickly and not make any difference to the genetic make-up of the population. If one person unwittingly decorates a pot in a slightly different way from the norm, this will not make any difference at all if there are many potters, unless some at least begin to deliberately copy the innovation.

Nevertheless, sometimes innovations are purposive. In the framework developed by Boyd and Richerson (1985) to describe processes of change in cultural traditions, purposeful innovation is referred to as 'guided variation': individuals change their way of doing something as a result of comparing the outcome of their existing method, most probably learned from their parents or another relative of the older generation, with that of a new method acquired by their own experimental, trial-and-error learning, and adopting the latter. For example, just because somebody has learned from their parents a particular way to make an arrowhead or the best time to plant a crop does not mean that they will always follow it. They may experiment with alternatives and start using one of them, especially if their current way of doing things is not very successful. For the individual concerned this amounts to a one-step combined innovation-selection procedure.

It should not be assumed that the element of intentionality in many innovations altogether vitiates the comparison between mutation and innovation. Just because somebody imagines that they have found an improved way of doing something does not mean that they really have, as the history of failed technological innovations shows. Moreover, even if a real improvement has been made, that does not necessarily mean that selection will act in its favour, as examples of technological 'lock-in' demonstrate. In other words, even if, at the level of the individual who produces it, innovation is a directed process, its ultimate fate in the population at large may have little to do with those initial individual intentions. It depends on selection processes.

However, things are more complicated than this as we can illustrate by taking a hypothetical archaeological example. We can imagine two different ways of hafting an axe blade present within a Neolithic population, one long-standing and widely prevalent, the other novel and little-used. These methods of axe-hafting can themselves be considered in population terms and their population trajectories traced through time as the two types compete with one another. The selective environment in which the competition takes place is the human population of axe makers and users. Decisions will be taken about which forms of axe haft to make and use in the light of a number of factors; for example, the size of the trees to be cut down (which may change as clearance proceeds and primary gives way to secondary forest); the raw material sources used (which may affect the form and size of the axe blade); the ways in which axes are held and used, and so on; all within a broad least-effort framework which assumes that people would prefer to spend less time and effort cutting down trees rather than more.

Nevertheless, we should not exaggerate the competitiveness of this process. It seems unlikely that when young adults reached the age of cutting down their first trees they took along axes hafted in six different ways and carried out a comparative performance analysis in terms of time taken, effort involved or the frequency of breakage. They would be far more likely to use the kind of axe haft a parent or some other older relative used, or the one that was most widely current. In many areas of life it pays to follow what others do, just diverting from this occasionally when it is really obvious that it is better to adopt an innovation. In other words, what we have is weak selection on ongoing cultural traditions with people as the environment and agents of selection.

In the case of the axes there is some relatively immediate indication of whether the hafting is at least adequate. However, even here people are most likely to simply adopt some existing pattern rather than experiment with alternatives. In some spheres of life, whether the consequences of a particular action are good or bad may not be at all obvious until long after the event. This adds a considerable element of uncertainty to the generation and adoption of novelty and argues in favour of adopting existing modes of behaviour whose consequences in older individuals can be observed, or simply accepting what one first learned from a member of the older generation. The result is that such practices may be largely insulated from any evaluation and continue undisturbed.

Like guided variation, this process (called 'directly-biased transmission' by Boyd and Richerson [1985]) is in one sense a kind of natural selection acting directly on cultural attributes, effected by human decision-making. That is to say, people make their judgements to continue with or to change what they do in terms of practical performance criteria. Such criteria – for example minimising effort in cutting down trees – are quite likely in the long run to contribute to the maximisation of survival probabilities and reproductive success. In this sense, people are trying to anticipate the effects of natural selection, in the strict biological sense of a process that results in individuals with certain attributes being more reproductively successful than others. However, in addition to any positive (or negative) contribution to people's reproductive success, the cultural attributes themselves are either more or less successful in spreading through the human population and maintaining themselves within it.

A rather different process which affects the frequency with which information is handed on to future generations, or even to next week, is what Boyd and Richerson call *conformist transmission*: the idea that for any particular practice people simply look around them and do what most other people are already doing. When in Rome, do as the Romans. In general, it seems a very good approach to adopt when deciding how to do something. It doesn't, for example, require the evaluation involved in direct bias or learning by trial-and-error oneself, and the consequent possibility of making a mistake. Furthermore, if most people are doing it, it must in principle be a good thing to do. However, it is important to note that it doesn't involve a reality check and that can be dangerous.

In relation to the rationality issue, the point is that people are always culturally situated. They are always making their decisions in the light of a particular cultural inheritance even when those decisions are intended (consciously or unconsciously) to be adaptively rational from the fitness point of view (Henrich 2001). Even optimal foraging theory presupposes the existence of particular technologies, as we noted above.

If there are many circumstances in which social learning provides the best means of individual adaptation, in the sense of increasing the chances of survival and reproductive success for the individuals who make use of it, does it have any down-side from this point of view? In fact, it does. An important result of the differences between the routes of genetic and cultural transmission is that cultural traits can spread through populations even when they have maladaptive consequences from the point of view of genetic transmission and reproductive success. This is the basis of the idea of the 'cultural virus' (e.g. Cullen 1996): cultural attributes that have the capacity to encourage their own adoption by others and thus increase their replicative success, without regard for the reproductive success of the individuals who adopt them. The idea is nicely encapsulated in Dan Dennett's (1995: 346) slogan: "A scholar is just a library's way of making another library." Or in George Williams' statement, "There is no more reason to expect a cultural practice transmitted between churchgoers to increase churchgoers' fitness than there is to expect a similarly transmitted flu virus to increase fitness" (Williams 1992: 15, cited in Dennett 1995: 361).

This is because the propagation of the practice does not depend on people reproducing themselves biologically but on their going to church. The two may even be entirely incompatible, as with the Shakers for instance. It is apparent that as soon as cultural transmission involves 'cultural parents' who are not biological parents – that is to say, in the jargon, when cultural and genetic transmission are asymmetric to one another – cultural transmission processes can lead to outcomes which over-ride the genetically advantageous ones. How would a process of natural selection in the course of human evolution ever give rise to such a phenomenon? We have seen the answer already. It lies in the fact that it does not necessarily pay people to continue doing things in the way they learned from their parents. They may do better – whether in terms of hunting, gathering, planting crops or gaining prestige – by copying someone else. The fact that the routes of cultural transmission and genetic transmission are different from one another means that successful responses to selective pressures on cultural traditions will not necessarily produce outcomes enhancing the survival and reproductive success of the individuals in the population concerned. The result is that histories of people and histories of cultural traditions are linked to one another but they are not the same thing, although they may come close to coinciding in certain circumstances, for example when there is strong vertical transmission from parents to offspring.

It should be clear by now that the properties of cultural transmission processes are such that the dynamic outcomes of their interactions through time are not easily predictable. It does not necessarily follow from the adoption of the perspective outlined above that the specific features of historical trajectories will inevitably be overwhelmed by the impact of natural selection, although they may be. The interplay of transmission and evolutionary forces is the key to understanding patterns of stability and change in the past.

INDIVIDUALS, UNITS OF ANALYSIS AND SOCIAL ORDERS

It will have become apparent already that the starting point for the evolutionary approach is the theoretical position known as methodological individualism. This is the view that larger scale entities emerge from interactions between individuals. Individuals exist in all societies, in the sense of living creatures with a specific genotype, developmental history, birth, lifespan and death, and propensities to achieve goals which have been favoured by natural selection. Even identical twins are not the same person because of variations in the course of phenotypic development. How communities construct and conceptualise these individuals in the course of their lifetime has varied with time and place. In some they have had considerable autonomy; in others they may be conceived as having no individuality at all. This latter situation is not an argument against the existence of individuals, as some believe. On the contrary, it is an argument for raising the question of why it is that such constructions of individuality vary. This is precisely the question Mary Douglas (1978) addressed when she suggested that societies could be characterised in terms of their position on two dimensions: 'group', the extent to which individuals are subordinated to group values; and 'grid', the extent to which societies have strong social categories which distinguish people from one another and affect what they can do. The Indian caste system would be an example of a society with a very high value on the grid dimension. Cults which demand total loyalty from their members, even to the extent of mass suicide, would be examples of societies at the high extreme of the group dimension.

Not dissimilar issues have arisen in evolutionary biology, concerning the identification of valid levels of individuality at which evolution can be said to occur. One of the key breakthroughs in understanding how evolutionary forces affect social behaviour was the rejection of the group selection view that individuals would act for the good of the species, for example by opting not to reproduce because they perceived that the local environment was already close to carrying capacity. It was shown that individuals that did so would lose out to individuals who put their own reproductive interests first. Accordingly, individuals in the basic sense defined above have to be our starting point in understanding the evolution of social behaviour: individuals with a specific genotype, developmental history, birth, lifespan and death, and propensities to achieve goals which have been favoured by natural selection. Nevertheless, the situation is not clear-cut, for a number of reasons. First of all, even though all the genes that characterise an individual have a common interest because they share a common fate, there is nevertheless evidence for so-called 'intra-genomic conflict'; that is to say, genes producing effects which are for their own benefit rather than for the benefit of the organism as a whole. Furthermore, the evidence for the existence of apparent altruism within animal societies does not make sense if individuals are the only relevant entities for evolutionary purposes, because no individual should put itself at risk for the sake of another. The key concept in resolving this – Hamilton's (1964) idea of inclusive fitness – inevitably has the effect of dispersing the individual in certain respects and is of course one of the pillars of the 'selfish gene' concept (Dawkins 1976). Furthermore, others have argued that, despite the demise of earlier concepts of group selection, selection between higher level entities than individuals is the main mechanism which produces major evolutionary change. This view is a key part of Eldredge and Gould's (1972) 'punctuated equilibrium' theory of biological evolution over geological time. It has been generalised by authors such as Sober and Wilson (1998) into the idea of multi-level selection. Finally, all theoretical schools, including those that are sceptical about other levels of evolutionary process than that of individual inclusive fitness, recognise that such interests may often be served by co-operating rather than competing with other individuals of the same species.

GAME THEORY

At this point we need to introduce a further theoretical concept. Interactions cannot be analysed by using the straightforward optimisation framework that has been implicit up to now because, when individuals interact, the best thing to do in a given set of circumstances depends on what the other person decides to do, all the more so if they have different interests. It is in the context of such interactions that the difference between people's intentions and the consequences of their actions become particularly apparent, as does the fact that we need to take account of both intentions and consequences if we are to understand human social life. The tools used to explore the implications of this sort of situation are those of *game theory*.

Perhaps the classic game is Prisoner's Dilemma, so called because the eponymous version of the game presupposes that two people who committed a crime together are being held by the police in separate cells and being asked to inform on each other. If neither of them informs, then the police will only have the evidence to convict them on a lesser crime, so each will get one year in prison. If one informs and the other does not, then the one who informs will get away free while the other will have to take all the blame and will get a three year sentence. If they both inform on each other, then they will share the blame and each get a sentence of two years. If the game is played only once, the only sensible thing to do is inform, since otherwise the outcome may be the worst possible; thus, both informing is the equilibrium result. On the other hand, if they had co-operated both would have done better.

The game is classic because it raises the key issue for the existence of societies: in what circumstances will people forgo a certain amount of self-interest to produce an outcome which is good for both of them, but not as good as it could have been for one of them at the expense of the other. A number of types of real world situations seem to correspond in structure to Prisoner's Dilemma. Perhaps the best known is the so-called 'Tragedy of the Commons', which can arise in the exploitation of common resources. Suppose a fishing ground is being over-fished. It would pay all concerned to stop fishing there for a year to allow stocks to recover. This is fine if everyone agrees to do it but if some people cheat and ignore the agreement they will get the benefit of everyone else's restraint. Unless some arrangement can be reached, the best available pay-off will be produced by carrying on fishing and obtaining at least some share of the diminishing resource.

Where games are repeated, however, and people can make use of their previous experience, contingently co-operative strategies can lead to the establishment of co-operation. The best known of such strategies is tit-for-tat (Axelrod 1984), in which players start by co-operating and then respond in kind to whatever their opponent played on the last occasion they met. This leads to co-operation and reciprocity, to the long-term benefit of those concerned, in that no other strategy can do better than it in terms of the pay-offs it provides. The problem from the point of view of understanding how societies work is that reciprocity tends to break down in these models when groups become larger than 6–10 individuals, because reciprocators can be infiltrated by selfish individuals who take advantage of them and gain better pay-offs as a result (Boyd and Richerson 1988). Nevertheless, there are various ways round this problem that raise interesting issues for the nature of co-operative forms of social organisation.

One possibility is that there is selection at the group level which is stronger than that at the individual level, thus leading to the differential survival of groups with greater degrees of co-operation. Another possibility is that co-operation could be maintained by sanctions, including sanctions on those who fail to apply sanctions when they should. Of course, someone has to pay the costs of punishment; and this presents another Prisoner's Dilemma. As Boone (1992) explains, one possibility is that there may be a special interest group within the larger population that has more to gain from the maintenance of group co-operation than the rest and is therefore willing to pay the extra costs to ensure this. Political entrepreneurs might be one such category of people.

However, there are other possible ways in which co-operation may be maintained without either group selection or the development of hierarchies; for example, if individuals use their memory of previous encounters to refuse to interact with those who have previously acted in a non-co-operative fashion. Indeed, this is one way of producing a more general phenomenon: the development of correlated game strategies (Skyrms 1996). If we do away with the assumption of random encounters between individuals and assume that similar strategies (and strategists) will meet one another more often than dissimilar ones, then, even with a small amount of such correlation between strategies, the possibility of selfish, non-co-operative states of equilibrium, i.e. states where these strategies do best, is greatly reduced. One way in which such correlation can occur is if co-operators can recognise fellow co-operators. Another is the case where similar individuals cluster together spatially. As a result of such correlation the short-term interests of classical economic game theory can be overcome in favour of co-operative interactions. Skyrms (1996) suggests that many human social institutions have the function of generating and maintaining such correlations.

These ideas have been taken forward by Bowles and Gintis (1998) in a study of the evolution of what they call pro-social norms, defined as norms, or rules of conduct, whose increased frequency in a population enhances the level of well-being of members of that population in Prisoner's Dilemma-type situations. It is here that we see the merging of structure and agency at the individual level. Bowles and Gintis focus their argument on the existence and nature of communities – organisations that lack centralised institutions capable of making decisions binding on their members. They are organisations in which people know one another, and within which people interact more than with members of other communities. The authors argue that community norms arise from structures of social interaction. These norms are not rules chosen in the context of trying to maximise some utility. On the contrary, many of them may not have been actively chosen at all. The key to understanding norms is not rationality but differential replication in the process of cultural transmission: some norms are copied, retained and adopted by many people; others are not.

Bowles and Gintis show that a variety of effects associated with frequent interaction with the same people lead to the emergence of pro-social norms which enhance the average well-being of members of the communities concerned, in terms of the pay-offs that individuals receive for particular kinds of behaviour. Populations whose interactions are structured in such a way that co-ordination problems are successfully overcome will tend to grow, to absorb other populations and to be copied by others. It is the effect, not the meaning-content of the norms as such, that matters.

Apart from its implications for an understanding of how co-operative communities can emerge and be maintained, Bowles and Gintis's game theory model, and others like it, has important implications for the assumptions on which game theory is based. Many people have objected to game theory on the grounds that it posits hyper-rational and perfectly informed individuals attempting to optimise as they interact. In Bowles and Gintis's model, however, a rough learning rule replaces conscious optimisation. All that is *required* is for individuals to be capable of recognising more successful forms of behaviour, in terms of the benefits they get from interacting with others in particular ways, and copying these. They are not perfectly rational and fully informed. On the contrary, they have access to only fragmentary information and have only a partial understanding of the processes they are involved in; they do not think very far ahead, but they are not completely irrational. They take action on the basis of expectations, and those actions in turn become a precedent influencing the behaviour of agents in the future.

The nature of social institutions

The account just presented gives us a powerful way of characterising social institutions; structure, in other words. Such institutions are the outcomes of individual interactions – game conventions. The game conventions prevalent at time t provide the pay-off structure for interactions at time $t + 1$. These outcomes are the best responses it is possible to give in a particular kind of interaction, conditional on other people sticking to the convention. Most people follow the conventions most of the time. However, not everyone does, and sometimes, even by chance, the new way of responding will take over and become a new convention. Institutional change may arise from internal or external, inter-group processes.

Most games have many potential equilibria, so that different societies whose members do not interact are likely to have different social institutions (equilibrium expected behaviour patterns); what is standard in one society may not be standard in another. Such inter-group differences in social institutions may be further accentuated by the conformist transmission of cultural behaviour patterns, as well as by sanctions against deviant behaviour. Furthermore, distinct social norms and institutions can be maintained by different groups even in the presence of considerable interaction between them (see e.g. McElreath *et al.* 2003). In other words, history matters.

At this point we need to sum up the argument so far concerning the relations between individuals and groups. If we do not start at the individual level, it is impossible to understand how and why groups form and why they have the character they do. We do not even see that co-ordination problems and their solution or otherwise represent a key aspect of human social interactions. The unrealistic rational actor assumptions of classical game theory can be abandoned; all we need are individuals that are not completely irrational in terms of their responses to the situations in which they find themselves. The social construction of the nature and autonomy of those individuals in specific societies is not something which undermines the concept of the individual but an aspect of the nature of local social norms, passed on by social learning. Social institutions are local equilibrium game outcomes arising out of interactions between individuals. They maintain their continuity through time as a result of the pay-offs they provide for group members. Because there is always a large number of possible equilibria, groups with different histories are quite likely to have different social institutions, although contact and competition may lead to the spread of more successful ones.

CONCLUSION

The issues that agency theory is trying to deal with are very similar to those that arise in the evolutionary analysis of human behaviour in general and social behaviour in particular. This is particularly the case with the evolutionary approach known as dual inheritance theory, which recognises the role of both genetically and culturally transmitted information in affecting what people do. Some aspects of people's lives really can be productively modelled using simple reproductive fitness criteria to generate predictions. What such models show is not the uniformity of behaviour but the often subtle ways in which it varies in response to relevant conditions. In general though, cultural transmission makes a big difference. People are always born and quickly enculturated into specific local social and cultural contexts which provide the starting point for their subsequent decisions. Moreover, the nature of evolutionary individuality is not straightforward; it can be dispersed among different people and cannot simply be seen as arising from the universal features of individual biological organisms. As far as social interactions are concerned, when people have long-standing relationships with one another, they obtain their best pay-offs by adjusting their courses of action to one another and their understanding of this in cost-benefit terms leads to the emergence of individual social norms which predispose people to interact in the ways most likely to bring local success. The fact that individual personalities and positions differ means populations will always generate and contain variation which provides the basis for future change.

Methodologically, the evolutionary approach to agency provides us with a theoretically well-founded set of expectations with which to approach the archaeological record, but that does not mean that they will always be met, for a variety of reasons including the differing routes of cultural and genetic transmission. Those expectations that have been most fully operationalised in archaeological terms are those based on optimal foraging theory, which provide a basis for assessing the outcomes of human action in relation to the criteria on which they are based – short term maximisation, it appears, in some cases (see e.g. Broughton 1997; Nagaoka 2002), a strategy in which individual intentions are central but the longer term outcomes unintended. In other areas there is much more work to be done, but whether we are trying to understand the appearance and disappearance of monumental display or the fluctuating occurrence of co-operation and conflict in prehistory, it is already clear that an evolutionary approach to agency in its social and cultural context can suggest new understandings which in no way detract from humans' humanity (see, for example, Shennan 2002).

References

Axelrod, R. 1984. *The Evolution of Cooperation*. New York: Basic Books.

Boone, J.L. 1992. Competition, conflict and development of social hierarchies. In E.A. Smith and B. Winterhalder (eds.) *Evolutionary Ecology and Human Behavior*, 301–38. New York: Aldine de Gruyter.

Bowles, S. and Gintis, H. 1998. The moral economy of community: structured populations and the evolution of pro-social norms. *Evolution and Human Behaviour*, 19, 3–25.

Boyd, R. and Richerson, P.J. 1985. *Culture and the Evolutionary Process*. Chicago, IL: University of Chicago Press.

Boyd, R. and Richerson, P.J. 1988. The evolution of reciprocity in sizeable groups. *Journal of Theoretical Biology*, 132, 337–56.

Broughton, J.M. 1997. Widening diet breadth, declining foraging efficiency, and prehistoric harvest pressure: ichthyofaunal evidence from the Emeryville Shellmound, California. *Antiquity*, 71, 845–62.

Cullen, B. 1996. Social interaction and viral phenomena. In J. Steele and S.J. Shennan (eds.) *The Archaeology of Human Ancestry: power, sex and tradition*, 420–33. London: Routledge.

Dawkins, R. 1976. *The Selfish Gene*. Oxford: Oxford University Press.

Dennett, D. 1995. *Darwin's Dangerous Idea*. London: Allen Lane, Penguin.

Dornan, J.L. 2002. Agency and archaeology: past, present, and future directions. *Journal of Archaeological Method and Theory*, 9, 303–29.

Douglas, M. 1978. *Cultural Bias*. London: Royal Anthropological Institute.

Eldredge, N. and Gould, S.J. 1972. Punctuated equilibria: an alternative to phyletic gradualism. In T.M.J. Schopf (ed.) *Models in Paleobiology*, 82–115. San Francisco, CA: Freeman, Cooper & Co.

Hamilton, W.D. 1964. The genetic evolution of social behaviour, I, II. *Journal of Theoretical Biology*, 7, 1–52.

Henrich, J. 2001. Cultural transmission and the diffusion of innovations. *American Anthropologist*, 103:4, 1–23.

Kelly, R.L. 1995. *The Foraging Spectrum: diversity in hunter-gatherer lifeways*. Washington, DC: Smithsonian Institution Press.

McElreath, R., Boyd, R. and Richerson, P.J. 2003. Shared norms and the evolution of ethnic markers. *Current Anthropology*, 44, 122–29.

Mithen, S. 1990. *Thoughtful Foragers*. Cambridge: Cambridge University Press.

Nagaoka, L. 2002. Explaining subsistence change in southern New Zealand using foraging theory models. *World Archaeology*, 34:1, 84–102.

Ruddle, K. 1993. The transmission of traditional ecological knowledge. In J. Inglis (ed.) *Traditional Ecological Knowledge: concepts and cases*, 17–31. Ottawa: Canadian Museum of Nature.

Shennan, S.J. 1989. Cultural transmission and cultural change. In S.E. van der Leeuw and R. Torrence (eds.) *What's New?* 330–46. London: Unwin Hyman.

Shennan, S.J. 1991. Tradition, rationality and cultural transmission. In R.W. Preucel (ed.) *Processual and Post-Processual Archaeologies: multiple ways of knowing the past*, 197–208. Carbondale, IL: Centre for Archaeological Investigations, Southern Illinois University (Occasional Paper No. 10).

Shennan, S.J. 2002. *Genes, Memes and Human History: Darwinian archaeology and cultural evolution*. London: Thames and Hudson.

Skyrms, B. 1996. *Evolution of the Social Contract*. Cambridge: Cambridge University Press.

Sober, E. and Wilson, D.S. 1998. *Unto Others: the evolution and psychology of unselfish behavior*. Cambridge, MA: Harvard University Press.

Williams, G.C. 1992. *Natural Selection: domains, levels and challenges*. Oxford: Oxford University Press.

CHAPTER 3

AGENCY AND COMMUNITY IN 4th CENTURY BRITAIN: DEVELOPING THE STRUCTURATIONIST PROJECT

Andrew Gardner

INTRODUCTION: AGENCY, INDIVIDUALISM AND SOCIETY

In this chapter, my aim is to explore the social aspects of agency, and in so doing to argue that we need to be flexible in our understanding of the constitution of agency in particular cultural contexts. The question of whether the widespread conception of agency in terms of knowledgable, reflexive actors is always an appropriate one, or whether there have in fact been different kinds of selfhood or subjectivity, has recently been raised by some archaeologists (Gero 2000; MacGregor 1994; cf. Meskell 1999: 25–26). Here, I would like to suggest ways forward with this problem, based particularly on a consideration of different scales of power and social identity. I will begin this argument by reviewing some of the problems with defining agency, and then move on to a substantive case study in which I will try to demonstrate that sensitivity to multiple scales of social interaction is one way of addressing these. I will also, in the conclusion of the chapter, suggest that variations in the way that humans engage with temporality and material culture are also critical to understanding how 'the self' might be constituted differentially in different cultural contexts, and argue that archaeologists are well placed to address these issues, which are clearly of much broader relevance across the social sciences.

As is clear from the other chapters in this volume, the concept of agency has appeared in a number of different guises in archaeology (see the Introduction; cf. also Dobres and Robb 2000). Certainly one of the most influential formulations, though, is the version proposed by Anthony Giddens, in a series of books written in the later 1970s and early 1980s (Giddens 1993 [1976], 1979, 1984). Although Giddens has since moved onto other – though not unrelated – concerns and structuration theory figures rather minimally on his LSE website (www.lse.ac.uk/giddens/default.htm), this body of work remains at the core of an ongoing debate in the social sciences (e.g. Bryant and Jary 2001; Parker 2000). Giddens' view of agency draws upon the work of a diverse group of what might be labelled 'micro-sociologists', such as Schutz (e.g. 1967), Goffman (e.g. 1990 [1959]) and Garfinkel (e.g. 1984 [1967]), interested in social relations on a small scale, particularly at the level of face-to-face interactions between individuals. From such a background, Giddens produces a model of agency which posits human beings as knowledgable and self-reflexive, capable of continuously monitoring their own behaviour. Within this approach, two elements are particularly important. One is a stratified model of consciousness, which separates the practical consciousness involved in performing very routine actions, from discursive consciousness, within which one is capable of talking about what one is doing (Giddens 1984: 5–8).

Secondly, Giddens defines agency not simply in terms of intentionality, as has been the tendency in much discussion of action within Anglo-American philosophy, but rather in terms of the power to act, in ways that can have both intentional and unintentional consequences (Giddens 1984: 8–14). This is, therefore, a sophisticated understanding of agency, made more so by Giddens' linkage of the concept to structure; that is the large-scale institutions of social life. As expressed in the duality of structure (Giddens 1984: 16–28), Giddens argues that actors are powerful inasmuch as they produce and reproduce the structures of social life, at the same time as being influenced by those structures in the ways that daily life is carried on, particularly through the rules and resources that they furnish. Indeed, this idea of *structuration*, which takes Giddens away from small-scale social theory into an attempt to bridge the gap between the micro and macro levels of analysis, is embedded in the idea of actors as knowledgable of the world around them, and able to monitor interactions and draw upon structures on a routine basis.

Giddens' conception of agency is, therefore, complex, and attempts to cover a great deal of ground. Power, motivation, intentionality and knowledgability are all dealt with, and through these a link is established to social structure. However, this understanding of agency has come under attack from a number of angles, and some of these critiques do prompt us to develop what is in many other respects a formidable and very useful body of social theory. A number of critics feel that Giddens' actors are too tightly bound to routines. Certainly, Giddens argues that daily routines are the main vehicle for the reproduction of the rules of social structures, in the form of institutions, and the monitoring of how effectively one is performing those routines is a key part of his model of agency (Giddens 1984: 60–64). Barbara Adam, however, rightly regards this approach, which is effectively dealing with the problem of social time, as over-emphasising repetition at the expense of variation and transformation. This is partly due to Giddens' use of Lévi-Strauss' ideas on 'reversible time' and of the time-geography of Torsten Hägerstrand, both perspectives which tend to homogenise temporality (Adam 1990: 25–29; cf. Gardner 2001a: 38–39). Anthony Cohen goes further into the implications of this routinisation in terms of power, writing that "the 'agency' which he [Giddens] allows to individuals gives them the power of reflexivity, but not of motivation: they seem doomed to be perpetrators rather than architects of action" (Cohen 1994: 21). This view has also been echoed in archaeology by Lynn Meskell (1999: 25).

On the other hand, Giddens has also been accused of over-emphasising the power of the individual actor, in the sense that this particular model of agency is taken to be universal, while in fact it is imbued with certain values peculiar to people – and particularly men – living in the modern West (Elliott 2001: 41;

Gregory 1989: 211–13). This has certainly been a point of critique within archaeology, with writers like Gavin MacGregor and Joan Gero drawing attention to the autonomous and individualistic nature of Giddens' agent, whose universal application has potentially dangerous political consequences (Gero 2000: 37–38; MacGregor 1994: 80–85; cf. also Berggren 2000). While these two sets of critiques may seem to be coming from different and somewhat contradictory angles, this does draw out the way in which Giddens' agents may indeed be the ideal representatives of late capitalism, embodying the tensions of our era between conformity and individualism (cf. Johnson 1999: 83).

What these analyses do offer, though, is the notion that there might be more than one kind of agency, and this is something in which archaeologists should take great interest (Barrett 2000: 62; Moore 2000: 261–62). The constitution of the human subject in different contexts might not conform to the model that Giddens offers, but involve different social and political relations, different relationships with temporality, and different kinds of embodiment and engagement with the material world. These three themes – sociality, temporality, and materiality – are essential in exploring different kinds of agency, though in this chapter I will focus only on the first (cf. Gardner 2001a and 2003). In particular, I wish to pursue a strand of criticism of structuration theory developed by Margaret Archer and Nicos Mouzelis. Both authors, in different ways, argue that while Giddens' duality of structure avoids the typical pitfalls of submerging agency within structure or vice versa, it actually merges the two somewhere in-between (what Archer terms 'central conflation'), producing weak and indistinctive understandings of both (Archer 1995: 93–134; Mouzelis 1995: 117–26; Parker 2000: 69–113). These critiques, then, stress the importance of social hierarchy, and of the multiplicity of scales of both agency and structure within social life, effectively arguing for the retention of a dualism of these concepts. While there are flaws in some of this critical commentary (e.g. Mouzelis' apparent failure to recognise the role of discursive consciousness [1995: 119–21]), and the appeal to dualism may be questioned (see Chapter 1, this volume), it is certainly appropriate to point out that Giddens' understanding of social relations is 'hierarchically flat' (Parker 2000: 105–08).

This is because of his limited attention to social roles or identities, and his rather weak definition of institutions as simply "the more enduring features of social life" (Giddens 1984: 24; cf. Gardner 2002). This drastically underplays the role of institutions as sources of agency, as we will see in the case study to be examined below, and desensitises us to the fact that 'agency' and 'structure' can be regarded as existing on multiple, interrelated scales. Actors are not to be equated with the micro-scale of social life, because some can be extremely powerful 'macro actors' – like the Roman emperor; similarly, structures or institutions can exist on micro-scales, and in this can blur the boundary between individual and collective sources of social power. Mouzelis' attention to micro, meso (or middle) and macro scales of agency and institution (1995: 26–27) provides us with a more nuanced approach to the relationship between agency and structure, and also opens the door to alternative ways for these elements to be related under different social conditions.

ARCHAEOLOGIES OF ACTION AND PRACTICE

Indeed, an examination of the relationships between different scales of social persona in different societies can be regarded as one way of investigating alternative conceptualisations of the self: how is 'the individual' defined in relation to different scales of institution or community? My intention here is not to deny individuality, but to make it a problematic concept for exploration, within a multi-layered understanding of social life (cf. Hirst and Woolley 1982: 95–139; Mauss 1979: 59–94). I would argue that archaeology is well placed to address this kind of issue, being capable not only of engaging with alternative cultural contexts to our own, but also of analysing things on multiple temporal and spatial scales. While a key feature of Giddensian sociology – the importance of practices as ways of doing things – can be used to link archaeological patterns with meaningful action, it is also possible to expand upon Giddens' work by relating these practices to different scales of sociality, and by being rather more specific about the hierarchical relationships between different kinds of institution. One potential pitfall here is that archaeological patterns very much tend to involve aggregations of actions, and therefore the ways in which individuals are important in a given context may be swamped by social phenomena of greater scales. This need not actually be a problem, however, as the following example should demonstrate, because an emphasis on what is shared and contested in a broad range of material practices at different temporal and spatial scales can highlight both very micro and very macro actors and institutions.

I hope to convey this by examining some of the patterns of different archaeological – and social – scales that intersect on certain late Roman military sites in Britain. This is a good context in which to work with the ideas outlined above, involving as it does the marked transformation of imperial institutions over a fairly short time (from the late 3rd to the early 5th centuries AD). As we will see, the military is a particularly significant – and well-evidenced – element in these transformations. A convenient place to begin to think about patterns of practices is the fort of Caernarfon, in north-west Wales (Fig. 3.1). Occupied from the late 1st century AD to the 5th, this site has been quite extensively excavated, with the two major phases being those directed by Mortimer Wheeler in the 1920s, and an investigation of the south-east corner in the 1970s (Casey et al. 1993; Wheeler 1924). While the material from the earlier excavations can only be examined at certain scales – though is by no means useless – the more recent research produced fairly high-resolution artefactual and stratigraphic data. I have used this, via a fairly basic application of GIS, to explore the relationships between small finds and contexts within this particular area. Comparing some of the various chronological, typological and stratigraphic aspects of this material, in terms of dates and types of artefacts, and dates and kinds of contexts, carries us quite a long way in establishing small-scale patterns, which can be compared with similar analyses from other sites (cf. Gardner 2002).

The south-eastern part of the fort is an area which, for much of the 4th century, was fairly open, and used for activities such as rubbish-dumping and the manufacture of artefacts – this following earlier phases of structures, by

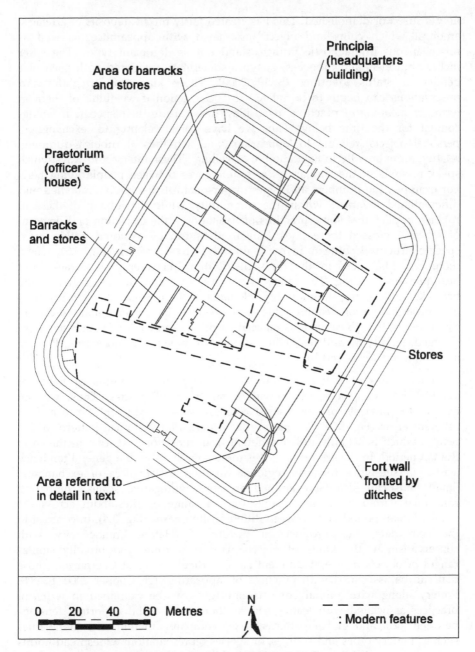

Fig. 3.1: Plan of Caernarfon, showing typical features of a Roman fort (plan after Casey *et al.* 1993: 8; Wheeler 1924: f.p. 186).

now disused or demolished. This has created fairly mixed deposits of artefacts, amongst which coins and objects associated with appearance, as well as miscellaneous undiagnostic fittings, stand out as dominant types. The latter include bracelets and brooches, of types sometimes associated with particular gender or status identities (Swift 2000). These kinds of straightforward observations can begin to be related to social action if we think of them in terms of meaningful practices, even if we leave aside their specific meaning-content for the time being. Thus we have coins, relating to 'exchanging', personal objects, relating to 'appearing', and activities of rubbish dumping, relating more broadly to habitation or 'dwelling'. These intersect in ways which speak to some of the similarities and differences between people living here. For example, the numbers and types of personal articles imply embodied and differentiated identities within the community, while the mixing of these in rubbish implies that some practices of habitation – the collection and disposal of refuse – crossed these lines. Similar ideas can be explored within more specific structural contexts in the legionary fortress at York (Fig. 3.2), where there are differences in the finds distributions between the barracks and headquarters building. The range of personal objects is much greater in the barracks, underlining the more official status of the *principia* through practices of deposition and/or cleaning. This status seems to have been enhanced during the course of the 4th century, as internal partitions and external routeways were changed, modifying and restricting routines of movement and access (Phillips and Heywood 1995a and b).

Other scales of patterning can also be explored in terms of fields of practice, involving comparison with a range of other sites. Thus, we can expand the analysis of coin-use to compare sites of different types and in different areas (Fig. 3.3). Caernarfon has a particular historical pattern in this regard, which is actually rather different from most forts, at least in the early Roman period. In the 4th century, it is more consistent with a general tendency across all site-types towards regional variation in practices of exchanging. Small finds can also be examined at more aggregative scales, comparing functional variation in assemblages from a range of sites, both across the whole Roman period and between different site phases (Fig. 3.4). In contrast to the coin data, this produces a picture of relative homogeneity, with conservatism in the kinds of objects used over time, and broadly similar ranges of objects in use at different sites, particularly, as at Caernarfon, those that can be associated with practices of 'appearing' (cf. Cooper 2000: 82–84). Pottery, along with animal bone assemblages, can be examined in terms of practices associated with 'eating'. Here, there seem to be important tensions between local and global patterns, if we compare different sites along lines such as pottery types and sources, or species representation: widespread norms of practice across Britain are mitigated by localised variations relating to smaller-scale preferences in supply and consumption. As with the other patterns, I would argue that positing these in terms of practices of eating opens up their interpretative potential (cf. Meadows 1994), allowing us to think about the contexts in which similarities and differences in ways of doing things can be discursively constituted as differences in identities.

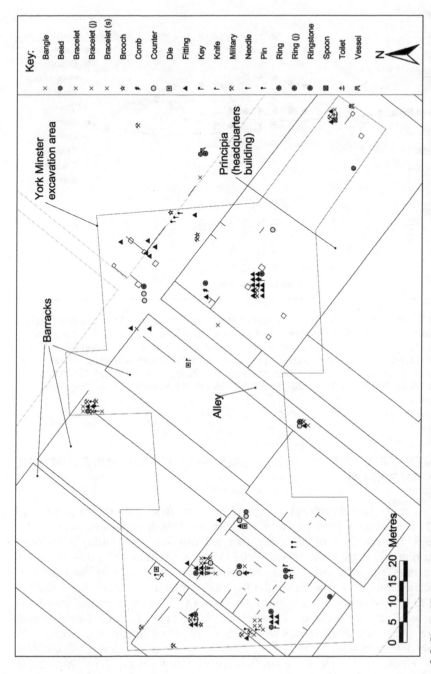

Fig. 3.2: Plan of the area of the York Minster excavations, in the central part of the fortress, showing the distribution of different small finds categories (after Monaghan 1997: Fig. 435; Ottaway 1996: Fig. 186; Phillips and Heywood 1995a: Fig. A; data from Price *et al.* 1995).

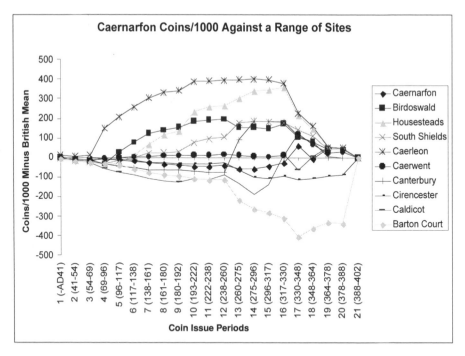

Fig. 3.3: Coin loss patterns from a range of sites, showing Caernarfon's place within a spectrum of military sites (Birdoswald – Caerleon) and towns/farms (Caerwent – Barton Court Farm). Each curve represents movement through time relative to the British Mean (i.e. an upward trend is above average, a downward trend below average, regardless of the absolute position of the points; see Reece 1995 for methodology). (Data from Boon 1988a; Gardner 2001c: 835–38, 855, 857–58, 860–61, 871–75, 887–90; King 1986.)

SCALES OF IDENTITY: INDIVIDUALS AND COMMUNITIES IN LATE ROMAN BRITAIN

Having made one significant interpretative step, from patterns to practices, I would like to move from practices to identities. This is important, because it is through the medium of identities that we can see how multiple scales of institution and agency interrelate. Social identities of different kinds – categories like gender, age, ethnicity, status, occupation, and arguably also 'the self' – are negotiated through similarities and differences in practice, and provide a medium for a great deal of social interaction. This is not to say that identities are always being explicitly constructed in everything that people do, but rather that even where specific identities are not salient, they still play a large part in defining the social constraints which affect how people 'go on' in interaction (Crossley 1996: 87–89; Elliott 2001: 31–36; Goffman 1990 [1959]: 136–40; cf. Giddens 1984: 22–23). A key feature of social identities is that they can be both fluid – because people have changing constellations of them – and fixed – that is, they serve to provide

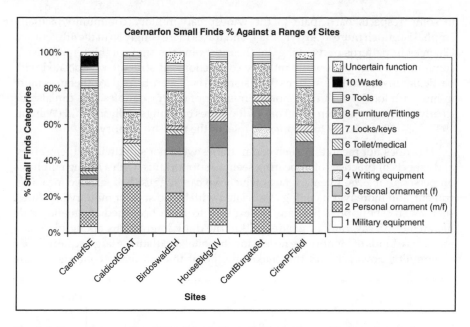

Fig. 3.4: Percentages of small finds from sites of different types (Caernarfon: fort; Caldicot: farm; Birdoswald and Housesteads: forts; Canterbury and Cirencester: towns). These are plotted according to functional categories, and show that most site assemblages are dominated by the same classes of finds (categories from Cool *et al.* 1995: 1626–47; data from Boon 1988b; Casey *et al.* 1993: 165–228; Jenkins 1951: 33–35; Rennie 1971: 79–84; Summerfield 1997: 269–321; Wilkes 1961: 294–98).

some structure and predictability to social interaction. In the latter sense, they can be regarded as institutionalised – abstracted from the complex and shifting currents of daily life – and thus very much as subject to hierarchies of power relations (Jenkins 1996: 90–138). In the patterns of practice I have described for late Roman fort communities in Britain, it is possible to detect different scales of identities, and pick out those that seem to have the most social resonance.

Before expanding upon these, it is important to note that there is also a body of textual material from a wider range of imperial contexts that can also be understood in terms of the construction of different levels of military identity (e.g. the writings of Ammianus Marcellinus; see Gardner 2001b). From this, as well as from phenomena such as the broad standardisation of fort architecture across the empire, it is obvious that the military was a macro-scale institution with strong links to state power. As such, and perhaps more in a social than an organisational sense, there was something of a community military identity across the empire (James 1999). Nonetheless, this community was internally sub-divided in a range of ways, both vertically and horizontally, and these produce a complex internal institutional hierarchy, which is even further complicated by the ways in which its external boundaries blur. The material patterns from sites like Caernarfon and York, which in some respects participate in the widespread military community, actually emphasise much more local dynamics, and this is increasingly so in the 4th century. Changes in patterns of dwelling are the most obvious signs of this, emphasising community rather than wider military connections, as structures associated with particular institutional functions (baths, streets etc.) were turned to other uses more in line with local priorities. Among a number of other examples, this can also be clearly seen in the conversion of one of the stores buildings at Birdoswald (Wilmott 1997: 203–09), probably to a domestic role, in the mid-4th century.

This does not mean that such communities were not sub-divided themselves, and aspects of practices of appearing seem to support this, with a strong emphasis on personal objects. Even artefacts which we can suggest had specific meaning-content, and moreover meanings associated with broad state or military identities, such as crossbow brooches, are more likely to have been tied to smaller-scale hierarchies of, say, rank or gender within the daily interactions taking place in a fort. These kinds of identity are no less institutionalised than the large-scale military community, however, and this makes the point that, in many contexts, we are

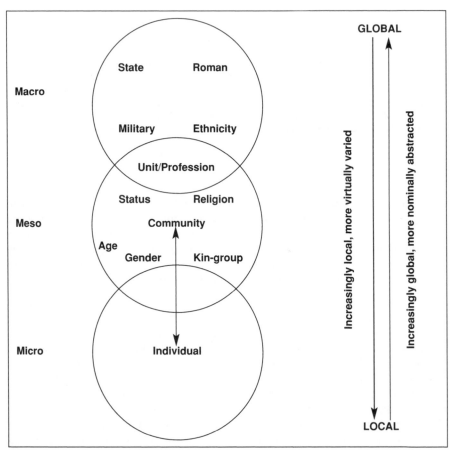

Fig. 3.5: A hierarchy of salient identity categories in late Roman-period Britain (after Gardner 2002: Fig. 7).

dealing with multiple scales and dimensions of institutions, within which actors – whether individuals or groups – have different degrees of power. This can perhaps be illustrated with a hierarchy of identities of varying scale which are relevant in this context (Fig. 3.5; cf. Gardner 2002: 345–46). This hierarchy is dynamic in the sense not only that different identities might be important in different contexts, but also that the power relationships between different collectivities are in flux. Late Roman state ideology emphasised order, homogeneity and control. This was articulated in motifs on coins stressing continuity, in law-codes (e.g. the Theodosian Code; Pharr 1952), and so forth. The material culture from Britain, in contrast, emphasises the continuity of local, particularly community traditions, and more fluidity with regard to practices linked to state power. Even where authority seems to be maintained, as in the central area at York, the very locality of this phenomenon (i.e. its exceptional character compared to other sites) underlines the general trend towards regionalisation. Although some of these changes could be seen in terms of Giddens' notion of unintended consequences of routine actions (1984: 8–14), one can also think of them in terms of different scales of collective agency. In this case, the small-scale institutions of individual communities were active forces in the decentralisation of the late Roman state.

But does the recognition of collective agency necessitate differences in the constitution of the self? In this particular context, and drawing upon other practices such as burial, the individual does not seem to be dispersed to any great extent, but there do seem to be significant connections between self and corporate identities which are perhaps different from those familiar to us, and arguably from those embedded within certain aspects of Giddens' conception of the human agent. This is not because there are no such connections for Giddens – as has been noted above, one critique is that he has enslaved actors to routines. Rather, it is because this routinisation is the primary connection between actors and institutions (e.g. Giddens 1984: 35–36); on the contrary, I think that, in the archaeology of late Roman Britain, we see the potential for social *change* in the agency of small-scale collectivities operating within larger institutional frameworks. Different levels of identity are made fixed or fluid by the activities of individuals operating together, and the community of place seems a particularly important focus for some of the practices that have been discussed here. Moreover, there are certainly other reasons for considering alternative 'technologies of the self' in the Roman world at large (cf. Mauss 1979: 75–89; Thomas 1989, 2000), among them the institution of slavery, concepts of civilisation and barbarism, practices of naming, and the importance of patronage relations and community engagement in defining the worth of individuals. Given that these had consequences in terms of power and knowledge, we might expect differences in the self-understanding of someone born into slavery as against someone born a semi-divine emperor.

CONCLUSION: THE SOCIAL (MATERIAL, TEMPORAL) CONSTITUTION OF AGENCY

Even though the argument pursued here has focused on the ways in which the Giddensian notion of agency is capable of modification or elaboration, this has still been done by working within a framework based firmly on some of Giddens' key ideas, such as the importance of practices in social life. Through thinking about hierarchies of identity, and the ways in which these may impact upon the self, I believe we can develop these ideas rather than reject them, and sharpen our sensitivity to noticeable differences in practices as well as routines. In essence, my aim in this chapter has been to flesh out Giddens' picture of the social world, through the themes of hierarchy, identity and community. These have the potential to open up variations in the constitution of the self, or at least to situate selves within a more complex and differentiated social order, where actors can be both micro and macro, and individual or collective (cf. Mouzelis 1995: 26–27; Parker 2000: 106). In addition to this overall theme of 'sociality' (cf. Mead 1938: 609, 654–56; Miller 1973: 188–91), I would suggest that there are two other dimensions along which archaeologists, in particular, can pursue the project of developing Structuration theory, and with it the Giddensian conception of agency. These are materiality and temporality.

Materiality is in many ways the most obvious, and a number of archaeologists have made the point that Giddens pays little attention to either embodiment or material culture (e.g. Barrett and Fewster 2000: 31; Meskell 1999: 25–26). Critics from other disciplines have made related observations, for instance geographers who feel that Giddens' understanding of space is not particularly sensitive to the meaningful qualities of place (Gregory 1989: 204). These critiques are well-founded, and in my examination of 4th century contexts from Britain I hope a sense of the engagement of material culture in identity negotiation at a range of different scales of practice has come through. Beyond this, there is certainly potential for alternative conceptualisations of the relationships between embodied people and things (Gardner 2003; cf. Miller 1994; Schiffer 1999; Thomas 1989; Tilley 1991). These relationships – which might be expressed in terms of processes of objectification, mediation and hybridisation – have been relatively under-emphasised in much social theory and philosophy, at least until very recently (Attfield 2000; Dant 1999; Graves-Brown (ed.) 2000; though see e.g. the earlier work of Mead [2002 (1932): 135–51; cf. McCarthy 1984] and Merleau-Ponty [1962: 348–402]). They are, however, likely to be critical elements in different technologies of the self. This is most apparent in situations where people are treated as things, as in the context of slavery, but such themes can also be explored in more generalised circumstances, where self-identities are formed through different hybrids of people and things (Urry 2000: 77–78; cf. Latour 2000). In 5th century Britain, for instance, there are striking changes in material culture which generate an impression of people who are archaeologically-invisible, in a period otherwise known as the 'Dark Ages' (or, less prejudicially, the post-Roman period). These changes are unlikely to be meaningless in the relationships between material culture and identities of different scales in this period (cf. Criado 1995), and therefore potentially in the definition of social personae.

Temporality is an altogether more difficult theme to pursue. While one of Giddens' major contributions to social theory is the central place he affords to time – along with space – in understanding the constitution of society, he is again restricted to certain kinds of time. The emphasis placed upon repetition, particularly in pre-modern societies, contains the danger of crushing change in such societies beneath the weight of tradition. With regard to modern societies, Giddens has a tendency to treat time as an abstract container for action, rather than as a field implicated within interaction (Adam 1990: 25–30; Gardner 2001a: 38–45; Meskell 1999: 26). This is a difficult concept to get across, mainly because our abstract, chronological understanding of time is so deeply embedded in our definition of the concept. However, when we think about the different ways in which we actually relate to temporality in daily life – the different tempos of activities, our different senses of time passing or of our relationship to past, present and future – we can begin to see how there are alternatives to clock time, even within our own society (Adam 1994). Temporality must be central to any understanding of agency in relation to either cognitive or social processes (Emirbayer and Mische 1998), and the variable way in which it is understood must also, therefore, be taken on board in exploring different constitutions of agency.

Sociality, materiality and temporality are, therefore, critical dimensions of agency along which we may be able to chart alternatives to the Giddensian understanding of this concept. Indeed, they can be envisaged as overlapping fields within which different kinds of agency – as a certain kind of relationship – can emerge, upon which can also be overlaid the three key modalities of action: reflective, habitual and affective (Fig. 3.6; cf. Chapter 1, this volume). It is

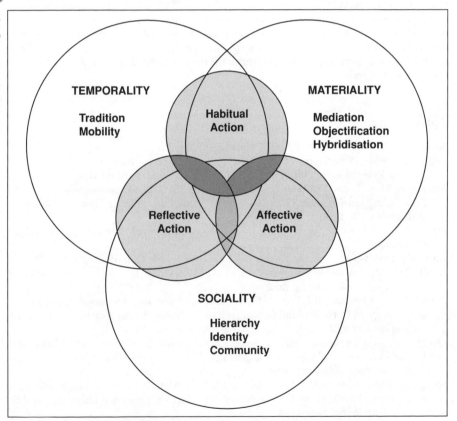

Fig. 3.6: A model of the three dimensions (temporal, social, material) along which human agency can be defined, overlaid with the three modalities of human action (habitual, reflective, affective).

important to note, in conclusion, that consideration of the notion of agency in this fashion is a political matter. The implications of making the definition of agency historically problematic are, therefore, also political, and indeed moral and ethical (cf. Taylor 1985: 15–114), since what is under scrutiny is something which has been posited as the very essence of human life. Once again, it seems, archaeologists place themselves in a position of ontological and political uncertainty, with no clear ground to make for. Are Giddens' agents more dangerous as models for human power than those situated in other contexts, like the Roman discourse of barbarism? In confronting these difficult issues, archaeologists have a genuine contribution to make to a broad and ongoing debate in the social sciences (e.g. Parker 2000: 102–25), and must therefore continue to discuss agency. The stakes are high, but if we recognise the distinction between our understandings of agency and those of past others, we free up the possibilities for archaeology as a politically-relevant social science in the present.

Acknowledgments

I would like to thank Mark Hassall, Jeremy Tanner, Richard Reece, Stephen Shennan, Matthew Johnson and Simon James for their advice and encouragement in the research upon which this chapter draws, which was funded by the Arts and Humanities Research Board of the British Academy. I would also like to thank Stephanie Koerner, Koji Mizoguchi and Bill Sillar for useful discussion of some of the themes of the chapter, and Peter Ucko for his continued support.

References

Adam, B. 1990. *Time and Social Theory*. Cambridge: Polity Press.

Adam, B. 1994. Perceptions of time. In T. Ingold (ed.) *Companion Encyclopedia of Anthropology: humanity, culture and social life*, 503–26. London: Routledge.

Ammianus Marcellinus. *The Later Roman Empire (AD 354–378)*. Harmondsworth: Penguin Books (Penguin Classics) (Translated by W. Hamilton, with an Introduction by A. Wallace-Hadrill, 1986).

Archer, M.S. 1995. *Realist Social Theory: the morphogenetic approach*. Cambridge: Cambridge University Press.

Attfield, J. 2000. *Wild Things: the material culture of everyday life*. Oxford: Berg.

Barrett, J.C. 2000. A thesis on agency. In M.-A. Dobres and J.E. Robb (eds.) *Agency in Archaeology*, 61–68. London: Routledge.

Barrett, J.C. and Fewster, K.J. 2000. Intimacy and structural transformation: Giddens and archaeology. In C. Holtorf and H. Karlsson (eds.) *Philosophy and Archaeological Practice: perspectives for the 21st century*, 25–33. Göteborg: Bricoleur Press.

Berggren, K. 2000. The knowledge-*able* agent? On the paradoxes of power. In C. Holtorf and H. Karlsson (eds.) *Philosophy and Archaeological Practice: perspectives for the 21st century*, 39–46. Göteborg: Bricoleur Press.

Boon, G.C. 1988a. The coins. In B.E. Vyner and D.W.H. Allen, A Romano-British settlement at Caldicot, Gwent, 91. In D.M. Robinson (ed.) *Biglis, Caldicot and Llandough*, 65–122. Oxford: BAR British Series 188.

Boon, G.C. 1988b. Miscellaneous finds. In B.E. Vyner and D.W.H. Allen, A Romano-British settlement at Caldicot, Gwent, 93–99. In D.M. Robinson (ed.) *Biglis, Caldicot and Llandough*, 65–122. Oxford: BAR British Series 188.

Bryant, C.G.A. and Jary, D. 2001. The uses of structuration theory: a typology. In C.G.A. Bryant and D. Jary (eds.) *The Contemporary Giddens: social theory in a globalizing age*, 43–61. Houndmills: Palgrave.

Casey, P.J., Davies, J.L. and Evans, J. (eds.) 1993. *Excavations at Segontium (Caernarfon) Roman Fort, 1975–1979*. London: C.B.A. Research Report 90.

Cohen, A.P. 1994. *Self Consciousness: an alternative anthropology of identity*. London: Routledge.

Cool, H.E.M., Lloyd-Morgan, G. and Hooley, A.D. 1995. *Finds from the Fortress*. York: Council for British Archaeology/York Archaeological Trust (The Archaeology of York: The Small Finds, 17/10).

Cooper, N. 2000. Rubbish counts: quantifying portable material culture in Roman Britain. In S. Pearce (ed.) *Researching Material Culture*, 75–86. Leicester: University of Leicester, School of Archaeological Studies (Material Culture Study Group, Occasional Paper No. 1).

Criado, F. 1995. The visibility of the archaeological record and the interpretation of social reality. In I. Hodder, M. Shanks, A. Alexandri, V. Buchli, J. Carman, J. Last, and G. Lucas (eds.) *Interpreting Archaeology*, 194–204. London: Routledge.

Crossley, N. 1996. *Intersubjectivity: the fabric of social becoming*. London: Sage Publications.

Dant, T. 1999. *Material Culture in the Social World*. Buckingham: Open University Press.

Dobres, M.-A. and Robb, J.E. 2000. Agency in archaeology: paradigm or platitude? In M.-A. Dobres and J.E. Robb (eds.) *Agency in Archaeology*, 3–17. London: Routledge.

Elliott, A. 2001. *Concepts of the Self*. Cambridge: Polity Press.

Emirbayer, M. and Mische, A. 1998. What is agency? *American Journal of Sociology*, 103.4, 962–1023.

Gardner, A. 2001a. The times of archaeology and archaeologies of time. *Papers from the Institute of Archaeology*, 12, 35–47.

Gardner, A. 2001b. Identities in the late Roman army: material and textual perspectives. In G. Davies, A. Gardner and K. Lockyear (eds.) *TRAC 2000: Proceedings of the 10th Annual Theoretical Roman Archaeology Conference, London 2000*, 35–47. Oxford: Oxbow Books.

Gardner, A. 2001c. 'Military' and 'Civilian' in Late Roman Britain: an Archaeology of Social Identity. Unpublished PhD thesis, Institute of Archaeology, UCL (University of London).

Gardner, A. 2002. Social identity and the duality of structure in late Roman-period Britain. *Journal of Social Archaeology*, 2:3, 323–51.

Gardner, A. 2003. Seeking a material turn: the artefactuality of the Roman empire. In G. Carr, E. Swift and J. Weekes (eds.) *TRAC 2002: Proceedings of the 12th Annual Theoretical Roman Archaeology Conference, Canterbury 2002*, 1–13. Oxford: Oxbow Books.

Garfinkel, H. 1984 [1967]. *Studies in Ethnomethodology*. Cambridge: Polity Press.

Gero, J.M. 2000. Troubled travels in agency and feminism. In M.-A. Dobres and J.E. Robb (eds.) *Agency in Archaeology*, 34–39. London: Routledge.

Giddens, A. 1979. *Central Problems in Social Theory: action, structure and contradiction in social analysis*. Houndmills: Macmillan.

Giddens, A. 1984. *The Constitution of Society*. Cambridge: Polity Press.

Giddens, A. 1993 [1976]. *New Rules of Sociological Method*. Cambridge: Polity Press (2nd edition).

Goffman, E. 1990 [1959]. *The Presentation of Self in Everyday Life*. Harmondsworth: Penguin.

Graves-Brown, P.M. (ed.) 2000. *Matter, materiality and modern culture*. London: Routledge.

Gregory, D. 1989. Presences and absences: time-space relations and structuration theory. In D. Held and J.B. Thompson (eds.) *Social Theory of Modern Societies: Anthony Giddens and his critics*, 185–214. Cambridge: Cambridge University Press.

Hirst, P. and Woolley, P. 1982. *Social Relations and Human Attributes*. London: Tavistock Publications.

James, S. 1999. The community of the soldiers: a major identity and centre of power in the Roman empire. In P. Baker, C. Forcey, S. Jundi and R. Witcher (eds.) *TRAC 98: Proceedings of the 8th Annual Theoretical Roman Archaeology Conference, Leicester 1998*, 14–25. Oxford: Oxbow Books.

Jenkins, F. 1951. *Roman Canterbury: an Account of the Excavations in Burgate in 1946–48*. London: Medici Society (Roman Canterbury V).

Jenkins, R. 1996. *Social Identity*. London: Routledge.

Johnson, M. 1999. *Archaeological Theory: an introduction*. Oxford: Blackwell.

King, C.E. 1986. Coins. In D. Miles (ed.) *Archaeology at Barton Court Farm, Abingdon, Oxon*, mf.5/B7–C5. London/Oxford: C.B.A. Research Report 50/Oxford Archaeological Unit Report 3.

Latour, B. 2000. The Berlin key or how to do words with things. In P.M. Graves-Brown (ed.) *Matter, materiality and modern culture*, 10–21. London: Routledge.

MacGregor, G. 1994. Post-processual archaeology: the hidden agenda of the secret agent. In I. Mackenzie (ed.) *Archaeological Theory: progress or posture?*, 79–91. Aldershot: Avebury (Worldwide Archaeology Series, 11).

Mauss, M. 1979. *Sociology and Psychology: essays*. London: Routledge and Kegan Paul (Translated by B. Brewster).

McCarthy, E.D. 1984. Toward a sociology of the physical world: George Herbert Mead on physical objects. *Studies in Symbolic Interaction*, 5, 105–21.

Mead, G.H. 1938. *The Philosophy of the Act*. Chicago, IL: University of Chicago Press (Edited with an Introduction by C.W. Morris).

Mead, G.H. 2002 [1932]. *The Philosophy of the Present*. Amherst, NY: Prometheus Books.

Meadows, K.I. 1994. You are what you eat: diet, identity and Romanisation. In S. Cottam, D. Dungworth, S. Scott and J. Taylor (eds.) *TRAC 94: Proceedings of the 4th Annual Theoretical Roman Archaeology Conference, Durham*, 133–40. Oxford: Oxbow Books.

Merleau-Ponty, M. 1962. *Phenomenology of Perception*. London: Routledge and Kegan Paul.

Meskell, L. 1999. *Archaeologies of Social Life*. Oxford: Blackwell.

Miller, D. 1994. Artefacts and the meaning of things. In T. Ingold (ed.) *Companion Encyclopedia of Anthropology: humanity, culture and social life*, 396–419. London: Routledge.

Miller, D.L. 1973. *George Herbert Mead: self, language and the world*. Austin, TX: University of Texas Press.

Monaghan, J. 1997. *Roman Pottery from York*. York: York Archaeological Trust/Council for British Archaeology (The Archaeology of York: The Pottery, 16/8).

Moore, H.L. 2000. Ethics and ontology: why agents and agency matter. In M.-A. Dobres and J.E. Robb (eds.) *Agency in Archaeology*, 259–63. London: Routledge.

Mouzelis, N. 1995. *Sociological Theory: What Went Wrong? Diagnosis and remedies*. London: Routledge.

Ottaway, P. 1996. *Excavations and Observations on the Defences and Adjacent Sites, 1971–90*. York: York Archaeological Trust/Council for British Archaeology (The Archaeology of York: The Legionary Fortress, 3/3).

Parker, J. 2000. *Structuration*. Buckingham: Open University Press.

Pharr, C. 1952. *The Theodosian Code and Novels and the Sirmondian Constitution*. Princeton, NJ: Princeton University Press (Translation, commentary, glossary and bibliography by C. Pharr with T.S. Davidson and M.B. Pharr; introduction by C. Dickerman Williams).

Phillips, D. and Heywood, B. 1995a. *Excavations at York Minster, Volume I: Roman to Norman: the Roman legionary fortress at York and its exploitation in the early Middle Ages A.D. 71–1070. Part 1: the site*. Swindon: Royal Commission on the Historical Monuments of England (Edited by M.O.H. Carver).

Phillips, D. and Heywood, B. 1995b. *Excavations at York Minster, Volume I: Roman to Norman: the Roman legionary fortress at York and its exploitation in the early Middle Ages AD 71–1070. Part 2: the finds*. Swindon: Royal Commission on the Historical Monuments of England (Edited by M.O.H. Carver).

Price, J., Henig, M., Manning, W.H., Lloyd-Morgan, G., Butcher, S.A., MacGregor, A.S. and Walton, P. 1995. Small finds reports. In D. Phillips and B. Heywood, *Excavations at York Minster, Volume I: Roman to Norman: the Roman legionary fortress at York and its exploitation in the early Middle Ages AD 71–1070. Part 2: the finds*, 346–432. Swindon: Royal Commission on the Historical Monuments of England (Edited by M.O.H. Carver).

Reece, R. 1995. Site-finds in Roman Britain. *Britannia*, 26, 179–206.

Rennie, D.M. 1971. Excavations in the Parsonage Field, Cirencester, 1958. *Transactions of the Bristol and Gloucestershire Archaeological Society*, 90, 64–94.

Schiffer, M. (with the assistance of A.R. Miller) 1999. A behavioral theory of meaning. In J.M. Skibo and G.M. Feinman (eds.) *Pottery and People: a dynamic interaction*, 199–217. Salt Lake City, UT: University of Utah Press.

Schutz, A. 1967. *The Phenomenology of the Social World*. Evanston, IL: Northwestern University Press.

Summerfield, J., with contributions from Allason-Jones, L., Bayley, J., Coulston, J.C.N., Davies, J., Edwards, G., Henig, M., Lloyd-Morgan, G., Mould, Q., Price, J., Cottam, S., Riddler, I. and Tomlin, R.S.O. 1997. The small finds. In T. Wilmott, *Birdoswald: Excavations of a Roman fort on Hadrian's Wall and its successor settlements: 1987–92*, 269–361. London: English Heritage (Archaeological Report 14).

Swift, E. 2000. *The End of the Western Roman Empire: an archaeological investigation*. Stroud: Tempus.

Taylor, C. 1985. *Human Agency and Language: philosophical papers 1*. Cambridge: Cambridge University Press.

Thomas, J. 1989. Technologies of the self and the constitution of the subject. *Archaeological Review from Cambridge*, 8:1, 101–07.

Thomas, J. 2000. Reconfiguring the social, reconfiguring the material. In M.B. Schiffer (ed.) *Social Theory in Archaeology*, 143–55. Salt Lake City, UT: University of Utah Press.

Tilley, C. 1991. Materialism and an archaeology of dissonance. *Scottish Archaeological Review*, 8, 14–22.

Urry, J. 2000. *Sociology Beyond Societies: mobilities for the twenty-first century*. London: Routledge.

Wheeler, R.E.M. 1924. *Segontium and the Roman Occupation of Wales*. London: The Honourable Society of Cymmrodorion.

Wilkes, J. 1961. Excavations in Housesteads Fort, 1960. *Archaeologia Aeliana*, 39 (Series 4), 279–301.

Wilmott, T. 1997. *Birdoswald: excavations of a Roman fort on Hadrian's Wall and its successor settlements: 1987–92*. London: English Heritage (Archaeological Report 14).

CHAPTER 4

'AGENCY' THEORY APPLIED: A STUDY OF LATER PREHISTORIC LITHIC ASSEMBLAGES FROM NORTHWEST PAKISTAN

Justin Morris

INTRODUCTION: DEFINING 'AGENCY'

At the broadest level, James Bell (1992: 30) distinguishes three types of explanation that are being applied within the "cognitive revolution" (an overall shift in method and theory) that is currently taking place in prehistoric archaeology: an 'holistic' approach in which the thoughts of individuals are *not* a significant factor in the development and structure of human social organisation; an 'individualistic' approach wherein the thoughts of individuals *are* considered a significant factor in such organisation; and an 'empathetic' approach which assumes that the inner experience of individuals is worthy of study for its own sake.

It is the individualistic approach that I am concerned with here, for I take this to be the approach within which agency theory is situated. Bell (1992: 38) goes on to identify two principal criticisms levelled at the 'individualistic' approach: (a) that human agency is not a legitimate study in scientific theories; and (b) that the method cannot be interpreted empirically. In order to debate these criticisms we need to define what we mean by 'agency' and how it can be practically integrated into an archaeological methodology. Marcia-Anne Dobres and John Robb (2000: 8) define four principles that underlie the study of agency:

- the material conditions of social life;
- the simultaneously constraining and enabling influence of social, symbolic and material structures and institutions, habituations, and beliefs;
- the importance of the motivations and actions of agents;
- the dialectic of structure and agency.

This provides a basis for the formulation of a working definition relevant to specific research questions. The material conditions of social life, social, symbolic and material structures, habituations, and beliefs are all aspects of an interpretation of the archaeological record that have been explored with the development of post-processual archaeology. However, the importance of the motivations and actions of agents and the dialectic of structure and agency are more abstract concepts that have only recently begun to be considered in archaeological contexts. This chapter aims to explore the potential for interpretation of the archaeological record from this latter standpoint through an examination of the relationship between lithic technology and social organisation during the fourth to third millennia BC in northwest Pakistan.

The potential for an interpretation or explanation based on agency and social structures depends greatly on the resolution of the data available to the archaeologist and the degree of detail that can be extracted from it. The archaeological dataset discussed here provides enough resolution to explore the intentions and hence choices made by individuals, but only at the scale of the settlement as a whole. In this research it is suggested that *intentions* are what characterise an agent and that *choices* are the outcome of these intentions. It is the choices that link the tangible archaeological record to an interpretation of that record in terms of the somewhat intangible motivations of agents. Therefore, whilst the dataset might not provide as much resolution as desired (such as evidence of a single core reduction event), it is perhaps more reflective of the data available to the majority of archaeologists working in South Asia and, indeed, beyond.

In order to accommodate this particular degree of resolution the collective ideas or motives of the group have become the focus, examined through their technological behaviour. The individual is generic. The site upon which I will concentrate (Sheri Khan Tarakai) was occupied during the fourth to third millennium BC and the material culture remains predominantly homogenous during this time, and so it is suggested that the social structures present at the site would also have remained predominantly unchanged over this period. Dobres (2000: 133) highlights the fact that the term "agent" is not necessarily synonymous with the individual, and considers a "community of practice" e.g. a group of technical labourers, to be as much an "agent" as each individual in the group. Reconstruction of individual event sequences, such as the *chaîne opératoire*, may make it possible to discern intentionality and decision-making without relating this to a particular individual.

DEFINING 'TECHNOLOGY'

Central to the approach to agency taken in this chapter is a particular approach to material culture or technology. Technology is a fundamental medium through which social relationships, power structures and worldviews are expressed and defined (Dobres and Hoffman 1994: 211). Many authors (such as Dobres [1995, 1996] and Mark Edmonds [1990]) have noted that traditionally the study of prehistoric technology has been structured around environmental conditions, such as the physical constraints imposed by the nature of raw materials, the functional requirements of the artefacts, and the overall adaptive strategies that were created to promote cultural survival through technological means.

Edmonds (1990: 56) suggests that, essentially, technology has been placed between people and nature, which denies any role for human agency in the act of material selection, production, and technological change. This is certainly true for a great deal of Anglophone research; however, anthropological theory has had a tremendous influence on the definition and application of technological studies within French archaeology. In particular the notion of the *chaîne opératoire*, as defined by André Leroi-Gourhan (1943), provides a basis from which numerous French scholars have explored the relationship between the material and the social, such as Pierre Lemonnier (1993), who retains a distinction between different aspects of technology – style and physical function – but emphasises that both have social dimensions.

In another approach, scholars such as Timothy Ingold (1990: 7) are exploring the concept of a deconstructed technology, broken down into a number of components. He distinguishes between technology and technique. Technique is embedded in the experience of particular subjects in the shaping of particular things (relating this to the capabilities of individuals), whereas technology consists of the knowledge of objective principles of mechanical functioning, which are capable of practical application. Therefore technique might be considered as 'style'.

Traditionally the variability among technological attributes or components has been examined in order to assess the complexity of social organisation. However, as Dobres (1996: 224) points out, these social dynamics also contributed to the shape of the technological system. Culture is therefore constructed of dynamic reflexive processes, which need to be studied using research programmes that allow for broader interpretative statements to be made.

To this end, Dobres (1995: 27) provides a definition of technology that highlights the social, material, and symbolic dimensions of material culture production, while acknowledging that how technology is defined structures what is studied as technological:

> Because all technologies depend on social relations of production, technology is properly defined as a materially grounded arena for dynamic social interaction involved in the planning, production, use, repair, and discard of material culture (Dobres 1995: 27).

'AGENCY' THEORY APPLIED

Lithic implements retain traces of the successive phases involved in their production very well, and are generally considered good indicators of the intentions of their makers and users. This is particularly true when compared to other forms of material culture such as ceramics, which require a greater degree of investment in terms of research resources to understand the production processes.

The application of the *chaîne opératoire* method has been adopted by increasing numbers of researchers, who have focused in particular on the stages of raw material reduction (Dobres and Hoffman 1994: 237). The framework of the *chaîne opératoire* method is well suited to linking the tangible and intangible aspects of embodied technological practice into a single whole (Dobres 2000: 155). Instead of delineating only stimulus and response constraints, such as those pertaining to the physics, chemistry, and mechanics of a raw material, the *chaîne opératoire* allows statements to be made about cognitive matters.

The *chaîne opératoire* approach recognises that technical gestures are performed in public domains and highlights the sequential nature of both material and social production (Dobres 2000: 155). The analysis of the reduction sequence has demonstrated that variability within lithic assemblages occurs throughout the production process, therefore opening up a much broader range of contexts within which this variability might be generated. Catherine Perlès (1992) discusses this in some detail. Differences between artefacts are no longer considered in exclusively typological terms, but also conceptual, technical, and economic. In turn, the underlying causal factors for such variation are likely to be equally as diverse, therefore dispelling the idea that individual explanations such as culture, or functional needs are solely responsible for artefact differentiation. This is not to say that the individual factors do not have some role to play; it is simply that more emphasis has to be given to understanding the degree of influence of that factor, or the likelihood of multiple factors (Perlès 1992: 224).

The *chaîne opératoire* research methodology places an emphasis on individual choice, which through the application of specific methods such as experimental studies can be more fully understood, as alternative strategies can be posited and the different potentials of each explored. Perlès (1992: 224) outlines a number of fundamental underlying propositions of her research, particularly that for any given task there will be a number of potential tools and techniques, with technical needs guiding the production of tools whilst the context (social and economic) limits the range of effective solutions. Only the *recurrent* choices of the options available throughout the manufacturing process can be analysed in terms of strategies, which will enable comparisons to be made between these strategies and the given variables of an archaeological situation (e.g. raw material availability), and therefore permit identification of those variables which have been the most constraining (Perlès 1992: 225).

Dobres (2000: 174) posits a series of questions that might be asked by an archaeologist inquiring into the social agency of ancient technological practice. Essentially she emphasises the notion that choices are made during the production process at a variety of social scales, e.g. individual, group, or settlement, but that these choices may not necessarily have been condoned by or reflect the broader production strategy of the culture. This is agency, the potential for individuals to make choices that do not necessarily reflect the broader strategy of a community – i.e. the ability to make choices for oneself. People make choices within different social contexts, which will be reflected within a technological system, which is enabled or constrained by particular social boundaries. This technological system may be identifiable within the archaeological record.

METHODOLOGY

Many models for interpreting technology from a social perspective are beginning to appear, such as those of Perlès (1992), and Hayden (1990). From these I have

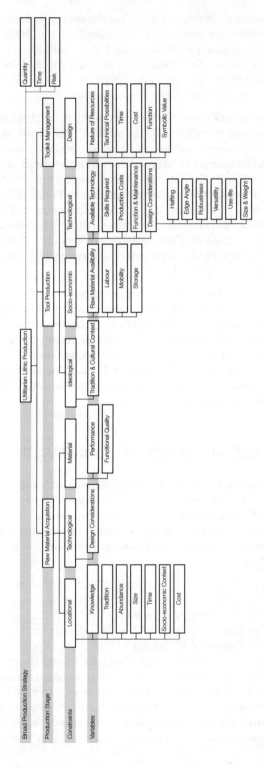

Fig. 4.1: An organisational chart of a lithic tool life cycle and its potential enabling and constraining variables.

developed an organisational chart (see Fig. 4.1) of the conceptual stages of a lithic life cycle, which provides the framework against which the lithic assemblage analysed from the study region can be compared and contrasted. The chart has been designed to emphasise the notions of enablement and constraint, as discussed by Giddens (1984: 169), and the potential for individuals to make technological choices, based on the theory discussed above.

The conceptual framework identifies four levels of a technological process, in this case lithic manufacture, though it could be applied to any form of technology. The 'broad production strategy' will be constrained overall by the variables of quantity (of end products needed), time (available for the entire strategy), and risk (such as that associated with failure). The broad production strategy is then broken down into three production stages (as detailed by Perlès [1992: 226]): raw material acquisition, tool production, and toolkit management. Each of these strategies is broken down into classes of constraints, within which are a number of constraining or enabling variables. Each variable is considered in relation to the technological attributes that are present within an assemblage, and the socio-economic context of the site as a whole.

A number of these variables have been included based on the agency theory framework. For instance, within the raw material acquisition stage, cultural constraints such as knowledge, tradition and time all contribute more broadly to an understanding of the social agency of technology. Likewise, during the tool production stage ideological constraints such as tradition and cultural context, socio-economic constraints such as labour and mobility, and technological constraints such as available technology and skills required could all be affected by the social context of this technological practice.

A CASE STUDY OF SOCIAL AGENCY THEORY IN PRACTICE

During the last four years I have had an opportunity to work in the Bannu Division of the Northwest Frontier Province of Pakistan, as a member of the Bannu Archaeological Project, investigating the later prehistoric cultural sequence of the region. Specifically, I have examined a number of lithic assemblages from archaeological sites in the region, one of which, from the site of Sheri Khan Tarakai, is discussed here.

Sheri Khan Tarakai is located approximately 17 km southwest of Bannu city (see Fig. 4.2) and is situated on a low alluvial terrace. The site consists of a surface scatter of cultural material covering an area of approximately 0.2 km^2, and in some areas a complex stratigraphy to a depth of 2.5 m. It is clear from the ceramics that the surface and stratified material all belong to one cultural phase. An absolute radiocarbon chronology has also been established which dates the site to between 4950 and 2460 Cal. BC. The preservation of the bio-archaeological remains is very poor, although sheep, goat and cattle bones have been identified, along with charred grains of domesticated barley. The material culture recovered from Sheri Khan Tarakai represents a clearly defined phase of occupation in the Bannu basin, referred to in this research as the 'SKT phase'.

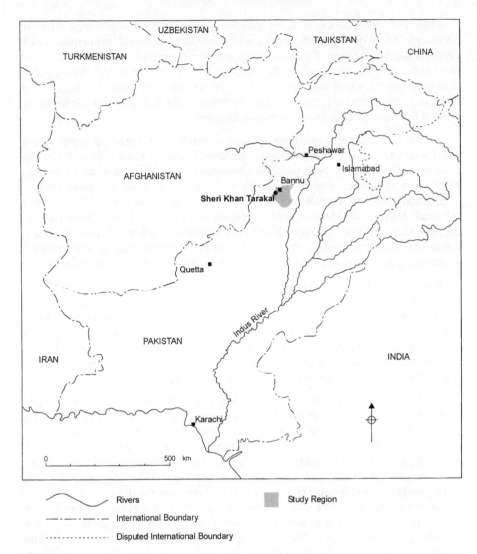

Fig. 4.2: The location of Sheri Khan Tarakai in northwest South Asia.

An overview of the entire assemblage suggests that the principal lithic technology at the site centred on core working, with the aim of producing a bladelet end product. The blades produced were ultimately retouched into geometric and non-geometric microlithic tools. However, the production of expedient tools throughout the core reduction process also seems to have taken place, resulting in the manufacture of artefacts such as scrapers, denticulates, and burins. The industry is suggestive of a utilitarian production system as opposed to anything more specialised such as the production of prestige goods. The full range of the *chaîne opératoire* is represented, suggesting that manufacture, use, and discard of the artefacts all took place at and around the site.

The raw material consists of river-worn pebbles of microcrystalline to cryptocrystalline quartz, with very small quantities of chemical impurities, which produce the wide range of colours seen, ranging from dark red to cream. These raw materials are predominantly classified as chert, although fine-grained limestone and a small amount of green jasper are also present. The chert is thought to have eroded from limestone bedrock in the hills and mountains to the west of the Bannu basin, in modern day Afghanistan.

At the raw material acquisition stage a number of variables would have constrained and enabled the production process. The socio-economic context of the settlement (a sedentary agro-pastoral community of which some members may have been nomadic) would have allowed plenty of time for raw material acquisition, and the overall cost of this stage of production would have been minimal. Additional evidence, such as the recovery of oak charcoal from the site, suggests that a system of exchange or a system that allowed people from the site to travel more distantly existed, and this has an important bearing on an interpretation of the social structures surrounding the lithic production process (see below).

Raw materials would have been widely available 'locally', within a 5 km radius of the site. However, it is also more than likely that they would have been available more distantly (30–50 km away), potentially at the location from which many of the raw materials deposited locally around the site were originally derived and subsequently transported in the river system. These more distant sources may or may not have provided raw material of a higher flaking quality due to decreased exposure to erosion and weathering.

There is no evidence for the use of better quality raw materials at the site; rather the raw materials recovered have a particularly poor performance (flaking quality). This suggests a low level of investment in raw material acquisition, and indicates that there was apparently a trade-off between the cost of raw material acquisition and flaking quality. Nevertheless, the raw materials still produced a sharp edge (as with any microcrystalline or cryptocrystalline quartz) and would have provided good functional qualities. It is clear from the debitage that the raw material nodules would have constrained the potential size of the end products to a maximum of 10–15 cm in length. However, river pebbles are ideally suited to bladelet production due to the fact that it is relatively easy to open a striking platform, and the natural morphology of the nodules lend themselves to the idealised morphology of bladelet cores.

The reduction sequence can be divided into five principal stages (see Fig. 4.3):

Stage 1: The initial working of the reduction sequence consisted of splitting the raw material pebbles, which resulted either in two half pebbles, or often in a large thick flake. A minimum of flaking was noted on some pieces at this stage prior to discard. All flaking seems to have been undertaken with a hard hammer.

Stage 2: The split pebbles (stage 2a), or thick flakes (stage 2b), were further knapped with a hard hammer, where the aim appears to have been the creation of a ridge down the side of the piece, and the working of the platform and face adjacent to the ridge. Many cores seem to have been abandoned at this stage with the consequent discard of numerous flakes.

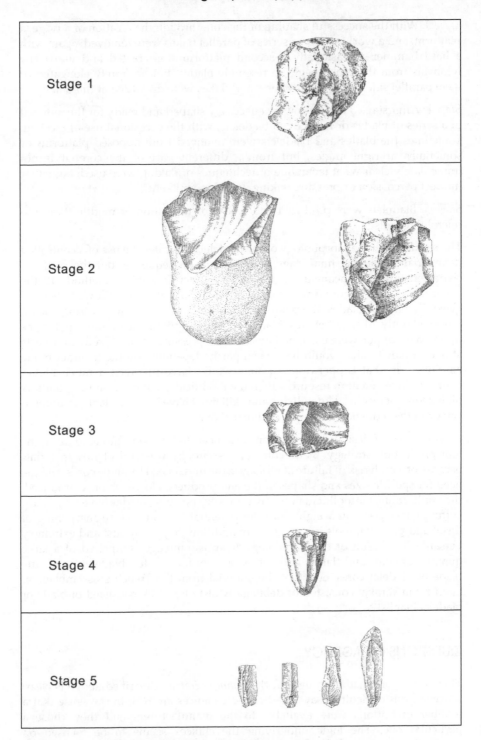

Stage 1

Stage 2

Stage 3

Stage 4

Stage 5

Fig. 4.3: The reduction strategy employed at Sheri Khan Tarakai.

Stage 3: With the successful shaping of the core through the creation of a ridge, a platform, and a working face, a series of parallel flakes were removed, again with a hard hammer. Occasionally a second platform was created and used. The removals from this stage begin to resemble blades, but are rarely elongated or have parallel sides. Again many cores and flakes were discarded at this stage.

Stage 4: After stage 3 the cores were effectively shaped and ready for the removal of a series of blades or more often bladelets, with the occasional use of cresting. Sometimes the blades and bladelets were removed from opposed platforms or sometimes at right angles, but from a different part of the core. It is not immediately clear what technique or techniques of flaking were used, but either indirect percussion or pressure flaking would seem likely.

Stage 5: Bladelets were produced and ready for utilisation or modification into microlithic tools.

The regularity of the morphology of the bladelets indicates the use of a controlled hammer mode in the final stage of the reduction sequence, but the platform characteristics are inconclusive as to the exact knapping method. If the experimental conclusions drawn by Jacques Pelegrin (1994) are followed, then the generally parallel blades, the plain butts and the low proportion of 'ring cracks' observed (only 20 of 173 blades/bladelets), suggest that bone or antler points, as opposed to copper, were used, perhaps through pressure flaking. Production costs at Sheri Khan Tarakai would have been partly dependent on the hammer mode employed, in that copper-tipped points would have involved a much higher degree of investment in resources than the modification of bone/antler points. A high degree of technical knowledge and skill must have been available, in order to carry out the reduction strategies outlined above.

A number of design considerations also need to be taken into account in the tool production strategy. Blade cores are essentially wasteful of raw materials because of a high risk of failure at all stages, the initial need to shape cores, and the need for specific sizes and shapes of the end products. However, once produced, the implications for toolkit maintenance are very positive. Blades have long sharp cutting edges per unit weight, and the potential for multiple re-sharpening of distal and proximal tools is very high. In addition they are robust and extremely versatile. The result of this technology is an assemblage comprised of a large quantity of cores and flakes, and comparatively few blades, bladelets, and true blade or bladelet cores. 80.9% of the material from the Trench 6 assemblage at Sheri Khan Tarakai consisted of debitage whilst only 7.3% consisted of blade or bladelet blanks.

QUESTIONS OF AGENCY

That choices are made throughout the *chaîne opératoire* described above is clear; however, it is difficult to say whether these choices are real, in the sense that a number of options were available to the manufacturers and they chose a particular one. The logic underlying the choices seems to be focused on materiality, such as the properties of the raw material itself (see Lemonnier 1993:

9–16 for a more detailed discussion of technology as a mediation between physical laws and the inventiveness of cultures). If arbitrary choices have been made during the production process then there is little evidence for this.

The strategy for the production and use of the lithic material seems to have been shared between the artisans manufacturing the lithic artefacts. There is no evidence for significant variability in this strategy through time. However, at the same time there is no evidence to suggest that variability was tolerated, favoured, or discouraged. The production strategy primarily constitutes the need to produce a bladelet core, which has the potential to produce a number of bladelets as opposed to an individual bladelet, and what differentiation there is seems to be directly linked to the quality of the raw material. The reduction strategy employed at Sheri Khan Tarakai is also apparent at other sites, suggesting that the required technical knowledge must have been widely available in the region.

A number of interpretations can be drawn regarding the social structures in place and their effect on the lithic technological process. As stated previously, the social context seems to have limited the procurement of raw materials from further afield whilst the additional material culture and environmental data from the site suggests that broader contacts with areas such as northern Baluchistan and northeastern Afghanistan did exist at the time. This decision not to acquire better quality raw materials from further afield suggests that a constraining social structure at Sheri Khan Tarakai was more dominant than the enabling economic structures that were clearly in place. However, defining the social structure or structures is more problematic. This choice or strategy may be part of a cultural tradition (of which there is no earlier data to compare with) or it could be a reflection of the decreasing social value of lithic technology as metal technology begins to appear (although there is little evidence to suggest that metal tools directly replaced the function of stone tools).

The fact that the artisans chose not to acquire better quality raw materials from further afield is a reflection of agency, but at the corporate level. A choice has been made regarding the acquisition of raw materials from the initial occupation of the settlement through to its abandonment. This is perhaps where agency theory has the most potential, at the corporate level, as regards its ability to meaningfully interpret the archaeological record. This is not a new finding, as Sillar (2002: 593–94) points out in his recent review of Dobres' work: archaeologists have only been able to focus on the site as a meaningful unit of analysis when interpreting the archaeological record from an agency perspective, as opposed to being able to link the motivations of individuals to the artefacts they produced.

In using agency theory to help define a practical methodology, it has been possible to draw a broader interpretation and develop a more complete narrative regarding the cultural framework in existence in northwest Pakistan during the fourth to third millennia BC (cf. Morris 2003). The adoption of this particular model has provided an opportunity to interpret the assemblage up to a point, in particular regarding the broader role of social structures and their effect upon the manufacturing process. However, it has proved difficult to draw interpretations beyond this scale. An understanding of the motivations of individuals seems to be reliant on an archaeological record that differentiates between the specific actions of individuals. In this case the archaeological data has simply not provided the degree of resolution needed.

However, even if the archaeological data consisted of a series of clearly defined individual knapping events, would we really be able to draw interpretations of intentionality based on the agency model defined previously, given that the variability present within this particular assemblage can be explained using a more simplistic model based upon issues of materiality and the quality of the raw material? Whilst it has been possible to isolate social and economic structures, defining those social structures is much more difficult. Because the economic structures are more readily accessible to interpretation by the archaeologist, a model of technological production based on economics is more likely to be accepted, even if the social structures clearly have a role to play. Agency theory encourages us to consider the importance of the motivations and actions of agents, but it is difficult to see how such an intangible concept can be made tangible through the archaeological data that has been examined here. Clearly technology is constrained and enabled by a series of structures, including social; however, the difficulty in isolating these structures in the archaeological record is considerable. Whilst it is still believed that the theoretical and methodological framework outlined in this chapter has potential, in the sense that it encourages us to think more broadly about the factors that might be responsible for the creation of a particular material assemblage, it is clear that the realisation of this potential depends very much on the nature of the archaeological record itself and practicalities such as data recovery strategies.

Of course it is also always possible that the archaeological data itself may simply not be suited to an interpretation that encompasses such abstract elements as the motivations of an individual. If the degree of resolution available is only at the scale of the site as a whole, then assemblages composed of utilitarian artefacts are less likely to provide evidence of being influenced by the motivations of individuals during the production process. More suitable would be artefacts that have an inherent social value, that provide evidence of ritual, or an opportunity to display power or status. These elements of material culture are far less ubiquitous across the archaeological landscape and are therefore more likely to represent anomalies as regards interpretation. The criticisms that Bell (1992: 38) highlights certainly seem to be valid in the sense that an agency model is not universally applicable and has several limitations, in particular when applied to utilitarian artefacts. This study has highlighted some practical aspects of the application of agency theory. It is clear that more simplistic explanatory models can be applied to the dataset in this instance, and that agency theory is probably more applicable to a specific range of artefactual material as opposed to its utilisation as a broad-based model of interpretation.

References

Bell, J. 1992. On capturing agency in theories about prehistory. In J.-C. Gardin and C.S. Peebles (eds.) *Representations in Archaeology*, 30–55. Bloomington and Indianapolis, IN: Indiana University Press.

Dobres, M.-A. 1995. Gender and prehistoric technology: on the social agency of technical strategies. *World Archaeology*, 27:1, 25–49.

Dobres, M.-A. 1996. Early thoughts on technology and cultural complexity: peopling the relationship. In D.A. Meyer, P.C. Dawson, and D.T. Hanna (eds.) *Debating Complexity: proceedings of the 26th annual Chacmool conference*, 224–40. Calgary: The Archaeological Association of the University of Calgary.

Dobres, M.-A. 2000. *Technology and Social Agency*. Oxford: Blackwell.

Dobres, M.-A. and Hoffman, C.R. 1994. Social agency and the dynamics of prehistoric technology. *Journal of Archaeological Method and Theory*, 1:3, 211–58.

Dobres, M.-A. and Robb, J.E. 2000. Agency in archaeology: paradigm or platitude? In M.-A. Dobres and J.E. Robb (eds.) *Agency in Archaeology*, 3–17. London: Routledge.

Edmonds, M. 1990. Description, understanding, and the *chaîne opératoire*. *Archaeological Review from Cambridge*, 9:1, 55–70.

Giddens, A. 1984. *The Constitution of Society: outline of the theory of structuration*. Cambridge: Polity Press.

Hayden, B. 1990. The right rub: hide working in high ranking households. In B. Graslund (ed.) *The Interpretive Possibilities of Microwear Studies*, 89–102. Uppsala: Societas Archaeologica Upsaliensis (AUN 14).

Ingold, T. 1990. Society, nature, and the concept of technology. *Archaeological Review from Cambridge*, 9:1, 5–17.

Lemonnier, P. 1993. Introduction. In P. Lemonnier (ed.) *Technological Choices: transformation in material cultures since the Neolithic*, 1–35. London: Routledge.

Leroi-Gourhan, A. 1943. *Evolution et Techniques: l'homme et la matière*. Paris: Albin Michel.

Morris, J.C. 2003. *Lithic technology and cultural change during the later prehistoric period of northwest South Asia*. Unpublished PhD thesis, University of London.

Pelegrin, J. 1994. Lithic technology in Harappan times. In A. Parpola and P. Koskikallio (eds.) *South Asian Archaeology 1993, II*, 587–98. Helsinki: Suomalainen Tiedeakatemia.

Perlès, C. 1992. In search of lithic strategies: a cognitive approach to prehistoric chipped stone assemblages. In J.-C. Gardin and C.S. Peebles (eds.) *Representations in Archaeology*, 223–47. Bloomington and Indianapolis, IN: Indiana University Press.

Sillar, B. 2002. Review of M.-A. Dobres (2000) 'Technology and Social Agency'. *Antiquity*, 76, 593–94.

CHAPTER 5

AGENCY, TECHNOLOGY, AND THE 'MUDDLE IN THE MIDDLE': THE CASE OF THE MIDDLE PALAEOLITHIC

Brad Gravina

INTRODUCTION

Gamble (1999) has suggested that Palaeolithic archaeology is in more of a need for theory than it is for facts. While it is without question that our research paradigms are enhanced with the development of new theoretical frameworks, the benefits derived from such advancement may not be felt equally across all periods. Such new theoretical insights are inevitably framed, not only within the diversification and elaboration of new philosophical and sociological influences, but also within the increasing sophistication and computerisation of recording and recovery techniques, which have dramatically improved both the quantity and quality of our data and its interpretative possibility. An increasing body of work operating within the theoretical framework of social agency, especially studies of prehistoric technology, is beginning to occupy a prominent place in the recent archaeological and anthropological literature (Dobres 1999, 2000; Dobres and Hoffman 1994; Pfaffenberger 1992; Lemonnier (ed.) 1993). However, given both the advancement in archaeological field techniques and the development of new theoretical approaches to the archaeological record, should we expect the compatibility of theory and practice to be universal in scale despite the context? This chapter presents an attempt to answer just such a question, framed within the context of the archaeological record of the Middle Palaeolithic. I should like it to be remembered that the problem of applicability does not imply redundancy because what is of interest here is a question of *scale* and *extent*, rather than *validity*.

In keeping with this theme of scale and extent of theoretical compatibility a synoptic approach to the major tenets of agency theory has been adopted with special attention to those that are of particular relevance to the study of prehistoric technology. Agency theory maintains that (after Dobres 2000: 96–97): (1) technologies are meaningful acts of social engagement in which worldviews are expressed and transformed; (2) technology produces personal, practical and cultural knowledge that is at once discursive, as well as non-discursive; (3) above all, technology is about people and their involvement in the social relations of production. This approach to technology and the gestures responsible for its realisation attempts to re-infuse the physical object back into the dynamic web of social relations responsible for its coming into being. Technology becomes a question of social values, power, politics and participation rather than simply artefact physics, raw material limits and availability, function, and efficiency.

Agency theory asks about technical decisions, competence, inclusion and knowledge and the relationship between individual and society.

The existence of differential competency has been documented both enthnographically among Lapp reindeer herders (Ingold 1993) and archaeologically at the Magdalenian site of Etiolles (Pigeot 1990). From the standpoint of technical agency, individual technical skill and display may be articulated to promote or hinder social standing or virtue (Dobres 2000). Social status is then created and reaffirmed, both tacitly and overtly, in relation to the importance of that technology to the community in its totality. Thus, material culture becomes a medium for differentiation not only in possession but in production and mastery. Further, we may view the individual in the light of technical and practical knowledge possessed. Community ideas about the possession and proscription of technical knowledge by individuals become politicised, by abstraction, into the concrete reality of technological production. Thus, singular technical agents are still embedded in and contributing to, knowledgably or not, the social community and context in which their action is framed: "the control of knowledge, like the control of resources, can be the arena for the negotiation of social power" (Dobres and Hoffman 1994: 234).

Situating technical agents within the framework of their community enables a questioning of what forces impinge, constrain, or prescribe material production or access to material resources. Anthony Giddens' (1984) structuration theory and Pierre Bourdieu's (1990 [1980]) concept of the 'habitus' provide an outline for attempting to account for the creation, maintenance, and transformation of the social forces that mediate and are mediated by social practice. In the context of practice theory, which has come to represent this orientation towards the study of production and re-production of the social, social structures are deemed to be "both the medium and the outcome of social interaction and are conceived of as the normative rules and social and material resources available to individuals ... and groups" (Dobres and Hoffman 1994: 222). In the 'structuration' model of social systems, order emerges through the actions of intelligent individuals (agents) acting according to the rules or structures of conduct governed by a set of material and social conditions prescribed by society. In that agents are aware of these conditions, the choice to abide by or challenge social norms leads to continuity or transformation in the structures of social action.

Bourdieu's concept of the 'habitus' places material and social production and consumption within historically and culturally specific contexts: "the habitus, a product of history, produces individual and collective practices – more history – in accordance with the schemes generated by history" (Bourdieu 1990 [1980]: 54). Material and social production become simultaneously produced, reproduced, or transformed through historically situated conditions:

> The conditionings associated with a particular class of conditions of existence produce habitus, systems of durable, transposable dispositions, structured structures predisposed to function as structuring structures, that is, as principles which generate and organise practices and representations without presupposing a conscious aiming at ends or express mastery of the operations necessary to obtain them (Bourdieu 1990 [1980]: 53).

In such a conception of the social system, individuals are not automatons going about their everyday material practice unaware or as mere products of an obedience to social rules, but they act reflexively, producing both unintended consequences and/or exacting significant conscious counter-strategies. Thus, even the most commonplace, pedestrian acts of social negotiation serve in some way to reify and embed individuals within conventionalised social categories. However, if we are to properly engage or work within the practice theory conception of social life we must guard against the objectification of agency as an analytical unit. Although we often deem the isolation of individual action, past and present, as the pinnacle of interpretative resolution, to conceive of agency as a "thing we hold [rather] than a capacity we are involved in exercising" (Thomas 2000: 150) is to run the risk of mistaking the trees for the forest.

As it stands, no consideration of social agency and technology would be complete, even within a synopsis such as this, without making mention of the *chaîne opératoire* approach to prehistoric technology. Although a majority of work utilising *chaîne opératoire* has been concerned with issues of language, cognition, or mental templates (Renfrew and Zubrow (eds.) 1994; Schlanger 1994), it is possible to extend this analytic method to "a consideration of the dynamic social milieus and artifice by which material acts were differentially pursued by technicians and variously organized work groups" (Dobres 1999: 124). Moving beyond considerations of cognition and language employing the *chaîne opératoire* methodology, following the step by step physical gestures of prehistoric technology from the very seeking of raw material to final discard permits us to investigate not only the various reduction strategies applied to such material, but the various levels of competence, knowledge, skills, and, further, individual-group interactions that frame and constrain these material actions. *Chaîne opératoire* research allows not only the reconstruction of the life histories of artefacts, but an insight into the history of life with those artefacts. However, to be used to their full analytical potential, it is important to situate *chaînes opératoires* within the social context of their unfolding.

Social agency theory, therefore, provides a framework for conceiving material culture beyond simple techno-typological and functional analysis. Such a framework posits "technology, as embodied material practice, [that is] a socially charged and materially grounded arena in which agents express value systems, and give meaning to the object world" (Dobres 2000: 162). In the following section, three Upper Palaeolithic case studies will be presented that are taken to be representative of this line of thinking. This brief theoretical synopsis, coupled with these case studies, should provide a baseline for the investigation into the scale of applicability that agency theory may have in addressing the problems and questions of the Middle Palaeolithic record.

CASE STUDIES: AGENCY THEORY IN PRACTICE

The Magdalenian site of Etiolles in the Paris Basin, given the extraordinary preservation of the deposits, has allowed for both the refitting of the *chaîne opératoire* of blade production in its entirety, as well as the recognition of a social division of space observed in the patterning of artefact clusters. This detailed refitting project has allowed the researchers to "recognize the handicraft of highly experienced knappers, which have been identified as genuine flint specialists, and, besides, the activities of novices and young members of the group" (Pigeot 1990: 127). These findings suggest that knowledge, skill and competence were articulated and regulated by society with the aim of producing fully accomplished individuals, and, further, that these components would have been integral to the maintenance and creation of personal identities and inter-personal relationships. Such findings were made possible by both the completeness of the reduction sequences present at the site and the isolation of various spatial movements, corrections, and skilled interventions by more accomplished, older members of the group through the course of a core's life. At Etiolles the social life of particular raw materials has made it possible "to link on-the-ground material practice to the dynamic processes of personhood and even politics" (Dobres 2000: 187). However, let it be remembered that it is the "the remarkable integrity of the deposits" (Pigeot 1990: 127), the completeness of the reduction sequences present at the site, and the clarity and unequivocal recognition of spatial patterns that, above all, have enabled these findings.

Sinclair's (2000) study of the Solutrean industries of France and Iberia investigates social agency and technology at the artefact-specific level, rather than at a site level, as at Etiolles. This work investigates the classic Solutrean tools, that is, the finely made bifacial leaf points and shouldered points, as enmeshed in technical practice and social action. Central to the argument is the relationship between the tools themselves and the level of practical knowledge possessed and enacted by individuals who made them. The author attempts to place Solutrean lithic technology within a *'constellation of knowledge'* that enables and frames particular material action. "It is properly a constellation of *knowledge* because the materials used, the implements and techniques that might be employed, and the desired end-points of use or manufacture, depend upon the knowledge that an individual has acquired of them" (Sinclair 2000: 200, emphasis in original). Thus, the variable expression and routinisation of tool use and manufacture observed in Solutrean lithic products becomes a possible locus of agency.

In this case the expression of technical knowledge, learned and expertly expressed, is deemed to be essential to the creation and reaffirmation of particularly esteemed dimensions of individual identities (Sinclair 2000). The manufacture of Solutrean bifacial foliates and shouldered points requires not only extended practice and acute awareness of appropriate raw material, but "the ability to co-ordinate a variety of techniques and monitor a number of changing variables" (Sinclair 2000: 206). The expression of these 'salient skills', embodied in the boldness and audacity of raw material exploitation, are considered by the author to denote actions vital to the creation and maintenance of individual identity. The suggestion that the completeness of some of the more substantial pieces may indicate that the bifacial points were, perhaps, never intended for practical use, to some degree substantiates the argument for their being objects of individualistic expression.

While I would not disagree that the complexity of these lithic items, compounded with the obvious technical skill and knowledge necessary for their manufacture, may have played a fundamental role in the generation and affirmation of individual identity, I should point out that it is the very existence of such items that has allowed for the investigation of social agency at the artefact-specific scale. The presence of these discrete and elaborate pieces creates a stark contrast with the tool forms associated with Middle Palaeolithic assemblages of the same region. This is a point that I will return to below. However, I am left to conclude that a major factor contributing to the applicability of agency theory in the Solutrean, which in this case is well argued and supported, lays not so much with theoretical ingenuity as it does with the sheer existence of, and synonymous skill associated with, these artefacts.

The last case study departs from an explicit concern with lithic economies and, instead, focuses on aspects of organic artefact design, manufacture use and repair at a number of Magdalenian sites in the Midi-Pyrenees region of France (Dobres 2000: 187–211). Four types of specific bone and antler artefacts (awls, spear points, harpoons, and needles) were assessed with a view to "evaluate whether technical treatment, knowledge and skill did or did not vary across and within artefact categories and in what specific ways" (Dobres 2000: 196). The research design of this investigation benefits from a non-site specific, regional approach to technical behaviour, as well as a detailed technical consideration of variability across multiple axes of material and artefact classes at multiple physical scales. Thus, by identifying patterns in manufacture intensity, end-product variability, and specific activities, both within sites and between sites, a model of individual technical disposition and its relation to overall Magdalenian technical and social structures emerges. While a majority of organic tool forms appear to be components of an over-arching Magdalenian technical complex which, perhaps, constrained or framed technical action, Magdalenian technical agents "appear to have displayed their differently learned skills of the trade, betrayed their incompetence, and tried out new or unusual techniques in rather subtle and covert ways; not in overt or gratuitous displays of self-promotion" (Dobres 2000: 209). Despite the rather demure expressions of individual agency in raw material transformation, these subtle material communications would intersect existing social and technical structures, invoking transformations in the social structure of technical behaviour.

These three case studies exemplify the application of social agency theory to prehistoric technology, both lithic and organic, and the quality and condition of the databases from which the conclusions were drawn. All of the above case studies have a number of factors in common that, theoretical and paradigmatic considerations aside, in some way permit or make possible the consideration of agency in prehistoric, and specifically Upper Palaeolithic technology. In the case of Etiolles, the undisturbed, pristine nature of the deposits, the clear identification of enriched spatial patterns, and the high-quality and complete core refits are important. With Sinclair's study of the Solutrean, it is both the undeniable nature of the bifacial and shouldered points as being both real and discrete, coupled with the inherent difficulty of their manufacture, that enable his conclusions. And finally, Dobres' study of Magdalenian organic tool forms is, to a large extent, made feasible not only by the existence of these discrete and real tool forms, but by their regional ubiquity and preservation at various stages of manufacture.

NEANDERTHAL AGENTS: A WAY THROUGH THE 'MUDDLE IN THE MIDDLE' OR THEORETICAL DEAD END?

The preceding two sections have presented the theoretical basis of agency theory and demonstrated its application in three Upper Palaeolithic case studies. In this final section an evaluation as to the scale at which Middle Palaeolithic technology can be meaningfully analysed within the framework of social agency theory will be presented. This evaluation will be conducted at three levels: (i) the level of the artefact (i.e. the end-product); (ii) at the level of the site; and, finally, (iii) at the level of primary flaking strategies. However, before looking at these aspects of Middle Palaeolithic technology I believe that some remarks concerning the nature of what we may generally call 'Neanderthal society' are essential to an understanding of the context in which we might seek to apply or uncover social agency.

What is the nature of Neanderthal social relations? In comparison to even the earliest Upper Palaeolithic period, the Middle Palaeolithic record bears witness to significantly smaller territories and population numbers. This, coupled with a less diverse set of utilised raw materials compared to later periods, would, to a fair extent, function to limit the diversification of social relations in Neanderthal communities to the extent that these are mediated by differentiated material culture. In contrast, the Upper Palaeolithic, as seen in the above case studies, would, almost implicitly, have seen both the expansion of everyday technical activities and raw material types, as well as the elaboration of manufacturing techniques which, together, would lead to new forms of group interaction and social dynamics (Gosden 1994: 182–86; Gamble 1999).

The explosion of symbolic behaviour observed in the Upper Palaeolithic record has popularly been attributed to the emergence of anatomically modern humans possessing the capacity for such displays. However, a consideration of the functional requirements necessary to carve bone and antler, engrave walls, or bore holes in jewellery suggests that "the essential genius of the Upper Palaeolithic was expanded technologically-assisted symbolism *per se,* rather than the emergence of the biological capacity for symbolism" (Gibson 1996: 41). Regardless of the underlying factors generating transition, the Upper Palaeolithic record emphasises considerable, and, in some aspects, completely new, changes in both the diversity of raw materials and tool typologies. Even the earliest Aurignacian in western Europe demonstrates …

> explicit evidence for radical changes in at least five or six separate aspects of behaviour: the technology and typology of stone tool production; the production of bone, antler and ivory artefacts; the emergence of varied and complex personal adornment; the 'explosion' of representational art and associated abstract ornamentation; and the emergence of greatly expanded networks for the distribution of marine shells and in some cases high-quality raw materials (Mellars 1996: 400).

These radical changes in technical and artistic activities may have given way to the emergence of new social formations and articulations wherein technology would have slotted into material and symbolic structures that were vital to the production of identities and communities. I would suggest that this elaboration of technological entities and activities in the Upper Palaeolithic provides ample grounds for an agentic or practice theory approach to the empirical data. The obvious contrast with the material record of the Middle Palaeolithic rings quite soundly. Furthermore, a majority of the ethnographic and ethnoarchaeological work (articles in Lemonnier (ed.) 1993; Dobres and Hoffman (eds.) 1999) that informs and frames the application of agency theory in archaeology has been carried out in contexts where developed symbolic behaviour enfolds co-operation between individuals and in society at large. This is not to say that looking for technical agency in non-symbolic or pre-modern contexts is a lost cause; rather it suggests that we should approach these contexts, in this case the Middle Palaeolithic, slightly more cautiously with attention to the scale at which we seek agency in technological endeavours. Perhaps a consideration of social agency in relation to organic and stone tool use in non-human primates can provide a touchstone for resolving this possible concern.

Bearing the above in mind, at what level or scale can we expect to be able to identify social agency in Middle Palaeolithic technology? Can we expect to look for agency in Mousterian stone tools as Sinclair (2000) has done with the French and Iberian Solutrean? I would suggest that looking for agency in this manner in the Mousterian would be difficult for a number of reasons. First, if we accept that there do indeed exist real and discrete tool forms in the Middle Palaeolithic, there are no such items that even remotely compare with the finely crafted bifacial and shouldered points typical of the Solutrean. Even the small bifaces associated with the Mousterian or Acheulean Tradition industrial facie of the French Middle Palaeolithic are crude in comparison. Further, virtually all the scraper and denticulate tool forms associated with the Middle Palaeolithic are not only known from much earlier periods, but are manufactured through extremely simple, almost elementary, secondary retouch methods. Given this, it would be tenuous to argue that the manufacture of Mousterian tool forms required high levels of technical knowledge or *savoir-faire*, which in turn could be articulated by individuals or groups in meaningful social strategies.

Secondly, Dibble (1987, 1988) has made a case that nearly all the documented variation in Middle Palaeolithic tool types can be attributed either to the tool's intended use or to successive modifications in the form and design of a tool through repeated edge rejuvenation and reworking. Thus, the lack of imposed shape, standardisation, and the general simplicity of Mousterian tool forms makes it more difficult to imagine their being instrumental in creating and manipulating identity and social merit in the ways that Sinclair has suggested for the Solutrean.

Finally, ethnographic work on stone tool-using societies suggests that "there is *absolutely no* empirically demonstrated or even apparent logical relationship between social, linguistic or mental characteristics and these types of tools" (Hayden 1993: 119; original emphasis). It is not by any length unreasonable to suggest that to some extent social or cultural values enabled, proscribed or framed stone tool production and use in the Middle Palaeolithic; rather, difficulty arises in attempting to isolate such factors in the archaeological record of the period. This difficulty is exacerbated not only by the ubiquity of Middle Palaeolithic tool forms across various regions, but by the near-complete lack of bone or antler industries with which stone tool production can be juxtaposed or connected at an interpretative or analytical level. Thus, in defiance of a technical agency approach to Middle Palaeolithic technology at the level of the artefact, the very nature of the tools themselves severely hampers the possibility of drawing any firm conclusions or building secure models of technical/social action.

To evaluate the extent to which social agency theory can be usefully adopted for the interpretation of Middle Palaeolithic technology, it is necessary to approach the archaeological record at the scale of the site. Studying the spatial patterning of occupational remains at individual sites is one of the most productive lines of inquiry for addressing questions of social and technological organisation, as well as economic activity. Detecting differences in activities in different areas of a small space may provide evidence referring to interpersonal social dynamics generated through or transformed by technological activities. Paul Pettitt's (1997) fairly comprehensive survey of a number of highest-resolution spatial data-sets from a number of European and Middle Eastern Middle Palaeolithic sites resulted in some extremely relevant conclusions regarding the nature of Neanderthal occupation traces. I will briefly summarise these findings and then explore their ramifications for an agency-based interpretative framework.

The high resolution data-sets that comprise the body of evidence surveyed by Pettitt has led him to the following conclusions regarding the nature of Middle Palaeolithic occupation horizons (Pettitt 1997: 219):

(1) The number of Neanderthal inhabitants at enclosed sites (i.e. caves and rockshelters) appears to have been relatively small and it is not inconceivable that a majority of the high resolution assemblages associated with these sites are the product of "a number of individuals in the context of solitary occupations" (Pettitt 1997: 219). Where isolated lithic scatters and refits can be recognised, most conform to either solitary knapping events, as at Maastricht-Belvedere (Schlanger 1994), or a small number of individuals involved in core reduction episodes around a central hearth. The latter situation results in what can be regarded as a 'hearth and scatter' assemblage. The size, and, to some degree, the complexity, of these spatial patterns may be due to the physical constraints imposed by the size and nature of the sites themselves, as well as the postulated extremely small groups making infrequent visits to these sites (Mellars 1996). Furthermore, given that the distribution of lithic debitage may represent palimpsests of occupational episodes it is very possible that any number of scatters may not be contemporaneous and, instead, may represent residue from successive site visits.

(2) The small number of sites that have yielded reasonably good spatial data have indicated that the "Neanderthal organization of space … seems to have been along very simple lines, which cannot be distinguished from non-human

carnivores" (Pettitt 1997: 219). This simple organisation of space appears to have been carried out on a number of somewhat similar levels. First, the separation of 'living' areas from refuse/dumping areas, as has been demonstrated at Kebara Cave, Israel (Bar-Yosef *et al.* 1992). Secondly, the spatial clustering of 'cutting tools' (i.e. backed knives, unretouched large flakes) in one area of a site, with 'scraping' forms grouping together in a separate area, as has been documented at the Chattelperronian levels of Saint Cezaire and the Typical Mousterian levels of Morin, Spain. This would indicate a simple division of task areas, probably predicated on the physical suitability of the site for accommodating tasks requiring these different tool functions (Pettitt 1997).

Probably one of the most informative sites, as far as spatial patterning is concerned, is Grotte Vaufrey, in the Dordogne region of France. The spatial distribution of burnt and heavily fragmented bone, lithic refits, and tools at this site cluster into three relatively distinct areas. These segregations have been interpreted as representing a brief occupational episode of 2–3 individuals introducing a carcass into the cave, lighting a fire for cooking purposes and manufacturing the necessary tools for the butchery of the carcass (Mellars 1996). While each cluster probably represents the activity of one individual, the overall pattern is consistent with the previous examples, that is, a simple dichotomised use of space within sites for different activities by individuals. Although the dichotomised use of space is likely to be structured by both the physical characteristics of the site as well as social ideas about the use of space, it is unlikely that these social structures were highly formalised. Rather, the behaviour responsible for the observed material patterns appears both "limited in variability and habitual in nature" (Pettitt 1997: 219).

The data currently available for Middle Palaeolithic spatial patterning strongly suggests that inferring the social or technical agency responsible for these material traces will be problematic at best. Although, as Dobres stipulates, *"one cannot excavate agency ... the static material remains of the archaeological record are the archaeologist's link for inferring the dynamic social processes accounting for them"* (Dobres 2000: 142, original emphasis). This is not to say that the lack of such a link necessarily implies the absence of agency; rather, where such links are discerned the interpretative possibilities of the data are greatly enhanced. Material residues of past behaviour can be highly informative, depending upon the question we are asking, but the case of the Middle Palaeolithic presents a limited data-set of what appears to be a simplistic use of space that was more likely governed by practical efficacy rather than social structures. Taphonomic and depositional concerns aside, where individual action and motivations can be recognised (although the latter appears highly unlikely for the Middle Palaeolithic), discerning similar and large scale inter-site contemporaneous action has proved elusive. Consequently, identifying inter-subjective dynamics through which Middle Palaeolithic hominids expressed themselves technically and hence, politically and socially, is beyond the limits of the present data resolution for the period. While it is understood that 'agency' does not implicitly indicate any particular individual, and that agency can be a collective expression of community worldviews and values, all action is played out in the context of the historically situated social arena. Given the limited material evidence, in terms of artefact types (i.e. organic and lithic), spatial patterning and internal site organisation, contextualising technical action is severely hampered. The reservations presented here are not philosophical, nor theoretical; rather they represent the simple pragmatics dictated by the state of our present database.

This being so, I would suggest that the extent to which the material evidence from this period is capable of helping us understand the relationship between social agency and technology at the scale of the 'site' is extremely restricted. This is not to say that technical knowledge, know-how and skill were not tangible components of social negotiation and community structure, but that they are just beyond the limits of the empirical data.

The discussion of Middle Palaeolithic tool forms and spatial patterning has brought to light the difficulties facing an agency methodology in these areas of research. Bearing this is mind, I would suggest that probably the most profitable scale at which we can approach agentic processes in the Middle Palaeolithic would be in primary flaking methods – more specifically, the Levallois reduction strategy. The Levallois reduction method comes to dominate Levantine lithic assemblages by at least 70,000 BP and, perhaps, as early as 250,000 BP (Meignen 1995). In Europe, Levallois methods begin to appear during the late Middle Pleistocene and persist until the last glaciation in various forms and intensities, disappearing with the last Neanderthal populations at approximately 35,000 BP (Pettitt 2003). A majority of research focusing on Levallois methods has been concerned with the recognition and interpretation of Levallois systematics and behavioural or cognitive implications of Levallois operational chains (articles in Dibble and Bar-Yosef (eds.) 1995; Schlanger 1994). Following the pioneering work of first F. Bordes and then E. Boeda an extensive and varied array of work has been conducted dealing with various aspects of Levallois lithic technology. However, little attention has been paid to the Levallois reduction strategy outside of its typo-technological 'Blackbox', that is, as a social phenomenon.

Schlanger's (1996) detailed and thought-provoking study of the comprehensively refitted Majorie's Core from the stage 7 site of Maastricht-Belvedere, in the Netherlands, provides a good point of departure in terms of content, as well as of the criticism it has elicited. Schlanger's approach to this particular reduction sequence is stated as being 'reactionary'; that is, against the 'standardised' conception of Levallois reduction strategies as being inherently preconceived and systematically planned as a "blueprint or script which would have been prior and prerequisite to its actual realization" (Schlanger 1996: 246). In de-emphasising systematic predetermination, the interaction of action and knowledge with material circumstance emerges. What surfaces from this analysis is not only that the separation of knowledge and action is untenable, but also a recognition of the interplay of knowledge and skill in overcoming raw material imperfections, as well as the knowledgable and fluid negotiation of the surface and distal convexities of the core 'in hand' as reduction unfolds (Schlanger 1996). Despite the new insights that this detailed analysis of this particular Levallois reduction sequence has furnished, it has been criticised by Dobres (2000: 184), who states that it "does not help us understand the social conditions within which Neanderthal technicians negotiated between material contingency and individual intentions, skills, and knowledge, [and] how such tricks of the trade were learned and passed on from generation to generation". Criticisms aside, what this study does demonstrate is that the Levallois technique inherently involves the fluid articulation of knowledge, perhaps differential knowledge, and the open-ended application of precision and skill that is reflexive and conscious, rather then hard-wired and thoughtless.

In the final part of this section I will attempt to present a coarse-grained framework in which these criticisms might be addressed, employing the archaeological record of one of the core areas of Middle Palaeolithic occupation, the Levantine region. The three Mousterian techno-complexes (Tabun B, C, D) associated with Levantine lithic assemblages all broadly fall within Bordes' 'typical Mousterian' facie as being characterised by variable percentages of side scrapers and the absence or extreme rarity of handaxes and backed knives. Thus the major differences between Levantine Middle Palaeolithic assemblages are demonstrated at the level of Levallois end-products, especially relative percentages of Levallois points, and the varying Levallois reduction strategies employed to realise these desires (Bar-Yosef 2000). Consequently, it can be safely inferred that Levallois techniques were not only the dominant form of core reduction and vital to economic and subsistence adaptations, but involved an articulation of technical knowledge and skill in which social and collective beliefs about material action were played out in the public domain.

This statement in hand, what might we be able to say about the role of Levallois in the everyday technical and social lives of Levantine hominids? Given the ubiquity of Levallois core and end-products within Levantine assemblages it is unlikely that the technique represented an exclusive knowledge and know-how limited to certain members of the groups. This is not the same as saying that *knowledge and skill to execute* are commensurate entities. While it is likely that all members of the group could and did perform Levallois, I would suggest that it is very possible that the skill to which this technique was displayed would not be equal in all members of the group. Experimental replication of the Levallois reduction strategy has demonstrated that among modern flintknappers there are very few "that ever achieve a Neanderthal's level of expertise in producing good Levallois cores or flakes, while the number of contemporary flintknappers that have successfully mastered the technique for producing good Levallois points probably numbers less than a score" (Hayden 1993: 118). I think that it is not too much to suggest that such a differential in skill was played out among Middle Palaeolithic hominids. The ability to display technical knowledge in the production of good Levallois points, and/or maximising a core's usefulness through skilful negotiations of raw material and core surface contingencies, would become a communicative medium in which personal and group identities were created, expressed, or realigned. Thus the Levallois technique becomes the locus of an interface between 'practical' and 'discursive' consciousness where individuals are able to produce articulate statements about society in general while still operating according to certain social rules and structures (Giddens 1984).

The ability to perform the Levallois flaking method, we may postulate, must involve the acquisition of new technical knowledge that would supplement existing knowledge concerning both the selection and handling of raw material. It is likely that there would be some semblance of an apprentice-expert relation that Pigeot (1990) has suggested to have been in place at Magdalenian Etiolles. However, I would disagree with Pigeot's assignment of differential expertise with gendered agents. In that the Levallois reduction strategy probably involved the assimilation of new knowledge, rather then new know-how, it may be more likely to be transmitted from relative to relative (Pelegrin 1990). In the instance of Levallois, I would suggest that the acquisition and performance, tacitly or overtly, of this technology would be a mechanism of social integration and inclusion, whereby members demonstrated their usefulness and fitness to the group through technical displays.

By removing Levallois lithic strategies from the typo-technological and systematising shelf in which it has been entrenched we may begin to see the parallel between material transformation and social circumstance that encases technical action. While the material record of the period will not permit an exact reconstruction of the dynamic social webs in which Levallois must have played an integral role, viewing the various guises of this technology as "arenas in which agents construct social identities and forge power relations while producing and using utilitarian objects and practical ends" (Dobres 1999: 129) at least provides a basis from which to better understand Late Pleistocene human groups and may, to some extent, help to cast light onto the persistence of the Levallois technique for such an extended period of time through oscillating environmental and climatic conditions in the Levant.

CONCLUSION

In this chapter I have attempted to assess the applicability of social agency theory to the archaeological record of the Middle Palaeolithic by examining three separate scales: artefacts, spatial patterning, and primary flaking methods. I have demonstrated that the nature of the material record in terms of spatial patterning and the character of Middle Palaeolithic tool types are not amenable to this conceptual framework. I have stressed that, although the dynamics of social agency are beyond the reach of present data-sets in relation to these scales of inquiry, this is not the same thing as denying that agentic and social processes were involved in framing and enabling technical action at these scales. Following this, I have argued that the most profitable scale at which to identify social agency in the Middle Palaeolithic is that of primary flaking techniques, and more specifically, the Levallois method. The skill and knowledge expressed in Levallois knapping may have contributed to the forging and affirmation of personal or group identities. While not under investigation here, I believe that in the future we should turn towards other aspects of Neanderthal behaviour. In particular, subsistence practices or methods might be explored from the point of view of social agency with an attempt to incorporate aspects of embodiment (i.e. the body as a form of technology that can be articulated through gestures or abilities that affirm or transform social positions). Finally, what might be of most significance, coming from the realisation of the relationship between agency and technology, at least in the Lower and Middle Palaeolithic, is the attitude towards technology that this methodology implies. I believe that a great benefit for our understanding of the Palaeolithic as a whole may be drawn from infusing the technologies of the period with a consideration of the social forces and circumstances that frame them, in conjunction with the economic and subsistence practices that form the majority of current research paradigms.

Acknowledgments

This paper is a modified version of coursework submitted in partial fulfilment of the degree of BSc in Archaeology at the Institute of Archaeology, UCL, and is used with the permission of the Head of Department.

References

Bar-Yosef, O. 2000. The middle and early Upper Paleolithic in Southwest Asia and neighboring regions. In O. Bar-Yosef and D. Pilbeam (eds.) *The Geography of Neandertals and Modern Humans in Europe and the Greater Mediterranean*, 107–56. Cambridge, MA: Harvard University (Peabody Museum Bulletin 8).

Bar-Yosef, O., Vandermeersch, B., Arensburg, B., Belfer-Cohen, A., Goldberg, P., Laville, H., Meignen, L., Rak, Y., Speth, J.D., Tchernov, E., Tillier, A.M. and Weiner, S. 1992. The excavation in Kebara Cave, Mt. Carmel. *Current Anthropology*, 33, 497–550.

Bourdieu, P. 1990 [1980]. *The Logic of Practice*. Cambridge: Cambridge University Press (Translated by R. Nice).

Dibble, H. 1987. The interpretation of Middle Paleolithic scraper morphology. *American Antiquity*, 52:1, 109–17.

Dibble, H. 1988. The interpretation of Middle Paleolithic scraper reduction patterns. In L. Binford and J.Ph. Rigaud (eds.) *L'Homme de Neandertal 4: La Technique*, 49–58. Liege: Etudes et Researches Archeologiques de l'Universite de Liege, no. 31.

Dibble, H. and Bar-Yosef, O. (eds.) 1995. *The Definition and Interpretation of Levallois Technology*. Madison, WI: Prehistory Press (Monographs in World Prehistory No. 23).

Dobres, M.-A. 1999. Technology's links and *chaînes*: the Processual unfolding of technique and technician. In M.-A. Dobres and C.R. Hoffman (eds.) *The Social Dynamics of Technology*, 124–46. Washington, DC: Smithsonian Institution Press.

Dobres, M.-A. 2000. *Technology and Social Agency*. Oxford: Blackwell.

Dobres, M.-A. and Hoffman, C.R. 1994. Social agency and the dynamics of prehistoric technology. *Journal of Archaeological Theory and Method*, 1:3, 211–58.

Dobres, M.-A. and Hoffman, C.R. (eds.) 1999. *The Social Dynamics of Technology*. Washington, DC: Smithsonian Institution Press.

Gamble, C. 1999. *The Palaeolithic Societies of Europe*. Cambridge: Cambridge University Press.

Giddens, A. 1984. *The Constitution of Society: outline of a theory of structuration*. Berkeley, CA: University of California Press.

Gibson, K. 1996. The biocultural human brain, seasonal migrations, and the emergence of the Upper Palaeolithic. In P. Mellars and K. Gibson (eds.) *Modelling the Early Human Mind*, 33–46. Cambridge: McDonald Institute Monographs.

Gosden, C. 1994. *Social Being and Time*. Oxford: Blackwell.

Hayden, B. 1993. The cultural capacities of Neandertals: a review and re-evaluation. *Journal of Human Evolution*, 24:2, 113–46.

Ingold, T. 1993. The Reindeerman's lasso. In P. Lemonnier (ed.) *Technical Choices: transformation in material cultures since the Neolithic*, 108–25. London: Routledge.

Lemonnier, P. (ed.) 1993. *Technical Choices: transformation in material cultures since the Neolithic*. London: Routledge.

Meignen, L. 1995. Levallois lithic production systems in the Middle Paleolithic of the Near East: the case of the unidirectional method. In H. Dibble and O. Bar-Yosef (eds.) *The Definition and Interpretation of Levallois Technology*, 361–79. Madison, WI: Prehistory Press (Monographs in World Archaeology No. 23).

Mellars, P. 1996. *The Neanderthal Legacy*. Princeton, NJ: Princeton University Press.

Pelegrin, J. 1990. Prehistoric lithic technology: some aspects of research. *Archaeological Review from Cambridge*, 9:1, 116–25.

Pettitt, P. 1997. High resolution Neanderthals? Interpreting Middle Palaeolithic intersite spatial data. *World Archaeology*, 29:2, 208–24.

Pettitt, P. 2003. The Mousterian in action: chronology, mobility, and Middle Palaeolithic variability. In N. Moloney and M.J. Shott (eds.) *Lithic Analysis at the Millenium*, 29–44. London: UCL Press.

Pigeot, N. 1990. Technical and social actors: flintknapping specialists and apprentices at Magdalenian Etiolles. *Archeological Review from Cambridge*, 9:1, 126–41.

Pfaffenberger, B. 1992. Social anthropology of technology. *Annual Review of Anthropology*, 21, 491–516.

Renfrew, C. and Zubrow, E.B. (eds.) 1994. *The Ancient Mind: elements of cognitive archaeology*. Cambridge: Cambridge University Press.

Schlanger, N. 1994. Mindful technology: unleashing the *chaîne opératoire* for an archaeology of mind. In C. Renfrew and E. Zubrow (eds.) *The Ancient Mind: elements of cognitive archaeology*. Cambridge: Cambridge University Press.

Schlanger, N. 1996. Understanding Levallois: lithic technology and cognitive archaeology. *Cambridge Archaeological Journal*, 6:2, 231–54.

Sinclair, A. 2000. Constellations of knowledge: human agency and material affordance in lithic technology. In M.-A. Dobres and J.E. Robb (eds.) *Agency in Archaeology*, 196–212. London: Routledge.

Thomas, J. 2000. Reconfiguring the social, reconfiguring the material. In M.B. Schiffer (ed.) *Social Theory in Archaeology*, 143–55. Salt Lake City, UT: University of Utah Press.

PART 2: AGENCY AND POWER

CHAPTER 6

DIRT, CLEANLINESS, AND SOCIAL STRUCTURE IN ANCIENT GREECE

Astrid Lindenlauf

INTRODUCTION

Dirt can be conceptualised as physical-concrete, but also as immaterial-abstract. It is generally held that beliefs on dirt and pollution concepts in ancient Greece (*konis, pinos, lyma, miasma, akomistie*), as well as the understanding of cleanliness and purification (*katharsis, komide*) saw changes from the Homeric to the Classical period. There is, however, a debate currently taking place regarding the quality and the degree of changes involved. It would be an oversimplification to characterise the changing conception of dirt as from material-concrete to immaterial-abstract. On the one hand, such a statement would ignore authors like Aischylos (*Ag.* 772–74), who, in a masterly fashion, opposed the physical-concrete, social and moral dimensions of *pinos* (dirt) and *chrysos* (gold) in terms of poverty and wealth, purity and rottenness, and goodness and badness. On the other, it would play down the crucial fact that the immaterial-abstract conceptualisation of dirt and pollution of the Classical period had strong material-concrete reference points (e.g. Herodotos 1.35.1; Aischylos *Eu.* 52, 280–81; Plato *Ti.* 22D; Aristophanes *V.* 118). At the other end of the scale, it would also disregard the symbolic overtones of dirt in the Homeric epics (cf. Vernant 1996; Parker 1996; Wöhrle 1996; *contra* Gillies 1925; Moulinier 1952; Rudhart 1958: 51; Mije 1991a, 1991b; Neumann 1992), as, for instance, when Odysseus cleansed away from his *oikos* (household) with sulphur and fire the traces of murder that had already been removed by his servants (Hom. *Od.* 22.436–94). Less ambiguous is the development of the conceptual framework of *miasma* that appears in c. 600 BC, in particular in the works of Alkaios and Solon, for the first time (Neumann 1992: 73, add. Solon *fr.* 23.10 [Franyó and Gan 1981]). However, in this chapter, I do not want to get caught up in such unfruitful discussion on particular kinds of dirt. Consequently, I will conceptualise all kinds of cleanliness and dirt simply as social symbols, and explore their role in the structuration of Greek society.

The need to integrate an understanding of dirt and its complementary opposite, cleanliness, into a holistic view of society has long been stressed. Douglas, in her influential book *Purity and Danger* (1995), for example, found the exploration of dirt to be an exciting undertaking that helped to uncover social classificatory systems and social tensions. Douglas' approach to the study of dirt is influenced by structuralism. She conceptualised culture as a system of classifications and a set of "institutional and intellectual productions built upon those systems of classification and performing further operations upon them" (Ortner 1984: 135), and also through her analogy of the physical and social body. Hodder (1982a, 1982b, 1990: esp. 127) applied Douglas' interpretative framework to various archaeological studies with a view to examining, through the distribution of physical dirt, the principal boundaries between the familiar and the strange, the 'self' and the 'other', in terms of ethical or social boundaries. However, whilst Douglas defined dirt as a "by-product of the creation of order", Hodder (1982a: 62–65, 66, 91; 1982b: 159–63) suggested that social and ethnic groups actively use their material culture to resolve their conflicts, communicate and manifest power relations or settle societal changes. That attitudes to cleanliness must also be examined within their cultural, social and historical context has been argued by Elias in *The Civilising Process* (1992), and later by Vigarello (1988), who applied the Eliasian framework to changing concepts of cleanliness in France since the Middle Ages. Owing to their interest in the long-term processes of social and political developments, Elias and Vigarello stressed that socio-political configurations and attitudes towards cleanliness as well as normative behaviour are constantly in flux. A diachronic perspective and analysis of the mechanisms behind, and social processes leading to, sanitary reforms were also at the heart of Corbin's (1994) study of "the history of sensibilities" in Europe. In contrast to Elias and Vigarello, however, Corbin stressed the active ways in which concepts of cleanliness and behavioural conditioning were used by people in power to maintain social differences, and he referred more to Foucault's theory of power (1977) than to Elias' 'civilising process'. In his treatment of chlorine, for example, Corbin (1994: esp. 143) emphasised the substantial effects of the introduction of chlorine in speeding up progress towards "the bourgeois control of the sense of smell", and he asserted that the 'secretions of poverty' were blamed for the cholera epidemic in 1832.

Conceptualising notions of cleanliness and dirt as social and historical categories, rather than cross-cultural and analytical, means that their understanding may differ from society to society and across time in a given society. This otherness has often not been accounted for by classicists. Consequently, ancient Greek habits have been judged from our modern European standards, on the one hand. Thus, Flacelière (1977: 368) concluded that ancient Greeks were not clean, because they did not brush their teeth, used no handkerchiefs and spat on the ground. On the other hand, ancient Greek cleaning practices have been associated with concepts of hygiene (for a definition cf. Hemker 1993: 256) and health, despite the existence of studies convincingly showing that concepts of cleanliness were not yet necessarily linked to concepts of health in ancient Greece (e.g. Kornexl 1970). Crouch (1993: 311, 321), for instance, assumed that the cleaning activities of Greek athletes ensured their health and well-being and that the bathing facility at Gortys was a health facility. In this chapter, I attempt to understand cleaning practices within their cultural context with a view to exploring ancient Greek concepts of cleanliness.

Different aspects of cleanliness and dirt in ancient Greece have been discussed in various archaeological, philological and historical studies, yet a cohesive history and sociology of cleanliness and dirt, taking into account the wider political, societal and symbolic implications, remains to be written for ancient Greece. The aspect of personal cleanliness has received most scholarly attention. Laser's (1983) and Wöhrle's (1996) articles on concepts of body care and personal cleanliness in the Homeric epics are socially informed, but they tackle mainly the Homeric epics and very rarely encompass comparative references to later periods. The publications of Hawley (1998) and Shanks (1992a, 1992b, 1999) address the issues of the meaning and symbolism of the beautification of the human body and cleaning processes, but again only within a very restricted time-span. Hawley's article on beauty and external appearance in classical tragedy illuminates primarily the symbolism and manipulation of the beautiful and clean female body in two tragedies by Euripides. Shanks' various contributions to the interpretation of art in the context of the emergence of the city-state were based on one category of material culture, the Corinthian *aryballoi*. In some respects, Ginouvès' (1962) basic book on *Balaneutiké* is more encompassing. Here, he discusses various social contexts and occasions for which cleansing practices were required in the ancient Greek world, and changes over time in cleaning practices. In other respects, however, his work is less informative, as Ginouvès does not tackle issues such as the structuration of ancient Greek society through cleansing practices, bathing equipment and notions of personal cleanliness. Lewandowski (1960: esp. 82–83), by contrast, discusses cleaning practices in his book on changing customs and moral standards in the ancient Greek world. Yet, his actual discussion of the literary and archaeological evidence is too superficial and eclectic to highlight changing patterns of cleanliness and purity. Finally, there are Neumann's (1992) and Parker's (1996) philological investigations into changing conceptualisations and understandings of cleanliness and dirt, which are interesting in their own right, but disrespect social theory. Apart from cleanliness with respect to the human body, other aspects of cleanliness have not received much scholarly attention, such as the intersection of cleanliness and work, space, and language.

Adopting an interdisciplinary perspective, which draws not only on a sociologically-informed archaeology, but also on material culture studies, this chapter will analyse cleanliness and dirt within the parameters of social power and time, incorporating literary and archaeological sources such as ancient texts, inscriptions, vase-paintings, and architectural remains. More specifically, it takes into account that social structure is the cause and result of ideas and principles of difference. This chapter also attempts to be sensitive towards fluctuations in human power balances and interdependencies across time, following the Eliasian and Foucauldian interpretative frameworks that are based on a relational theory of power (cf. Arnason 1987; Featherstone 1987: 203). However, in contrast to the Eliasian processual conceptualisation of socio-political changes, I believe that individuals and social groups play an active part in them and, therefore, that social structure is both a medium for and an outcome of people's ideas, and differences (cf. Giddens' process of structuration, 1979, 1984; Shanks 1999: 20). That ancient Greeks understood themselves as 'knowledgable agents' interacting with other subjects and actively constructing and manipulating other people's world views as early as the Classical period, becomes clear from the oft-cited passage in the work of Thukydides (6.16.1–3, cf. Linders 1997: 32 with n. 13), in which Alkibiades financed more than one chariot in the Olympic games, so that

Athens would appear more powerful than it actually was. Here, I will also analyse the parameters of the embodied agent, identity and the self – categories briefly tackled by Foucault and analytically addressed in Turner's sophisticated sociological reading of the same (Elliott 2001: 97–99). In Elias' model, the embodied self as being fundamental to social action is of no importance, and the self plays a role only in the sense of being constituted by processes of internalisation of mechanisms of social control. By contrast, owing to my emphasis on the active social agent, I do not conceive of power as moving only one way. Thus, I will not only explore how far the body is crucial to an individual subject's sense of self, but also the manner in which the self relates and interacts with others.

The time-span considered ranges from the Homeric period to the Classical period. Later sources are occasionally encompassed, as in the section dealing with the attempts of *polis* authorities to keep public places tidy. The standard periodisation deriving from political history is used except with regard to the Homeric period. The society and time described in the Homeric epics is referred to simply as the Homeric period, as the epics are an "organic amalgam", based on the experience of the "Gleichzeitigkeit des Ungleichzeitigen" (simultaneity of the non-contemporary; cf. Sherratt 1990; Raaflaub 1998: esp. 188). The time-span under discussion covers a critical phase of socio-political transformations, characterised by changing power distributions, dynamic social relations and increasing integration. This can be summarised as follows: Greek society in the age of Homer and Hesiod may be described as a pre-*polis* society, in which the *oikos* (household) was of greater importance than the *polis* (city; city-community). During the course of the Archaic period, the domestication of the hero and the process of social integration of the aristocracy on the one hand, and the increasing care and interest in the community and the *polis* on the other, led to the depersonalisation of the exercise of power, a monopolisation of physical force by the *polis*, and changes in ethics and values, from individual-centred to community-centred ideals (Spahn 1977; Finley 1992: 121; Walter 1993: esp. 211–19). By the 4th century BC, the citizen was the ideal and the norm in this configuration of the *polis*-community, and the *demos* set the normative ideals and limits which were not to be crossed, at least in Athens (cf. Zanker 1995).

A diachronic perspective can offer fascinating insights into changing concepts of cleanliness and the ways in which notions of cleanliness and dirt served to empower and privilege some, whilst marginalising others. The interplay of cleanliness and dirt with social structure across time can be explored by understanding agency on both an individual and an inter-group level. Owing to the great socio-political changes in the period under discussion, the inter-group level is of particular interest. The questions posed here are as follows: which social groups articulated relative social status with reference to cleanliness or dirt? Did the changing composition of the groups in power or those who considered themselves as superior result in changing understandings and conceptualisations of cleanliness and dirt? Although these questions need to be posed, they are often not easy to answer due to the fragmentary sources. For Homeric society, for example, social stratification into the *dmoai* and the aristocrats has long been acknowledged, but the exact social status of each group is disputed. Whilst Laser

(1983: S142–43) and Wöhrle (1996: 159) assumed that the *dmoai* were slaves, Morris (1987: 178) followed Finley and stated that they were by no means slaves, but rather the lowest members of the estate-household. Similarly, Theognis, who lived in the second half of the 6th century, divided Greek society into *deloi* (58 [West]) and *agathoi* and *esthloi* respectively (57), characterising the former as socially underprivileged and the latter as socially privileged. Yet, he did not provide an exact social profile for these groups. The precise meaning of the term *penia*, used by Theognis in connection with the *deloi*, has been much discussed. Jameson (1992: 143, 145) argued most persuasively that this term seems not to refer to paupers and indigents in a modern sense, but more precisely to those who have to work for a living.

The social stratification of some Greek *poleis* in later times is better known. Athenian society of the Classical period, for example, seems to have been divided into two broad legal and social classes, the slave and the free (Edmondson 2000: V). During the heyday of classical Athenian democracy, they were equal in the sense that they were both liable for punishment. Yet, the Athenians involved in the political process enforced a definite differentiation between slave and citizen by distinguishing, for instance, the penalties according to socio-political status and forbidding slaves to act as witnesses in lawsuits (Edmondson 2000: VI). The complexity of these legally defined classes, however, and the degree to which they were stratified have only recently received scholarly attention (Edmondson 2000: V). Those people counted among the free included individuals as diverse as leading political figures such as Pericles, resident aliens or metics, transient foreigners, and bastards. Among the slaves were those who were privately owned by individuals and those who were publicly owned, i.e. the property of the state (cf. Edmondson 2000: VI). Consequently, I shall attempt to uncover the extent to which the members of these two legally-defined groups actively used notions of cleanliness and dirt to demarcate themselves from each other, and to communicate and constitute social status within these groups.

State formation processes became socially and politically significant from the Archaic period, as discussed above, and especially in Athens, one of the best documented of ancient Greek cities. Thus, in addition to the individual and the inter-group level, I will also analyse the significance of the social values of cleanliness and dirt on the intra-state level. More specifically, I shall examine the points when issues related to personal cleanliness and clean public places were high on the agenda of the *polis* authorities, and when those in power used cleanliness as a discipline of social control, in the Foucauldian sense.

This chapter is divided into four sections. First, I will analyse the understanding of cleaning practices through time and the way in which the human body served to define the self and constitute social relations, inequalities and oppression with a view to exploring how far the social reproduction of ancient Greece also involved the social reproduction of appropriate bodies (cf. Shilling 1993: 125). Secondly, I shall discuss the social recognition of people who worked with or removed dirty substances or performed tasks classified as dirty. Thirdly, I intend to study the intersection of social status and control with the cleanliness of houses and public places. Finally, following on from Foucault's concentration upon discourse and language, I will end by exploring the link between dirt and language.

CLEANING PRACTICES, CLEANLINESS AND THE BODY

In the Homeric epics, Homeric society is characterised as hierarchical. Social status is communicated through the wealth of the *oikos*, including the size of houses (*Od.* 20.122) and the value of artefacts (*Od.* 7.173 vs. 13.437), but also through an order of appearance that allowed the relevant social and economic facts to be read from external signs. Bodily marks of distinction and symbolic representation of identity included the quality of clothes (*Od.* 13.218 vs. 4.245) and the degree of *komide*. The concept of *komide* can be best translated as 'body-care', encompassing, among other social activities, washing practices; it was linked to *aglaie*, a sense of beauty, brilliance or brightness (e.g. *Od.* 18.180). Grooming (and cleanliness) were linked to social status in a range of ways: people like seamen, beggars, vagabonds, and *dmoai* were characterised as lacking in body-care (e.g. Hom. *Od.* 14.124, 21.284, 24.248–57). They were squalid and unwashed (*Od.* 19.72) and clad in defiled clothes (*Od.* 13.435). Visible manifestations of the level of the *komide* of the elite (*agathoi*), which were valid among Greek and non-Greek nobles, included clean and freshly-washed clothes in a good condition (*Od.* 4.750, 759, 13.218) and an anointed body (*Od.* 15.332). Nausikaa stated that freshly washed clothes were part of the proper appearance of the elite and constituted a "good report" on individuals (*Od.* 6.29–30; for the ideal of *kalokagathia* cf. Bourriot 1995). In addition to the cleanliness of the entire body, special attention was drawn to the cleanliness of the feet, hands and the heads of male nobles (*Od.* 15.332; Laser 1983: S148–53); they could signify a well-groomed person as a *pars pro toto*. The divine level of *komide* was characterised by constant grooming (*Od.* 8.450–53). An exact description of the appearance of gods was not given, but they may be thought of as clad in clean and divine clothes from which fragrant oil of a supreme quality would constantly drip (*Il.* 14.172; *Od.* 5.230–31, 7.107).

Frequent references to the bodies of aristocrats as anointed imply that *komide* played a constituent role in defining the self-image of the aristocracy (cf. Laser 1983: S136–48). A possible reason why an anointed body provided a fundamental criterion for social status may have been because it was thought of as a shining body, and thus linked to the positive values of radiance, heroism, light and illumination, as opposed to the negative values of shadow, darkness and death (cf. Vernant 1990). *Komide* was considered by the gods and the elite as basic a component of life as eating (*Il.* 19.303–08, 346). Negligence of cleanliness would not allow the elite to live up to the demanding code of physical excellence (*Od.* 8.232–33), whilst a high degree of personal grooming contributed to a "good report" (*Od.* 6.29–30). The vehemence with which the leading Achaeans urged Achilles, who was grieving for his dead companion Patroklos, to wash the clotted blood from his body, as well as the eagerness with which Achilles attempted to befoul the dead corpse of Hektor (*Il.* 22.405, 23.24–26, 24.17–18), and the concern of the gods for the standards of body-care due to a dead member of the elite (*Il.* 23.185–87, 24.418–23), all hint at the importance of cleanliness among this group.

The extensive descriptions of hot baths for the male elite and gods imply that the cleaning process was as important for the construction and maintenance of social hierarchy as its visible results. The only socially accepted way of achieving cleanliness was through a cleaning process that involved conspicuous consumption, because a typical aristocratic bathing complex consisted ideally of the following five elements (cf. Arend 1933: 68–72, 124–26): (1) a hot-water bath with precious vessels either in a fixed or portable bathtub and assistants, (2) anointment with oil or ambrosia, (3) new clothes, (4) a meal or wine, and (5) rest. Members of the elite could make minimal efforts at cleaning themselves, such as washing away their sweat in the sea. They had, however, to indulge in a hot bath afterwards in order to be not merely washed but clean, as the bathing sequence of Diomedes and Odysseus indicates (*Il.* 10.572–79).

In a society in which social status was regulated by outward appearance, highly structured rules and conventions governed the human body. Thus, the Homeric elite only gave up the distinguishing marks of body-care in exceptional circumstances, such as grief (*Od.* 18.173–84; Wöhrle 1996: 155) and when in disguise (*Od.* 4.244–50), while it was relaxed when adopting modes of appearance and cleanliness typical for the divine realm (*Od.* 2.5, 5.255–63). By contrast, deities who frequently adopted human features, appearing either as nobles or as beggars, seem to have been far more relaxed in temporarily accepting lower standards of body-care (*Od.* 13.221–27, 287–90). The significance of a hot bath in constituting the status of the *agathoi* becomes evident when Odysseus, after the murder of his wife's suitors, preserves the exclusivity of a hot bath and fresh clothes for himself and his son (*Od.* 23.131, 142, 154–63). Here, the bath marks the transition from being a person begging for alms to being a member of the social elite (*Od.* 17.501–02 vs. 19.321–22).

Until almost the close of the Archaic period (630–480 BC), archaeological sources such as vase paintings and a greater variety of literary sources, namely the works by Hesiod and Semonides, provide glimpses of the interplay of cleanliness and social power. In contrast to Homer who attempted to think in the past, archaic poetry analyses the present. The bard and farmer Hesiod gives, in his *Works and Days*, a personal and altogether unheroic account of life at an archaic Boeotian *oikos* of farmers around 700 BC, somewhere in between the postulated extremes of a poor, underprivileged or dependent peasant (Morris 1987: 175; Stein-Hölkeskamp 1992: 40; Himmelmann 1996: 52) and a wealthy aristocrat (Tandy 1997: 205–06, cf. Isager and Skydsgaard 1995: 84). He creates the impression (520, 746–47 [for a convincing interpretation of this passage cf. Dean-Jones 1994: 230 rather than Ginouvès 1962: 265 n. 1]) that the constitution of status and power in relation to cleanliness and dirt outside of the *oikos* was of no importance in everyday life, whilst power in the household was manifested by unrestricted access to bathing facilities. In addition, Hesiod regarded cleaning processes rather as metaphors for gender powers than metaphors for tensions between social strata. However, the conceptual link between bath, pleasure and consumption in contrast to hard work and productivity, first expressed by Homer with the image of the well-cared-for aristocrat who rests his feet on a footstool (*Od.* 4.136), still exists, even if presented in a new engendered framework (cf. Parker 1996: 293; Zeitlin 1996).

Semonides (*fr.* 7 [West], 10A [West]), who has a more aristocratic background than Hesiod, seems to discuss issues of cleanliness in the Homeric sense of the term as appearance and self-presentation in his poems of the second half of the 7th century. As in the Homeric epics, notions of cleanliness and dirt are linked to social order and the human body is seen as a symbol to communicate social status and group-identity: when Semonides stated (*fr.* 7) that the degree of cleanliness of a 'mare-woman' may suit the upper-elite but is unsuitable for men of his status, he was acknowledging that different degrees of personal cleanliness characterised different social strata. Thus, it may be concluded that Semonides would probably agree with Homer that *aglaie*, and permanent *komide* were restricted to the upper-elite and that a satisfactory level of concern for cleanliness was about right for people like himself. Yet, in contrast to Homer, Semonides leaves no doubt that he does not hold this extreme form of beautification (*aglaizein*) in high esteem, as he criticises those obsessed with outer appearance for neglecting their duties within the *oikos* and family values, including the preparation of food, keeping the house in order and removing *kopros* (animal and/or human excrement). Similarly, he disregards women and men who are unwashed, unkempt and unlaundered (*akosmos*) alike, as they stand for disorder, wildness and danger (cf. Wöhrle 1996: 164). With his emphasis on the 'mean' as the ideal and his perception of deviations from the norm as unacceptable he anticipates the Aristotelian 'doctrine' of the mean. To what extent Semonides' symbolism of cleanliness and dirt is original is difficult to say. Fragments of other ancient authors survive which draw on metaphors of women (cf. Lloyd-Jones 1975; Franyó and Gan 1981: 8). Thus, it is possible, even likely, that Semonides' creative act consisted of presenting generally accepted social norms in an artful form. This would suggest that in the Archaic period, the Greeks used embodied ideas of cleanliness and dirt with a view to exercising social control over others.

For the purposes of this chapter, an additional source of interest is a group of Archaic/early Classical vase-paintings that was produced for symposiasts (Figs. 6.1–6.2). These vases depict naked female figures, possibly *hetairai* (courtesans), washing and beautifying themselves and transforming their bodies into objects of desire (cf. Manakidou 1992–93; Lewis 2002). If it is accepted that images created interactive relationships with the viewer (e.g. Lissarrague 1990 [1987]: esp. 107–22; Schäfer 1997: 45–49), it is likely that these washing scenes were produced with the purpose of playing an active role in structuring the expectations of the symposiasts towards the female participants of a symposion, the courtesans. The depiction of women washing themselves as a 'pretext' to depict naked women was not restricted to the Archaic period. Classical depictions of bathing goddesses draw on the well-established notion of bathing and washing hair as something that aroused men's sexual desire and invited sexual intercourse (Hawley 1998: 49, add. Diogenes Laertios 6.66). One such example is a red figure *pelike* (Simon 1981: pl. 52), by the Marsyas Painter, depicting Peleus catching sight of Thetis bathing and washing her hair; that he will succeed in seducing/raping her is indicated by the Eros crowning Peleus (Fig. 6.3). Further Classical and Hellenistic examples include certain representations of Aphrodite, preparing to take a bath, with whom men would fall in love and desire intercourse. Post-classical stories of men crying

Fig. 6.1: Attic red figure stamnos, Munich, Antikensammlung, AS 2411, c. 440/30 BC (drawing by M.-L. Charalambi, after Lewis 2002: 148 fig. 4.12).

Fig. 6.2: Attic red figure kylix, Brussels, Musées royaux d'Art et d'Histoire, A 889, c. 480 BC (drawing by M.-L. Charalambi, after Simon 1981: fig. 135).

Fig. 6.3: Attic red figure pelike, London, British Museum, E 424,
c. 340 BC (drawing by M.-L. Charalambi, after Simon 1981: pl. 52).

over the statue of the Aphrodite of Knidos, having sex with it and staining it with
semen, on the one hand, and the selling of pornographic images of this statue, on
the other, testify that it had a lasting impact on men and became the object of male
admiration and desire (cf. Davidson 1998: caption to fig. of Aphrodite of Knidos;
Zanker 1998: 74).

By the end of the Classical period (480–323 BC), a clean appearance together
with other aristocratic privileges such as participation in symposia (cf. Eder 1992;
Sutton 2000: 181) had also become the concern of lower, if not of all, social strata.
Bodily cleanliness appears to have been part of the value code of all Greeks,
including prostitutes and slaves, shaping their modes of living and ideals (cf.
Theophrastos *Char.* 10.14, 19.3–4). An increased awareness of cleanliness among
the population can, for example, be deduced from a passage in Aristophanes'
Plutos (729) where Kario emphasises that Asklepios wiped the eyelids of a patient
with a "perfectly clean rag". The degree to which bathing came to be taken for
granted as an element of everyday life becomes evident in the casual way in
which a visit to the public baths or bathing is mentioned in the literary sources
(Aristophanes *Eq.* 50–51, 1061; Eubulos *fr.* 123 [Kassel and Austin]; Theophrastos
Char. 27.14; Diogenes Laertios 6.40) and in the critical comments made about

ordinary people who do not wash in the comedies of Aristophanes (*Pl.* 1061–62), and Theophrastos' *Characters* (19.5; cf. Leppin 2002: 44). The process of the democratisation of cleanliness, it seems, went hand in hand with what Ginouvès (1962: 102) has termed the simplification of washing activities from the 5th century BC, and the provision of public baths (Aristophanes *Nu.* 1045–62; Isaios, cited in Isager and Skydsgaard 1995: 101), which enabled the *demos* to engage in and live up to new standards of cleanliness.

Despite these literary references to the democratisation of cleanliness, notions of cleanliness and the components of the cleaning process still served as a symbolic demonstration of superior social status, albeit in a more subtle way. Public baths that could guarantee bodily cleanliness for everyone had a bad reputation and were said to be frequented by socially disreputable figures (Lewandowski 1960: 82). Diogenes even went as far as claiming that the public baths were dirty and that whoever bathed there would have to go somewhere else to get clean (Diogenes Laertios 6.47). Socially-acceptable cleanliness resulted from washing at home (Hermippos *fr.* 68 [Kassel and Austin]; Athenaios 590F), ideally in a room set apart for exclusively this purpose (for Olynthos cf. Lohmann 1992: 35; for Priene cf. Höpfner and Schwandner 1994: 202). That private bathrooms indeed indicated a new form of social differentiation is supported by the fact that only rich farmsteads such as the so-called Dema House and house A at Draphi, both located within Attika (Jones 1975: 102, fig. 13, 113), were equipped with bathrooms. A more body-orientated and Homeric means of constructing and sustaining group-identity and social difference was, in Xenophon's understanding (*Sym.* 2.4), the quality of perfumes and oils used; the underlying logic for the preference of olive oil over perfumes seems to have been that everybody could buy perfumes, but the scent of the olive oil used in the gymnasium distinguished those who had the privilege to have access to the socially-restricted space of the gymnasium from those who did not.

For other realms, Foucault (1992) could show that self-control, self-awareness and self-mastery – as opposed to control over someone else or being controlled by someone else – defined the ethical regime of the classical age. This is less clear from the point of view of cleanliness for two reasons. First, changes that may be interpreted as an increase in self-restraint can be seen in the trend towards excessive daily cleansing practices already from the Archaic period rather than from the Classical period. Secondly, the state seems to have taken over the monopoly of power by the Classical period.

Neglecting bodily cleanliness was not necessarily exclusively associated with low social status or plain economic necessity. An active way in which the negative social connotation of a dirty outer appearance served to create social difference was employed, for example, by the philosophical fringe group of the Cynics. They, for ideological reasons (cf. Diogenes Laertios 6.22), played with and deliberately chose a lifestyle characteristic of people that Thompson (1979: 93) would classify as "social rubbish" in order to protest against and challenge commonly accepted norms. The Cynics surely held their way of life in high esteem, but the very label Cynic, meaning dog-like, shameless and animal-like (cf. Lindenlauf 2001: 87), seems to allude to the way they were perceived by non-followers. In fact, their appearance recalls the description of disgusting (*bdeluktropos*) monsters such as Gorgon-like creatures as well as the Cyclops (Aischylos *Eu.* 52–54; Aristophanes *Pl.* 296–300; cf. Heath 1999: 35).

To sum up, in all periods under discussion, ancient Greeks were preoccupied with the cultivation of the self and the creation of social differentiation in and through bodily cleanliness and body care. The making of individual and group identities was highly structured by rules and conventions regulating the proper outer appearance of people and the degree of conspicuous consumption involved in the washing process. Yet the means with which social differentiation was communicated differed across time and from individual to individual. Whilst precious bathing equipment and a well-groomed appearance were characteristic for the aristocracy in the highly-structured Homeric society, a separate bathroom functioned as a social marker in the more democratic *poleis*. Personal cleanliness and a dirty appearance respectively were symbols of social reproduction and of social differentiation, tensions, and conflicts between people of different social status. Social groups who aimed at distinguishing themselves from other groups included aristocrats, from the lower social orders, consisting of seamen, beggars, vagabonds and *dmoai* (Homer); the rich, from the poorer (bathrooms); and athletic male citizens, from slaves and lazy male citizens (Xenephon). Greek society was also structured with reference to cleanliness and dirt into different social groups (Cynics and ordinary people), or different genders (Hesiod; vase-paintings). Over time, the development of the *polis* brought about changes in the concept of cleanliness, the simplification of cleaning activities and the provision of public bathing facilities.

So far, I have analysed the intersection of bodily cleanliness with social structures, reproduction and power. In the following section, I will examine critically the link between low social status and cleaning tasks and work relating to dirty substances.

DIRT AND WORK

"Removing other people's dirt"

Removing other people's dirt as one's primary job indicated, as in many other cultures, a low social position in the ancient Greek world; this also holds true for Homeric society (cf. Brock 1994). Much of the menial labour related to washing with water was women's work (cf. Lefkowitz 1982: 27). In the majority of cases, the nobly-born head of an aristocratic household would restrict her duties to those of supervision, and delegate tasks to the female servants, as described in the palaces of Hektor and Alkinous (*Il.* 22.442–44; *Od.* 8.426–57). Washing practices, which some high-status women regarded as being prestigious enough to be involved in, albeit with the aid of their female servants, included the washing of textiles (*Od.* 6.25–33). This interest may be explained on the basis of the social significance of textiles in general (*Il.* 3.125–28, 22.440–41; *Od.* 3.348; cf. Mansfield 1985; Barber 1992: 106), and of freshly washed garments in particular (*Od.* 6.26–30, 60–61).

The performance of cleaning as an everyday activity and/or to earn one's living was also typical for men of low, including servile, social status. Thus, Odysseus, disguised as an old beggar, thought it appropriate to serve nobly-born people, whose functions included mixing wine, cutting meat, chopping firewood and cleaning tables before feasts (*Od.* 1.109–12, 15.322–24). Other cleaning tasks which meaner men carried out for the noble included the cleaning out of stables (*Od.* 17.223). The only cleansing task in which a male head of the *oikos* was actively involved was the symbolic cleaning of houses with special purificatory agents (*Od.* 22.481–82). In all other cases, his role was restricted to the supervision of cleaning activities. His primary concern appears to have been the cleanliness of the stables, though, in exceptional circumstances, he also seems to have taken over the organisation and supervision of cleansing operations within the *megaron* (*Od.* 22.430–94, esp. 436–39).

Permanent occupations associated with providing a clean environment (for other people) were also considered to be disreputable jobs, and were primarily carried out by slaves and free people of lower social status performing menial wage labour in the Archaic and Classical periods. Thus, school-cleaners (Demosthenes 18.258), people doing the laundry (cf. above; add. possibly *IG* I³ 794; II² 2934) and bath-attendants in private and public baths (Hippocrates *Epid.* 4.32; Philipp 1990: 88; Brock 1994: 341 with n. 32, add. Aristophanes *Eq.* 1403, *Ra.* 710; cf. Anderson 1991: 151 with n. 10) were generally regarded as performing demeaning tasks, and these tended to be people of servile status. Similarly, the removal of the corpses of people who had died on the Athenian streets was regarded too demeaning a job to be carried out by a state official (Aristotle *Ath.* 50.2). Slaves also seem to have been the group of people who almost exclusively performed cleansing tasks within the sanctuaries (Graf 1978: 61–62; Bömer 1990: 216, add. Hammond and Walbank 1988: 202). Only the symbolic purification of altars before sacrifices, and of cult-statues, was performed by priests, *astynomoi* and people of the upper social classes (cf. Parker 1996: 27). As in the Homeric period, the washing of clothes appears to have been the exclusive domain of women. The Pan-painter made this point quite explicitly, creating an opposition between the male and the female realm of activities (Fig. 6.4a/b). Two women are depicted in his laundry-scene, one of whom is characterised by her hairdress and her clothing as a female servant. This working scene serves as a counterpart to the reverse that carries an image of two men simply standing in 'conversation', or a man engaging in 'conversation' with a (young) woman.

The job of the cesspool/sewage picker (*koprologoi*) of Athens had a low social reputation in the opinion of some characters in Aristophanes' comedies (*Pax* 16–25). More specifically, the household slaves of Trygaios considered the most disgusting part of this job to be its direct contact with *kopros* (all kinds of excrement), which they characterised as a noxious-smelling substance. They regarded the task of the *koprologos* as so revolting that they are said to have seen it as being beneath their dignity (*Pax* 9–16). The documentary sources offer only a limited amount of direct evidence about the social identity of *koprologoi*, but some modern scholars have convincingly argued that *koprologoi* were not public slaves, but private entrepreneurs (Owens 1983: 48–50; Ault 1993; Alcock *et al.* 1994: 149; Ault 1994: 221; Liebeschuetz 2000: 56) or people working for a private agency

Fig. 6.4a/b: Attic red figure pelike, Paris, Musée du Louvre, G 547, c. 470 BC (drawing by M.-L. Charalambi, after Pekridou-Gorecki 1989: 53 fig. 27 and CVA Louvre 8 pl. 46, 3).

(Durm 1910: 515); they were controlled by the state, but operated independently of public institutions. Whereas the term 'private entrepreneur' seems to imply that free men worked as *koprologoi*, the term 'private agency' would permit slaves and free men to work for an entrepreneur. Consequently, the cesspool/sewage pickers were either of the same legal status as the household slaves or even higher. In this light, Aristophanes' comments on the intolerable stench of excrement gain new significance, as his intent here may have been to bring discredit upon the *koprologoi*. If so, their stench may be defined as social in Corbin's (1994: 39–40, 142–50, 232) sense of the term. The social conceptualisation of *koprologoi* as an "archetype of stench" (Corbin 1994: 146, 196) may be supported by Thiercy's (1993) observation that Aristophanes actively employed odours in order to create a symbolic order of the world (cf. Dirt and language, below). Whether Aristophanes' creation of social hierarchy with reference to stench is original, or whether it merely reflects the opinion of a certain social group, is difficult to say. More important, however, is the fact that Aristophanes could expect his main target group, male citizens (Moraw 2002: 147), to acknowledge and to understand his linkage of stench with low social reputation.

Working with dirt

Occupations involving contact with physical dirt tend to have had a low social reputation. Coal miners and blacksmiths who returned from their jobs covered with coal-dust or begrimed with smoke seem to have been marginal and despised people; other people disliked even looking at them (Hom. *Od.* 13.435; cf. Demosthenes 54.4). Dirt could include stench in the Classical period. Thus, labour involving contact with putrid substances, as in the case of *koprologoi*, was categorised as demeaning. Although little is known about the social recognition of tanners and tanneries in pre-Hellenistic Greece (Parker 1996: 53), I believe that it is reasonable to assume that the former were also an 'archetype of stench' in Corbin's (1994: 142–50) sense of the term, as there are a number of references to the unpleasant and vile odours set free in tanneries (cf. Blümner 1875: 262 n. 1;

Burford 1985 [1972]: 93). It is reasonable to link the stench associated with tanners and tanneries with the use of bodily emissions in the process of tanning (cf. Forbes 1996: 4). If so, some of the insults which Aristophanes (*Eq.* 309) hurled at Kleon, whom he describes as a tanner and leather-seller, such as being a *borborotaraxis*, churner of dirt, may have alluded to his contact with urine (cf. Dirt and language, below).

To conclude, the context alone did not determine attitudes towards and the value attached to cleaning activities. The frequency of, and the degree of symbolism involved in, a cleaning activity may therefore be identified as important factors that determined the social value of cleansing practices and which social group would perform them. Thus, the cleansing of textiles and cult-statues as well as the removal of pollution were considered too prestigious to be left to the low social orders. The social groups who performed dirty work included male public and private slaves and possibly also free citizens.

In this section I have explored the relationship of dirty jobs with low social status or recognition, and in the next section shall discuss the link between physical and social dirt with respect to spatial cleanliness. By exploring the measures undertaken by the *polis* authorities to keep public places tidy, I shall illuminate the use of cleanliness as an instrument of state control.

SPATIAL CLEANLINESS

At home

Although Homer described cleansing scenes in the *oikos* of Odysseus (cf. Wickert-Micknat 1982: R59), it is unclear whether the entire *megaron* was tidied and cleaned on a regular basis, since the cleaning activities depicted were carried out before and after specific events. It may be concluded that cleanliness was not restricted to the human body, but extended to the aristocratic and divine spheres in a spatial sense. Passages which support this position include occasional references to laying tables (*Od.* 1.109–12, 17.32) and Hephaistos' efforts to provide his divine visitor a tidy environment (*Il.* 18.412–17). Dirt, by contrast, seems to have been characteristic for the living (and working) environment of servants in Homeric society: female servants, for example, slept on the bare ground covered with a layer of ash (*Od.* 11.190–91). Little literary evidence concerning the cleanliness of private houses of the Archaic period has survived. Semonides (*fr.* 7 [West]) gives the impression that order (*kosmos*) and cleanliness (absence of *borboros* [mud] and *kopros* [excrement]) were crucial aspects of the domestic realm. As with bodily cleanliness, Semonides has a clear understanding of what a clean house should look like and criticises those who do not live up to his ideals. A clean house was also the ideal in the Classical period, but it is not clear whether it was still indicative of social status. Thus, Aristophanes (*Ach.* 71–72) criticised the squalid living conditions of the refugees who lived in *forutos* (whatever the wind carries along), and Plato considered dirty living conditions as socially unacceptable (Diogenes Laertios 6.26, after Vögler 1997: 48). Interestingly, the presence or absence of vermin was not considered a social marker, probably because all *oikoi* were infested by vermin (cf. Davies and Kathirithamby 1986: 46–47, 149, 168–76; Beavis 1983: 91–120, 240–42).

In public places

The earliest evidence for *polis* authorities taking an interest in the cleanliness of public places goes back to the pre-*polis* period. The Athenian tyrant Peisistratos is said to have purified the island of Delos by removing the graves in the vicinity to the sacred place of Apollo, enforcing his understanding of sacred purity upon his fellows (Herodotos 1.64; Thukydides 3.104.1). The next documented measure to ensure public cleanliness was issued by the Athenian assembly (*demos*) and is dated to between 508 and 498 BC. In the so-called Hekatompedon inscriptions (*IG* I³ 1, 4B; cf. Németh 1993, 1994a, 1994b), the *polis* authority was concerned not only with mastering sacred places, but also with structuring and regulating the lives of the cult personnel. Other direct sources documenting the interest of *polis* authorities in keeping public spaces tidy were the construction of public toilets (Gross 1964: col. 851). The construction of public drainage systems, which are regarded as sewers in the modern literature (e.g. Crouch 1993: 22, 27) cannot be interpreted as measures undertaken by *polis* authorities, as their primary function was as drains for rain water (Liebeschuetz 2000: 57).

For the subsequent periods, evidence is more plentiful. Many city authorities were concerned with shielding off the sacred from all sorts of dirt (Dillon 1997). The majority of regulations relating to disposal from the Classical period were concerned with keeping *kopros* out of the *temenoi* and temples (Sokolowski 1962: 24.8–9, 50, 53.7–9; Sokolowski 1969: 57.6, 67.28–30, 115.4, 116.4–5, 14–17; *IG* XI 2 146.76–79; cf. Plato *Lg.* 764B). In addition to *kopros*, *spodos* (ashes; Sokolowski 1962: 24.8–9, 53.7–9) and *ekkatharmata* (liquid deriving from the cleansing of intestines (?) after the sacrificial procedure; Sokolowski 1962: 111, after Németh 1994b: 64 n. 45) were regarded as intolerable in connection with the sacred, as was social dirt such as men who prostituted themselves, cowards and murderers (Parker 1996: 74–75, 104–05; Pimpl 1997: 117–22). In addition to sanctuaries, other public places were also of interest to the *polis* authorities. One inscription, the so-called Piraios inscription of 320/19 BC (*IG* II² 380.36–40), can be restored as a behavioural code prohibiting defecation in the *agora* and the streets of Piraios. In the *Athenaion Politaia*, Aristotle (50) noted that Athens and Piraios were kept free of corpses and all kinds of excrement, and Plutarchos (*Mor.* 811B) gives evidence that the city authorities of 4th-century Thebes were also concerned with organising the disposal of urban waste. The *telmarch* was engaged in supervising the alleys for the removal of dung and the draining off of waste water in the streets. A much later astynomic law survived at Pergamon (*OGIS* 483; cf. Liebeschuetz 2000: 55) and prescribed that the owner of a house was to keep the part of the street close to the house clean. It is noteworthy that no dumping restrictions for cemeteries have survived.

These legislative provisions set out a normative code of social behaviour. Obviously, they were deemed "necessary", as Dillon (1997: 127) has rightly noted. However, it is less clear when these behavioural rules were first formulated, and which social groups or interests were competing in their formulation. As to the first point, it is not clear whether the inscriptions announced new regulations or whether they were simply an expression of the democratic ideology, making accessible for all those who could read regulations which were already known and socially accepted. In the first case, the erection of the inscriptions under discussion would constitute an attempt to unify the plurality of discourses towards a normative consensus; in the second case, the laws would have been socially accepted, yet not internalised by everyone. That there was still some degree of dispute regarding the cleanliness of public places at the time when the legislative provisions were fixed in stone can be deduced from the passages which either promise a monetary reward to encourage the informer to report before the *boule* or those which threaten witnesses who fail to report to the council.

As regards the second point – the question of who was involved in defining these norms – in democratic cities such as Classical Athens those in power and dominating political and social discourse were the male citizens in the assembly. Through the Hekatompedon-inscriptions, these individuals attempted to condition and control the behaviour of cult personnel. The other regulations concern visitors to the sanctuaries, including citizens and slaves, men and women, inhabitants of a *polis* and strangers. In these cases, the disposal regulations may be interpreted as an attempt by those in power to impose the new *polis* ideology, namely the increasing significance of the community (*koine*; *demosion*) and the territory of the *polis* (as against the pre-*polis* ideology, in which only the *oikos* and the individual (*to idion*) mattered), upon individuals of all social strata, including fellow-citizens, and to control individual behaviour and the interpretation of law (cf. Ober 1991: 76–86). This official ideology of the *polis*, which is based on the public/state-private/individual dichotomy, is well attested as structuring other realms of social and political life of the Greek city. Consequently, the ratification of the laws can be reinterpreted as reflecting the struggle between opposed interests of Athenian citizens, which Hansen (1999: 88) described as the opposition between the individual as a private persona and the individual as a citizen, since the *polis* was identical with the sum of its citizens.

To sum up, the perception of sanctuaries as places with distinguishing modes of cleanliness can be deduced from a number of prohibitions mentioned in the sacred laws regulating disposal within them and prohibiting access, for example, to social outcasts such as murderers. Sanctuaries were also marked out by *perirrhanteria* (basins for lustral water), as places of special religious and political importance, i.e. as *temenoi* – places cut off from the surrounding area (cf. Pimpl 1997: 49–65). The unusual standards of cleanliness and the scale of surviving legislative regulation concerning sacred spaces suggest that *polis* authorities cared more for sanctuaries than for other public places. This preoccupation of *polis* ideology with public sanctuaries can be explained by the distinguishing role sanctuaries played in the political and social life of every Greek *polis* (cf. Polignac 1995: esp. 184). In addition, sanctuaries played a significant role in integrating members of the civic community and in creating new forms of solidarity, because they provided the place in which citizens and other inhabitants of the civic territory could participate in the *polis* cults. They were also the places where the official history of a *polis* was constructed through the erection of public and private monuments and the destruction of statues of political leaders who had fallen into disregard.

Thus, the concept of the cleanliness of 'private' and 'public' spaces played, for individuals and *polis* authorities, a significant role in communicating social status and importance. Those in charge took measures to keep public spaces tidy and forced the entire community to follow their ideals and norms. Whilst Peisistratos acted against a specific social group, the assemblies of the democratic *poleis* directed their social power against everybody who disregarded the interests of the community.

DIRT AND LANGUAGE

Foul language and verbal abuse relating to dirt can best be studied through Greek comedy, especially the comedies of Aristophanes (427–388 BC). His work is not only the most complete, but he also explicitly classified his world according to good and bad with reference to notions of cleanliness and dirt (cf. Thiercy 1993). In addition to the examples discussed by Thiercy, Aristophanes' characterisations of the elderly and cowards are good examples of his usage of dirt as a metaphor for inferiority and unmanliness. More specifically, to the usually-listed sufferings of old people such as loss of strength (e.g. Hesiod *Op.* 110–17; Semonides *fr.* 1.1–13 [West]; Mimnermos 2.10–15 [West]; Pindar *P.* 10.41), contributing to the low esteem in which old age was commonly held in ancient Greece (e.g. Hesiod *Op.* 90–93; Aristophanes *Pl.* 265–66, *Rh.* 1360B), Aristophanes added the incontinence of old men (cf. Henderson 1991: 189 no. 400, 191 no. 408, 194 no. 420). As for fear and cowardice, Herodotos (7.140.3) and Plato (*Phdr.* 254C) associated them with the uncontrolled discharge of sweat. For Aristophanes, by contrast, the conceptual and associative link of sweat with fear was not drastic enough to express his lack of esteem. He, therefore, employed the visual and verbal metaphor of cowards who dirtied themselves, possibly deriving from the archaic sub-culture, if the inscription *Ko[pr]is* on one of the archaic clay tablets found at the sanctuary of Poseidon at Penteskouphia has been correctly read and interpreted (cf. Giuliani 1998: 631 with n. 5).

Various degrees of linking people with dirt in order to make a symbolic statement on the social esteem in which they are held by Aristophanes can be distinguished in his comedies, including associations of people with filthy habits and stench as well as insults of being dirty, in the sense of having internalised dirt into their mental personae. Thus, Aristophanes frequently hurled the accusation of the neglect of personal cleanliness, since this could be used to criticise, mock and marginalise people (e.g. *Av.* 1282, 1554). Another way of associating people with dirt in order to express the low social esteem in which individuals or social groups were held is related to the verb *propelakizein*, to bespatter with mud (e.g. *Th.* 386). By far the most common invectives in the first category were scatophagous insults (e.g. *Eq.* 1397–408, *Pax* 48; cf. Henderson 1991: 192 no. 414, 193 no. 417). They refer to consumers of excrement and indicate extremely low behaviour. How disrespected scatophagy was can be deduced from a statement by Pheidippides that not even Socrates, a frequent satirical target, would eat animal dung, filthy though he was (*Nu.* 1431–32).

Other invectives characterised people as *borborotaraxis*, churner of dirt, *borborope*, filth-hole, and *borborokoites*, (someone) lying in dirt (Aristophanes *Eq.*

308; Hipponax 135B [West]; *Batr.* 230; cf. Henderson 1991: 192 no. 414). Certain people were also referred to as greedy beggars (*molobros*) or addressed as filthy and disgusting types who shout loudly (Homer *Od.* 18.26; Aristophanes *Eq.* 303). Aristophanes' (*Pax* 48, 753, *Eq.* 308) favourite target of insults, Kleon, whom he accused of being scatophagous, a hurler of filthy-minded threats, and a churner of filth, was considered worthy of being called the worst-smelling person of all, *bdeluroteros*. That Aristophanes was expressing his own opinion in his assault on Kleon, rather than documenting a view common among his audience, can be deduced from the fact that Kleon played a relatively small part in comedies other than those of Aristophanes (Halliwell 1993: 332–33). When phrases containing associations and comparisons with dirt, personal uncleanliness and/or unpleasant smells did not suffice to express feelings of disgust about a person, Aristophanes deprived them of their humanity. In his opinion (*Pax* 804–14), the *choregos* Melanthios was no better than a fish-molestor whose armpits smelled like a he-goat.

The second category of insults – internalisation of dirt into the mental persona – included phrases such as hurler of *apeilas borborothumas*, filthy-minded threats (*Pax* 753, cf. Henderson 1991: 192 no. 414). Occasionally (cf. Henderson 1991: 193 no. 417), a person was also said to be a container for dirt, or to have become dirt.

A comparable language characterised forensic speeches. Here, accused persons were called, for example, foul wretch, unclean of body or an unclean scoundrel in order to represent their behaviour, habits and lifestyle as socially unacceptable (Aeschines 1.54, 2.88; Demosthenes 19.199). An even more powerful and aggressive means of expressing feelings of dislike about a person was through a combination of an animal-metaphor with dirt. Demosthenes (25.58), for instance, used the phrase "an unclean beast whose touch pollutes".

To sum up, Aristophanes created his social world by linking disgusting, detestable and abominable individuals, places and objects with all kinds of dirt, including bad odours. This was not a genuine creation, as can be deduced from Semonides' poem and Detienne's structural study (1985: esp. 93) of the ancient Greek world. Aristophanes' dirt-metaphors were directed against specific individuals, including Kleon, Socrates and Melanthios, whilst others were directed against specific social groups, such as elderly men. The metaphorical association and equation of a person with dirt were techniques which were also employed by court-room speakers in order to cast doubt on the integrity, humanity and morals of their opponents and to express their antipathy. If this kind of verbal abuse was characteristic for the stage and the court-room, then it is likely that it was quite widespread among their audiences (male citizens as well as some foreigners, slaves, and possibly women and boys) too.

CONCLUSIONS

I have shown that ancient Greeks engaged with issues of cleanliness and dirt in different aspects of human life, namely the human body, work, space and language, in all periods under discussion and that these concepts were bound up with networks of power. Both social concepts saw a shift in emphasis across time, in different social contexts and literary genres, but not in their social value. Whereas cleanliness was a concept with high social appeal, as it was linked to the positive values of radiance, heroism, light, prestige and superiority, dirt was associated with low social status, inferiority, animals, and monsters and with social outcasts such as murderers. Exceptions to this rule occurred only rarely (e.g. the symbolic removal of dirt; the Cynics). Cleanliness and dirt were constituting parts of the symbolic representation of the identity of individuals, social groups of different legal status, sexes and social prestige and the *polis*. They were also a means to construct, manipulate and sustain social power, privilege and status, on the one hand, and to reinforce and legitimise inequalities in Greek society on the individual, inter-social and intra-state level on the other. Individuals who used concepts of cleanliness and dirt for the negotiation of their social differences and hierarchies included Odysseus, Aristophanes, the accuser and the counsel of the defence; social groups that defined agency with reference to particular bodily attitudes included plutocrats vs. poorer people (bathrooms), men exercising in gymnasia vs. slaves and lazy citizens (Xenophon), private household slaves vs. private entrepreneurs or private slaves working for an agency (Aristophanes *Pax*), and men vs. women (Hesiod). An institutionalistion of agency occurred, I have argued, when democratic *polis* authorities provided public baths to ensure that all social strata could live up to the ideal of a clean citizen and when they ratified regulations in order to keep public spaces clean with a view to safeguarding the interests of the *polis* ideology.

References

Ancient works are abbreviated as in LSJ (Liddell, T.H.G., Scott, R. and Jones, H.S. (eds.) 1951. A Greek-English Lexicon. Oxford: Clarendon Press [9th edition] with Suppl. [Oxford, 1968]).

Alcock, S., Cherry, J.F. and Davis, J.L. 1994. Intensive survey, agricultural practice and the Classical landscape of Greece. In I. Morris (ed.) *Classical Greece: ancient histories and modern archaeologies*, 137–70. Cambridge: Cambridge University Press.

Anderson, C.A. 1991. The Dream – Oracles of Athena, Knights 1090–95. *Transactions of the American Philological Association*, 121, 149–55.

Arend, W. 1933. *Die typischen Scenen bei Homer*. Berlin: Weidmann (Problemata 7).

Arnason, J. 1987. Figurational sociology as a counter-paradigm. *Theory, Culture and Society*, 4, 429–56.

Ault, B.A. 1993. Koprones and oil presses: domestic installations related to agricultural productivity and processing at Classical Halieis. *American Journal of Archaeology*, 97, 324–25.

Ault, B.A. 1994. *Classical Houses and Households: an architectural and artifactual case study from Halieis, Greece*. Ann Arbor, MI: UMI.

Barber, E.J.W. 1992. The *peplos* of Athena. In J. Neils (ed.) *Goddess and Polis: the Panathenaic Festival in ancient Athens*, 103–18. Princeton, NJ: Princeton University Press.

Beavis, I.C. 1983. *Insects and other Invertebrates in Classical Antiquity*. Oxford: Alden Press.

Blümner, H. 1875. *Technologie und Terminologie der Gewerbe und Künste bei Griechen und Römern*. Leipzig: B.G. Teubner.

Bömer, F. 1990. *Untersuchungen über die Religion der Sklaven in Griechenland und Rom. 3. Die wichtigsten Kulte der griechischen Welt*. Stuttgart: F. Steiner (Forschungen zur antiken Sklaverei 14.3; 2nd edition).

Bourriot, F. 1995. *Kalos kagathos – kalokagathia. D'un terme de propagande de Sophistes à une notion sociale et philosophique. Étude d'Histoire Athénienne*, 2 vols. Hildesheim: Olms (Spudasmata 58).

Brock, R. 1994. The labour of women in Classical Athens. *Classical Quarterly*, 88, 336–46.

Burford, A.M. 1985 [1972]. *Künstler und Handwerk in Griechenland und Rom*. Mainz: P. von Zabern (Kulturgeschichte der antiken Welt 24; Translated from English).

Corbin, A. 1994. *The Foul and the Fragrant: odour and the French social imagination*. London: Picador (Translated from French).

Crouch, D.P. 1993. *Water Management in Ancient Greek Cities*. Oxford: Oxford University Press.

Davidson, J.N. 1998. *Courtesans and Fishcakes: the consuming passions of Classical Athens*. London: Fontana Press.

Davies, M. and Kathirithamby, J. 1986. *Greek Insects*. Oxford: Oxford University Press.

Dean-Jones, L.A. 1994. *Women's Bodies in Classical Greek Society*. Oxford: Clarendon Press.

Detienne, M. 1985. *The Gardens of Adonis: spices in Greek mythology*. Princeton, NJ: Princeton University Press (Translated from French).

Dillon, M.P.J. 1997. The ecology of the Greek sanctuary. *Zeitschrift für Papyrologie und Epigraphik*, 118, 113–27.

Douglas, M. 1995. *Purity and Danger: an analysis of the concepts of pollution and taboo*. London: Routledge.

Durm, J. 1910. *Die Baukunst der Griechen*. Leipzig: A. Kröner (Handbuch der Architektur 2.1; 3rd edition).

Eder, W. 1992. Polis und Politai. Die Auflösung des Adelsstaates und die Entwicklung des Polisbürgers. In I. Wehgartner (ed.) *Euphronios und seine Zeit. Kolloquium in Berlin am 19./20. April 1991, anläßlich der Ausstellung Euphronios, der Maler*, 24–38. Berlin: Staatliche Museen zu Berlin.

Edmondson, J. 2000. Preface. In V. Hunter and J. Edmondson (eds.) *Law and Social Status in Classical Athens*, V–VII. Oxford: Oxford University Press.

Elias, N. 1992. *Über den Prozeß der Zivilisation. Soziogenetische und psychogenetische Untersuchungen. Wandlungen der Gesellschaft. Entwurf zu einer Theorie der Zivilisation*, 2 vols. Frankfurt/M.: Suhrkamp (17th edition).

Elliott, A. 2001. *Concepts of the Self*. Cambridge: Polity Press.

Featherstone, M. 1987. Norbert Elias and Figurational Sociology: some prefatory remarks. *Theory, Culture and Society*, 4, 197–211.

Finley, M.I. 1992. *Die Welt des Odysseus* (Reihe Campus 1061). Frankfurt: Campus (Translated from English).

Flacelière, R. 1977. *Griechenland: Leben und Kultur in klassischer Zeit*. Stuttgart: Reclam (Translated from French).

Forbes, R.J. 1996. *Studies in Ancient Technology 5*. Leiden: E.J. Brill.

Foucault, M. 1977. *Discipline and Punish*. London: Allen Lane (Translated from French).

Foucault, M. 1992. *The Use of Pleasure (The History of Sexuality 2)*. London: Penguin (Translated from French).

Franyó, Z. and Gan, P. 1981. *Frühgriechische Lyriker 1. Die frühen Elegiker*. Berlin: Akademie (Schriften und Quellen der alten Welt 24.1; 2nd edition).

Giddens, A. 1979. *Central Problems in Social Theory*. London: Macmillan.

Giddens, A. 1984. *The Constitution of Society*. Cambridge: Polity Press.

Gillies, M.M. 1925. Purification in Homer. *Classical Quarterly*, 19, 71–75.

Giuliani, L. 1998. [Review of] Himmelmann, N. 1994. Realistische Themen in der griechischen Kunst der archaischen und klassischen Zeit. Berlin and New York: W. de Gruyter. *Gnomon*, 70, 628–38.

Ginouvès, R. 1962. *Balaneutikè. Recherches sur le bain dans l'antiquité grecque*. Paris: E. de Boccard.

Graf, F. 1978. Die lokrischen Mädchen. *Studi e Materiali di Storia delle Religioni*, 2, 61–79.

Gross, W.H. 1964. Bedürfnisanstalten. In K. Ziegler and W. Sontheimer (eds.) *Der Kleine Pauly 1*, col. 851–52. Stuttgart: A. Druckenmüller.

Halliwell, S. 1993. Comedy and publicity in the society of the polis. In A.H. Sommerstein, S. Halliwell, J. Henderson *et al.* (eds.) *Tragedy, Comedy and the Polis. Papers from the Greek Drama Conference Nottingham, 18–20 July 1990*, 321–40. Bari: Levante Editori (Collana di Studi e Testi 11).

Hammond, N.G.L. and Walbank, F.W. 1988. *A History of Macedonia 3: 336–167 BC*. Oxford: Clarendon Press.

Hansen, H.M. 1999. The opposition between the public and the private. In H.M. Hansen (ed.) *Polis and City-state: an ancient concept and its modern equivalent. Symposium, January 9, 1988*, 86–91. Copenhagen: Munksgaard (Acts of the Copenhagen Polis Centre 5; Historisk-filosofiske Meddelelser 76).

Hawley, R. 1998. The dynamics of beauty in Classical Greece. In D. Montserrat (ed.) *Changing Bodies – Changing Meanings: studies on the human body in antiquity*, 37–54. London: Routledge.

Heath, H. 1999. Disentangling the beast: humans and other animals in Aeschylus' Oresteia. *Journal of Hellenic Studies*, 119, 17–47.

Hemker, C. 1993. *Altorientalische Kanalisation: Untersuchungen zu Be- und Entwässerungsanlagen im mesopotamisch – syrisch – anatolischen Raum (ADOG 22)*, 2 vols. Munster: Agenda.

Henderson, J. 1991. *The Maculate Muse: obscene language in Attic comedy*. Oxford: Oxford University Press (2nd edition).

Himmelmann, N. 1996. Banausen und Künstler. In N. Himmelmann (ed.) *Minima Archaeologica: Utopie und Wirklichkeit der Antike*, 46–53. Mainz: P. von Zabern (Kulturgeschichte der antiken Welt 68).

Hodder, I. 1982a. *The Present Past: an introduction to Anthropology for Archaeologists*. London: B.T. Batsford Ltd.

Hodder, I. 1982b. *Symbols in Action: ethnoarchaeological studies of material culture*. Cambridge: Cambridge University Press.

Hodder, I. 1990. *The Domestication of Europe: structure and contingency in Neolithic societies*. Cambridge: Basil Blackwell.

Höpfner, W. and Schwandner, E.-L. 1994. *Haus und Stadt im klassischen Griechenland*. Munich: Deutscher Kunstverlag (Wohnen in der klassischen Polis 1; 2nd edition).

IG = *Inscriptiones Graecae*.

Isager, S. and Skydsgaard, J.E. 1995. *Ancient Greek Agriculture: an introduction*. London: Routledge.

Jameson, M.H. 1992. Agricultural labor in Ancient Greece. In B. Wells (ed.) *Agriculture in Ancient Greece. Proceedings of the Seventh International Symposium at the Swedish Institute at Athens, 16–7 May 1990 (ActaAth 42)*, 135–46. Göteborg: P. Åströms Förlag.

Jones, J.E. 1975. Town and country houses of Attica in Classical times. In H. Mussche, P. Spitaels and F. Goemaere-De Poerck (eds.) *Thorikos and the Laurion in Archaic and Classical Times*, 230–41. Princeton, NJ: American School at Athens (*Miscellanea Graeca* 1).

Kassel, R. and Austin C. (eds.) 1983–1995. *Poetae Comici Graeci*. Berlin: W. de Gruyter.

Kornexl, E. 1970. *Begriff und Einschätzung der Gesundheit des Körpers in der griechischen Literatur von ihren Anfängen bis zum Hellenismus*. Innsbruck and Munich: Universitätsverlag Wagner (Commentationes Aenipontanae 21).

Laser, S. 1983. Medizin und Körperpflege. In H.-G. Buchholz (ed.) *Archaeologica Homerica 3*, S135–88. Göttingen: Vandenhoeck and Ruprecht.

Lefkowitz, M. 1982. *Women's Life in Greece and Rome*. Baltimore: John Hopkins University Press.

Leppin, H. 2002. Theophrasts "Charaktere" und die Bürgermentalität in Athen im Übergang zum Hellenismus. *Klio*, 84, 37–56.

Lewandowski, H. 1960. *Licht's Sittengeschichte Griechenlands*. Munich: C.H. Beck.

Lewis, S. 2002. *The Athenian Woman: an iconographic handbook*. London: Routledge.

Liebeschuetz, W. 2000. Rubbish disposal in Greek and Roman cities. In X. Dupré Raventós and J.-A. Remolà (eds.) *Sordes Urbis: La eliminación de residuos en la ciudad romana. Actas de la reunión de Roma, 15–16 de Noviembre de 1996*, 51–61. Rome: L'Erma di Bretschneider (Bibliotheca Italica/Monografías de la Escuela Española de Historia y Arqueología en Roma 24).

Lindenlauf, A. 2001. Thrown away like rubbish – disposal of the dead in Ancient Greece. *Papers from the Institute of Archaeology*, 12, 86–99.

Linders, T. 1997. Gaben an die Götter oder Goldreserve? In W. Höpfner (ed.) *Kult und Kultbauten auf der Akropolis (Schriften des Seminars für Klassische Archäologie der Freien Universität Berlin)*, 31–36. Berlin: E. Wasmuth.

Lissarrague, F. 1990 [1987]. *The Aesthetics of the Greek Banquet: Images of wine and ritual*. Princeton, NJ: Princeton University Press (Translated from French).

Lloyd-Jones, H. 1975. *Females of the Species: Semonides on women*. London: Duckworth.

Lohmann, H. 1992. Agriculture and country life in Classical Attica. In B. Wells (ed.) *Agriculture in Ancient Greece. Proceedings of the Seventh International Symposium at the Swedish Institute at Athens, 16–7 May 1990 (ActaAth 42)*, 29–57. Göteborg: P. Åströms Förlag.

Manakidou, E. 1992–93. Athenerinnen in schwarzfigurigen Brunnenhausszenen. *Hephaistos*, 11–12, 51–91.

Mansfield, J.M. 1985. *The Robe of Athena and the Panathenaic Peplos*. PhD thesis, University of California at Berkeley. Ann Arbor, MI: UMI.

Mije, S. R. van der, 1991a. Kathairo. In W. Böhler (ed.) *Lexikon des frühgriechischen Epos 2*, col. 1271–72. Göttingen: Vandenhoeck and Ruprecht.

Mije, S. R. van der, 1991b. Katharos. In W. Böhler (ed.) *Lexikon des frühgriechischen Epos 2*, col. 1272. Göttingen: Vandenhoeck and Ruprecht.

Moraw, S. 2002. Das Publikum – Der mündige Bürger als Ideal. In S. Moraw and E. Nölle (eds.) *Die Geburt des Theaters in der griechischen Antike*, 146–53. Mainz: P. von Zabern.

Morris, I. 1987. *Burial and Ancient Society: the rise of the Greek city-state*. Cambridge: Cambridge University Press (New Studies in Archaeology).

Moulinier, L. 1952. *Le pur et l'impur dans la pensée et la sensibilité des Grecs jusqu'à la fin du IVe siècle avant J-C*. Paris: Klincksieck.

Németh, G. 1993. Übersetzung und Datierung der Hekatompedon-Inschrift. *Jahrbuch des Deutschen Archäologischen Instituts*, 108, 76–81.

Németh, G. 1994a. Hekatompedon-Probleme. *Zeitschrift für Papyrologie und Epigraphik*, 101, 215–18.

Németh, G. 1994b. Med' onthon egbalen. Regulations concerning everyday life in a Greek Temenos. In R. Hägg (ed.) *Ancient Greek Cult Practice from the Epigraphical Evidence. Proceedings of the Second International Seminar on Ancient Greek Cult, organized by the Swedish Institute at Athens, 22–24 November 1991 (ActaAth 13)*, 59–64. Stockholm: P. Åströms Förlag.

Neumann, G. 1992. Katharos 'Rein' und seine Sippe in den ältesten griechischen Texten. Beobachtungen zu Bedeutung und Etymologie. In H. Froning, T. Hölscher and H. Mielsch (eds.) *Kotinos: Festschrift für E. Simon*, 71–75. Mainz: P. von Zabern.

Ober, J. 1991. *Mass and Elite in Democratic Athens: rhetoric, ideology, and the power of the people*. Princeton, NJ: Princeton University Press.

OGIS = Dittenberger, W. 1903–05. *Orientis Graeci inscriptiones selectae*, 2 vols. Leipzig: B.G. Teubner.

Ortner, S.B. 1984. Theory in Anthropology since the Sixties. *Comparative Studies in Society and History*, 26, 12–166.

Owens, E.J. 1983. The Koprones at Athens in the fifth and fourth centuries BC. *Classical Quarterly*, 33, 44–50.

Parker, R. 1996. *Miasma: pollution and purification in early Greek religion*. Oxford: Clarendon Press.

Pekridou-Gorecki, A. 1989. *Mode im antiken Griechenland*. Munich: C.H. Beck (Beck's Archäologische Bibliothek).

Philipp, H. 1990. Handwerker und bildende Künstler in der griechischen Gesellschaft. In H. Beck, P.C. Bol and M. Beuckling (eds.) *Polyklet: Der Bildhauer der griechischen Klassik. Ausstellung im Liebieghaus, Museum alter Plastik, Frankfurt am Main*, 79–110. Mainz: P. von Zabern.

Pimpl, H. 1997. *Perirrhanteria und Louteria: Entwicklung und Verwendung großer Marmor- und Kalksteinbecken auf figürlichem und säulenartigem Untersatz in Griechenland*. Berlin: Dr. Köster (Wissenschaftliche Schriftenreihe. Archäologie 3).

Polignac, F. de 1995. *Cults, Territory, and the Origins of the Greek City-state*. Chicago, IL: University of Chicago Press (Translated from French).

Raaflaub, K.A. 1998. A historian's headache: how to read Homeric society? In N. Fisher and H. van Wees (eds.) *Archaic Greece: new approaches and new evidence*, 169–93. London: Duckworth.

Rudhart, J. 1958. *Notions fondamentales de la pensée religieuse et actes constitutifs du culte dans la Grèce classique. Étude preliminaire pour aider à la comprehension de la pieté athenienne au IVème siecle*. Genève: E. Droz.

Schäfer, A. 1997. *Unterhaltung beim griechischen Symposion: Darbietung, Spiele und Wettkämpfe von homerischer bis spätklassischer Zeit*. Mainz: P. von Zabern.

Shanks, M. 1992a. Some recent approaches to style and social reconstruction in Classical Archaeology. *Archaeological Review from Cambridge*, 11, 48–53.

Shanks, M. 1992b. Style and design of a perfume jar from an Archaic Greek city state. *Journal of European Archaeology*, 1, 77–106.

Shanks, M. 1999. *Art and the Early Greek State: an interpretive archaeology*. Cambridge: Cambridge University Press (New Studies in Archaeology).

Sherratt, E.S. 1990. Reading the texts: archaeology and the Homeric question. *Antiquity*, 64, 807–24.

Shilling, C. 1993. *The Body and Social Theory*. London: Sage.

Simon, E. 1981. *Griechische Vasenmalerei*. Mainz: P. von Zabern (2nd edition).

Sokolowski, F. 1962. *Lois sacrées des cités grecques. Supplément*. Paris: E. de Boccard (Ecole Française d'Athènes: travaux et mémoires des anciens membres étrangers de l'Ecole et de divers savants 11).

Sokolowski, F. 1969. *Lois sacreés de cités grecques*. Paris: E. de Boccard (Ecole Française d'Athènes: travaux et mémoires des anciens membres étrangers de l'Ecole et de divers savants 18).

Spahn, P. 1977. *Mittelschicht und Polisbildung*. Frankfurt: P. Lang (European University Studies, Series 3. History and Auxiliary Sciences 100).

Stein-Hölkeskamp, E. 1992. Lebensstil als Selbstdarstellung. Aristokraten beim Symposium. In I. Wehgartner (ed.) *Euphronios und seine Zeit. Kolloquium in Berlin am 19./20. April 1991, anläßlich der Ausstelllung Euphronios, der Maler*, 39–48. Berlin: Staatliche Museen zu Berlin.

Sutton, R.F. 2000. The good, the base, and the ugly: the drunken orgy in Attic vase painting and the Athenian self. In B. Cohen (ed.) *Not the Classical Ideal: Athens and the construction of the other in Greek art*, 180–202. Leiden: E.J. Brill.

Tandy, D.W. 1997. *Warriors into Traders: the power of the market in early Greece*. Berkeley, CA and Los Angeles, CA: University of California Press (Classics and Contemporary Thought 5).

Thiercy, P. 1993. Les odeurs de la polis ou le 'nez' d'Aristophane. In A.H. Sommerstein, S. Halliwell, J. Henderson *et al.* (eds.) *Tragedy, Comedy and the Polis. Papers from the Greek Drama Conference, Nottingham, 18–20 July 1990*, 505–26. Bari: Levante Editori (Collana di Studi e Test 11).

Thompson, M. 1979. *Rubbish Theory: the creation and destruction of value*. Oxford: Oxford University Press.

Vernant, J.-P. 1990. Dim body, dazzling body. In M. Feher (ed.) *Fragments for a History of the Human Body 1*, 18–47. New York: Urzone Inc.

Vernant, J.-P. 1996. The pure and the impure. In J.-P. Vernant (ed.) *Myth and Society in Ancient Greece*, 121–41. New York: Zone Books (Translated from French).

Vigarello, G. 1988. *Concepts of Cleanliness: changing attitudes in France since the Middle Ages*. Cambridge: Cambridge University Press (Translated from French).

Vögler, G. 1997. *Öko-Griechen und grüne Römer?* Dusseldorf and Zurich: Artemis and Winkler.

Walter, U. 1993. *An der Polis teilhaben: Bürgerstaat und Zugehörigkeit im archaischen Griechenland*. Stuttgart: Steiner (Historia Einzelschriften 82).

West, M.L. 1998. *Iambi et Elegi Graeci 1*. Oxford: Oxford University Press.

Wickert-Micknat, G. 1982. Die Frau. In H.-G. Buchholz (ed.) *Archaeologica Homerica 3*, R1–147. Göttingen: Vandenhoeck and Ruprecht.

Wöhrle, G. 1996. Körperpflege und körperliche Sauberkeit als Merkmale sozialer Differenziertheit in den homerischen Epen. *Gymnasium*, 103, 151–65.

Zanker, P. 1995. *Die Maske des Sokrates. Das Bild des Intellektuellen in der antiken Kunst*. Munich: C.H. Beck.

Zanker, P. 1998. *Eine Kunst für die Sinne: Zur Bilderwelt des Dionysos und der Aphrodite*. Berlin: K. Wagenbach (Kleine Kulturwissenschaftliche Bibliothek 62).

Zeitlin, F. 1996. Signifying difference: the case of Hesiod's Pandora. In F. Zeitlin (ed.) *Playing the Other: gender and society in Classical Greek literature*, 53–86. Chicago, IL: University of Chicago Press (Women in Culture and Society).

CHAPTER 7

EXAMINING THE ROLE OF AGENCY IN HUNTER–GATHERER CULTURAL TRANSMISSION

Peter Jordan

INTRODUCTION

This chapter draws on the concept of 'agency' to investigate the sacred places and material culture of two communities of high latitude hunter-gatherers, one located in the ethnohistorical present, the other in the prehistoric past (Fig. 7.1). Two contrasting constructions of agency are identified in the literature. In Socioecology a focus on agency generates insights into the diversity of forager behaviour in terms of the relative 'efficiency' of their adaptive strategies, in relation to a local resource environment. The second reading of agency emphasises cultural and symbolic dimensions to this kind of adaptation, that is, the negotiated and historically contingent nature of social interaction, which is viewed in terms of transactions in symbolic meanings rather than quantifiable exchanges of goods and services. It will be argued that while this second 'practice-based' reading of agency has come to enjoy considerable currency in the wider anthropological and archaeological literature, hunter-gatherer studies have tended to remain aloof to these developments, so that foragers continue to be

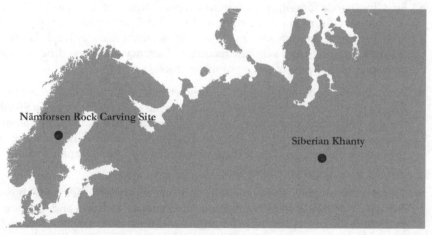

Fig. 7.1: Location map of ethnographic and archaeological case studies described in the text (Siberian Khanty and Nämforsen).

portrayed exclusively in ecologically adaptive terms. This chapter argues that the analytical concept of landscape represents an ideal framework within which these divergent readings of agency may be combined, thereby strengthening the insights generated by both.

As a sub-theme the chapter explores the relationship between agency and material culture. A key shortcoming of practice theories, for example, has been their failure to theorise adequately the semiotic role of material artefacts and built structures in social interaction:

- This conceptual impoverishment has hindered the ability of archaeologists to reconstruct human agency as a producer, inhabitant and consumer of the material residues of prehistory. Consequently, archaeologists searching for access routes into a more meaningfully-constituted prehistoric past have struggled with this analytical gap, and have drawn – with debatable levels of success – on a diverse body of literary theory to advance their interpretation of material culture.

- A further handicap for archaeologists working from 'material culture upwards' has been the dearth of suitable ethnographic studies exploring the role of artefacts in social interaction, especially those investigating the material culture of mobile foraging communities from more resolutely social, symbolic and ecological landscape perspectives. Anthropologists, for their part, have always been able to rely on direct engagement with the human subjects of study and so the inspiration to explore the material dimensions to human interaction, at least from a semiotic perspective, has never had the same impetus.

In short, the relationships between agency, material culture and landscape are poorly understood in both ethnographic and archaeological contexts. This chapter addresses these concerns and makes three general contributions to the study of material culture and landscape:

- First, for mobile foraging communities, it generates models exploring the roles of material culture in (a) the community's social and symbolic reproduction and (b) the veneration and material transformation of 'natural' landscape features. Adaptive and semiotic readings of agency are given different scales of emphasis in the examination of these processes.

- Secondly, as heuristic frameworks, these ethnographic models are applied to the interpretation of the prehistoric rock carving site of Nämforsen in Sweden, thereby enhancing our understanding of the site's role both (a) in the wider resource landscape and (b) for the prehistoric communities visiting and producing the images carved there.[1] Four forms of ethnographic analogy are employed as bridging arguments.

- Thirdly, developing these models and interpretations demands broader engagements with the theorisation of material culture and agency. In particular, the concept of material culture as a form of text is soundly rejected. By working through the ethnographic and archaeological case-studies it will be argued that the textual metaphor promotes the quest for timeless essential meanings, thereby diverting attention from the production and interpretation of places or artefacts through the actions of historically-situated agency.

To conclude, the final goal of this chapter is to generate a more sophisticated understanding of the relationship between material culture and human agency within the symbolic and resource landscapes of mobile foraging communities.

SOCIETY, STRUCTURE AND AGENCY

Research into human societies has tended to adopt one of two mutually exclusive perspectives, which conceptualise society in terms of either:

- structural and/or organic models – where pre-existing social, symbolic, economic, ethnic or environmental conditions determine the actions of either the individuals and/or groups that make up a society; or

- the knowledgable actions, strategies and achievements of the individuals comprising society – human agency.

More recently there has been a gradual shift in analytical focus away from an emphasis on the static, timeless and often deterministic social and symbolic *structures* that have been argued to mould society and the course of human history. Instead, a growing interest in patterns of interaction between individuals making up society has emphasised the dynamic and transformative social *processes* that these cumulative exchanges and engagements generate. Interaction theories, however, do not form a coherent body of theory, but divide further along one of the deeper fault lines running through the humanistic sciences. Enlightenment explanation – *'erklären'* – can be broadly contrasted to interpretative understanding – *'verstehen'*. As I have noted elsewhere (Jordan 2003), causal explanation is characterised by a programme of empirical investigation, the recording of statistical regularities in human behaviour and an underlying quest to develop general laws, which are argued to be valid in all historical and cultural contexts (Layton 1997: 184–86). With the intellectual objective being the formulation of an objective (etic) truth of how the world works (see Harris 1979) much practical and theoretical inspiration for this research is drawn from the natural sciences, rather than the humanities. Yet herein lies an area of immense theoretical contention, for many practising in the human sciences have argued that their subject matter – human beings and human culture – differ qualitatively from that of the natural sciences. In contrast to the pursuit of (etic) explanation, the alternative project of interpretative (emic) understanding is based around observing "meaningful interaction, in order to discover meanings specific to that time and place and which actors attributed to their own and others' behaviour" (Layton 1997: 184). Clifford Geertz, a key theorist of interpretative approaches, has argued that:

> the concept of culture I espouse . . . is essentially a semiotic one. Believing, with Max Weber, that man is an animal suspended in webs of significance he himself has spun, I take culture to be those webs, and the analysis of it to be therefore not an experimental science in search of laws but an interpretive one in search of meaning (Geertz 1973: 5).

These divergent perspectives – explanation versus understanding – emphasise different dimensions to the constitution of society (Layton 1997: 184), and can loosely be grouped (cf. Jordan 2003) into (a) materialist and (b) semiotic schools of anthropology:

- Materialist anthropology (socioecology): social life is constituted by transactional 'moves' in material goods and services in relation to the rule bound strategies of individuals. The outcomes of these games are generally independent of the intentions and strategies of individual players but generate stable forms of social organisation and interaction, which are rendered explicable in terms of general laws of human behaviour. Whilst Socioecology developed alongside (a) Marxist-inspired investigations of the control of labour and access to productive resources within colonial relationships (see Asad 1973), and (b) neo-evolutionary and 'vulgar materialist' approaches to social change (Harris 1979; Steward 1973 [1955]; White 1973 [1949]), both approaches are united by the general tenet that material conditions determine, to various extents, forms of human consciousness (Layton 1997: 131).

- Semiotic anthropology: social interaction is argued to be analogous to 'language' such that individuals conceive and interpret their social interactions symbolically: human interaction is, above all, meaningfully constituted. This emphasis on meaning rather than matter blends older traditions of interpretative sociology, cultural relativism (in a Boasian sense) and historical particularism to form a loosely defined postmodernist anthropology. In contrast to the Socioecological approaches outlined above, social life is studied as cultural transactions in (semiotic) meanings, rather than in (material) substance (Layton 1997: 184). While these postmodernist approaches emphasise that society is constituted by symbolic interaction they develop and extend the insights of Lévi Strauss, who argued that culture be investigated as a science of communication. His main thesis was that there are "unconscious but structured regularities [in] human thought" which represent "cognitive models of reality", and while the same kinds of mental processes occur in all individuals, the particular manifestations of these processes will vary according to cultural and historical context. In other words, "man comprehends his universe and orients his behaviour on the basis of these structures" (Bohannen and Glazer 1973: 372–73), with patterns in social interaction the "outward manifestation of such cognitive structures" (Layton 1997: 63).

To summarise, in broad terms two contrasting models of human agency emerge, one loosely defined as the neo-Darwinian agency of Socioecology; the second, the agency of practice theory, with its closer associations with symbolic and interpretative approaches. neo-Darwinian approaches tend to emphasise the constitution of interaction in terms of measurable exchanges in goods and services while postmodernist anthropology conceives of social interaction in terms of transactions in meanings rather than physical substance. Moreover, in the latter case the anthropologist cannot measure these subjective meanings, but must interpret them through a careful hermeneutic process (Layton 1997: 184).

NEO-DARWINIAN AGENCY

At a general level socioecology investigates the non-directional evolutionary (Darwinian) selection of learned (as opposed to genetically acquired) behaviours in human populations in terms of reproductive success: "[Socioecology] attempts to explain variation in patterns of human behaviour in terms of the consequences of behaviour in particular environments" (Layton 1997: 158). Socioecological research focuses on the behavioural strategies followed by individual agents, the idea being that successful social and/or resource procurement strategies will reward particular individuals with increased reproductive success, enabling these more successful 'winning' behaviours to spread at the expense of less successful strategies, which presumably die out with the unlucky, undernourished and undersexed individuals who insist on maintaining them. Anthropological calculation of long-term reproductive success is empirically problematic and researchers have tended to focus on measuring a suite of 'proxy currencies' with which to gauge the relative efficiency of adaptive strategies (Smith and Winterhalder 1981: 3). Clearly, there may be no deterministic link between culture and the ecological habitat, although intervening variables – technology, material culture and economic relations – may be argued to form indirect linkages between patterns of sociocultural life and the local resource environment (Smith and Winterhalder 1981: 3). In complex urban and state-based societies these linkages will be much more elaborate and so hunter-gatherers have tended to be the favoured human populations for this kind of research. First, this socioecological interest in foragers can be argued to stem from the fact that hunting and gathering adaptations have characterised much of human history, but, secondly, hunter-gatherers are assumed to live closest to a state of pristine subsistence (Hardesty 1977) – it's simply easier to model links between human society and environment when there are fewer variables to build into the analytical models. For example, as Winterhalder and Smith (1981: ix) argue:

> human foragers provide an excellent subject for socioecological analysis ... they exhibit a strong degree of interaction with the local environment (as opposed to a regional and global economy), and a limited inclination to modify that environment ... the subsistence patterns of human foragers are fairly analogous to those of other species and thus more easily studied with ecological models.

The big question, of course, is whether humans actually perceive the world in these maximising terms. Critics have argued that this evolutionary construction of agency is inherently dehumanising: individuals are argued to know too much yet do too little – they are unable to 'act' voluntarily but are doomed to 're-act' passively to external environmental constraints (Clark 2000). Moreover, the tendency in Socioecology to focus on short-term and local strategies downplays the essential historicity and contingency of human action and strips away the influence of antecedent cultural and social influences on agency. For example, research with a strong socioecological bias has promoted images of pristine and isolated hunter-gatherers inhabiting ahistorical resource landscapes (e.g. Binford 1978; Lee 1968, 1969; Winterhalder and Smith (eds.) 1981 etc., but see Bhanu 1992; Solway and Lee 1990; Trigger 1989: 335; Wilmsen and Denbow 1990; Woodburn 1988; Zvelebil 1998).

More recently, however, processes of cultural transmission have received increasing attention from evolutionary theorists (Boyd and Richerson 1985; Cavalli-Sforza and Feldman 1981; Shennan 2000 etc.) who start from the premise that cultural behaviour and cultural attributes, like language, are transmitted in ways that are both (a) akin to genetic transmission and (b) essentially distinct (see discussions in Layton 2000). Social learning is argued to be the key process in cultural transmission but individuals are also conceived as being able to monitor and change their behaviour in relation to the actions of others. In other words, this cultural analogy with Darwinian theory opens up a series of hypotheses about the specific role of human agency in cultural transmission. Humans are inherently cultural beings, but the transmission of their cultural perceptions and practices spreads according to a suite of clearly defined processes. Evolutionary agency is not a biological approach to human culture; rather it draws inspiration from biology to postulate explanatory mechanisms and processes by which change and stability come about (Shennan 1996). Clearly, many of these purported mechanisms resonate closely with other practice-based constructions of agency outlined below. Shennan goes on to argue that the emergence of this dual inheritance movement (i.e. culture plus genes) within neo-Darwinism has:

> produced a parallel emphasis on the importance of the individual, including a role for individual intentionality, a distinction between cultural and genetic transmission, and a detailed analysis of the properties of cultural transmission and of the various processes which act upon it ... a Darwinian approach to human societies and cultures need not, and indeed must not, be reductionist, and ... history has a vital role in the understanding of particular situations (Shennan 1996: 295).

To conclude, Socioecological perspectives *do* appear equipped to (a) identify broader adaptive limits (Layton 2000) and (b) establish objective means of evaluating patterns of behaviour. Contrasts with practice-based conceptions of agency ultimately stem back to the desire to pursue knowledge as a form of explanation or interpretative understanding. At the same time, there remain many spheres of potentially fruitful engagement between neo-Darwinian schools and practice theorists, especially around the theorisation of agency, social action and cultural transmission (Shennan 1996). However, for the scope of this chapter I will retain the distinction between the essentially materialist scope of Socioecological approaches and the more semiotic focus of agency/ practice theories.

AGENCY/PRACTICE THEORIES

The 'agency' concept of the social theorists emphasises conflict, contradiction, meanings and the importance of history (Shennan 1996: 295). With these research interests agency/practice theories investigate how cultural meanings and social structures are constructed and transformed through actors' knowledgable dealings with others, a process loosely termed social practice (praxis). In contrast, structuralism, structural functionalism and the (Geertzian) analogy of culture as text (Silverman 1990: 124) all adopt a holistic perspective on human populations, whereby the conduct of individuals is determined by their place in the wider social or symbolic system. For example, within the framework of the textual metaphor for culture there are 'fixed public meanings' which interlocutors execute according to predetermined scripts (Silverman 1990: 124, 127). Individuals may be the users of that system (i.e. engage in *'parole'*), but they cannot transform the underlying or overarching structures (the *'langue'*).

Agency/practice theories stress that the key structural elements in social systems are not fixed – or ever in a 'finished' format – but are being constantly reproduced, generating an inherent state of fluidity, termed 'structuration' (Giddens 1984) or 'becoming' (Pred 1985). With the shift towards trying to understand this process of historical becoming the analytical emphasis refocuses on the meaningful construction of lifestyles – how individuals and groups embody the social and symbolic system in which they dwell, how they are guided by it, yet, through novel performances and particular strategies, are able to alter or transform it (Bourdieu 1977; Giddens 1984). These praxis-based models of society emphasise potential for 'internally' driven social change: cultural meanings and social structures are not fixed, but are negotiated by human agency through time. Each individual is thereby empowered to either accept – or radically transform – the historical legacy they inherit. This dynamic perspective is lost to anthropologists and other social theorists who seek to isolate normative and timeless social structures (Layton 1997: 204). Similarly, the suggestion that there might be a Durkheimian collective social consciousness now appears overly simplistic, with an 'atom-ised' society cast in a perpetual state of negotiation and improvisation (Giddens 1984; Layton 1997: 185, 204). This is not the place to provide an extensive review of practice theories. Instead I would like to consider three salient themes in the literature:

- The temporality of social practices

- The poor theorisation of material culture

- 'Scales' of agency.

Giddens (1984) brands his coarser-grained set of ontological tools *structuration* theory, the foundations of which lie "at the intersection between theories of action and theories of collectivities" (Cohen 1990: 34). Inherent jargon aside, Giddens' model of society rests on acknowledging (a) the structure-agency duality, and (b) the time-space constitution of social practices:

- Society is portrayed as an accomplishment of agents (human individuals) who have a good knowledge of what they are doing. As such, they are not 'cultural dopes' (Garfinkel in Outhwaite 1990: 64) but are partially aware of the consequences and conditions of what they do in their daily lives (Giddens 1984: 281). The conduct of social practice forms the 'point' in the structuration process where "structure and agency are empirically and experientially indistinguishable" (Parker 2000: 103). Through routine practices individuals recreate particular social, symbolic and institutional structures, which guide – but do not determine – further patterns of social interaction (Giddens 1984: 282): within the workings of this structure-agency duality historical continuity is likely, although radical change remains a possibility.

- With its focus on routine practices structuration theory coaxes social analysis away from abstraction and towards a focus on the spatial and temporal dimensions to the workings of agency. Structuration theory recognises that social systems "consist of routinized, practice-embedded, social encounters" that are "situated in time-space and organised in a skilled and knowledgeable fashion by human agents" (Pred 1990: 122).

As Cohen (1990: 34) has argued, Giddens presents us with a raft of intellectual tools and resources (e.g. distanciation, co-presence, regionalisation) with which to conceptualise social interaction. As such, structuration theory – and its foundational concepts – represents what Cohen terms an "ontology of potentials" (Cohen 1990: 34):

> they do not refer to empirical events, but, rather, to generic human capacities and conditions through which social life is constituted, patterned, reproduced and changed ... they admit manifold variations in the way that social life is constituted in disparate historical settings and on different occasions.

Although Gregory argues that some of the early formulations of structuration theory were at "forbidding heights of abstraction" and have since, as a research programme, moved to "more concrete terrain" (1989: 185), Giddens' work has been consistently criticised for its poor theorisation of the material contexts of interaction, which are "reduced to frozen back drops" (Pred 1990: 126). This is surprising given that the:

> ... production of space, the em-place-ment of durable artefacts, the establishment and transformation of settings, is both the medium and outcome of human agency and social relations, both the medium and outcome of 'structuration processes' (Pred 1990: 126).

Bourdieu's work is relevant here because he traces out a route-way to similar sets of agency/practice conclusions, although via some long and richly worked ethnographic case-studies. The key concept in Bourdieu's work is that of *habitus* – a practical consciousness and/or set of cultural dispositions, which are acquired in early life through a process of experience and explicit socialisation into a given cultural context (Bourdieu 1977: 87, 93–94). They go on to underlie and condition all subsequent social and learning experiences but may be reflexively adjusted over the lifetime of the individual in relation to objective reality (Jenkins 1992: 80). The term *habitus* is employed to signify a habitual state or condition, especially of the body. In this sense *habitus* exists in individual agents as a set of acquired and durable cultural dispositions. *Habitus* is neither conscious, nor unconscious, but is expressed (and reproduced) through embodied and routinised social practices.

Perhaps because of its empirical roots – rather than overarching theory – Bourdieu's work goes some way in addressing the key shortcoming of Giddensian structuration theory: its poor theorisation of material culture. With Giddens failing to account for the "particular material conditions within which social practices are situated" Bourdieu's work illustrates how "the material world, permanent and decaying, constructed and demolished, exchanged and accumulated, is a potentially powerful system of signification" (Barrett 1988: 9). The ethnographic evidence Bourdieu draws upon is rich and insightful, and explores beautifully the processes by which cultural continuity may come about, with each fresh generation raised within the material, social and symbolic spaces of the last. This local and empirical basis to his theorisation of agency has meant that Bourdieu's work has won long-standing appeal amongst anthropologists whose focus has traditionally been the "micro-specificities of day-to-day routines and practices" (Moore 1996: ix). However, the ethnography is perhaps too rich, too localised and too normative in its portrayal of remote and traditional Berber lifeways, this increased emphasis on concrete cultural contextualities ultimately generating significant divergences with Giddens' structuration theory. For example, Parker (2000: 107) points out different trajectories in the relationship between structure and agency:

> For Giddens, every 'instantiating' moment is one of unspecificable change and the unexpected. For Bourdieu, what people do in moments of practice is highly predictable and reproductive.

Where, then, to place the controversial balance between the transformative capacity of a more 'atomistic' Giddensian agency and the more deterministic nature of Bourdieu's *habitus*, mired as it apparently is in the acquisition of pre-existing cultural traits and traditions? This difficult issue has implications for the analysis of social collectives, for what are we really talking about when we employ the term 'agency' as a conceptual tool? Are we focusing on given *individuals* or the *processes* of interaction amongst many individuals? As Jenkins notes, *habitus* also refers to a collective social phenomenon which is the "shared body of dispositions, classificatory categories and generative schemes ... the outcome of collective history" (Jenkins 1992: 81), which unites particular groups in society. Individuals must fit into the social, material and symbolic spaces created and inhabited by preceding generations and from them construct their own sense of gender and identity. Giddens' work becomes a little threadbare at this point, and Parker goes so far as to argue that "since he lacks any concepts of social structures as specific kinds of relations between collectives", Giddens has "no concept of the collective basis of agency" (Parker 2000: 106). In contrast to the Anglo-American tendency to associate agency with the individual we sense here the potential for a broader-scale reading of human agency, loosely defined as the 'group agency' of particular communities' historical trajectories:

> agency is less about the intentional exercise of personal interests and more about a cultural process through which personhood and a sense of 'groupness' are negotiated, constructed and transformed ... an agency of social collectives (Dobres and Robb 2000: 11).

As I shall argue below, both 'scales' of agency have important but different roles to play in ethnographic and anthropological interpretation.

To summarise, I have drawn a general distinction between two forms of agency. A key strength of socioecological approaches is their capacity to identify the range and complexity of adaptive strategies in particular historical as well as ecological resource environments. Practice theory is essentially more descriptive. This construction of agency does not explain *why* change or continuity comes about but it does present us with a set of conceptual tools for interpreting *how* (Cohen 1990: 34). In the remaining sections of the chapter I would like to draw on insights from both constructions of agency to focus on the complex inter-relationships between human action, material culture and local resource environments.

AGENCY AND ANTHROPOLOGY: A SIBERIAN CASE-STUDY

If the practice-based reading of agency is about human interaction, about carrying history forward through the expression and reworking of social and symbolic structures, then what role do artefacts and built structures play in these cumulative social engagements? In particular historical contexts, how does agency inhabit, transform and perceive the broader physical terrain? Anthropologists can go out into the world and study these complex relationships through interviews and participant observation, drawing on the ethnohistorical literature to extend their insights back in time. For archaeologists, detailed insights into the richness and variety of these human:artefact and human:landscape relationships are of particular interest because they provide the important sources of ethnographic analogy from which all interpretations of the past begin (Wylie 1985).

My initial motivation for studying the Siberian Khanty was to explore how these small-scale and semi-nomadic indigenous communities create, use and deposit material culture. From the outset it became clear that understanding the specific symbolism of Khanty artefacts and built structures lay beyond making close reference to their social and symbolic contexts of use. First, any form of social interaction – and its material correlates – stretches through time and over inhabited topographic spaces. Moreover, appreciation of the spatial dimensions to social interaction are made more pressing by the fact that these Siberian communities are essentially mobile, inhabiting taiga landscapes of forest, lake, river and bog. Patterns of community agglomeration and dispersal resonate closely with the strong boreal seasonality and the varied availability of food species in different parts of the landscape at different times of the year. Lines of access run through the forest or along the waterways, changing abruptly with the break-up of river ice or the first autumn snows. Life is a process of constant journeying, sometimes alone, sometimes in small task groups; the scales of the terrain are vast and human material transformations of this forested environment are minimal.

The Khanty are one of the few hunter-gatherer communities outside Australia for which there are detailed ethnographic and ethnohistorical data concerning the ritual use of space (Layton, in Jordan 2003: xiv). For these communities the landscape is inhabited by living persons, different generations of divine beings and the human dead, whose presence in key locations informs patterns of human territoriality and long-term resource procurement. Campsites and base settlements are never dwelt in permanently, but, like cemeteries and sacred places, are encountered and visited at particular times within the seasonal round. At other times, sacred sites and cemeteries are strictly avoided and activities conducted in their proximity demand certain prescribed patterns of movement. Khanty communities are reproduced through this complex choreography of movement, a stream of social interactions with the materiality of the world. Individuals locate themselves within the social, material and symbolic spaces constructed by preceding generations, recreating or transforming them, and thereby constructing their own senses of gender and identity.

For the Khanty, at least, daily existence is precarious and vulnerable, not because they are unskilled in their procurement activities, but because the resources they take from the world belong to other spiritual agencies. Every person and social group is, at all times, and in all places, bound into a complex web of relationships and obligations to divine beings, who aid, protect and support them (Jordan 2001). It is impossible to move through life without reference to these other agencies and dangerous to ignore them. Communion with them is vital but, to open channels of communication, *material offerings* must be made of goods altered by human agency, which are deposited at special holy sites. These acts of communion involve visits to sacred sites, which are often, but not exclusively, places of special natural beauty, or topographic salience – islands, hills and promontories.

Different categories of place derive their meanings from the symbolism of the artefacts deposited and practices conducted there. Artefacts, in turn, derive their meaning from their sources of procurement, from their social use and from their final deposition at key places or areas of the landscape, which are often charged with a particular symbolism as a result of the activities conducted there. From the study's initial focus on material culture emerged a set of rich insights into the way in which communities along one river bring meaning to, or 'enculturate', what we might regard as 'natural' landscape features. The study detailed how Khanty hunter-fisher-gatherers inhabit culturally constructed landscapes, the ultimate realisation being that landscape too is a form of material culture (Jordan 2003).

The study explored the intersections of two scales of agency:

- The first focused on the ways in which particular individuals were enculturated into and were then able to transform existing social, symbolic and material spaces, thereby gaining senses of identity and gender.

- The second adopted a larger scale and explored a communal trans-generational sense of agency (cf. Ingold 1993), inhabiting a broader landscape over the *longue durée* and singling out key locales of the natural world for special veneration.

I have argued elsewhere that ritual activity around Siberian Khanty sacred sites has many characteristics of a dialogue between human persons and spiritual agencies. Apart from direct interventions by shamans, communication between these domains is only possible though the media of artefact creation and deposition (Jordan 2001, 2003). From the human side, communication is conducted through visits to sacred places. Each *ritualised* offering and visit marks thanks for, and anticipation of, health, welfare and hunting success. The subsequent intervention of divine agencies either provides or denies these desires to humans during the conduct of their *routine* activity during the seasonal round. Thus, the significance of events at holy sites cannot be separated entirely from the stream of activity taking place in the wider inhabited landscapes. While these two dimensions comprise an unfolding negotiation between humans and divine agencies, it is human beings who carry with them the memories and significance of these exchanges as they bind holy sites into the seasonal round through embodied movements. In this manner, particular knowledges and symbolism may find their focus in physical places of special veneration, yet the (re)creation of those meanings at those places, and within the context of wider inhabited spaces, is embodied within particular individuals and the broader collective memory.

Drawing on the concept of 'group agency' four themes emerge from this Siberian Khanty case-study:

- The constitution of mobile Khanty life-ways is closely linked to the exploitation of ecological resources in a high latitude environment characterised by strong seasonality.

- Khanty society is reproduced through routine and ritual practices at key locales. Behaviour at holy sites has a more rigid format than at cemeteries and dwelling sites, and because people of all ages are involved in the visits, the rituals and places act as central corridors of cultural transmission.

- For the Khanty, life can be viewed as a dialogue between people and places of power. Artefacts deposited at sites store up, as residues of communication, the symbolism that the place, image or artefact has carried on the wider seasonal round.

- There is a key temporal dimension to agency as it produces, perceives, handles and deposits material culture. Meanings are expressed at these moments of engagement and are carried forward and transformed through social reproduction, through the *longue durée* of communal agency. Artefacts, however, pass in and out of these flows of practice. Their meanings, however, lie within these flows, at moments of creation, use or deposition.

AGENCY AND ARCHAEOLOGY

In this section I would like to apply these agency-based conceptual frameworks to the interpretation of prehistoric rock art. The carved images at Nämforsen, Sweden, constitute clear evidence of the existence of a symbolic dimension to hunter-gatherer activities, yet interpreting their local and wider landscape significance constitutes a major interpretative challenge. From exploring the place of material culture within the social practices of one historical context (the ethnographic present), we must study social practices from the surviving material remains of another historical period (the prehistoric past). It is perhaps because the concept of agency has been endorsed by theorists across the archaeological spectrum – from phenomenology to evolutionary ecology (Dobres and Robb 2000: 1) – that it would be easier here to focus on broad- scale adaptive and resource procurement strategies than on the more subjective dimensions to the past. "Analyzing agency through archaeological remains poses undeniable challenges" (Dobres and Robb 2000: 12), and nowhere are these challenges more acute than in the interpretation of rock art, widely acknowledged as being a "most difficult subject" (Bradley 1993: xii). For these reasons, ethnographic studies of 'communal agency' like that outlined above are of greater utility for archaeology because they enable an extended focus on non-subsistence dimensions of existence, and, furthermore, enlarge the potential frame of analysis from the micro-specificities of the immediate and the individual to encompass longer term processes of 'becoming' (cf. Pred 1985). Moreover, the insights generated by larger scale group agency perspectives tend to resonate more closely with the coarser resolution of archaeological data-sets (cf. Ingold 1993).

MOVING ON

The heuristic frameworks outlined above are brought to the prehistoric site to open out a 'thicker' understanding of the site's significance. My aim here is to understand *how* the images – and the ideas associated with them – were produced and re-produced as part of a long-term cultural tradition. I will argue that the carvings are not just a passive text to be read or 'unlocked' but are the product of repeated actions and practices, forming a key arena of social and symbolic reproduction. These actions demanded repeated visits, the repeated journeys binding the significance of Nämforsen into the lives of local communities, and thereby binding the sacred site into wider routine landscapes.

But with what justification can these heuristic frameworks be drawn from one social context and applied to another? The inevitable reliance on ethnographic analogy for all forms of archaeological interpretation is inherently problematic (Wylie 1985), and the communities in question are separated by thousands of miles and several millennia. However, a particularly strong case can be built for the use of Siberian analogies in the interpretation of the Fennoscandian archaeological record (see Zvelebil 1997; Zvelebil and Jordan 1999). There are four bridging arguments which can be drawn on here to open out a suite of linkages:

- Both communities inhabit similar high latitude environments where convergence in adaptive strategies is encouraged. In temperate and boreal ecosystems hunter-gatherer subsistence strategies are guided by the strong seasonality and the uneven distribution of resources over the landscape at different times of the year. Residential mobility is encouraged – alongside food- and social storage and inter-group trade and reciprocity – as a typical solution to the summer concentration of fish, sea mammals and migratory waterbirds at water-edges and a more dispersed range of hunted furbearer resources over the winter landscape.

- Relationships between similar sets of material culture are being compared; that is, a similar range of exploited resources, similar landscape features like rivers and special topographic features, clearly sacred sites, and artefacts and images associated with both the ritual and routine spheres.

- The analogy employed is a direct historical analogy based on the assumption of historical continuity and that "similarities between two chronologically distant societies have more validity if they share the same historical trajectory and geographic region" (Zvelebil and Jordan 1999: 102). Moreover, Khanty language belongs to the same group of Uralic languages as that of the Proto-Finnic speakers, who now occupy much of northern Fennoscandia, colonising the area soon after deglaciation. Zvelebil and Jordan (1999: 103) also note that "in addition to cultural and historical links there may also be genetic and linguistic affinity as well".

- Moving on from this point it can be argued that both groups may have shared a similar circumpolar cosmology, which, broadly defined, involves nature being perceived in various ways as being a 'giving environment'. Its bounty is bestowed either unconditionally or conditionally, with interaction between human and spiritual domains guided, in the latter case, by concepts of reciprocity. Resources are replenished in a cyclical way, generally as a result of ritual interaction between human and spiritual agents (Bird-David 1990, 1992; Ingold 1986; Zvelebil 1997; Zvelebil and Jordan 1999).

The major rock carving site of Nämforsen, located in northern Sweden, was produced by hunter-fisher-gatherers between 3000 and 1500 BC in a social climate of growing contact and exchange with adjacent farming communities (Tilley 1991; Zvelebil 1997; Zvelebil and Jordan 1999). Although the site has received considerable attention in the literature (e.g. Hallström 1960; Malmer 1975; Forsberg 1993; Zvelebil 1997; Zvelebil and Jordan 1999), *Material Culture and Text: The Art of Ambiguity* by Tilley (1991) is of particular interest for the current chapter:

- First, when published, it represented a watershed book (Janik 1999), and remains relatively unique, in that it constituted the application of interpretative (post-processual) research methodologies to hunter-fisher-gatherer archaeological data. Indeed, the European Mesolithic has traditionally been investigated through a more economic and environmentally deterministic lens (van Gijn and Zvelebil 1997; Zvelebil 1998). Tilley's monograph was a pioneering attempt to understand the cosmology of these prehistoric foragers via detailed analysis of meaningfully constituted material culture.

- Secondly, he employed the tenet of 'material culture as text' in his analysis, approaching the carvings as a problematic text in need of translation. As will be discussed, this choice of analytical framework generates problematic implications for the theorisation of agency and temporality in prehistoric contexts.

The rock carvings are located at rapids on the River Ångerman, in northern Sweden. The rapids form the last barrier before the river enters the sea and are situated at the junction of the interior uplands and the coastal plain. The site is 40 km from the mouth of the river and about 140 km from open sea, so that, when produced, the carvings were located at the end of a long narrow inlet open to the sea (Hallström 1960; Malmer 1975; Tilley 1991; Zvelebil 1997; Zvelebil and Jordan 1999). A massive accumulation of motifs – almost 2,000 – were carved and pecked into the rocky surfaces of the river banks, but mainly on the two islands in the centre of the rapids (Fig. 7.2). It appears that the images were produced by hunter-fisher-gatherer communities in the broad time period between 3000 and 1500 BC (Zvelebil 1997: 39).

The carvings are representational rather than abstract and consist mainly of elk and boat images, which predominate in all of the rock carving areas (Fig. 7.3). People, fish, shoe-soles and tool or scythe-like images are also present. The main themes which appear to run through this collection of images are as follows:

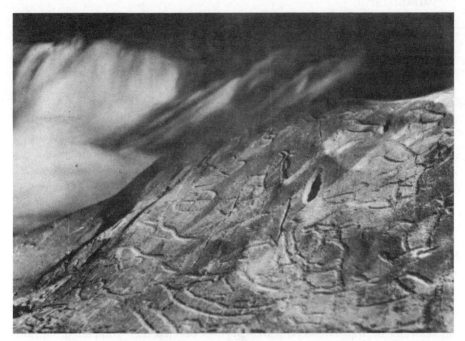

Fig. 7.2: Example of the rock carvings at Nämforsen (Hallström 1960: pl. 124).

Fig. 7.3: Detail of the images (Hallström 1960: pl. 81).

- There is a distinct lack of hierarchical structure in the depictions.

- The same kinds of image are repeated over and over again, often overlapping, but also merging (e.g. boats with elk prows, etc.).

- Images of the same broad group show great individual variation in their particular style.

Arranging the images into a relative chronology is problematic. They were probably executed over many centuries, although it is not known whether this was a continuous or discontinuous process. Tilley argues that these temporal ambiguities are part of the timelessness of the text in that the same images are used again and again:

> That it is impossible to provide any detailed relative chronology for any individual elk, boat, shoe sole, etc. is not just our contemporary 'failing': it may be telling us something of profound importance about the carved designs and their associations (Tilley 1991: 85).

He continues:

> On any individual carving surface it may still be the case that some motifs were carved first and others added later. Regardless of this, what we see today are the 'completed' and subsequently eroded carving surfaces. Irrespective of the time of execution of individual forms, at some stage they *must all have acted together as symbolic units* on individual rock surfaces and this is the palimpsest which we can perhaps best begin to understand (Tilley 1991: 86, emphasis added).

Tilley draws on the linguistic theories of Saussure to define the dense concentration of carving elements within topographically defined 'pages' as a text, which, via the application of appropriate theoretical frameworks, can successfully be translated. With the carvings defined as a completed text, the problem becomes one of translating underlying meanings rather than actions. In three parallel interpretations three decodings are presented. The first draws on structuralist theories to make the fairly unlikely assertion that the carvings are a 'tribal encyclopaedia', while the third suggests that the 'textual' panels record secret knowledge, and are then used to maintain power relations of elder males over youngsters and females. The second – and most convincing – interpretation draws on Siberian ethnography; here Tilley develops the idea of an interpretative circle, in which there is a conversation between people, i.e. him and the (prehistoric) 'Other', in a "dialogic process of otherness". We move on from the text as a system of signs to the idea of a text as a "structured totality which is irreducible to the sentences of which it is made up" (Tilley 1991: 119). Importantly, and indeed inspiringly, Tilley uses the Evenk ethnography (Tilley 1991: 128 – and see translations from Russian ethnohistorical sources in Michael (ed.) 1963) to gain entry into the prehistoric community's worldview, dressing up this use of analogical reasoning as an "approach to fusing horizons, gaining an entry point into meaning" (Tilley 1991: 126).

The prehistoric communities undoubtedly had mythology and folklore about elk, rapids and rivers. Tilley reworks snippets from his larder of ethnographic anecdotes so that the "link with Sel'kup Evenk Mythology is almost exact" (Tilley 1991: 136). But the problem here is twofold: first, we are left with no sense of *how* this Evenk symbolism is linked to actual practices, or to how these practices might lead to the material transformation of topographic features singled out for special veneration. Any sense of agency is absent from this ethnography and we end by blanketing the prehistoric past with a quilt of static and abstracted images from the (ethnohistoric) present. This problem is exacerbated by the use of the textual metaphor for material culture: following his burst of ethnographic inspiration Tilley loops back into a portrayal of the images as "a visual statement of myths, cosmic categories and associations held to structure both the supernatural world and human existence" (Tilley 1991: 145). There are "herds of elks and herds of boats, massive accumulations of animals and huge ships, both of which it is doubtful ever existed" (Tilley 1991: 144). Moreover, Nämforsen provides fundamental ideas about social relations (Tilley 1991: 147) and:

> forms the only rock carving location in northern Sweden in which *the cosmology of the world is laid out in full* and in the process of which the different clans using the ritual areas of the rock carvings became integrated and related to each other (Tilley 1991: 148, emphasis added).

The carvings are adverts "for and of a cosmological system" (Tilley 1991: 147). Just like the Evenk in the Soviet monographs (see Michael (ed.) 1963) we have the essentials of a prehistoric society laid out for our convenience and classification. Tilley is essentially reading from one normative ethnographic text in order to create another. Both are devoid of any sense of historically-constituted agency.

At the end of his suite of interpretations Tilley argues that he has aimed to write a 'producer' text, which deliberately offers no firm conclusions about the site, but instead aims to draw from the reader "a response: another text" (Tilley 1991: 183). Yet by circulating so many tightly argued interpretations and shrouding them in a cloud of inherent relativism Tilley wards off much potential for direct critical response. I remember reading the book in the mid-1990s and being particularly inspired by Tilley's novel use of Siberian Evenk ethnographic analogy to investigate the carvings' wider symbolism. In fact, these descriptions were instrumental in despatching me to Siberia to investigate the material culture and symbolic landscapes of the Khanty, another group of West Siberian hunter-gatherers. Following fieldwork, readings of *Material Culture and Text* brought a sense of unease, which circulated around Tilley's concept of material culture as a kind of text. His use of this metaphor had important implications for the conceptualisation of both agency and various forms of temporality. This results in two shortcomings; first, the production of the carvings is ignored – they are in a completed state rather than in a state of *becoming* (cf. Pred 1985; Ingold 1993); secondly, there is no seasonal or biographical sense of temporality around the carvings. Returning agency and temporality to the analysis enables alternative interpretations:

• The site is returned to its location in a broader resource landscape.

• The actions associated with the inhabitation of this landscape establish the seasonal rhythms within which (a) the site was visited and (b) the images were carved.

• The Khanty ethnographic analogy is employed to suggest more specific insights into the site's symbolism. The carved panels are argued to represent the material media of successive acts of communication, rather than a single carved message waiting to be interpreted.

Turned around, this approach emphasises the importance of translating a grammar of social practice rather than embarking on the misguided quest for the symbolic grammar of a timeless text.

(1) Nämforsen as place

There is a suite of temporalities relating to the carvings, and an appreciation of these relationships can be derived from an understanding of the actions of the collective human agency inhabiting the wider resource landscape (Fig. 7.4). Malmer notes that upstream from Nämforsen is a "remarkable concentration of dwelling sites" (1975: 42). Indeed the residential site of Nämforsen, located on the bank, close to the rapids, appears to have been central to some 600 contemporary sites within the Ångerman river system (Zvelebil 1997: 39), and was discontinuously occupied from 3000 BC to the Iron Age, with the main period of occupation being the late stone age, 2500–2000 BC. Zvelebil also describes how fishing and the procurement of elk, beaver and waterfowl were the main subsistence occupations and were practised through both residential and logistical mobility. The sites near Nämforsen were at the juncture between mountains and the coastal plain and finds of bones from pike, salmon, seal and water birds – resources procured in summer and spring – suggest seasonal occupation during the summer part of the year. Conversely, the bones of elk, usually hunted in winter, are absent. Nämforsen appears to have been a summer fishing, fowling and aggregation site in the practical 'resource' landscape (Zvelebil 1997: 39; see also: Zvelebil and Rowly-Conwy 1989). Malmer (1975: 44–45) and Hallström (1960: 373) also suggest that the site was a major point of contact, where furs and hides were exchanged with farming traders from the south.

Fig. 7.4: Landscape location of Nämforsen (Hallström 1960: pl. 64).

In this wider region Nämforsen is but one of a number of rock carving/ painting sites, the nearest being some 60–70 km distant. Tilley (1991: 92) notes "a striking series of regularities in the location" of other sets of carvings in the wider region. Most are found near water (lakes, streams, rivers, waterfalls) and some are located on islands near rapids in a direct analogy to the Nämforsen site. Moreover, while the lake carvings are at the waterline, those near waterfalls are either splashed or submerged depending on the water height.

A major point to note here is that Nämforsen, in its original social, symbolic and subsistence context, was bound into a wider network of routine and ritual sites by patterns of seasonal movement and regional exchange. Prehistoric forager populations living in the Ångerman river area appear to have dispersed for hunting elk in the winter and practised spring and summer aggregation at rich salmon fishing sites like the Nämforsen rapids, but also at analogous locations like Stornorrfors. Moreover, the seasonal abundance of predictable and concentrated fish resources allowed the temporary concentration of population to levels impossible at other times of the year.

(2) Nämforsen as material culture

Tilley treats the images of Nämforsen as a problematic text to be read through *translation*, thereby compressing the biographies of the carvings, the actors and the site itself into the structures of one interrelated text. The text is translated, not the practices that produced, venerated and interpreted those images over successive generations. Temporality is thereby collapsed, advancing us into bizarre debates about the possibility of (pre)historic changes in elk herding behaviour in relation to the 'cosmological' herds of elk or boats (Tilley 1991: 63–64), even though each individual carved image displays great variety in relative style and competence.

This approach blinds us to the possibility of routine carving of the images by different hands in a tradition passed over many generations. Moreover, it is at the times spent away from the site that the forms of knowledge, authority and power associated with the significance of Nämforsen are drawn upon, upheld and, indeed, recreated. Nämforsen is being visited seasonally year after year, with groups residing here, fishing, and visiting the carving site. When local life ways are traced out in this manner, the interlocking mass of carved symbols, each slightly different, take on a slightly different association. Each carving is produced within the circular temporality of repeated seasonal visits, which, in linear time, form part of a longer-term tradition of adding carvings to the site. We must therefore make a conceptual distinction between an act of carving which *produces* another stone image and *re-produces* the symbolism associated with that act, and the act of visiting the site on a year to year basis, which *re-inscribes* the *place*, not the *image*, into the collective agency of the people. We are left with a sense of distinction between the biography of Nämforsen as a very special place and focus of special attention, and the cursory or ephemeral significance of individual carvings as the results of specific instances of creative acts conducted repeatedly by successive generations over extended time-spans.

If we understand how temporal relationships link past social practices to the carvings, we will realise that these images are not 'cosmological scenes' or 'herds' of elk and boats. The carving surfaces are repositories of the material results of the same actions year after year. The carvings, each elk or boat slightly different, are the media through which actors reproduce cosmological concepts, bound up with the groups visiting the site during the summer. Unlike humans whose biographies unfold through time and space, the biography of each carved image is immobile, carved by hands and then unchanging, unmoving.

(3) Nämforsen's carvings as a medium of communication

Mechanisms of meaning

Thus far we have explored *how* the site came to have meaning: we have yet to explore *what* those meanings were. And here we face two interpretative options, one more conservative, and drawing on only generalised ethnographic analogy, the second more ambitious in its use of direct historical analogy, and thereby more vulnerable. Following the first option we should not really be asking about actual meanings but should seek to return the images into wider flows of prehistoric practice. In a study of carvings by the Madagascan Zafimaniry, Maurice Bloch has argued that images cut into wooden support posts at the centre of houses form ". . . a celebration of the material . . . and of a successful life which continues to expand and reproduce . . ." (Bloch 1995: 215). Although the images can be casually named in terms of 'the moon' or 'rain', the carvings have no particular symbolism – rather, informants say they make the wood 'beautiful'. Bloch argues that their real significance is drawn from the *times* in particular personal histories at which the artefacts are executed, and from their spatial *location* within the house, a key domain of community life and sphere of cultural transmission.

The cascading rapids and islands at Nämforsen possess a special kind of atmosphere, characterised by the rigidity and silence of the rock amongst the constant movement, energy and noise of the water. Among the wider suite of rock carving sites in the broader region we note strong associations with water – with waterfalls, running water, rapids and islands in those rapids (see Tilley 1991: 92). We may suggest that these places were also notable for possessing a special kind of energy, and, perhaps most significantly, this energy was acknowledged, venerated and enhanced by the addition of material designs. Thus, as a locus in the natural landscape singled out by prehistoric communities for special attention over an extended time period, we can suggest that the site of Nämforsen may have been one (or more) of the following:

- A corridor of spiritual communication, linking a number of worlds or domains.

- A place of special significance, which empowered the wider social collective with procurement ability or reproductive success on the course of its seasonal round.

- A spiritual keeper of the local area or river basin.

Thus, Nämforsen was, at one and the same time, both a site of spiritual communion and a place for social aggregation around a major and predictable resource. Nämforsen may be similar to Khanty ritual sites in that groups and individuals are congregating there, making and sustaining particular meanings, taking these knowledges away to other places and times, and returning with expectations. At Nämforsen too, human actors are engaged in sustaining a material and embodied dialogue of exchange, mediated by the act of carving, between vulnerable human communities and powerful spirits. The significance of carving is derived from the position which the act occupies within the temporality of the seasonal round, and within particular biographies, but also from its position within the landscape. Understanding the carvings is not about a quest for a relational grammar within the palimpsest of icons. It is about a quest for the *grammar of praxis*, which locates the site within a wider landscape, and the acts of carving and veneration within the biography of individuals and communities.

Specific symbolism

At Nämforsen, however, I believe that the carvings are about the expression of a richer symbolism, one that also links the islands into the wider landscape via the signification of the images. Tilley is scornful of the notion that large masses of elk are depicted at Nämforsen because of their dietary importance to the local community. This would immediately subscribe to a position in which "human culture is grounded in biological necessity" (1991: 49). This position ignores the fact that these prehistoric engagements with elk, the main meat species hunted in the sites around Nämforsen, may have been conceived in terms that were as much social and symbolic as they were biological. Indeed, elk bones in the area appear to have been carefully burnt, suggesting particular beliefs in relation to carcass treatment. Moreover, insights from Khanty ethnography reveal how the conduct of tasks associated with the hunting and consumption of elk and other animals, and the appropriate deposition of the bones is central to the creation of particular gender identities and the enculturation of spaces around the settlement (Jordan 2001). The consumption of meat often prompts the recounting of hunt details, these stories making reference to the wider landscape and its tenure by particular groups and individuals. The rich imagery of the elk is a metaphor for much more than biological necessity and has symbolic associations with general welfare and hunting success as the head is ritually consumed at Khanty holy sites. The key point is that cosmologies – in order to have meaning – are not abstracted, overarching and deterministic phenomena, but are bound up with the practical conduct of life.

In the ongoing routine and ritual dialogue between human and spiritual domains the creation of elk images at Nämforsen may serve as the material media for symbolic exchange. During the seasonal round the community has taken (been granted) food from the world. Making carvings at the sacred site is a way of offering something in return, a fulfilment of reciprocal obligations, a way of informing the spiritual agencies that gratitude is felt for the elk (and other animals or resources) who have been procured. While Tilley argues that "hunting magic theories can be rejected outright" (1991: 53), the term 'magic' immediately disregards the rich networks of symbolism associated with ideas of birth, death and rejuvenation, the desire to tend particular human:spirit relationships and culturally specific ways of dwelling in the world.

Another dimension to this concept of exchange can be pursued if it is recalled that, for the Khanty, the classification of animate articles includes those objects whose form resembles that of living beings (e.g. a bear-shaped stone is treated as a living bear, able to tell fortunes). Moreover, there is a tradition in venerating anthropomorphic rock outcrops in Fennoscandia suggesting more general parallels in the treatment of material culture, throughout the wider region (Nuñez 1995). Thus, when prehistoric communities repeatedly carved the images onto the rocks of the islands, they may have been creating *living* elk, at a particular, and spiritually charged, locus in the landscape. Most of the carvings face south, to the middle sun (Tilley 1991: 138) and the nearer they are to the rapids the closer they are to the water, suggesting some deliberate intention to place them as close as possible to sources of movement and energy.

Most *animate* objects of Khanty material culture (like Khanty ritual dolls) require a master, or the fulfilment of some form of obligation towards them. Thus, when the elk, fish, birds and other images are carved at Nämforsen, this may represent life being *created* (or replaced) for the spirit-master keeper of other game, who either resides at, or can be contacted from, the island carving sites. In turn, and through time and seasonal movement into other areas of the landscape, the spirit reciprocates by despatching further game to the human collective. Carved wooden and lead images of various game animals are 'sacrificed' to Khanty holy spirits in the hope that this will affect hunting success (Karjalainen 1922: 70–73; Kulemzin and Lukina 1977: 131–32). At Nämforsen, the acts of carving may have formed part of a more general spring festival of world revival as communities were gathering for the coming fishing season. The temporality of these material acts of creation appears to have been linked closely to movements around the landscape and seasonal phases of community aggregation around dependable resource points.

The second most frequent design class at Nämforsen comprises the outlines of boats, some with crew, some without. For the Khanty, boats and rivers are charged with symbolism associated with the dead and the journey of the souls of the deceased to the last world, which lay downstream, at the mouth of the River Ob' (Chernetsov 1963; Balzer 1979, 1980; Zvelebil and Jordan 1999). Dug-out canoe burials appear to have been the standard form of burial for the peoples of western Siberia even before the colonial period (Semenova 1998). The image of a boat with no paddle, without a means of propulsion, is associated specifically with preparations for the journey of the dead to the next world (Kulemzin 1995: 73–74). In the same way, sleds are sometimes left on graves in order to assist the soul of the dead on their journey to the next world (Semenova 1998). Khanty souls of the deceased are sometimes unable, or unwilling, to depart for the next world, and may wreak havoc in the world of the living. Every effort is made by the community of the living to maintain clan links with the dead, yet at the same time ensure their smooth departure to the next world. The bird, moving through the seasons, from north to south, also has strong associations with souls and death and we should note that the Khanty carve a bird at the graves of children (see Zvelebil and Jordan 1999).

At Nämforsen, none of the boats has paddles. They cannot be powered or steered, but only drift downstream, out of the control of the crew. The act of carving boats or birds may have facilitated transport for the souls of the deceased. Alternatively, in a world characterised by exchanges between the domains of humans and spirits, the carving of the boats and crews may have (a) formed symbolic tokens, placing real boats and crews under the protection of the spirits resident at the site, or (b) been 'given' to the rapids in the form of a metaphoric sacrifice, so that the waters would not take the boats and lives of those fishing the waters throughout the following season.

DISCUSSION

In this chapter I have drawn on two readings of agency. In the first case-study these theories were applied to an ethnographic study of Khanty landscape enculturation. A series of heuristic frameworks were drawn from this material and then applied to the interpretation of a complex prehistoric carving site. What does this exercise contribute to (a) the interpretation of the Nämforsen carvings, and (b) the general conceptualisation of material culture in the archaeological record?

(a) The re-interpretation stresses that Nämforsen constituted an important fishing location and the islands a sacred carving site, which lay slightly outside and away from the areas of routine activity. These places were bound into the wider inhabitation of the landscape by the seasonal aggregation and dispersal of communities in the conduct of their procurement round. Individual carvings acted as the media of exchange between human society and divine or spiritual agencies, which either resided at the site, or were accessible to human requests for assistance from it. This carving site was a place where people came to 'touch worlds', the act of *carving* the images being of central importance in this, but also acting as a means of setting up relations of power and exclusion in relation to the specific ritual knowledges and practices associated with the site. The palimpsest of images – immovable communicative media – were a legacy of attempts by the wider mobile community to ensure health, welfare and hunting success for the social collective as well as the departure of the souls of the dead to the other world. Differing timescales can be detected, including the *circular* seasonal time of repeated visits, which add fresh carvings and adjust the collective and individual associations with, and symbolism of, the site. It is within this timescale that new designs are added alongside the old, representing innovations and adjustments within a linear and *long-term* tradition of carving the rock surfaces at the site.

(b) At a second level, the investigation has enabled a critique of textual approaches to prehistoric material culture. Rather than seeking to translate the objective meanings of material texts, attention should be given to *how* particular sets of meanings are created and sustained through embodied social practices as they are spun out through time and space. This demands consideration of how the material conditions of the prehistoric past were created and inhabited by social actors bound recursively into webs of meaning, power and symbolism. Furthermore, the treatment of material culture as a text tends to collapse different forms of temporality (personal, seasonal and historical), each fundamental to an understanding of the intricate processes producing the archaeological record, in favour of a univocal set of meanings associated with a single timeless textual record.

CONCLUSIONS

This chapter has ranged widely over social theory, the ethnohistoric present and the prehistoric past. At its core has been a detailed consideration of the relationships between material culture, cognitive and ecological landscapes and different conceptualisations of human agency. Key themes have been:

- The importance of combining complimentary insights from different readings of agency in order to reveal that "Ritual landscapes ... possess symbolic, ancestral and temporal significance, which is complementary to, and dialectically interactive with the practical, economic landscapes" (Zvelebil and Jordan 1999: 105). Broader understandings of resource procurement strategies in mobile communities expand the discussion outwards to (a) incorporate wider landscape inhabitation, especially by seasonally mobile groups, and (b) thereby inject a range of temporalities essential to both human action and the production, perception, use and deposition of material culture.

- The existence of different scales of human agency. These range from the reified individual to the looser concept of agency as long-term process (cf. Ingold 1993).

- The rejection of textual approaches to material culture and human action: temporality is collapsed and a role for agency actively denied.

- The need for ethnographic studies of material culture and ritual landscapes (ethnoarchaeology) which employ adequate theories of human agency, thereby enhancing their utility to archaeologists as potential sources of ethnographic analogy.

Note

1   In this chapter I seek to explore how studies of material culture and landscape enculturation in contemporary societies can stimulate and enrich our conceptualisation of the prehistoric past. There is, of course, a whole raft of complex ethical issues at stake in the academic exercise of appropriating a modern indigenous community's culture, reducing it to simplified a-historical sketches, and then drawing analogies between the present and the past. I have presented a richer and fuller portrait of the Khanty in other

publications, where history, colonialism and struggles with oil companies over land rights receive a much fuller discussion (see Jordan 2003, etc.). For more information on current struggles between mineral extractors and indigenous groups in Siberia see Wiget and Balalaeva 1997 (a and b) and for a full survey of oil industry impacts on traditional Khanty communities, see Wiget 1999.

Acknowledgments

Limited sections in the present discussion of society, structure and agency appeared in Chapters 1 and 2 of Jordan 2003 (*Material Culture and Sacred Landscape: the anthropology of the Siberian Khanty*) and have been edited and adapted for inclusion in the present chapter. Acknowledgments to the Russian and Khanty communities who assisted me in this Siberian research are listed in full in this monograph. The investigation of Nämforsen (including the critique of Tilley's 1991 monograph) formed the final chapter in a Doctoral thesis written at the Department of Archaeology and Prehistory, University of Sheffield between 1997 and 2000 and I recall particularly insightful discussions with Mel Giles and Michael Lane regarding both the site and *Material Culture and Text: the art of ambiguity*. Useful comments and feedback were also provided by the thesis examiners, Mark Edmonds and Richard Bradley. Finally, a special thanks to Marek Zvelebil for sparking a long-term research interest in Siberia and circum-polar hunting, gathering and reindeer cultures.

References

Asad, T. 1973. *Anthropology and the Colonial Encounter*. London: Ithaca Press.

Balzer, M.M. 1979. *Strategies of Ethnic Survival: interactions of Russians and Khanty (Ostiak) in twentieth century Siberia*. PhD thesis, Anthropology Dept., Bryn Mawr College, University of Michigan.

Balzer, M.M. 1980. The route to eternity: cultural persistence and change in Siberian Khanty burial ritual. *Arctic Anthropology*, 17:1, 77–89.

Barrett, J.C. 1988. Fields of discourse: reconstituting a social archaeology. *Critique of Anthropology*, 7:3, 5–16.

Bhanu, A.B. 1992. Boundaries, obligations and reciprocity: levels of territoriality among the Cholanaicken of South India. In M.J. Casimir and A. Rao (eds.) *Mobility and Territoriality: social and spatial boundaries among foragers, fishers, pastoralists and peripatetics*, 29–54. Oxford: Berg.

Binford, L.R. 1978. *Nunamiut Ethnoarchaeology*. London: Academic Press.

Bird-David, N. 1990. The giving environment: another perspective on the economic system of gatherer-hunters. *Current Anthropology*, 31:2, 189–96.

Bird-David, N. 1992. Beyond the hunting and gathering mode of subsistence: culture-sensitive observations on the Nayaka and other modern hunter-gatherers. *Man* (N.S.) 27: 19–44.

Bloch, M. 1995. Questions not to ask of Malagasy carvings. In I. Hodder, M. Shanks, A. Alexandri, V. Buchli, J. Carman, J. Last and G. Lucas (eds.) *Interpreting Archaeology: finding meaning in the past*, 212–15. London: Routledge.

Bourdieu, P. 1977. *Outline of a Theory of Practice*. Cambridge: Cambridge University Press.

Boyd, R. and Richerson, P. 1985. *Culture and the Evolutionary Process*. Chicago, IL: University of Chicago Press.

Bradley, R. 1993. *Altering the Earth: the origins of monuments in Britain and Continental Europe*. Edinburgh: Society of Antiquaries of Scotland.

Cavalli-Sforza, L. and Feldman, M. 1981. *Cultural Transmission and Evolution: a quantitative approach*. Princeton, NJ: Princeton University Press.

Chernetsov, V.N. 1963. Ideas of the soul amongst Ob-Ugrians. *Anthropology of the North*, 4:13–14, 3–45.

Clark J.E. 2000. Towards a better explanation of hereditary inequality: a critical assessment of natural and historic human agents. In M.-A. Dobres and J.E. Robb (eds.) *Agency in Archaeology*, 92–112. London: Routledge.

Cohen, I.J. 1990. Structuration theory and social order: five issues in brief. In J. Clark, C. Modgil and S. Modgil (eds.) *Anthony Giddens: consensus and controversy*, 33–45. London: The Falmer Press.

Dobres, M.-A., and Robb, J.E. 2000. Agency in archaeology: paradigm or platitude? In M.-A. Dobres and J. Robb (eds.) *Agency in Archaeology*, 3–17. London: Routledge.

Forsberg, L. 1993. En kronologisk analys av ristningarna i Nämforsen. In L. Forsberg and T.B. Larsson (eds.) *Ekonomi och näringsformer I nordisk bronsålder*, 195–246. Umeå: Studia Archaeologica Universitatis umensis 3.

Geertz, C. 1973. *The Interpretation of Culture*. London: Hutchinson.

Giddens, A. 1984. *The Constitution of Society*. Berkeley and Los Angeles, CA: University of California Press.

Gregory, D. 1989. Presences and absences: time-space relations and structuration theory. In D. Held and J.B. Thompson (eds.) *Social Theory of Modern Societies: Anthony Giddens and his critics*, 185–214. Cambridge: Cambridge University Press.

Hallström, G. 1960. *Monumental Art of Northern Sweden from the Stone Age: Nämforsen and other localities*. Stockholm: Almqvist and Wiksell.

Hardesty, D.L. 1977. *Ecological Anthropology*. New York: John Wiley and Sons.

Harris, M. 1979. *Cultural Materialism: the struggle for a science of culture*. New York: Random House.

Ingold, T. 1986. *The Appropriation of Nature*. Manchester: Manchester University Press.

Ingold, T. 1993. The temporality of the landscape. *World Archaeology*, 25:2, 153–74.

Janik, L. 1999. Rock art as visual representation – or how to travel to Sweden without Christopher Tilley. In J. Goldhahn (ed.) *Rock Art as Social Representation*, 129–40. Oxford: Archaeopress (BAR International Series 794).

Jenkins, R. 1992. *Pierre Bourdieu*. London: Routledge.

Jordan, P. 2001. Ideology, material culture and Khanty ritual landscapes in western Siberia. In K.J. Fewster and M. Zvelebil (eds.) *Ethnoarchaeology and Hunter Gatherers: Pictures at an Exhibition*, 25–42. Oxford: Archaeopress (BAR International Series 955).

Jordan, P. 2003. *Material Culture and Sacred Landscape: the anthropology of the Siberian Khanty*. Walnut Creek, CA: AltaMira Press.

Karjalainen, K.F. 1922. *Die Religion der Jugra-Völker (Volume II)*. Helsinki: Suomalainen Tiedeakatemia.

Kulemzin, V.M. 1995. Mirovozzrencheskie aspekty okhoty i rybolovstva. In N.V. Lukina (ed.) *Istoriia i Kul'tura Khantov*, 65–76. Tomsk: Izdatel'stvo Tomskogo Universiteta.

Kulemzin, V.M. and Lukina, N.V. 1977. *Vasiugansko-Vakhovskie Khanty v kontse XIX – nachale XX vv*. Tomsk: Izdatel'stvo Tomskogo Universiteta.

Layton, R. 1997. *An Introduction to Theory in Anthropology*. Cambridge: Cambridge University Press.

Layton, R. 2000. *Anthropology and History in Franche-Comte: a critique of social theory*. Oxford: Oxford University Press.

Lee, R.B. 1968. What hunters do for a living, or, how to make out on scarce resources. In R.B. Lee and I. DeVore (eds.) *Man the Hunter*, 30–48. Chicago: Aldine.

Lee, R.B. 1969. *The !Kung San*. New York: Cambridge University Press.

Malmer, M.P. 1975. The rock carvings at Nämforsen, Angermanland, Sweden as a problem of maritime adaptation and circumpolar relations. In W. Fitzhugh (ed.) *Prehistoric Adaptations in the Circumpolar Zone*. The Hague: Mouton.

Michael, H (ed.) 1963. *Studies in Siberian Shamansim*. Arctic Institute of North America, Toronto: University of Toronto Press (Translations from the Russian sources).

Moore, H.L. 1996. *Space, Text, and Gender: an anthropological study of the Marakwet of Kenya*. New York and London: Guilford Press (2nd edition).

Nuñez, M. 1995. Reflections on Finnish rock art and ethnohistorical data. *Fennoscandia Archaeologica*, 12, 123–35.

Outhwaite, W. 1990. Agency and structure. In J. Clark, C. Modgil and S. Modgil (eds.) *Anthony Giddens: consensus and controversy*, 63–72. London: The Falmer Press.

Parker, J. 2000. *Structuration*. Buckingham: Open University Press.

Pred, A. 1985. The social becomes the spatial, the spatial becomes the social: enclosures, social change and the becoming of place in the Swedish province of Skåne. In D. Gregory and J. Urry (eds.) *Social Relations and Spatial Structures*, 337–65. London: Macmillan.

Pred, A. 1990. Context and bodies in flux: some comments on space and time in the writings of Anthony Giddens. In J. Clark, C. Modgil and S. Modgil (eds.) *Anthony Giddens: consensus and controversy*, 117–29. London: The Falmer Press.

Semenova, V.I. 1998. K voprosu o vremeni proiskhozhdeniia olenevodstva u vostochnykh Khantov (po arkheologicheckim istochnikam). In *Matererialy XI Zapadno-Sibirskoi Arkheolo-etnograficheskoi Konferentsii, Tomsk. Sistema Zhizneobespecheniia Traditsionnykh Obshchest v Drevnosti i Sovremennosti. Teoria, Metodologiia, Praktika*, 136–39. Tomsk: Izdatel'stvo Tomskogo Universiteta.

Shennan, S. 1996. Cultural transmission and cultural change. In R. Preucel and I. Hodder (eds.) *Contemporary Archaeology in Theory*, 282–96. Oxford: Blackwell.

Shennan, S. 2000. Population, culture history and the dynamics of culture change. *Current Anthropology*, 4:5, 811–35.

Silverman, E.K. 1990. Clifford Geertz: towards a more 'thick' understanding. In C. Tilley (ed.) *Reading Material Culture: Structuralism, Hermeneutics and Post-Structuralism*, 121–62. Oxford: Basil Blackwell.

Smith, E.A. and Winterhalder, B. 1981. New perspectives on hunter-gatherer socioecology. In B. Winterhalder and E.A. Smith (eds.) *Hunter-Gather Foraging Strategies: ethnographic and archaeological analyses*, 1–12. Chicago, IL: University of Chicago Press.

Solway, J.S. and Lee, R.B. 1990. Foragers, genuine or spurious? *Current Anthropology*, 31:2, 109–45.

Steward, J. 1973 [1955]. The concept and method of cultural ecology. In P. Bohannan and M. Glazer (eds.) *High Points in Anthropology*, 321–32. New York: Alfred A. Knopf.

Tilley C. 1991. *Material Culture and Text: the art of ambiguity*. London: Routledge.

Trigger, B. 1989. *A History of Archaeological Thought*. Cambridge: Cambridge University Press.

Van Gijn, A. and Zvelebil, M. 1997. *Ideology and Social Structures of Stone Age Communities in Europe*. Leiden: Faculty of Archaeology, Leiden University (Analecta Praehistorica Leidensia 29).

White, L.A. 1973 [1949]. Energy and the evolution of culture. In P. Bohannan and M. Glazer (eds.) *High Points in Anthropology*, 336–55. New York: Alfred A. Knopf.

Wiget, A. and Balalaeva, O. 1997a. Saving Siberia's Khanty from oil development. *Surviving Together*, 46 (Spring), 22–25.

Wiget, A. and Balalaeva, O. 1997b. Black snow, oil and the Khanty of West Siberia. *Cultural Survival Quarterly*, 20, 13–15.

Wiget, A. (ed.) 1999. *Ocherki Istorii Traditsionnogo Zemlepol'zovaniia Khantov*. Yekaterinburg: Tezis.

Wilmsen, E.N. and Denbow, J.R. 1990. Paradigmatic history of San-people and current attempts at revision. *Current Anthropology*, 31:5, 489–524.

Winterhalder, B. and Smith, E.A. (eds.) 1981. *Hunter-Gather Foraging Strategies: ethnographic and archaeological analyses*. Chicago, IL: University of Chicago Press.

Woodburn, J. 1988. African hunter-gatherer social organisation: is it best understood as a product of encapsulation? In T. Ingold, D. Riches and J. Woodburn (eds.) *Hunters and Gatherers: history, evolution and social change (Volume 1)*, 31–64. Oxford: Berg.

Wylie, A. 1985. The reaction against analogy. *Advances in Archaeological Method and Theory*, 8, 63–112.

Zvelebil, M. 1997. Hunter-gatherer ritual landscapes: spatial organisation, social structure and ideology among hunter-gatherers of northern Europe and western Siberia. In *Ideology and Social Structures of Stone Age Communities in Europe*, 33–50. Leiden: Faculty of Archaeology, Leiden University (Analecta Praehistorica Leidensia 29).

Zvelebil, M. 1998. What's in a name: the Mesolithic, the Neolithic, and social change at the Mesolithic-Neolithic transition. In M. Edmonds and C. Richards (eds.) *Understanding the Neolithic of Northwest Europe*, 1–36. Glasgow: Cruithne Press.

Zvelebil, M. and Jordan, P. 1999. Hunter fisher gatherer ritual landscapes: questions of time, space and presentation. In J. Goldhahn (ed.) *Rock Art as Social Representation*, 101–27. Oxford: Archaeopress (BAR International Series 794).

Zvelebil, M. and Rowly-Conwy, P. 1989. Saving it for later: storage by prehistoric hunter-gatherers in Europe. In P. Halstead and J. O'Shea (eds.) *Bad Year Economics: cultural responses to risk and uncertainty*, 111–26. Cambridge: Cambridge University Press.

CHAPTER 8

IDENTIFYING AND DEFINING AGENCY IN A POLITICAL CONTEXT

Fiona J.L. Handley and Tim Schadla-Hall

INTRODUCTION

Within the Humanities, in particular, the use of the term 'agency' has become a matter of debate in recent years, and problems of definition and of whether there are different types of agency have dominated what has become an increasingly theoretical agenda. Indeed, within what might be termed the 'soft' sciences, 'agency' and its elusive and burgeoning definitions seems to have become a multi-purpose and consequently hollow term, lacking a core meaning – a little like the term 'cultural heritage' – and used, the less kindly-disposed might suggest, by those who find clarity and definition a challenge. In this chapter we want to return to the use of the term in a more Marxist (see Kamenka (ed.) 1983: 155–58; 287) and utilitarian sense, examining the realities of *what people do*. This chapter is concerned with an analysis of agency within large organisations, specifically the British Government and its various Departments of State, and Non-Departmental Public Bodies (NDPBs), such as English Heritage. These bodies control the political, and subsequently financial, environment within which most forms of archaeological activity take place in the UK – whether within university departments, archaeological units, or museum and conservation bodies. We hope that this chapter contributes to the critical debate which has shadowed the use of agency theory in archaeology, and which highlights the position of agency theory, and hence archaeology's use of it, within modern Western society's concern with the individual. The activities of agents and the role of agency within this wider framework, as well as their consequent impacts, are far too often ignored within the context of our own professional activities.

First, we want to demonstrate that Government, although an external agency to the practice, process and use of archaeology, is critical to the way in which archaeology performs and operates. The strategic direction of policy is critical to the way in which archaeology is conducted, even though it is a long way down the 'food chain'. All aspects of archaeological activity are affected by policy direction, and an understanding of this is ultimately of crucial importance to decision-making in archaeological and heritage organisations, with regard to their future direction. Archaeologists or those with archaeological interests do not control the framework within which such directions are promulgated, but they affect all of us.

Secondly, we shall attempt to examine the mechanisms by which policy emerges – particularly through consideration of those policies that affect archaeology – and suggest that even in Government, and contrary to common perception, most policy is created by a very small number of unseen agents, who are normally unidentifiable and unaccountable. We argue that real agency and real power operate through these individuals.

Finally, we argue that it should be of more than passing interest, both in the training of archaeologists and within the research areas that they study, for these processes to be better understood. Archaeologists need to recognise both the importance of external agencies and also the fact that the direction that archaeology takes is often not moulded by archaeologists as agents (even though they frequently think it is). Archaeology is essentially a non-economic field of endeavour in the sense that it has no product that has a monetary value. This in turn means that the resources that are applied to it will always be limited – and that the ways in which these limited resources are applied should be fully understood.

CREATING POLICIES FOR ARCHAEOLOGICAL ACTIVITY

The creation of what we shall term meta-agencies – those that generate the big agendas which are external to archaeology – is controlled by the organisation and process of Government; in this case we are referring to the 'UK Government' in its widest sense. All activity in a modern nation state in the 21st century is to some degree controlled by the availability of resources, so that in one sense at least one could argue that what takes place is controlled by the finance available. In other words – as we are constantly reminded by the media – it is the Treasury that controls all that happens. This being accepted, there is a series of areas of decision-making that must be understood. Meta-agencies – for want of a better term – create the 'big' agendas, and the main origin for these is the British Government. It creates policy that is derived from manifesto pledges and aspirations. Ultimately these are made explicit through primary and secondary legislation in Parliament. However, there are often areas where legislation is not necessary and where changes in the implementation of activity, as well as in policy direction, can be achieved within the framework of Government by altering policies internally. These changes are frequently implemented within, and by, the professional Civil Service which is responsible for carrying out policy on behalf of Government. For example, the Secretary of State has powers under the Treasure Act 1996 "... by order, for the purposes of section 1(1)(b)" to "designate any class of object which he considers to be of outstanding historical, archaeological, or cultural importance" (DNH 1997). This requires an order to be made by statutory instrument, which has to be laid before both Houses of Parliament and needs to be approved by a resolution in each. Such an instrument was made in 2002, and was drawn up by the civil servants after lengthy consultation, and approved by the minister, thus extending the definition of treasure. In this case the Order extending the Treasure Act 1996 was debated in both houses in July and October.

However, in the case of the introduction of the Iraq (United Nations Sanctions) Order 2003 (SI 2003/1519) on 12 June 2003 there was no debate. Despite the fact that the Dealing in Cultural Objects (Offences) Bill was being considered in Parliament at the same time and that there was a link between the two, this Order in Council was not discussed. It could be argued that this was an urgently required order, although it seems more likely that it was rushed through speedily both to prevent debate and to deflect any criticism about the looting of Iraqi antiquities. PPGs can be treated in a similar way: no debate is needed (see below). Working Groups and similar bodies set up to promote Government policy, whilst ultimately requiring ministerial support for any actions that they might encourage, can be immensely influential in this respect, and can often make decisions and recommend policy changes that have far-reaching consequences.

The Labour Government of 1997 made it clear from the outset that it wished to promote a series of policy objectives, and encourage their development – principally education, social inclusion, community and access. Immediately upon taking up the reins of power, every attempt was made to bend the existing activities of Government towards developing policies to include all of these aims. This happened across all departments of State. There is a considerable degree of work that can be, and was, done to promote these objectives without any legislation at all, simply by having the relevant departments' civil servants draw up new guidelines. For example, the Department for Culture, Media and Sport (DCMS) produced a whole series of publications (e.g. DCMS 1999, DCMS 2000) on promoting access and social inclusion in the areas of activity for which it was responsible in policy terms, which were in turn immediately seized upon by the DCMS's client bodies, and where possible implemented or applied as rapidly as possible. The museums sector, for instance, had already made claims that it was promoting social inclusion, and began to develop measures to demonstrate this fact (see below). The origins of the policy objective of social inclusion lie embedded in the pre-1997 policy development of the New Labour platform. Whilst there are those who have questioned its validity, it nevertheless became a key area of Governmental policy. A point that is also well known, but worth making in the context of this chapter, is that it is important to take into account that all policy objectives, no matter how broad, need ultimately to be demonstrated as being achieved. Initially this is often expressed in terms of targets drawn up as Public Service Agreements (PSAs), which appear at the beginning of Departmental Annual Reports (e.g. DCMS 2002: 29–31). This brings in a second area of policy and also of agency – that of the quantification or measurement of results. It is not our intention here to discuss the problems of demonstrating that a particular policy objective has been achieved through the application of a series of agreed measures (an approach first developed by the previous Conservative administration, but further developed by the Labour administration). We wish to note, however, that while ministers may well approve the measures selected for showing that specific policy objectives are being met, it is normally civil servants (often having taken advice) who create them.

Non-Departmental Public Bodies are well aware of the need to align themselves with the current policy objectives of any Government. Indeed, where possible, they will seek access to both ministers and civil servants to ensure that they can both influence policy direction and, where possible, secure favourable policy and legislation. Whilst NDPBs and other organisations can lobby appropriate ministers, the most successful pressures are probably exerted via the civil servants of, for example, the DCMS. Such discussions are necessarily outside the spotlight of public attention, and the exact nature of what goes on remains opaque. Both sides have agendas. From the civil servant's point of view, the aim is to make the organisations fulfil Government objectives without compromising their arm's length relationship, or appearing to pander to pressure groups, or approving anything that results in the expenditure of additional money, which might damage agreed financial targets. Organisations also want to keep their independence, yet influence policy to their advantage. In practice a reciprocal relationship is established whereby organisations that fulfil Government aims become closer to civil servants, who have the power to develop favourable policy. Policy, however, is the key and without being able to influence the agents responsible for creating policy all that archaeologists can do is attempt to join in the general flow and turn it to their advantage.

Once created, policy becomes a paradigm of both change and assessment that dictates a whole string of lower level organisations into subtly organising and realigning their efforts, especially if they have not been able to influence the general policy development. For example, recent Government policy has focused on the importance of social inclusion and life-long learning, and this is directly reflected in the report *Renaissance in the Regions* produced by Resource (2001), an NDPB that is responsible for museums, libraries and archives. This report makes a case for increasing resources for regional museums and predicts that the bulk of new funding for the next five years will be under the headings of social inclusion, education and access, and not, for example, under collections and displays. One of the interesting points about *Renaissance* is that its conclusions were organisational and structural (e.g. remedying fragmentation, and rationalisation of collections and resources, etc.), yet the first phase of funding addressed none of these long-term issues. Instead it focused exclusively on short-term initiatives relating to schoolchildren and communities. The Government has a modernisation agenda within which *Renaissance*'s organisational and structural goals would comfortably fit, and this was (along with children and communities) one of the DCMS's three priority areas under its PSA (DCMS 2002: 26-30). Thus it makes a case for funding which is directly in line with the current Government policy. Surely this is an example of agency at work? National museums have been instructed to produce measures that demonstrate their success in promoting social inclusion, because they are directly funded by the DCMS (Selwood (ed.) 2001: 354). Whether or not they are the best measures or have been effective is another matter – it seems from the measures that they have adopted, or have been forced to adopt, that they have not actually widened social inclusion at all (House of Commons Select Committee 2002: 25). More worrying is the current debate on what 'social inclusion' actually means and whether it is even a sensible approach to the nation's problems.

The impact of Government policy – again on an NDPB within the DCMS's control – is illustrated by the opening sentence of a report by English Heritage, *Power of Place* (English Heritage 2000: 4). This states, "*Power of Place* is about the future of England's historic environment, its role in people's lives and its contribution to the cultural and economic well-being of the nation". This can be read as an almost direct response to what the Labour Party wrote in its 1997 manifesto: "the arts, culture and sport are central to the task of recreating the sense of community, identity and civic pride that should define our country" (Labour Party 1997: 30). Thus, the power of meta-agency on the biggest consumer of Government funding for archaeology in the UK is plain for all to see. English Heritage now places a series of social inclusion goals on its website.

After meta-policy is determined, it is then adapted and aligned to suit the needs of particular organisations, and it is here that we need to understand the process in more detail. Somehow, general policy statements have to be incorporated into the language (this is particularly important) and written substance of an organisation. The case of sustainability provides a good example: it began as an international scheme to protect the habitats of migratory birds, entered international policy at the Rio Summit, was brought down to a local level as Local Agenda 21, and was taken on as a Manifesto Commitment by the Labour Party. The importance of this policy, or concept, was demonstrated by the way that environmental organisations responded to it, by making sustainability apply to their remit through the rewording of current projects, the rewriting of overall goals, the initiation of new projects, and by stating very clearly the contribution of the organisation to the policy's aims. A good example of this is the English Heritage and Civil Service input into the writing of *Sustaining the Historic Environment* (English Heritage 1997). This document was perhaps one of the first that English Heritage had a hand in with the clear aim of aligning archaeological policy with overall Government policy. It did this by shifting its emphasis from a relatively academic and bureaucratic approach to a much more publicly accessible stance.

This example hints at one of the underlying features of the announcement of broad policy directions. Government does not need to force bodies – especially NDPBs – to realign. On the contrary, organisations realign themselves to compete for Government favours and funding, and to 'prove' that they can fulfil policy in the face of Government scepticism. For archaeology and heritage organisations, this was particularly the case with the arrival of the 'New' Labour Government in 1997 – the consequences of which are still reverberating. Statements such as Chris Smith's claim that "heritage is as much about the future as the past" (Smith 1998: 69), and Tony Blair's report to the Party conference in 1994 that "this party is a living movement not a historical monument" (Blair 1996: 19), made it clear that historical monuments were objects that the Labour Party did not desire to be associated with. The low priority of the historic environment in Government agendas, especially in the early days of this Labour Government, was striking, and it left heritage organisations, represented in the last years of the Conservative Government by a (then) Department for National Heritage, in a somewhat marginalised position. The department soon changed its name to the Department for Culture, Media and Sport, and heritage organisations had to realign themselves rapidly, not just to respond to Government policy directives, but also to justify their funding – and attempt to reclaim their importance – within Government thinking. It is important to stress that this would also have necessitated ensuring that the relevant civil servants were aware of the role that these organisations might play in developing Government policies, so that they could achieve relevance. For example, in 1998, the Social Exclusion Unit set up 18 cross-Governmental Policy Action Teams (PATs) led by different Whitehall departments, all involved in looking at neighbourhood regeneration. The DCMS led PAT 10, to investigate the contribution of Arts, Sport and Leisure. Notably, there was no contribution representing the historic environment, a situation which led the conservation group SAVE Britain's Heritage to strongly criticise the Social Exclusion Unit, and to produce an agenda for the contributions that the historic environment could make to regeneration, which was supported by 20 heritage organisations, including the Council for British Archaeology, ICOMOS UK and the National Trust (SAVE Britain's Heritage 1998).

The success of all areas of archaeological endeavour will be affected by the overall policy of Government and those agents and agencies that create the policies – policy advisers and, to an extent, civil servants. Archaeologists are unlikely to get near the 'high level' agents, who are creating broad and often opaque objectives. They are likely to be able to both communicate with and meet those at a departmental level who are responsible for ensuring delivery of policies through a series of 'lower level' initiatives and policies, and they are likely to be either 'victims' or agents themselves within these processes. We have attempted to use examples in the heritage field in this section, and have concentrated on only one department of State (DCMS), but it is important to remember that archaeology is affected by, and interacts with, a whole series of Government departments, which do not apparently communicate in a joined-up way (APPAG 2003:10–11).

AGENTS AND POLICIES

Agency theory in archaeology has been a way for the past to become comprehensible to us, not just as a series of events, but also as a world of socially- and physically-embodied people. Importantly, it gives us a structure for understanding past human behaviour that does not preclude us from thinking about what it was like to be a person in that time and place. In contrast with this feeling of immediacy, even intimacy, with people in the past, organisations such as Government agencies and NDPBs appear to be the opposite: faceless, monolithic, emotionless and corporate. Individuals only, and even then rarely, appear as 'leaders' – Directors or front-bench politicians.

One issue here that is of particular interest is the role of DCMS in relation to its various Agencies and NDPBs. A logical and transparent structure would be one in which a Government minister makes policy and then delegates implementation to the appropriate Agency/NDPB. Traditionally, DCMS and its predecessor bodies left making policy to these Agencies/NDPBs (the classic 'arm's length' principle), but at the same time sought to influence those policies. A good example of this is National Lottery distribution, where the distributing bodies, such as the Heritage Lottery Fund, are intended to be independent, but are nevertheless constrained by a whole series of DCMS Policy Directives and Financial Memoranda that directly and indirectly affect their activities. Thus influence – in this case from DCMS – is increasingly overt and yet also opaque. For example, the recent proposals for reforming the protection of the historic environment, published in *Protecting our Historic Environment: making the system work better* (DCMS 2003) suggest that English Heritage should take over responsibilities currently held by ministers. This is a further example of an inconsistent approach concerning where responsibility should lie, and further muddies the waters as to whether the arm's length principle remains a valid or even consistent concept. In turn it is worth asking who is really making decisions, and why?

However, this apparent facelessness and impenetrability belies the true nature of the way these organisations work. In creating policy, or incorporating policy directives from other institutions, an organisation creates a written policy statement that deliberately smoothes over the transition of language and ideas. This is done using a particular style of writing that is uncritical, does not acknowledge the context of the change or why it has been done, and in fact is designed to suppress any suggestion that there may be an individual with an opinion who wrote it. We have become so accustomed to this kind of corporate talk that we no longer examine it critically but accept that it was 'written by a committee'. But how realistic is it to think that an organisation can 'write' a policy direction? It is rare enough for a committee to be able to write a document. Ultimately, it is down to one or two people to act as agents, either by writing the policy or gaining a clear agenda that allows them to influence others in the writing.

A recent example of this is again the report *Power of Place* (English Heritage 2000). According to Sir Neil Cossons in the Preface:

> The review has been led by a 20-strong steering group representing a wide range of interests. Well over 100 people have contributed to five specialist working groups ... Detailed consultation papers were issued in June ... and we have received and analysed over 600 responses. We have commissioned MORI to carry out a major survey ... (English Heritage 2000: 1).

But whilst this started out as a democratic and open exercise, it was subsequently written up into report form by a small group of people who decided what went into it – for an agenda that still isn't clear. What started off as an exercise involving wide participation and maximum consultation suddenly changed to a small group creating a series of policies that might well have suited the DCMS, but certainly did not meet with universal approval from the archaeological interests of the country as a whole.

Another important example of how meta-policy affects specific policy is provided by the creation of the Planning Policy Guidance Note 16 (PPG16), which appeared in 1990 (Department of the Environment 1990). PPG16 is one of a series of planning guidelines that could be introduced by the then Secretary of State for the Environment (without primary legislation) under the provisions of the Town and Country Planning Act 1990. Its impact was to change the organisation of archaeology in the UK, and particularly England, to the extent that any archaeologist returning to the UK after a break of 20 years would not recognise the current structure of archaeology as even remotely connected with what he/she had known in the 1980s or earlier. Essentially, since its introduction, funding for archaeological investigation and analysis of results has probably trebled, at least, and there are now far more archaeologists employed than ever before (Aitchison 1999). The results of excavations still, arguably, provide the raw material for allowing work in the subject to progress. To understand how this transformation in British archaeology came about it is necessary to place the appearance of PPG16 in context.

Funding for archaeology increased rapidly during the heady days of rescue archaeology in the 1970s. This increase was relatively small in terms of national expenditure, and came about when pressure was applied through a successful and sustained campaign by archaeological organisations (Jones 1984; Barker 1987). This expansion in archaeological funding was also accompanied by a growth in the number of university departments of archaeology (Millett 1987), which is still continuing and is itself the consequence of decisions made by the Department for Education and its successor bodies in terms of funding the higher education sector – another area of agency! It is worth noting that archaeology also benefited from the economic downturn of the late 1970s and early 1980s, in the form of job creation schemes; these also helped to increase the funding for archaeological activity (Aitchison 2000).

The increased funding was found to meet the perceived threat to archaeology, particularly from development. It was supplied through what became the Directorate of Ancient Monuments and Historic Buildings (DAMHB), which had incorporated the Inspectorate of Ancient Monuments (IAM). Both the IAM and the DAMHB were part of the Department of the Environment (DoE), and all its employees were civil servants, answerable to the Secretary of State through the DoE's permanent secretary.

In 1984, under the provisions of the National Heritage Act 1983, the Historic Buildings and Monuments Commission for England was created as an NDPB, with its own board of Commissioners. It adopted the 'trading name' of English Heritage, and, with many of the executive powers of the IAM and the DAMHB, continued the development of a series of somewhat haphazardly-created archaeological units that approximately covered the country by the early 1980s (Spoerry 1991). These relied to a great extent on funding from Government, ultimately through the DoE.

The problem of damage to the historic environment was recognised by the passing of the Ancient Monuments and Archaeological Areas Act 1979 in the dying days of the Labour Government. Among its provisions it allowed the creation of Archaeological Areas. Initially, five were designated, although the Secretary of State for the Environment was empowered to add others. Basically, this Act laid out a series of requirements for developers to allow archaeologists access to sites that had archaeological importance for specified periods of time before development could take place. Unfortunately the Act did not specify who would pay for archaeological works required, and as a result it had little effect on ensuring that more work could be carried out. There have been no new designations since the Act was passed. It was rapidly recognised as flawed (see Cookson 2000: 138–40), and indeed the excellent – and now apparently forgotten – consultative paper

Protecting our Past (DNH and Welsh Office 1996) suggested that it be scrapped. This paper was a casualty of different influences coming into play during the lead-up to the 1997 General Election. However, it did demonstrate the close connection established between the planning process, development and ultimately the need for mitigation of damage to archaeological material. This connection meant that there was a constant series of negotiations between the DAMHB and local authorities to ensure, through a system of tapered funding, that archaeological posts were increasingly lodged within planning structures, and particularly in county planning departments. This process was by no means uniform or instantaneous, but it was accompanied by the development of the concept of protecting the environment – and particularly the historic environment – through the planning process. The DoE was responsible for all planning legislation in Parliament, and in the early 1980s increasing concern was being expressed about environmental damage resulting from development as the economy revived. In Thatcherite Britain the concept of making the polluter pay became increasingly acceptable as the decade wore on.

This tied in with the fact that the increasing absorption of archaeology into the planning process meant that the Government was having to pay – directly through its own coffers, or indirectly through those of local government – for more and more archaeological activity. For some time, first DAMHB and then English Heritage had been wrestling with the problem of how to fund archaeological activity, and although there were developments, such as the use of 'planning gain' whereby a *quid pro quo* was agreed between planners and developers to allow development to take place (this was applied particularly effectively in London), there was no uniform approach to such exercises. Matters were brought to a head in the late 1980s by two particular incidents, both in London. The first was at the Huggin Hill Bath site in the City, where the developer was not prepared to allow archaeologists to complete their work (Eccles 1990: 151). This was shortly followed by the discovery of the late 16th century Rose Theatre in Southwark, which resulted in a massive public outcry and demonstrations aimed against the developers, amongst others. There were several debates and questions raised in Parliament about the issue and even the then Prime Minister, Margaret Thatcher, was heard to make pledges about the future of the theatre (Eccles 1990: 170).

It was clear – and had been recognised well before the Rose Theatre debacle – that something had to be done to ensure that there was sufficient future funding available for archaeology, as well as sufficient time to carry out appropriate work. A number of members of English Heritage had already been working on a solution that would inevitably mean using the planning process (pers. comm. D. Morgan-Evans, M. Parker-Pearson, A. Saunders). There was added urgency in the DoE to sort out the situation so that the Government would not be embarrassed by any more Rose Theatres. In the Rose case there would have been severe costs, far in excess of the annual budget of English Heritage, because within the letter of the law the developer had already allowed time on the site for the archaeologists and was in danger of losing money on a capital development scheme (Eccles 1990: 234). The DAMHB had a solution, and the DoE had a mechanism for delivering the solution – introducing another PPG. However it was not the archaeologists who were responsible for the ultimate form that PPG16 took; it was the senior civil servants who produced it in the DoE, even if they did take advice from the archaeologists. The Government at the time was committed to offering choice through competitive tendering wherever and whenever possible – this was a key policy for the then-governing (Conservative) party.

Competitive tendering introduced market forces, and was intended to drive down costs of services within the public sector, and was applied eventually across the whole of the EU (HM Treasury 1993). The DoE was able to ensure that developers would be prepared to meet the costs of archaeological investigation and associated works – there was no significant outcry from that quarter about the new PPG – and presumably any subsequent costs could be passed on to the ultimate purchaser. As a *quid pro quo* it was made clear that it would be possible for a developer to use any competent archaeological body that he/she wished to select to advise and carry out the work required. Thus competitive tendering was introduced in to archaeology. The publication and approval of PPG16 resulted in the end of local authority and DoE-funded units, and created an open market for archaeology. It is worth considering that the then archaeological establishment, with few exceptions, did little to analyse the underlying reasons for this change and instead spent their time re-aligning their activities (see e.g. Swain (ed.) 1991). The effect was to hasten the development of a professional archaeologists' association, and also to increase the placement of archaeology and archaeologists within planning departments (the so-called Curators). The drift of funding created by the application of the 'polluter pays' principle meant that these archaeologists – normally county archaeologists – were placed at the centre of archaeological activity.

County archaeologists are expected to act as 'curators' of the archaeological resource, making appropriate recommendations on the treatment of any threat to an archaeological site from a proposed development, and also to advise the planning authority on the steps required to mitigate such a threat – as a last resort, through excavation. They normally also advise on appropriate archaeological contractors and specify the measures required to satisfy archaeological requirements in advance of development. At the same time, the movement of archaeology increasingly into the planning sphere ensured that the control of archaeological works was ultimately the responsibility of a department of State (the DoE) that had considerable control over the archaeological resource because of its dominance in terms of planning legislation. One might argue that this development freed the Government from much of its previous responsibility for funding archaeological work, but at the same time it resulted in archaeological activity being made merely a tool of the planning and development process. It might be possible to argue that specific incidents such as the Rose Theatre precipitated this move, but a combination of growing concerns about the environment and the booming economy in the late 1980s, together with the broad policy of encouraging competition in all areas of Government activity, were also agents.

In little more than a decade after the introduction of PPG16, the levels of funding for archaeological activity increased several fold, as did archaeological activity itself and employment of archaeologists both by units and in the form of consultants (Aitchison 2000). In addition, the number and diversity of archaeological finds increased. Archaeology has become a relatively important factor within the planning process. Thus, there were consequences of PPG16 that benefited archaeology – for example the massive increase in funding and the amount of archaeology that was to be done in the country (see for example Aitchison 2000: esp. 23–24) – and it is these consequences that were highlighted by those archaeologists most responsible for the development of the policy (see e.g. Wainwright 1993). In addition, it saved the DoE from having to find ever-increasing sums to pay for both units and excavations whilst ensuring, through the network of county archaeologists, some form, however dubious, of quality control.

There were many, however, who decried the development of PPG16, and saw it as acting against the research interests of archaeology (e.g. Biddle 1994), especially in terms of creating specific research strategies; the funding available for archaeology would not be used to pursue research questions but merely to serve the needs of developers. Others saw it as inimical to the public interest in terms of the possibility of sharing in the results of archaeology (Ascherson 1994; Faulkner 2000). It is difficult to be certain what was in the minds of the original creators of PPG16, but we can be fairly sure that the public interest was not at the forefront. In addition, a further consequence has been to make the process of archaeology a competitive commercial activity that is effectively regulated by county archaeologists (as a result of national Governmental policy). It seems unlikely that those civil servants who developed PPG16, and the Secretary of State who approved the PPG, were aware of these potential consequences, some of which were recently investigated by the All-Party Parliamentary Archaeology Group (see e.g. APPAG 2003: 20–21). It has also been suggested that there is an increasing split between the universities who train archaeologists and conduct research, and the commercial sector that has developed a different set of requirements from both the archaeologists that it employs and from potential audiences other than those (i.e. commercial clients) to whom their work is primarily being presented. In turn, one of the (unforeseen) effects of PPG16 has been to raise the question of who is supposed to benefit from the results of archaeology – the commercial sector, or the public at large?

It is worth noting that the creation of the Department for National Heritage (DNH, subsequently DCMS) meant that the all-powerful DoE was replaced by the newly formed DNH as the sponsoring department of English Heritage after the 1992 General Election. This in turn led to English Heritage answering to DNH/DCMS, which remained responsible for much of the law underpinning the statutory duties of English Heritage. In this case the creation of a new relationship through a new department meant that, unlike the other environmental NDPBs with statutory responsibilities – like English Nature and its successor bodies – English Heritage has to some extent been removed from direct contact with the source of much of its legislative powers. This was certainly not envisaged at the time that PPG16 was developed. Here is another area in which decision- and policy-making become more difficult to understand, as *Force for our Future* (DCMS 2001), the Government's response to *Power of Place* (English Heritage 2000), was jointly published by the Secretaries of State for Culture, Media and Sport and for Transport, Local Government and the Regions (DTLR), DoE's successor department (in turn now the Department of Environment, Transport and the Regions). This department is responsible for planning, housing, transport and the constitutional framework within which most decisions affecting the historic environment are made, and the joint publication apparently recognises the key role of that department in respect of the historic environment. However, the extent to which a relationship does exist, how far it extends, and how much it is reflected in that department's policy is unclear.

Currently PPG16 and PPG15 (which post-dates PPG16 (DoE 1994) and deals with the built historic environment) are being reviewed by the Office of the Deputy Prime Minister, which has taken on many of the former DoE's responsibilities. It is intended to produce a new Policy Planning Statement (PPS) on the historic environment to replace both of these PPGs. Such a review is long overdue – after all, the original PPG16 has remained unrevised for nearly 15 years. Recently the minister responsible announced that consultation on the new proposed PPS has been deferred until Spring 2004 (having previously been expected in 2003; further details unavailable at the time of going to press) because of new proposals that stem from recommendations made by English Heritage which are included in a new paper, *Protecting our Historic Environment: making the system work better* (DCMS 2003). This means in turn that any revision will involve a more complex process than the original PPG16, in which again the final decisions are likely to be made not by archaeologists, but within the wider context of overall Governmental policy directions. There will be a number of identifiable agents involved in the process, and also public consultation, but the end product will be a complex, behind-the-scenes result that will be created as a result of the actions of lobbying and interest groups.

Another example of the working of agency in the context of the practice of archaeology, on a much smaller scale, is the appearance of the Battlefields Register as a policy development by English Heritage in 1990. The DAMHB, like most parts of Government, used to draw up a list of major tasks to be worked on annually. Such lists represented a form of measurement and monitoring that gave an indication that tasks were being performed. Although there had been a number of demands for the protection of historic battlefield sites in England for some time, the need to create a register in this case came not from an English Heritage initiative but from a senior DoE civil servant who had apparently been on holiday with a book on battlefields and returned to suggest that it was time for a battlefields register. This was then added to the list of tasks that DAMHB had to undertake (D. Morgan-Evans, pers. comm.). The register was produced and still exists today (although there is no statutory protection for battlefields *per se*). This example is worth offering because it underlines how decisions and initiatives, however worthy, often require outside and invisible agency in order for them to happen at all. More importantly it was an individual decision. Many of the policy results that affect the direction of our activities as archaeologists, although presented as rational and necessary, are in fact created by almost-invisible figures.

The point that we want to make clear is that it is difficult to identify the agents who actually create policy. This is not just because the process of decision-making remains opaque but also because the decisions are often made by agents who rarely admit that they are responsible. One of the most remarkable essays on the ways in which agents operate in Government – both civil servants and advisers – comes in the context of the well-documented scheme to develop the poll tax, which was an ill-fated attempt to replace domestic rates with a new form of local taxation. Butler, Adonis and Travers (1994) have illustrated the way in which civil servants and politicians created this particular policy in detail. It is the agents who mould, at both meta- and more local levels, what we do. Ultimately, we can question how much control meta-agencies really have, but the issue is perhaps not that we do not appreciate the extent of that control (which as politically-engaged archaeologists we like to think we do), but rather that the mechanisms which create control are obscured. We can spot the links. For example:

Funding bodies answering to Government social inclusion policy

+

archaeologists wanting money

=

community archaeology,

but the nature of these links is on a more complex scale than we imagine. The links between bodies advising Government policy, Government policy-makers, policy-makers in non-Governmental bodies that issue funding or grant contracts, and the people who write the applications in archaeology units or departments or museums, perhaps involve far fewer people than the size of these organisations would suggest. And this number is likely to be even smaller if, as is often unofficially the case, Government advisors and organisations distributing Government funds belong to the same body.

Here is a completely hypothetical scenario, based on a minimal number of, say, two people, creating policy in a series of organisations. Two people from the education committee of Organisation Number One advise the Government on, say, the direction of education in museums. Using this information, two members of the Civil Service (often seeking informal advice) write the Green Paper on Education in Museums, which becomes the guideline for the actions of Organisation Number Two. However, if we accept that this is the same organisation as Number One, which is unofficially the case, they already have a clear understanding of the direction to pursue, because they advised on it. So that's four people. To push this scenario further, we move to Bigtown Museum where, from the Government guidelines, and the latest policy report of the advisory organisation/funding body, the head of education and the head of archaeology sit down and write their funding application for an exhibition on archaeology …

In this minimal and hypothetical case, only six people are involved in creating and transferring policy from Government to archaeology. But, more importantly, we know who the head of interpretation and the head of archaeology at Bigtown Museum are – and we can pretty much guess what their agenda is in that situation: to get money for an exhibition. However, the other four we have no idea about, and we are not allowed to know who they are, and what their motivations are, or what pressures have been brought to bear on them. We don't know their agenda, and we have no way of finding it out.

CONCLUSION

It seems ambitious to suggest that we will ever know who the key agents in decisions affecting archaeology are, much less that we will ever be able to recognise the nature and sources of the pressures and influences that were brought to bear during the policy-making process. The pruning of the Freedom of Information Act, which would have given right of access to information held by public authorities, and would have allowed far greater insight into a whole range of decision-making, suggests that any change is a long way off, and it will remain difficult, if not impossible, to identify exactly how many decisions that concern us are reached. We should continue to scrutinise and worry the organisations that control archaeology. The networks that exist even within such a small-scale activity as archaeology will always to some extent elude us, and those who implement policy are naturally much easier to identify than those who create policy. Nevertheless, in a majority of cases the directions and areas that archaeology pursues are inextricably bound up with policy-creation and implementation. For this reason alone it is important that we both understand and seek to influence these processes. In terms of national legislation (and there is precious little archaeological legislation in the UK) and its effects, it is critical that archaeologists acquire a far better understanding of the agents who create policy. They are normally not archaeologists.

The most perverse point that this short chapter attempts to raise is that a Government policy such as the concept of social inclusion, which attempts to bridge the gap between individuals and society, is both a result of contemporary academic research including – perhaps especially – agency theory, and is a protagonist of furthering such ideas through the influence that the policy has. The circularity of this situation is beyond the scope of this paper, but the most important thing to consider is that rather than this process being driven by the weight of organisational power, it is in fact driven and interpreted by a few, but often powerful, individuals primarily within the core of Government. The power that such individuals have is not derived from the knowledge that they might (or might not) have of archaeology and its activities, but from the positions that they occupy within decision-making bodies, or indeed the influences and networks within which they operate. Policies often depend on individuals. It is difficult to gain access to policy-makers and examine what they do, but it is even harder to investigate how thoroughly policies are thought through before they are implemented.

Acknowledgments

We are grateful to many colleagues, particularly Adrian Babbidge and David Morgan-Evans, for their comments on this proleptic paper. However, we remain responsible for any errors or mistakes.

References

Aitchison, K. 1999. *Profiling the Profession: a survey of archaeological jobs and job profiles in the UK.* London: Council for British Archaeology, English Heritage and The Institute of Field Archaeologists.

Aitchison, K. 2000. The Funding of Archaeological Practice in England. *Cultural Trends*, 39, 2–32.

APPAG, 2003. *The Current State of Archaeology in the United Kingdom. First Report of the All-Party Parliamentary Archaeology Group.* London: All-Party Parliamentary Archaeology Group.

Ascherson, N. 1994. The villages of Kent have more to lament than the Channel rail link. *The Independent*, 6 February.

Barker, P.A. 1987. Rescue: antenatal, birth and early years. In H. Mytum and K. Waugh (eds.) *Rescue Archaeology – What's Next?*, 7–10. York: Department of Archaeology, University of York/Rescue.

Biddle, M. 1994. *What Future for British Archaeology?* Oxford: Oxbow Books (Oxbow Lecture 1).

Blair, T. 1996. *A New Statesman Special Selection from New Britain: my vision of a young country.* London: Fourth Estate.

Butler, D., Adonis, A. and Travers, T. 1994. *Failure in the British Government: the politics of the poll tax.* Oxford: Oxford University Press.

Cookson, N. 2000. *Archaeological Heritage Law.* Chichester: Barry Rose Law Publishers.

DCMS, 1999. *A Report to the Social Exclusion Unit: arts and sport.* London: DCMS.

DCMS, 2000. *Centres for Social Change: museums, galleries and archives for all.* London: DCMS.

DCMS, 2001. *The Historic Environment: a force for our future.* London: DCMS.

DCMS, 2002. *Department for Culture Media and Sport Annual Report (2 vols).* London: DCMS.

DCMS, 2003. *Protecting our Historic Environment: making the system work better – consultation paper.* London: DCMS.

Department of the Environment, 1990. *Planning Policy Guidance Note 16, Archaeology and Planning (PPG16).* London: HMSO.

Department of the Environment, 1994. *Planning Policy Guidance Note 15, Planning and the Historic Environment (PPG15).* London: HMSO.

DNH, 1997. *The Treasure Act 1996. Code of Practice (England and Wales).* London: Department for National Heritage.

DNH and Welsh Office, 1996. *Protecting Our Past.* London: Department for National Heritage and The Welsh Office.

Eccles, C. 1990. *The Rose Theatre.* London: Nick Hern Books.

English Heritage, 1997. *Sustaining the Historic Environment: new perspectives on the future.* London: English Heritage.

English Heritage, 2000. *Power of Place: the future of the historic environment.* London: English Heritage.

Faulkner, N. 2000. Archaeology from below. *Public Archaeology*, 1.1, 21–33.

HM Treasury, 1993. *The Competitive Tendering Process.* Guidance Note 40, The Central Purchasing Unit. London: HM Treasury.

House of Commons Select Committee, 2002. *Select Committee on Culture, Media and Sport: national museums and galleries – funding and free admission.* London: HMSO.

Jones, B. 1984. *Past Imperfect: the story of rescue archaeology.* London: Heinemann.

Kamenka, E. (ed.) 1983. *The Portable Karl Marx.* Harmondsworth: Penguin.

Labour Party, 1997. *New Labour: because Britain deserves better.* London: The Labour Party.

Millett, M. 1987. Universities and the future of Archaeology in Britain. In H. Mytum and K. Waugh (eds.) *Rescue Archaeology – What's Next?*, 29–34. York: Department of Archaeology, University of York and Rescue.

Resource, 2001. *Renaissance in the Regions: a new vision for England's museums*. London: Resource.

SAVE Britain's Heritage, 1998. *Catalytic Conversion – REVIVE Historic Buildings to Regenerate Communities*. London: SAVE Britain's Heritage.

Selwood, S. (ed.) 2001. *The UK Cultural Sector: profiles and policy issues*. London: Policy Studies Institute.

Smith, C. 1998. *Creative Britain*. London: Faber and Faber.

Spoerry, P. 1991. *The Structure and Funding of British Archaeology*. Hertford: Rescue.

Swain, H. (ed.) 1991. *Competitive Tendering in Archaeology*. Hertford: Rescue/SCAUM.

Wainwright, G. 1993. The management of change: archaeology and planning. *Antiquity*, 67, 416–21.

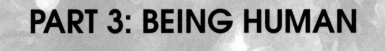

PART 3: BEING HUMAN

CHAPTER 9

ACTS OF GOD AND ACTIVE MATERIAL CULTURE: AGENCY AND COMMITMENT IN THE ANDES

Bill Sillar

INTRODUCTION

A sacrifice or offering is predicated on the assumption that it is part of a two-way process. The people making the sacrifice assume that a rational being will sense the offering, and they hope that in presenting a suitable gift in an acceptable manner they can express thanks for prior benevolence or persuade this being to reciprocate in an appropriate way. In the Andes such offerings have ranged from a few leaves of coca to large sacrifices including the lives of animals and people. In making these offerings Andean people are interacting with the dead, mountain deities, saints and sacred objects and requesting these knowledgable beings to intervene in the world to the benefit of the supplicant. It is relatively easy for a critical observer from outside the culture to see this as the tragic outcome of misguided animistic beliefs. Truly modern rationalist readers may group this with belief in astrology, divine kingship, shamanism, the virgin birth, and life after death, claiming that all of these attribute non-existent powers to non-sentient materials or imagined beings. Most sociologists (following Durkheim, Weber and Marx) would silently assume the falsity of these beliefs and concentrate on assessing how such ritual practices bound the society together, structured the social and economic world, or justified exploitation by a dominant elite. This is also the position adopted by Giddens (1984) who assumes that agency rests solely within the reflexive practice of knowledgable human beings, everything else being part of the structure within which people are socialised and which people's actions continually reproduce and transform. This chapter seeks to question that assumption by using examples from recent ethnographic work, as well as historical and archaeological evidence, to demonstrate the importance of offerings made to ancestors and sacred places in the Andes. This analytical approach could perpetuate the external gaze of the scientific observer capable of identifying who the 'real' human agents are, but I start by assuming that the world is full of agency beyond that of human individuals. Throughout I stress an animistic approach that attributes agency to the landscape and the material world. This approach has major implications for the application of agency theory, particularly within archaeology.

AGENCY AND THE 'SUPERNATURAL'

The majority of people in the world today devote some of their time to interacting with deities, ancestors, sacred places and sacred objects; all these people talk (pray) and make gifts (offerings) to beings that rational science has dismissed as illusory. The specific nature of these beings and the accepted ways of interacting with them vary enormously cross-culturally, and these beliefs are frequently very closely related to the means of subsistence and social organisation of the people concerned. In fact this variety, and the cultural specificity, of religious beliefs has been used as one of the strongest reasons to dismiss them as illusory. Has science not shown us that such religious beliefs and cosmologies are mistakenly attributing human qualities to universal natural forces? Have sociologists not demonstrated that religious ideologies primarily function to perpetuate current social hierarchies and institutions? But, if that is true, then my and your cosmologies are also a product of our social and economic world. Perhaps the beliefs in an animate world populated by ancestors and spirits, beliefs shared by the majority of the human species, are as valid as the egocentric vision of sociology. This article asks you to reconsider one of the central assumptions of sociology, 'the loneliness of being' (the conclusion that Nietzsche came to after proclaiming that 'God is dead', expressing the assumption that humans are the only conscious agents in the world [Hollingdale (ed.) 1977: 202–03]). I ask you to re-populate the world with animate and sentient beings that get involved in people's daily lives, that take an interest in our activities, and that influence the outcome of our actions. Acknowledging these beings requires you to extend any commitments you may already have to your family, friends and community, to include the dead and the animate beings of your surrounding landscape.

For many people this will require a major change in perspective, so let me start by considering a potential example in your own life. You are visiting the grave of your parents or grandparents. Would you walk over it? What is it that stops you? Respect for the dead? Do you really believe that their decomposing body is unaware of your actions, or are you concerned for *their* feelings (even though they are dead)? It could be argued that this is just social conditioning, but you are reacting to a specific place and your knowledge of who is buried there. Perhaps you find this a suitable moment to express some of your frustrations: 'why have you left me to deal with the house?' 'My brother's being so difficult at the moment.' Are you communicating with the dead? If your family has lived here for a few generations then the graveyard probably houses other relatives; while visiting Dad's recent grave you would also see those of his brother and your grandparents; perhaps you are aware of three or four previous generations of the family. Visiting the grave may be a weekly or seasonal activity, combined with going to church, walking the dog or a birthday celebration; particular moments when it seems appropriate to recall the memory of loved ones. This can happen without going to their grave – you may be equally affected by finding your deceased father's coat, favourite cup or photograph. Although we feel affected, we usually explain these as internal processes (seeing and handling the object prompts memories which trigger emotions, all caused by neurons firing in the brain). We are unaccustomed to thinking of this as the dead acting on us. If you did accept that your experiences were the direct effect of the presence of the ancestors then you would begin to see the world very differently and may feel the need to act differently within it. Not just the graveyard, but every house, shop, street, field and hill would be animated by the people who had lived and worked there, though of course this would be very directly related to the specific activities you and they were involved in (while working in the garden you may remember how your mother planted the tree after your sister was born). You may not be aware of all of the individuals from the past, but the collective presence of all those ancestors would surround you every day. In this animated world you can't just live 'off the land', it's no good just adding fertiliser to maximise the yield; you live 'in the world' asking your late mother, the garden soil and the rain to nurture your apple tree and coaxing the ancestors and other animate forces into generosity by the provision of tasty gifts. If you can conceive of yourself as a part of this living, dynamic and interested world then you are approaching something similar to Andean animism. Animism is the belief that aspects of the world, including plants, landscape features and climatic phenomena, are endowed with 'life' or 'spirit', and in the Andean highlands this combines with the active presence of the ancestors to provide an animate world that is shared with living humans (Allen 1988; Cobo 1990 [1653]; MacCormack 1991).

In the first part of this chapter I describe various ways in which people in the Andes have prepared offerings and used these to interact with the ever-present active power of ancestors, animate places and other (super)natural beings. This is used to demonstrate the variety and extent of offerings that Andean people make in order to communicate with the animate world around them. In part 2, I explore the significance of ancestral beings and the making of offerings for a reconsideration of agency within structuration theory and its application within archaeology.

PART 1: ANDEAN ANIMISM AND THE GIVING OF OFFERINGS

Feeding commitments

A good way to begin a discussion of the role of offerings in the Andes is to share a little food and drink! One of the major ways that people express and reproduce strong social bonds is through the giving and receiving of food and drink. Isbell (1977) used the words of one of her informants to describe the people who help to prepare food and drink for a festival, as well as those who participate in the ritual by eating, drinking and making libations to the saints and mountain gods: they are "those who love me". Over a longer period the day-to-day feeding of a child with the food produced by the household incorporates them into the family and can be used to adopt a child. "Those who eat together in the same household share the same flesh in a quite literal sense: they are made of the same stuff" (Weismantel 1993: 10). "Material substances like food are important in the process of changing a foreign child into one's own flesh and blood, but so too is time . . . It is when young Iza's boy has eaten so many meals with the family that his whole body is made of the same flesh as theirs, when he talks and laughs and gestures like the other Iza children, that the bond [of family] will be unquestioned and real" (Weismantel 1993: 11–12). One of the reasons that these foods are so powerful is because the maize and potatoes were grown in the fields of the ancestors (van den Berg 1989), and the meat comes from flocks cared for by the mountain deities (Flores-Ochoa 1979). The pre-Christian ancestors (the *machu*) continue to live in a parallel world and at night they continue to provide *wanu* (fertiliser) and help to cultivate the community's fields, which were once their own (Allen 1988: 56). In some communities potatoes must be peeled because their outer skin is the dried blood of ancestors and to eat it would be a cannibalistic act (Arnold 1988: 454). The food is quite literally the source of kinship and should be treated with care.

In the Andes, the social commitment involved in the repeated giving and receiving of food and drink is extended to communicate with the dead and the deities. Prior to starting many tasks, such as planting a field or making pottery (Fig. 9.1), it is desirable to sit and chew some coca, or make a libation with alcohol, in order to request the relevant deity or spirit's permission and support. These acts express an Andean conception of 'mutual consumption' where only if people feed the dead, the land and the deities can they expect to be fed in return. Swenson (2003: 258) has recently referred to this as a 'consumptive-reproductive dialectic' to emphasise how, in order to consume the bounty of the earth provided by divine forces, the latter need to be nourished by the making of offerings: what Bloch (1992) refers to as the 'consumption of vitality'. In the Andes such offerings may be 'sent' through three major routes: by blowing, pouring or sprinkling the essence (*sami*) of the offering; by burning it in a fire (*dispachu*); or by consuming through the body of a participant through a form of force-feeding (Allen 1982: 191). These same techniques are also reported for the Inka (Cobo 1990 [1653]: 115–17) along with the occasional use of human sacrifices. Gose (1986) suggests that Andean people see the consumption of goods and, at the most generous level, people, as acts of sacrifice that bind the household or the community together. It is in giving these sacrifices to be consumed by the animate mother earth (*Pachamama*), the mountain deities, and miraculous saints, that each household can hope to be fed and nurtured. For instance, many offerings are made to *Tata Pumpuri* (a miraculous image of Santiago/Saint James) on 25 July. The nature of these offerings varies greatly, but various devotees explained to me that the offerings are made because *Tata Pumpuri* is hungry and he may be generous to those who feed him, but if he is not fed, then he may bring disease and misfortune. During the night of 24–25 July, hundreds of devotees sit inside the church of Pumpuri (Northern Potosi, Bolivia) making offerings to Santiago by continually inviting each other to take the cigarettes, coca and alcohol that they have brought and consume them *for Tata Pumpuri*. Santiago is the patron saint of ritual specialists called *curanderos* or *yatiris*, many of whom state that they took up this calling after being struck by lightning sent by Santiago, and on the following day these *curanderos* are asked by devotees who are supplicating Santiago to be cured of some ailment to assist them in making larger offerings. These include the sacrifice of sheep whose necks are cut so that their blood can be collected into two bowls and then thrown onto the tower of the church. The animal is then skinned and jointed, taking care not to break its bones, and the meat is then boiled without

Fig. 9.1: Seq'ueracay, Dept. of Cuzco, Peru: before starting to work, the potter makes a libation (*t'inka*) with sugar cane alcohol on each of the four corners of the stone slab he will use as a support when forming his pottery, thus sending the essence of the drink (*sami*) to the local *Apus*. Prior to starting many tasks, such as agricultural activities, it is desirable to sit and chew some coca, or make a libation, requesting the permission and support of the *Pachamama*, the *Apus* or the saints (© Bill Sillar).

salt. Although the devotees put large amounts of the meat into their mouths they state that they are eating it for *Tata Pumpuri*; for this reason it is not salted or butchered as it would be for a human meal and throwing the blood onto the church tower directs it to the 'true' consumer. Various authors (e.g. Isbell 1985 [1978]; Abercrombie 1986; Allen 1988) stress how this heightened consumption of food and drink is seen as an obligation, because it is by over-consuming that the offering is made. Thus, to refuse to eat or drink is not only to refuse to enter into a debt relationship with the host, but also a refusal to give to the deities. According to Titu Kusi (1985 [1570]: 2, cited in Randall 1987: 165) the worst offence of the Spanish Conquistadors was to have thrown to the ground a drink of chicha (maize beer) offered to them by the Inka Atahuallpa.[1]

Socialising children within an animate world

The material world is animate, and like the ancestors it is sentient and needs feeding. The house is alive and from its inception various offerings are given to the building and the ground on which it stands. The building must be fed and nurtured just as it feeds and nurtures the occupants. "Each house lives because she is formed out of the living earth, ritually enlivened during the *wasichayay* (house-raising) and warmed by the fires of her internal stove, the *q'uncha*" (Allen 1988: 44). In Pumpuri a llama foetus is buried in the foundations with offerings of coca, and *q'uwa* at the four corners. Before constructing the roof, the blood from a sacrificial sheep is splattered on the four corners (*iskina*) of the room, and when the soup is brought in after the roofing, the two servers also splatter some of this on to the four corners. The people who helped to roof it are invited to drink and make copious libations of chicha in paired drinking cups (*turuwasus*), as well as being given food, alcohol and coca (Fig. 9.2; cf. Fig. 9.3). The house should then be danced in for two days and nights. All this serves to animate and feed the house and awaken its spirit, and from this time on the residents continue to make libations to the house spirit (*iskina*) at all major events, and send further libations from a distance when they journey away from the house, for instance on trading trips (Sillar 2000; cf. Abercrombie 1986; Lecoq 1987; Platt 1986; Allen 1988; Arnold 1988).

Children frequently participate in these rituals from an early age, and look forward to them with eager anticipation. For instance, at *Todos Santos* in Pumpuri children help to make the bread figures in the shapes of babies, the sun, and the moon that are placed on the altar for the dead. Similarly Allen (1988) describes the atmosphere surrounding the preparation of a *dispachu*, a burnt offering, in which children commonly participate, as more like the excitement kids usually bring to Christmas morning than the solemnity of a church service. All this leads to knowledge of the rituals, their meaning and intent, as well as an attachment to them and the various entities at which they are directed (the house, the animals, the dead, the fields), so that early adulthood involves taking on the obligation to make ritual offerings prior to many activities. Young women who wish to improve their weaving skills sometimes visit shrines dedicated to the Virgin (the patron of weavers) to pray for help in the craft. For instance, at the chapel of the Virgin in Arani (Cochabamba, Bolivia), on the night of 23 August, hundreds of

Fig. 9.2: Pumpuri, Dept. of Potosi, Bolivia: drinking chicha from a pair of *turuwasus* during a house-roofing ceremony. *Turuwasus* are named after the pairs of carved wooden bulls that appear within the chicha as it is being drunk, recalling how people and animals first emerged out of their origin places of lakes and caves. *Turuwasus* are usually used in pairs, apart from during *Todos Santos* when participants are drinking with the dead. By pouring a small libation on the ground and naming the recipient before he starts to drink, chicha forms one of the major routes of communication between the living people and the animated world of the dead and deities around them (© Bill Sillar).

miniature weavings are pinned to the hem of the Virgin's dress and scattered around her feet. I was told that these were made by *imillas* (young, unmarried women) who were asking the Virgin's help in gaining proficiency in these skills (cf. Allen 1988: 196).

In Raqchi, Dept. of Cuzco, Peru, the *k'intuqwi* offering is made on the night of San Luis (24/25 August) when household members chew coca, and make libations over a ritual cloth. Next to this cloth are placed the *illas*, carved figures or just pebbles that represent animals, houses, or crop plants (Fig. 9.4). These are living beings that come as gifts (indeed the children) of the mountain deities (*Apus*) and must be protected so that they can be looked after by each generation (cf. Flores-Ochoa 1976; Isbell 1977: 105). *Illas* are a source of life and productivity and during rituals they are said to be drinking the chicha and chewing the coca that they are given in the offerings (Allen 1988: 54, 150). The offering consists of carefully preparing each *k'intu* of three coca leaves and blowing the essence to a variety of entities. The naming of offering recipients starts with the house, hearth

Fig. 9.3: Early colonial drawing by the indigenous writer Guamán Poma de Ayala (1988 (1584–1615): 248). The caption is titled 'Iuni, Havca Cvsvi' (June festival for the end of the harvest). The text at the feet of the Inka reads 'Veve con el sol en la fiesta del sol' (drinking with the sun during the festival of the sun – IntiRaymi). Guamán Poma uses the European convention of a devil figure taking the Inka's second drinking vessel up for the sun to drink from.

and stores, and the family members themselves both living and dead. Each field worked by the family and each bit of pasture land or path used by their animals is named, and the clay mines, roads and market places that the household members commonly visit – all to do with the productivity of the household. One person, almost always a male, performs this ritual, blowing the invocations over each *k'intu* of three coca leaves before placing them onto the cloth or paper. But other

Fig. 9.4: Raqchi, Dept. of Cuzco, Peru: preparing a *k'intuqwi* offering (24 August 1995). The man is placing a *k'intu* (three coca leaves) onto a piece of white paper which already has maize kernels, carnation petals, llama fat and lead images on it. The miniatures (*illas*) are positioned on the ritual cloth in front of the man, next to two small bottles of sugar cane alcohol and wine and a little jug of chicha. His wife is helping to select coca leaves and helps by chewing coca and making libations as well as reminding her husband of fields, places and people that he might forget. The essence of each *k'intu* (a group of three coca leaves) is directed at important entities of the household. After preparing the offering (which takes between two and three hours) the bundles of coca leaves are taken into the household patio or one of the household's fields to be consumed in a fire (© Bill Sillar).

household members, including children, also participate by selecting coca leaves for the offering, and older members chew their coca, and make libations (*t'inka*). Once they are prepared, one of the bundles of coca leaves is taken into the household patio to be burnt and the other is taken to one of the household's main fields to be consumed in a fire. The household's *illas* are then carefully stored away until the next offering needs to be prepared.

The ritual importance of miniatures is, I believe, partly drawn from their association with children and play (Sillar 1996). Just as children learn their skills as a gift from the saints or mountain deities (*Apus*), in rituals, playing is appropriated as a way for people to communicate and make gifts to the deities (Figs. 9.5, 9.6), and the *illas* are even seen as the children of the *Apu*. Thus miniature pots and animal figures have become a part of the language with which people communicate with the supernatural, and through which they can petition for help and assistance. A miniature can be used as an offering or sacrifice, but it

Fig. 9.5: Pebble houses at Calvario above the shrine of el Señor de Huanca, 14 September 1995 (Dept. of Cuzco, Peru). Miniature houses are built out of pebbles at many shrines and mountain passes as offerings to the mountains and miraculous saints. Small twigs represent trees and some pebble animals are put in their corral. Increasingly, two-storeyed constructions are made with television aerials and garages. These houses are both a gift to the miraculous shrine and indicate a request for a similar (full scale) house and herd of animals of the devotee's own (© Bill Sillar).

can also be the vehicle that transfers offerings from people to the *Apus* and which brings fecundity back from the *Apus* to the herds.

Reciprocity with the animate earth

The exploitation of the earth's resources (such as soil, stone, clay, salt, gold, silver, copper, and tin) form an important part of the 'Andean moral economy' (Sallnow 1989). Sallnow used this term because the 'value' of such minerals and the 'cost' of their extraction can't simply be measured in terms of energy expenditure, because their extraction is conceived of as the removal of a material that belongs to the mountain gods (the *Apus* and *Wamani*). "Typically, these notions cast gold mining as an illicit, amoral and ritually dangerous activity, in which the successful prospector may well pay for his new-found wealth with his life" (Sallnow 1989: 209). The mountain gods 'own' the flocks of grazing animals and the mineral wealth, and *Pachamama* 'owns' the earth and the crops that grow from it. People may take from these resources but in return they must feed the ancestors, the animate earth and the deities with offerings; the earth does not bear fruit without such offerings (van den Berg 1989, 1990). "The fertility which the *Apus* and the

Fig. 9.6: Devotees at the shrine of el Señor de Huanca, Dept. of Cuzco, Peru: 14 September 1995. Devotees use the wax from candles to signal requests from the miraculous image of Christ; wax images of houses, trucks, children and animals can be seen on the wall. The shrine of el Señor de Huanca is located at the base of the Inka *huaca* and present day *Apu*, Mount Pachatusan. Christ first appeared in a miraculous apparition in 1674 when a vision of Christ's scourging was seen, and in 1718 Christ appeared as a doctor to cure a Spanish mine owner inflicted by an epidemic (Sallnow 1987) (© Bill Sillar).

Pachamama bestow on the soil and the protection they extend to humans and livestock are conditional, given only in return for periodic offerings" (Sallnow 1989: 211). In the case of mining, these ideas are best illustrated by Nash's (1979) study of the tin miners of Oruro, who make a daily offering to *Tío* (the spirit owner of the mine) consisting of coca, alcohol and cigarettes, and sacrifice llamas at major festivals (cf. Figs. 9.7, 9.8). Nash discusses how these rituals became a major focus for the development of strong militant political action by the miners.

Hernández Príncipe's account of 1622 described the offerings made prior to the Spanish Conquest by Olleros, the fourth sub-*ayllu* of Recuay, that consisted of two groups of potters from different regions, who were settled there by the Inkas. The people of Olleros worshipped the deity *Huari* in underground caverns, and each year they made two *capac huchas* (human sacrifices) of children who were sealed into deep shaft tombs. This offering was explicitly made to ensure good clay for their pottery (Zuidema 1989: 130–35, 149–50). All these areas of productivity, and extraction from the earth, are only possible through the generosity of the earth and mountain deities, and unless the deities are fed with offerings they will stop feeding the people (Fig. 9.9). This also has implications for people who are 'over' productive. Someone who is the benefactor of profuse production (of their crops, herds, or mining) could only achieve this through a 'special relationship' with the deities, and, because the deities are ambivalent rather than benign, this is a dangerous relationship that may earn the benefactor respect, but which may also be a source of fear and danger to the rest of the community. The only way to justify abundant production is through abundant consumption. Those who produce well are under strong social sanction to contribute most to community festivals (which are also a form of offering to the deities) by taking on the saint's *cargos*. This could be seen as an aspect of Foster's (1965) suggestion that peasants have an image of 'limited good' which reduces their drive for innovation, investment and expansion. However, this can also be seen as a strategy of investing the benefits of accumulated wealth in developing and extending social relations with living people and the animate world of ancestors and (super)natural beings, effectively building on the household's social capital and commitments (as a compliment to their increased stores or financial capital).

Hernández Príncipe (see Silverblatt 1987: 94–101) also described how the leader of the village of Ocros, Caque Poma, and his people constructed an irrigation canal with the help of other neighbouring villages. Because of this, the Inka elevated him to the position of *curaca* (mayor) over the other villages, and allowed him to sacrifice his own daughter in the *Capacocha* for the Sun deity. The *Capacocha* is an important ritual, where young boys and girls were sacrificed to various deities of the empire in order to bind the deity, the Inka and the local population into a system of reciprocal obligations. Some of these children were sacrificed in the Inka capital of Cuzco while many others helped to articulate Cuzco's relationship with the rest of the empire as the provinces sent designated children to be received and feted in Cuzco before returning to their home province where they were sacrificed (Duviols 1976). Caque Poma and his daughter went to Cuzco in a pilgrimage of homage to the Inka rulers, giving reverence to the gods of the Inkas, the Sun and Lightning and to the mummies of the royal dynasty; she then returned to her own community to be sacrificed. Here Hernández Príncipe

Fig. 9.7: Inside a mine, Potosi, Dept. of Potosi, Bolivia. A clay image of *El Tio* (the supernatural owner of the mine) is surrounded by offerings of coca, alcohol and cigarettes made by the miners before they start work each day (© Bill Sillar).

Fig. 9.8: Anonymous 17th century painting of the mountain of Potosi as the Virgin Mary, in the collection of the Museo Casa de la Moneda, Potosi, Bolivia. The Mountain Mary is being crowned by the Holy Trinity, with Pope Paul III and Charles V of Spain depicted on either side of the globe. The church undoubtedly sanctioned this sincretic image in its attempts to explain and make relevant Christian doctrine to Andean people and to reclaim some of the power attributed to the animate landscape of the Andes. In 1599, Padre José de Arriaga had written complaining about the idolatrous practices of the Indians in Potosi, because since time immemorial they had expressed an extraordinary devotion to two mountains through the making of offerings and sacrifices and by consulting the demon of the mountain about their doubts (Gisbert 1994: 19–20) (© Bill Sillar).

Fig. 9.9: Illustration from Guamán Poma (1988 [1584–1615]:
274). The caption is titled 'Idolos I Vacas de los Condesvios'
(Idols and *huacas* of the province of Contisuyu), with the
huaca, shrine or sacred place, of Corpona shown on the
left of the drawing and two kneeling supplicants giving a
child and an animal as offerings. In the page of text
accompanying this, Guamán Poma lists the various *huacas*
in the province of Contisuyu and the offerings made
including gold, silver, 12-year-old children, exotic feathers,
coca, spondyllus shells, blood and meat, stating that to this
day people continue to eat blood and crude meat in such rituals.

reports the final words of the girl: "Finish now with me, for the celebrations which
were made in my honour in Cuzco were more than enough" (Silverblatt 1987: 98);
then she was lowered into a shaft tomb to be walled-in alive. This tomb was dug
into the top of the mountain where the storehouses (*collcas*) for the produce of the
newly irrigated lands were. In time the sacrificed daughter herself became one of
the most venerated *huacas* (local deities) of her region. As a woman, sacrificed to
the Sun, and connected to the irrigation and production of the land, it is not
surprising that she embodied the forces of fertility and her powers were related to
maize production and health. But her sacrifice had also played an important role

in the promotion of her family. Not only was Caque Poma raised to the elevated status of *curaca* but, because he had shown his family's willingness to be subject to Cuzco, the Inkas continued to promote subsequent *curacas* for the area from his family. Because of this, Caque Poma's own mummy was venerated as the most important ancestral figure. The tomb that had been dedicated to him was destroyed by Hernández Príncipe who reports finding Caque Poma in the centre with the mummies of his ancestors and descendants on either side (Zuidema 1989: 126).

Among the sacred places that received human sacrifices, the low hill of Huanacaure near Cuzco was the cult centre for one of the Inka's own ancestors and the children sacrificed here were from the Inka's own lineage (Pedro Cieza de León (1554) cited in MacCormack 1991: 105, 199). Huanacaure is a hill just outside Cuzco which was greatly revered because it was a focal point in an origin myth which described how the four founding Inka brothers and sisters came out of a cave at Pacariqtambo and climbed the hill of Huanacaure. The second brother, Ayar Uchu, was turned to stone on this hill-top and in the process he became the major *huaca* (cult object) of the Inka priests. This hill became an important centre for Inka ritual, including the offering of human sacrifice, and at no time was this more important than for the initiation rights of the Inka nobles celebrated during the major annual festival of Capac Raymi, lasting from November into December. Cobo (1990 [1653]: 74) reported the Spanish destruction of this site which, he commented, was "among the most important shrines of the whole kingdom". "After the Spanish arrived, they removed a great quantity of gold and silver from this shrine but paid no attention to the idol [of Huanacaure], because it was, as I have said, a rough stone."

The living dead

In Pumpuri, Northern Potosi, Bolivia, 1 November is referred to as *Uchu*, meaning hot or spicy, after a series of dishes that contain spiced hot chilli peppers that are prepared for the dead on this day when the soul (*alma*) of the dead person will return to their old house (Fig. 9.10). In the household with whom I spent the night of *Todos Santos* in 1991 (Sillar 2000: 120–23), the father had died slightly less than a year before and his son presided over the room into which guests were invited. A *tumba* (a structure of two to four steps covered in a black cloth) was set up in what was normally the storeroom of the deceased's house and a large human figure made of bread (*tanta wawa*) was put onto the top level with the initials of the deceased on it. On entering the house compound each person was invited to say a prayer standing bareheaded by the *tumba* and to make a libation of some chicha onto the base of the *tumba* before drinking to (and with) the deceased. When participants had sat down they were given more alcohol and coca by the host, and each time this was given out some was always placed on the *tumba* for the deceased, as were portions of the food that was also served to visitors. In the evening we went round to the field behind the house (to face west, in the direction where the sun was going down). Embers from the cooking hearth were taken on a large sherd to start a small fire in the field, which we circled three times before throwing a half-full plastic bucket of chicha to the west, to the *alma* of the deceased

Fig. 9.10: Pumpuri, Dept. of Potosi, Bolivia, night of 1 November 1990. A relatively simple *tumba* or *misa* placed in the storeroom of a house, awaiting the return of the soul (*alma or angelita*) of a one year old child who had died two years previously. This offering of food for the dead includes sacks of toasted maize and beans, bread babies (*t'anta wawas*), plates of *uchu*, *ch'uñu* and egg, also cups of chicha, wine and alcohol, coca leaves and a small hunk of roasted meat (*kanka*) (© Bill Sillar).

to welcome him home. We then returned to the house and another fire was started in the centre of the patio which we circled three times saying '*saludo*' to the *alma* that had just arrived, while passing a single large gourd round from which everyone drank some chicha.

The second day (*Dispachu*, 2 November) is spent visiting the graves in the cemetery, when most community members go to the cemetery and visit each grave where they recite three prayers each for the deceased (Fig. 9.11). Adults are then given some chicha or alcohol with which to make a libation, and occasionally some coca to chew, and everybody is given toasted beans and maize (*habas jank'a* and *sara jank'a*) or bread from the *tumba*. All the food must be eaten since it has been prepared for the dead and the living are eating it on their behalf.

Much of the next week is then spent visiting households in the area and participating in what is both sociable and ritual drinking using ritual drinking vessels. The form and decoration of these drinking vessels (which express strong ideological concepts) help to direct this communication. Similarly, Sterner (1989) comments that the majority of the symbolic messaging, expressed by the form and the decoration of the African pottery she studied, was directed at the spirit world. In the celebration of *Todos Santos*, food and drink is the essential medium of

Fig. 9.11: Pumpuri, Dept. of Potosi, Bolivia, evening of 2 November 1990. The men are starting to dismantle a *tumba*, the temporary structure built over the grave of the deceased on which jars of chicha and bottles of alcohol, as well as sacks of toasted beans, toasted maize and bread are placed. These food offerings are given to the many adults and children who come to the graveyard to recite prayers for the dead and welcome them back to the community. A large *t'anta wawa* (bread baby) can be seen on the upper-level of the *tumba* that is being dismantled (© Bill Sillar).

communication between the living and the dead. The provision of this food and drink is a duty of the living, and they invite others to feast with their dead and welcome them home. *Todos Santos* is a festival of renewal and fertility at the start of the growing season (cf. Harris 1982; Van den Berg 1989; Rösing 1991). During the prayers in the cemetery the dead are requested to make the crops grow. Rain falling at the beginning of November is said to be the tears of the *angelitus* (dead children) as they return (Andrew Orta pers. comm.). Feeding the dead, drinking copious amounts of chicha and playing music are all directed towards the bringing of the rains (Stobart 1995), and many of the libations made on the following days are for *Virjiña/Pachamama* to protect and nurture the crops.

Within Inka society the actual bodies of the dead played an active role in society (Fig. 9.12). It is clear that the Inka elite (possibly unlike many earlier and contemporary Andean cultures) put a particular focus on creating and maintaining the memory of deceased individuals through the recitation of life histories and various personifications of the Inka in the form of mummies, bundles that incorporated hair and nail clippings of the deceased and stone or metal images referred to as *huauque*, or brothers, who sometimes replaced or acted for the Inka while they were still alive (Kaulicke 2000). When one of the ruling Inka died, his estate remained the property of the deceased and was administered

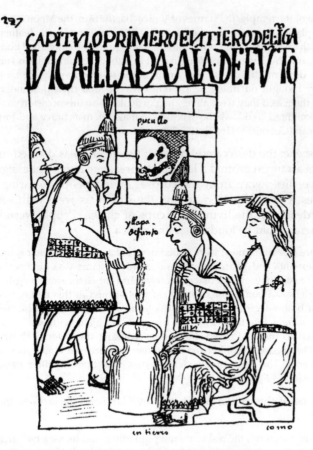

Fig. 9.12: Illustration from Guamán Poma (1988 (1584–1615): 289). The caption reads 'Capítulo Primero, Entiero del Inga/Inca Illapa Aia Defunto' (First chapter, The Inka *illapa*/his dead corpse). The Inka ruler's mummy is referred to as *illapa*, lightning, possibly expressing his role as communicator between the living and the sacred sky deities. The living Inka is seen holding two cups of chicha, and is pouring one into the jar located in front of the mummies of the dead Inka and his wife; behind them is a funeral tower (*pucullo*) with the bones of ancestors inside it. Guamán Poma elaborates upon this in his description of the month of November as *Aya Marcay quilla* (month of carrying the dead). "In this month they take out the dead from their tombs that they call *pucullo* and they give them (food) to eat and (chicha) to drink and they dress them in their richest clothes and put feathers on their head and sing and dance with them" (Guamán Poma 1988 (1584–1615): 259, author's translation).

by his family (*panaca*) who would use it especially to provide the necessary food, drink, and clothes etc. for the frequent ceremonies and rituals in the Inka capital (Cobo 1990 [1653]: 39–43). At these the mummified bodies of the dead Inkas were brought into the main square and, through the intermediaries of the deceased's living family and retinue, the dead Inka (*mallki*) could offer drink to the living Inka ruler and other lords incorporated into the Inka empire as well as the mummies of the other dead Inkas and the statues of deities.

In the Plaza of the temple, the statues of Viracocha, the Sun, the Moon, and Thunder would be placed on some low benches that were adorned with feathers. Those charged with this duty would bring into the said square the embalmed bodies of the dead lords, and this [custom] of bringing out in public the said idols and embalmed bodies was done on this day as well on all of the solemn days of the months. The reason they brought out these dead bodies was so that their descendants could drink with them as if they were alive, and particularly on this occasion so that those who were knighted could ask the deceased to make them as brave and fortunate as they had been (Cobo 1990 [1653]: 127–28).

Imagine the scene: the desiccated bodies of the dead Inkas dressed in their most ornate clothes arranged around a large open area, one attendant assigned to each body to wave flies away from the corpse. Living people wearing somewhat similar clothes would be seated around the square as well, with servers going between the dead and the living with cups of chicha. People would be getting drunk and there would be loud music and dance.

In the square [the mummies] were seated in a row according to their seniority, and there the servants and guardians ate and drank. A flame was kindled before the deceased of a certain firewood that was carved and cut all the same length. The food set before the dead bodies for them to eat was burned in this flame. Also placed before these bodies were large tumblers made of gold and silver, like pitchers, which were called *vilques*. Into these tumblers they put the chicha with which they would drink a toast to their deceased, but before drinking they would show it to the deceased. The deceased would toast each other; the deceased would toast the living and vice versa. The toast of the dead bodies was done in their name by the attendants (Cobo 1990 [1653]: 40).

The importance of this is clarified for us by Garcilaso de la Vega (see Figs. 9.3, 9.12):

Then the king stood up, the rest remaining squatting, and he took two great golden vessels which they call *aquilla*, full of the beverage they drink. He performed this rite in the name of his father, the Sun, as his first-born, and invited him to drink with the vessel in his right hand. This the Sun was supposed to do, and the Inka invited all his kinsmen to drink too. This custom of inviting one and another to drink was the greatest and most usual demonstration of condescension on the part of the superior toward his inferior, and of the friendship of friends for one another. After the invitation to drink the Inka poured the contents of the vessel in his right hand, which was dedicated to the Sun, into a gold basin, and from the basin it flowed along a beautifully made stone-work channel which ran from the square to the house of the Sun. It was thus as if the Sun had drunk the liquid. From the vessel in his left hand the Inka swallowed a draught, which was his portion, and then shared what was left among the other Inkas, giving each of them a little in a small bowl of silver or gold which was ready to receive it (Garcilaso de la Vega 1989 [1612]: 358–59).

History, power and a changing relationship with the gods

The way in which people engage with the wider community of non-human beings changes through their life, from the play of children, through the learning of skills (including the making of offerings), taking on the roles of household head or community leader, and the transformations that take place during and after death. But the succession of changes in any one individual's engagement with these animate beings varies greatly, depending on the historical circumstances, the social and economic position of the person making the offering, their skill in preparing and performing the ritual, and which local and regional forces/deities they engage with. I do not wish to suggest an unchanging essentialism within the practice of Andean animism. I have compared and contrasted modern examples of offerings with examples recorded in the early historical literature describing comparable offerings at the elite level of Inka society. There are significant issues of power-politics that are maintained and manipulated during these rituals and their explanation. Religion and ritual are almost by definition areas of unequal knowledge where power and the ability to act lie with those who claim access to restricted knowledge and skills, and they play an important part in promoting, transforming and challenging political hierarchies and socio-economic change. Recent work on Moche archaeology clearly demonstrates a strongly hierarchised society where ritual offerings, including human sacrifice, appear to have played a significant role in expressing elite authority (Alva 2001; Swenson 2003). It is becoming increasingly clear that the final phase of Moche 4, during which the large-scale sacrifices at Huaca de la Luna took place at the time of a major el Niño event (Bourget 2001), saw a major change in political structure with a renewed focus on the deities, particularly marine creatures, rather than the elite religious functionaries in the iconography (Castillo 2001; Donnan 2003).

The relationship with the landscape also changes over time. During the Moche period our evidence for sacrifice and offerings is largely located within major ceremonial centres such as Huaca de la Luna, but during the *capacocha* ritual, children were sacrificed on the high peaks of the Andean mountain tops, suggesting an audacious engagement with these entities as the Inka drew upon the power of the great mountain deities, the sun and the moon to integrate the empire (Reinhard 1992, 1996). The Inka state's religious infrastructure and its focus on the sun and the moon collapsed in the generation following the Spanish conquest, but the Spanish were horrified by the *Toqui Onqoy* movement where adherents forsook the Christian training offered by the Spanish and called upon the ancient pre-Inka *huacas* to rise up again and thwart the Christian gods and kill the European colonisers. "The huacas were walking about in the air, dried out and starving, because the Indians were not feeding them or pouring chicha." "Now the *huacas* did not enter rocks or clouds or springs in order to speak, but instead embodied themselves in the Indians and made them speak. And [they ordered the Indians] to keep their houses swept and in readiness in case one of the *huacas* desired to seek shelter there" (both quotations from Molina [1573] cited and translated by MacCormack 1991: 182–83). In more modern contexts Peter Gose (1994) has argued that Andean cosmologies and particularly the praxis of ritual offerings are central to the understanding and negotiation of class relations in Peru, where the rich landholders may occupy a privileged position, but are equally bound by the capricious reciprocity of sacrifice. One example Gose cites is Platt's (1983) analysis of how the Macha captured their local *haciendado* in the Chayanta uprising of 1927. The *haciendado* was killed, his flesh was devoured by the campesinos and his bones were offered to their most important mountain (much as I have described the sheep sacrifice made to Tata Pumpuri, some 30 km away) as "the haciendado no longer enjoyed the mountain's backing; hence he should be returned to it as an offering" (Gose 1994: 241). There can be no doubt that religious beliefs in the Andes have been a major focus for social and political change; these animistic beliefs have given motivation and purpose to help direct people's actions and any consideration of agency in the Andes must acknowledge the powerful force that these beliefs have had in maintaining and transforming Andean society.

PART 2: THEORISING NON-HUMAN AGENCY AND COMMITMENT

There is little doubting the depth of commitment that many Andean people have to non-human agency, the wide variety of forms that such animate forces take and the wide range of methods used to communicate with and feed these beings. These people do not suffer from 'the loneliness of being'. In attributing active power to objects, ancestors and the landscape they reject the modernist split between dynamic knowledgable people and an inanimate un-motivated material world. People show their commitment to these entities through the making of offerings, often through frequent activities such as chewing coca, walking, drinking and eating, although the scale and elaboration of the ritual performance of these offerings may become heightened at particular moments. It would be a mistake to separate these offerings from other forms of reciprocity. People's relationships with the animate world are social and economic; agriculture, mining, construction work, and storage each involve bringing together groups of people to engage with the animate world – they are each essential quotidian and ritual activities at one and the same time. For many highland Andean people, their ability to survive depends on maintaining good active reciprocal relationships with other members of the community including the animate powers of the Andean world. Each offering provides a further demonstration of their continuing commitment to the mountains, fields, houses and ancestors they depend on for their livelihood.

In the second half of this chapter I wish to reconsider Giddens' (1984) concept of agency in relation to these Andean perspectives. How should a consideration of these beliefs in the animate powers of the Andean world affect the concept of agency put forward in structuration theory? I argue that Giddens' ideas were largely constructed from the viewpoint of 20th century Western modernity, and, as is common with most sociology, it is only able to deal with people's religious beliefs by dismissing the supernatural focus of these rituals as illusory and concentrating on the social and economic function of the religious practices. In fact many sceptical readers will wish to point out that the mere fact that some people in the Andes think that mountains are living entities, and that *people* make offerings, does not mean that the mountains really have power to act knowledgably and transform the world. I must admit to my own difficulties in formulating a response to this point. When I am sitting in my office in London writing, I too am sceptical about the truth of these claims, even though I can remember being fully involved and emotionally engaged in making libations to my dead father when in Pumpuri, and I have prepared *k'intus* in Raqchi, blowing the essence of the coca leaves to protect my family and my home in the UK. Actions and beliefs that are meaningful and appropriate within the practical and emotional context of living with a family in the Andes, or even during a conversation in London, become difficult to express and justify within the logic of a Western scientific rationale. The use of linear argument and the rigorous questioning of evidence that is central to academic writing starts by assuming nothing beyond the physicality of the material world and the society of human beings, and fails to find proof for anything as socially-involved as a mountain deity or as knowledgable as the patron saint of weaving, whereas for many people around the world their engagement with the physical world allows them to experience it as animate, and they do not feel the need for any proof beyond this experiential level. This is the fundamental problem presented when considering apparently incompatible explanations for the world and our place in it. While such ontological relativism presents an insoluble predicament in philosophy, it seems to be easily accommodated within people's lives and daily practice. On a day-to-day basis it is usually more important to say and do appropriate things that are meaningful within a specific social or ritual context but, unlike an academic article, we are not necessarily judged by the overall coherence of these activities or the logical progression of our lives. One of the reasons that it is impossible to disprove most religious beliefs to the satisfaction of believers is precisely because many believers find it perfectly acceptable to change the basis of their explanation in relation to the circumstance.

Given the slippery logic and fundamentally different assumption underlying many religious beliefs it is not surprising that most sociological analysis adopts a 'pragmatic' approach that does not try to judge the truth or rationale of the religious beliefs, but prefers to concentrate on looking at the social and economic effects of ritual practice. So, even if you do not believe in the active role of ancestors, mountains and animate objects, then it must be accepted that these beliefs form a major part of the cosmological structure, and shape the material actions, of billions of people. However, if we ignore the religious commitment and focus our analysis on how ritual practices were used to structure and justify inequality or contributed to the economic organisation, it is very easy to assume that the purpose of these actions was primarily social aggrandisement and wealth creation when this represents only one aspect of the motivation behind people's actions (cf. Tarlow 1999: 23–24). There is a need for our theoretical constructs to handle the all-pervading way in which religious beliefs and cosmologies shape people's lives in a more sensitive way than simply dismissing them as false consciousness. What are we looking for when we seek to interpret 'agency' through an analysis of archaeological materials? Firstly, let me assure readers that I am not suggesting that we should be trying to identify archaeological evidence for the existence of the gods. However, I hope that the foregoing discussion has convinced you that many people do not see individual human agency as the only creative and active force in the world. This should help us to realise that Giddens' formulation of structuration theory is very culturally-specific and that we need to be somewhat more wide-ranging in our consideration of agency when studying other times and other cultures. The concept of the 'individual' is significantly altered when each person is composed out of ancestral foods, and when you know that putting food into your mouth can feed the dead and the saints. The definition of the self is very different when you know that you will continue to inhabit the world after you stop breathing. Your aims and intentions are greatly affected when you are concerned about how mountains and ancestors perceive your actions, even though you are alone on the hillside. Your social, economic and political organisations are structured differently when they incorporate mummies, stone deities and astral bodies as knowledgable, rich and powerful beings within your social hierarchy.

Sociology and the analysis of religion

Human beings seem to have an inherent desire to understand and explain the world that surrounds them; it is perhaps for this reason that Linnaeus classified us as *homo sapiens* – the only species defined as 'sapient', wise or knowledgable. Human actions are rationally determined after thought and reflection (unlike animals that behave instinctively, or plants and minerals that merely respond to specific physical conditions). This perspective is not just the product of scientific study and Enlightenment philosophy; it has become a tenet of much recent Christianity. Christianity and Judaism claim that God made man in his own image, that people were given dominion over all animals and plants, and that God liberated people from his control by giving them self-will and the ability to choose within their knowledge of good and evil. People become the only knowledgable and moral actors who have control over the world they live in. Modern Christianity has gone to some lengths to explain why an omnipotent God does not intervene for the clear benefit of his devotees. This means that a Christian can also be a scientist, able and willing to study the laws of nature without any expectation of finding direct evidence of God's active participation. In many ways the 'Enlightenment project' succeeded by narrowing down the parameters within which it was acceptable to analyse and explain the world. The aim of much scientific analysis appears to be to reduce the vast complexity of the world to a small number of universal laws and processes. Although evolutionary biology starts from the premise that *homo sapiens* are just another animal species, we have developed different disciplines to study and explain the natural and material world from the study of the social world of the human animal. Giddens' agency theory assumes that we are studying how knowledgable individuals act within the society created by human beings and the inanimate physical resource that is the rest of the world. This is a very 'modern' ideological construct, one that patronises and perpetuates our self-centred assumption that humans are the only autonomous subjects. It is the ideal vision for a liberal, democratic capitalism that removes the will of God and replaces it by putting the self-will of the human individual at the centre of creation. It is almost the exact opposite of some Andean concepts that consider the saints and mountain deities as the source of knowledge which people may acquire as individual skills, but only through the personal commitment of visiting springs and pilgrimage sites and the making of suitable offerings (cf. Stobart 2003).

For most social theorists the idea of mountains or ancestors as active agents that intervene in the social world of human beings would be considered as a false consciousness, a masking ideology that projects the human condition of social relations onto the objects of the material world and attributes social organisation to the mythical activities of gods (Feuerbach's alienation). Marx (1970 [1864]) stated that religion mainly served to justify the interests of the ruling group; Durkheim (1976 [1912]) discussed how religious ceremonies and rituals functioned to bind groups together; and Weber (1976 [1904]) identified how specific religious beliefs helped to direct social and economic change.

How do we define other people's religious beliefs; how do we discriminate between their beliefs and other areas of knowledge? One tendency is to study the society and describe all the practical activities, separating out those bits of their cosmology and behaviour that we can't accept as rational or necessary and calling them religious 'beliefs' and 'rituals'. Tylor's (1913) original description of animism adopts this approach by referring to it as the tendency to attribute supernatural characteristics to natural phenomena. But, as Evans-Pritchard (1965) pointed out, it is mainly our overconfident scientific approach that permits us to decide what are rational and what are irrational beliefs, or discriminate between natural and supernatural forces:

> [M]any people are convinced that deaths are caused by witchcraft. To speak of witchcraft being for these peoples a supernatural agency hardly reflects their own view of the matter, since from their point of view nothing could be more natural (Evans Pritchard 1965: 109).

In the Andean highlands it is also meaningless to separate the natural mountain from the mountain deity, and as we have seen, people's subsistence activities take place within the moral economy of their relationship with these *Apus*. This was part of the reason for developing the cultural relativism approach championed by Franz Boas, which aimed to study each society as a unique product of their particular circumstances and evaluate and explain the culture in terms of its own values in order to avoid judging it from the perspective of our own beliefs and values. Sociology, and Giddens' structuration theory in particular, seems to have been more arrogant in taking certain core values, such as the inanimate nature of the material world, for granted.

One of the reasons why many analysts have assumed that religious beliefs are illusory is because the specific beliefs are frequently intimately related to the modes of subsistence and social organisation of the practitioner (with totemism and shamanism more associated with hunter-gatherers, and monotheistic religions being dominant in larger scale urban societies). Many sociologists assumed that because such beliefs vary in relation to economic and political structures they are illusory social constructs. However, this assumption of a direct link between specific forms of belief and socio-economic contexts is in part a product of anthropology's early desire to classify and simplify the world. Such approaches to religion partly originate in Tylor's (1913) evolutionary assumption that animism was an aspect of primitive religion destined for extinction, but animism, ancestor worship and spiritualism continue to be practiced alongside, and within, major religions such as Christianity, Islam and Science. The coca offerings and feeding of the dead described at the start of this chapter were made by practicing Christians who are active participants within 21st century capitalism. A sociologist might look at ancestor worship and a belief in the *Apus* and see them as ideological constructs expressing aspects of the social organisation of a small-scale agricultural society. But, many Andean people would say that this was largely due to the analyst's lack of intimacy with the ancestors and the land that the Andean farmer experiences as an animate world in which diverse non-human beings take a critical interest in what people are doing. They would find it perverse for everyone to share the same ritual focus, or make the same offerings. For them it is entirely logical that an urban shop proprietor will prepare different offerings to a farmer, truck drivers will take their vehicle to specific pilgrimage sites to have it blessed, bankers will want to sponsor the most prestigious saint's *cargo* in the city, and the president of Peru will go to Machu Pichu to request the assistance of all the *Apus* during his inauguration. These differences are considered appropriate expressions of people's personal engagement with the specific animate forces that most directly influence their activities and their social status. As archaeologists and heritage managers around the world have had to acknowledge, many of the archaeological sites and 'beauty spots' they wish to preserve and display are sacred places which are recognised and used by different people (stakeholders) in different ways, and we need to accommodate this range of beliefs rather than enforcing a singular view of the place's significance (Anyon and Ferguson 1995; McBryde 1997; Ucko 2000). Native Americans and Aboriginal Australians have been particularly proactive in forcing archaeologists to give greater weight to their indigenous beliefs and value systems, as Whitedeer (1997: 42) has argued: "archaeologists must allow sacred considerations to influence its practice."

Material agents and structuring structures

The central tenet of structuration theory is that individual people are competent agents who act knowledgably in the world. The materiality of this 'world' is barely mentioned. The 'structure' usually refers to social structures such as politics, economics and religion, with some consideration given to manufacture and consumption, but there is little discussion of the climate, topography, flora and fauna within which people act. It is through the material acts of walking, planting, herding, building, making and consuming that the social structures of politics, economics and religion are reproduced and transformed. It is through the varied ways in which people act within the environment (the animate world) that the social comes into being. In a recent article critically evaluating the benefits of using structuration theory within archaeology, Barrett (2001) has commented on the need to incorporate the active role of material culture into this theory. In one section he gives a favourable interpretation of Giddens: "we rely upon clues to guide our actions, finding a familiarity and security by recognizing our place in the world, and to this extent material conditions can be regarded as 'both medium and outcome of the practices they recursively organise' [Giddens 1984: 25]. Material conditions are therefore an active component of the structural properties of the social system" (Barrett 2001: 152). However, it is Barrett who sees the material world as 'active'; Giddens' own work seems to suggest that he sees these material conditions as the setting for people's actions – what he might term the 'resources' – but he gives little evidence that he would consider it as the active agent that causes reproduction or change. Also this seems a very urban and middle-class vision of the 'material conditions'; many people living in the harsh landscape of the Andean altiplano do not consider this as being 'organised' by their practice, they consider the Andean landscape to be capricious and more in control of them than vice versa. To a large extent structuration theory has been fine-tuned for the complexities of the high density world of media-driven industrial capitalism. Does it need to be reconsidered in relation to distinctive environments and cultures?

Schiffer (1999) has recently emphasised how human life consists of ceaseless and varied interactions among people and myriad kinds of things. We continually rely on the use of artefacts for the most intimate and essential of our biological and social needs, and many of our abstract concepts are developed through seeing, touching and making objects (Mithen 2001). Material culture is an intimate part of our (human) being; without this corporeal and conceptual intimacy with the material world we would not be human. Perhaps it is this which makes us 'knowledgable', *homo sapiens*? In some ways this is not a new claim for archaeology; for Gordon Childe (1981 [1956]) it was clear that the gradual development of human knowledge and society came about in direct relation to changes in technology and the use of material culture – *Man Makes Himself*. Here it is pertinent to remember Hegel's description of alienation as the process through which the artisan has been slowly removed from a personal relationship and control over his creations, until we reach a stage where the commodified product of industrial labour is beyond the worker's control. Andean animism reclaims a personal relationship with the material world, where the use of 'resources' is justified through the making of offerings. Our 'objective' scientific rationale has also alienated us from this intimate relationship. We choose to ignore our continuing interdependence with the dead and the landscape; in doing so we have alienated ourselves from a personal relationship with the animate world that surrounds us and we claim to be the unique knowledgable and animate force in an otherwise in-animate, un-thoughtful and un-loving world.

A focus on human agency may suggest that society is continually brought into being by individual human actions, while society surrounds the individual providing them with the rules and resources through which they can act. Giddens tries to break down the conceptual boundary between the subjective individual and the objective world. By using the concept of the 'duality of structure' he saw the subjective agent and objective structure as mutually interdependent – neither one exists without the other (1984: 25–28). To some extent 'the duality of structure' is a refusal to define or delimit what, or who, makes up the structure or the agents. In a somewhat similar vein, many Andean people would highlight the role that the ancestors, the saints and the mountain deities have played in creating and nurturing the people, animals and crops. It could be argued that the Andean attribution of agency to mountains and ancestors is a more encompassing version of Giddens' 'duality of structure'. As Giddens is at pains to point out, the individual human agent is continually shaped by the larger social structures that surround them. Andean people have identified and described this structure as the animate power of the ancestors and the landscape, which they experience as ambivalent forces which are interacted with through the provision of offerings.

Every action relies on a multiplicity of earlier activities that provide the 'rules and resources' through which the individual can act. For instance, the planting of some maize requires not just the seeds and the tools to open up the soil, but also the prior clearing of the fields, the agricultural knowledge and skills, and generations of crop domestication and nurturing. Within Andean perception, acknowledging this is acknowledging the continuing presence of the ancestors and mountain deities. But, within structuration theory, Giddens (1981: 100) explains this through the concept of 'distanciation'. Distanciation is used to describe a range of techniques through which agents can make a difference at some distance to the subject. Giddens draws particular attention to storage systems as techniques through which people can anticipate and prepare for potential hardship in the future. In this way ancestors continue to act upon the living long after they are dead, in much the same way as Giddens' publications can act on me at some distance from his physical person. As with the actions of any individual, these may be misread or misunderstood by other observers, and they are just as prone to unintended consequences. Given Giddens' attention to storage systems it is particularly appropriate that much Andean ritual focuses on the stores of food and seeds as well as the husbandry and marking of livestock. These are the vital resources which the ancestors and living forces of the earth have given for this generation to benefit from, but also to nurture and maintain for future generations. Perhaps, in seeing these stores and the dead ancestors who cleared the fields as active living entities, Andean people are merely personifying the action at a distance that Giddens calls distanciation. To a large extent I am willing to accept this argument. But, I hesitate for two reasons. First, there is an evident cultural superiority involved in assuming we can see behind the illusory explanation offered by Andean people to the reality of the social constructs they have created; how can we be sure that our analysis is correct? Secondly, precisely because Andean people consider these entities to be sentient living beings, their world is structured differently. I do not perform sacrifices in front of my copies of Giddens' books, but Andean people do make offerings to the mountains, the dead and their house compounds. The motivation and purpose of people's actions are fundamentally altered because of these beliefs in non-human agency.

Commitments: the reason Andean people make offerings

Most Andean rituals are born out of a concern to protect what is already cherished (children, animals, land, houses, relatives, deities etc.) and out of people's aspirations for the future. At the same time these rituals reaffirm and strengthen sentiment, or attachment, in the participants. This helps to explain why an apparently incoherent set of religious beliefs and ideas, as well as the enormous variation in the specific form, timing and ingredients of rituals, continues to be maintained and developed. It is, in part, the very localised sharing of ideas and practices that makes them both powerful and personally meaningful. The exact form and function of these rituals is rarely articulated by the participants, partly because the meaning is contained within the sentiments of the event itself: the interaction between the people, the active process of composing the offering, and the emotive recalling of the various recipients (ancestors, places, and saints) the offering is directed to. None of this may ever be expressed in abstraction; it is in the moment of ritual interaction that it is *experienced*.

John Barrett has recently suggested (pers. comm.) that the dominant anthropological focus on exchange has diverted our attention from a more fundamental concern within society, that of commitment. I am in full agreement with the need to consider commitment, as it is people's commitments that provide them with the motivation to make gifts or undertake work. Such commitments extend beyond the loyalty people may have for each other, to include the obligations and desires they may have for their homes, their ancestors, their fields, and their gods. Rituals are frequently central to people's commitments because they become the focus for generating and expressing personal sentiment for cultural ideals such as marriage and the home (Sillar 2000: 39–40). Throughout their lives people are constantly adopting and transforming these commitments as they bind themselves into ever-changing relationships, and one of the commitments that the living make to the dead is to cultivate and maintain their memories of them (cf. Kaulicke 2000; Tarlow 1999).

Commitments are primarily expressed through exchange, and in the Andes this can be seen in the ideals related to feeding (of children, work parties, houses, ancestors, and deities) and in the commitments of labour exchange (e.g. *ayni*, *mink'a* and *faena*; cf. Alberti and Mayer 1974). Society is structured by each individual's commitment to other individuals, social groups, institutions, activities, places and beings. This provides the motivation for people to act, including the making of offerings. For instance, the weaving of cloth has always been one of the most labour- intensive and valued activities in the Andes, and much of this cloth is woven to express commitment, such as a mother weaving the clothes for a son's wedding. It is perhaps not surprising, then, that high-quality woven cloth was also one of the most prestigious burnt offerings that was made by the Inka, and new clothes were woven to adorn the dead (Murra 1989). Offerings are made to request support in protecting the people and things that the supplicant holds most dear, and a central purpose of Andean rituals is to engender and promote the commitment that the ancestors and the deities have to the people making the offerings.

It is partly due to the inter-relationships that commitments create that the boundary between individual and corporate agency is not clear. For instance, Andean pilgrimage is frequently done by a group sent as a delegation by the community for the community's benefit (Randall 1982; Sallnow 1987). There is not the focus on individual salvation or individual penance that is more common in European pilgrimage. Within archaeology this has obvious implications for corporate activities such as the building of a house or a monument, where it is the group's shared commitment to each other, as well as their commitment to the activity of building and presumably the intended function of the structure, that facilitates their blending of their individual agencies within a corporate goal. To a very large extent the field boundaries, houses, burials, and monuments that we investigate are a material manifestation of people's commitments – both their willingness to work together as a group and as a direct reflection of their priorities and concerns.

The landscape and material world of the Andes is actively engaged in supporting life – without the ancestors and *Pachamama* crops would not grow. The mountains care for and maintain the llama and alpaca herds, and the saints teach people how to weave. Occasionally these active beings intervene in the world in a dramatic way to cause change through earthquakes, lightning, floods and pestilence. If agency is that which exerts a causal force, these are extreme demonstrations of the agency of the animate powers of the Andean landscape. But Andean offerings are rarely used to request major changes to the world; quite the opposite – almost all ritual activity is focused on maintaining balance. Perhaps we should describe it as maintaining the structure? The largest and most elaborate sacrifices are associated with major periods of turmoil. Thus the human sacrifices at the Huaca de la Luna seem to have been made during a major el Niño event (Bourget 2001), while Inka child sacrifices were either made in response to the trauma of disease, war or famine, or upon the death or inauguration of an Inka ruler (Cobo 1990 [1653]). It is possible that even these 'extreme' cases were similar to the day-to-day offering of coca leaves and alcohol, where the aim seems to have been to request the deities and (super)natural forces to maintain order. The success of sacrifice is not measured in change (unless it is the halting of a major disaster) but rather in the continuity of daily life. For this reason, making offerings does not negate the need for people to plant and harvest crops. In fact it is probably a mistake to separate the offering from 'productive' activity, as labour, particularly that of agricultural work, may also be seen as a ritual activity (Laurencich-Minelli 1991). Thus physical labour, material investment and ritual offerings are all combined within people's commitment to their fields, crops, households and ancestors.

Individual motivation (the driving force behind human agency?)

Identifying agency depends on how and where we identify knowledgable intent. One of the fundamental reasons that it is usually considered possible to separate human agency from natural processes, is that human action is predicated on a conscious directed action whereas natural processes are unmotivated. Without considering people's motivation we risk perpetuating a concept of society where the reproduction of social forms appears inevitable rather than as the result of individual choices and aspirations. I see this as one of the major advantages of utilising Giddens' concept of agency within archaeology. Rather than trying to explain all social organisation and cultural change at the level of gross cultural interaction (e.g. the invasion and diffusion within cultural historical archaeology), or at the level of universal laws (e.g. environmental determinism within processual archaeology), agency theory seeks to incorporate a role for socially-informed individuals who act knowledgably to reproduce and transform the society they live in.

The importance of motivation and intent in directing agency raises a problem for archaeology. It is difficult enough to identify the intentions and motives behind people's actions in the present; what hope can there be for discovering the purpose and reason that informed the actions of people who are long dead? It is perhaps for this reason that Barrett's reformulation of structuration theory for archaeology has deliberately tried to avoid being drawn into a focus on individuals and personal motivations. "The individual does not now become the basic unit of our analysis, nor are we primarily concerned with individual motivations, nor do we begin analysis with a consideration of an individual action, nor do we see societies as being nothing more than the cumulative product of individual actions" (Barrett 2001: 149). There is a methodological problem here. Although the theory, and our knowledge of social processes, acknowledges the importance of individual motivation, we also accept that we are incapable of retrieving the thoughts and intentions of dead people (although this is something that the Inka seemed to have less of a problem with). But I don't think we should let this methodological problem undermine the importance of recognising that it is individual motivation that drives a large part of social reproduction and social change. We may not be able to get into the mind of the person in the past, but if we don't consider their motivation we can only talk about how they re-acted to problems, not about 'knowledgable' people acting with intent. For this reason an archaeology of agency is an archaeology of the future: by this I mean that rather than seeing people as unmotivated automatons who unconsciously maintain tradition (the cultural historical approach – an archaeology of the past), or people who merely react to changes in their environment (the systems approach – an archaeology of the present), we see them as motivated people who consciously think about the purpose of their actions and choose to maintain or change their circumstances by acting (not merely re-acting) upon the world as knowledgable agents trying to influence and shape their future. Like Father Bernabe Cobo, meditating on the problem of human sacrifice amongst the Inkas at the start of the 17th century, unless we give some credence to people's motivations and beliefs we will not be able to explain activities that are so fundamentally different to our own:

> Their religion was so firmly established, universally received, and amazingly strict that they offered and sacrificed even their own children and their own property by burning it, as was their custom. Therefore, it cannot be presumed that their acts were empty gestures, because human nature would not allow them to kill their own children and jeopardize their property so happily if they did not expect some reward for what they were doing or if they did not believe that they were sending their children to a better place than the one they had here. And it is evident that for people to produce exterior signs of happiness in making these sacrifices, in their own minds they believed without any doubt that the sacrifices were not made in vain. Thus there is no question that these acts were conditioned by some hope. People who would kill their own children and destroy their own property would be acting more like animals than human beings, unless they felt that such acts were somehow useful (Cobo 1990 [1653]: 8).

Human agency, faith and commitment in archaeology

Medical science accepts that faith in the physician is enormously powerful: the so-called 'placebo effect'. This is why the assessment of new drugs requires 'double blind' testing so that neither patient nor doctor knows which are the 'real' drugs. But imagine having enough faith to allow someone to cut open your chest and remove your beating heart! Only with the reassurance of the wider community and demonstrable success of the ritual would you trust a surgeon to perform a bypass, or an Aztec priest to sacrifice you. Presumably it is faith that there is the promise of a better life after this gruesome deed that explains why people put themselves under the metal scalpel or the obsidian blade. Such faith is a social construct; it depends on a number of people sharing knowledge and reinforcing the individual's commitment and belief in the efficacy of these rites.

Many readers will want to argue that I have presented no evidence for ancestors, deities, objects or places actively transforming the world, only the faith of Andean people, who believe that the material world around them is structured and maintained by these beings. But, is this not equally true of archaeologists looking for *human* agency? Agency theory in archaeology remains primarily an act of faith by archaeologists who believe that society and the material world was shaped by human intentionality. In fact we have little evidence to fully demonstrate this, and many sceptics still assume that the environment and long-term evolutionary processes have been much more important in shaping the development of human culture than the illusionary self-will of individual members of the species. What evidence do we have for the centrality of human agency within social change? I would suggest that this is primarily based on a personal commitment to value the individuality and creativity of each human being within an acknowledgment of the powerful influence exerted by the wider society of which we are all a part. This is precisely what Giddens is expressing within structuration theory: the mutual interdependence between the individual and the wider social structure in which we are embedded. But Giddens and I would think that, wouldn't we! It is the primary social construct of the liberal society in which he and I were brought up. These ideals are enshrined in the Human Rights Charter of the United Nations and the American Declaration of Independence. "We hold these truths to be self-evident, that all men are created equal, that they are endowed by their Creator with certain unalienable Rights, that among them are Life, Liberty, and the pursuit of Happiness ..." In fact Thomas Jefferson's original version began, "We take these truths to be sacred and undeniable ..." (Mason 2003). I do not want my comments to be seen as sarcasm. I genuinely do believe in the creative potential of every human being to act knowledgably within the social and material environment of which they form a part. But I think we should be honest and accept that this emphasis on individual agency, in contrast to environmental, cultural, or divine determinism is an article of faith and political commitment. Fortunately, people have fought so hard to uphold and develop these ideals over more than two centuries that we are now brought up and educated within a world that is increasingly shaped by the unquestioned assumption of individual rights as the foundation of civil society.

Perceptions of agency are themselves historical/cultural constructs that vary – in so doing they affect how, why and in what ways people act. Perhaps the most fundamental of social constructs is the individual's perception of what they are able to do and how they relate to the rest of the social and material world around them. A belief in the active engagement of non-human beings within the world obviously affects the social construct of the individual, the social world (which includes non-humans) and appropriate and effective ways of acting in that world (such as people giving themselves in sacrifice). It is my contention that we need to give greater consideration to how people's ideologies will have affected their perception of themselves as individuals, their experience of the world and their motivation for acting. As Gordon Childe recognised, if we wish to study past societies, or even past environments, "it is not a question of determining what a twentieth-century university professor would have observed four, fourty or four hundred centuries ago" (Childe 1949: 8). "The environment to which a society actually adjusts itself is not the material environment that natural science can reconstruct and observe as an external object, but the society's collective representation of that environment – that is, part of its culture" (Childe 1949: 23). This is all the more relevant when we are dealing not just with how people perceived their environment, but also how they perceived themselves, their individuality, their knowledge, and their ability to act in the world.

I have not addressed the problematic issue of how archaeologists can access the cosmologies and motivations of people in prehistory, although I would suggest that we have a growing number of studies that have tried to access past cosmologies and the purpose of rituals (e.g. Bradley 1998; Marcus and Flannery 1994). But perhaps the best guide to people's cosmologies and their motivations is to consider the commitment that was expressed in building the structures and using the artefacts that we study. While this does not deny that such activities may have played a role in the manipulations of power by social elites, we should not limit people's intentions to such political machinations, and pay greater attention to how these 'investments' strengthened commitments between the living as well as with the dead and the deities (cf. Tarlow 1999). Agency cannot be applied as a universal – we need to consider it as a social and ideological/cosmological construct. Without this we are in danger of populating the past with modern, liberal, materialist individuals, just like ourselves. The methodology for identifying human agency within the archaeological record has largely focused upon the bodies of deceased individuals, or identifying evidence for directed physical action – such as the knapping of flints or the building of large monuments. But in the end this tells us little about the relationship between motivated people and the larger structures that they were a part of. I suspect that only after we grapple with the important, but archaeologically elusive, question of people's motivations and beliefs will we be able to see the humanity of the men, women and children who made the stone tools and shared the commitment needed to work together and build the monuments we study. In mapping the changing focus of people's commitments over time, we can investigate how such commitments extend beyond the near-universal concerns for close relatives to include animals, ancestors, animate landscapes, and other beliefs.

Note

1   This recalls the offence taken by the Spanish when Atahuallpa threw down from his litter the breviary offered to him by the priest Valverde, an act that some authors suggest was taken as the signal and justification for the Spanish attack upon the Inka (Hemming 1983: 41). At this time neither culture could have understood the other sufficiently to see the significance, and offence to the gods, that these spontaneous reactions held. Alternatively it may have been only in the aftermath of the conquest that these acts were 'recalled' in order to provide religious justification for war.

Acknowledgments

The ethnographic research upon which this chapter is based has been funded at various stages by the Fitzwilliam Trust Research Fund; The Anthony Wilkin Fund; Crowther-Beynon Fund, The McDonald Institute for Archaeological Research; a Leverhulme Special Research Fellowship; the University of Wales at Lampeter; and the Institute of Archaeology, University College London. I received permission to carry out my research, essential letters of introduction and support from the Instituto Nacional de Cultura's offices in Lima and Cuzco and the Museo Nacional de Etnografía y Folklore in La Paz. By far my largest debt goes to the communities in Peru and Bolivia who permitted me to live amongst them, fed me, and gently educated me about the important things in life. A few people have been particularly important in educating me in the issues covered in this article: Emillano Colque in Seq'ueracay, Juan Cabeces in Pumpuri, Honorata Rodríguez, Eochino Sankka, and Maximo Amaru in Raqchi, and Henry Stobart in Ascot. I would also like to thank Adam Brumm for his constructive criticism of this chapter and suggested improvements. Finally, I received essential encouragement to complete the chapter and critical comment on an earlier draft from Andrew Gardner.

References

Abercrombie, T. 1986. *The Politics of Sacrifice: an Aymara cosmology in action.* PhD thesis, University of Chicago, IL.

Alberti, G. and Mayer, E. 1974. Reciprocidad Andina: ayer y hoy. In G. Alberti and E. Mayer (eds.) *Reciprocidad e intercambio en los Andes Peruanos*, 13–36. Lima: Instituto de Estudios Peruanos.

Allen, C.J. 1982. Body and soul in Quechua thought. *Journal of Latin American Lore*, 8:2, 179–96.

Allen, C.J. 1988. *The Hold Life Has: coca and cultural identity in an Andean community.* Washington, DC: Smithsonian Institution Press.

Alva, W. 2001. The royal tombs of Sipan: art and power in Moche society. In J. Pillsbury (ed.) *Moche Art and Archaeology in Ancient Peru*, 223–45. New Haven, CT: Yale University Press (Studies in the History of Art 63; Centre for Advanced Study of the Visual Arts Symposium Papers XL, National Gallery of Art, Washington).

Anyon, R. and Ferguson, T.J. 1995. Cultural resources management at the Pueblo of Zuni, New Mexico, USA. *Antiquity*, 69, 913–30.

Arnold, D.Y. 1988. *Matrilineal Practice in a Patrilineal Setting: ritual and metaphors of kinship in an Andean ayllu.* PhD thesis, University College London (University of London).

Barrett, J. 2001. Agency, the duality of structure, and the problem of the archaeological record. In I. Hodder (ed.) *Archaeological Theory Today*, 141–64. Cambridge: Polity Press.

Bloch, M. 1992. *Prey into Hunter: the politics of religious experience.* Cambridge: Cambridge University Press.

Bourget, S. 2001. Rituals of sacrifice: its practice at Huaca de la Luna and its representation in Moche iconography. In J. Pillsbury (ed.) *Moche Art and Archaeology in Ancient Peru*, 89–110. New Haven: Yale University Press.

Bradley, R. 1998. *The Passage of Arms: an archaeological analysis of prehistoric hoard and votive deposits.* Oxford: Oxbow Books.

Castillo, L.J. 2001. The last of the Mochicas: a view from the Jequetepeque Valley. In J. Pillsbury (ed.) *Moche Art and Archaeology in Ancient Peru*, 307–32. New Haven: Yale University Press.

Childe, V.G. 1949. *Social Worlds of Knowledge. The L.T. Hobhouse Memorial Trust Lecture, No. 19, delivered 12th May 1948.* London: Geoffrey Cumberlege/Oxford University Press.

Childe, V.G. 1981 [1956]. *Man Makes Himself*. London: Moonraker Press and Pitman Publishing Ltd.

Cobo, B. 1990 [1653]. *Inca Religion and Customs*. Austin, TX: University of Texas Press (Translated and edited by Roland Hamilton).

Donnan, C. 2003. *The Long Duration and Subsequent Collapse of Moche Borders*. Paper given at Objects of Contention: Boundaries, Interaction and Appropriation in the Andes: the 8th annual Sainsbury Research Unit Seminars, University of East Anglia, Norwich, 9–10 May 2003.

Durkheim, E. 1976 [1912]. *The Elementary Forms of Religious Life*. London: Allen and Unwin.

Duviols, P. 1976. La Capacocha. *Allpanchis Phuturinqa*, 9, 11–58.

Evans-Pritchard, E. 1965. *Theories of Primitive Religion*. Oxford: Clarendon Press.

Flores-Ochoa, J.A. 1976. Enqa, enqaychu, illay y khuya rumi: aspectos mágico-religiosos entre pastores. *Journal of Latin American Lore*, 2:1, 115–34.

Flores-Ochoa, J.A. 1979. *Pastoralists of the Andes*. Philadelphia, PA: Institute for the Study of Human Issues (Translated by R. Bolton).

Foster, G.M. 1965. Peasant society and the image of Limited Good. *American Anthropologist*, 67, 293–315.

Garcilaso de la Vega. 1989 [1612]. *Royal Commentaries of the Incas and General History of Peru*. Austin, TX: University of Texas Press (Translated by H.V. Livermore).

Giddens, A. 1981. *A Contemporary Critique of Historical Materialism*. London: Macmillan.

Giddens, A. 1984. *The Constitution of Society*. Cambridge: Polity Press.

Gisbert, T. 1994. *Iconografía y Mitos Indigenas en el Arte*. Editorial Gisbert y Cia: Fundacion BHN, La Paz.

Gose, P. 1986. Sacrifice and the commodity form in the Andes. *Man*, 21, 296–310.

Gose, P. 1994. *Deathly Waters and Hungry Mountains: agrarian ritual and class formation in an Andean town*. Toronto: University of Toronto Press.

Guamán Poma de Ayala, F. 1988 [1584–1615]. *El primer nueva corónica y buen gobierno*. Siglo Veintiuno Editores, México.

Harris, O. 1982. The dead and the devils among the Bolivian Laymi. In M. Bloch and J. Parry (eds.) *Death and the Regeneration of Life*, 45–73. Cambridge: Cambridge University Press.

Hemming, J. 1983. *The Conquest of the Incas*. Harmondsworth: Penguin.

Hollingdale, R.J. (ed.) 1977. *A Nietzsche Reader*. Harmondsworth: Penguin.

Isbell, B.J. 1977. "Those who love me": an analysis of Andean kinship and reciprocity within a ritual context. In R. Bolton and E. Mayer (eds.) *Andean Kinship and Marriage*, 81–105. Special publication of the American Anthropological Association No. 7.

Isbell, B.J. 1985 [1978]. *To Defend Ourselves: ecology and ritual in an Andean village*. Prospect Heights, IL: Waveland Press.

Kaulicke, P. 2000. *Memoria y Muerte en el Perú Antiguo*. Lima: Fondo Editorial del Pontificia Universidad Católica del Perú.

Laurencich-Minelli, L. 1991. El trabajo como forma de culto estatal en el Imperio Inca. In: M.S. Ziólkowski (ed.) *El Culto Estatal del Imperio Inca*, 55–58. Memorias del 46° Congreso Internacional de Americanistas Symposio ARC-2 Amsterdam 1988. Centro de Estudios Latinoameicanos, Universidad de Varsovia.

Lecoq, P. 1987. Caravanes de lamas, sel et échanges dans une communauté de Potosi, en Bolivie. *Bulletin de l'Institut Français d'Etudes Andines*, 16:3–4, 1–38.

MacCormack, S. 1991. *Religion in the Andes: vision and imagination in early colonial Peru*. Princeton, NJ: Princeton University Press.

Marcus, J. and Flannery, K.V. 1994. Ancient Zapotec ritual and religion: an application of the direct historical approach. In C. Renfrew and E.B.W. Zubrow (eds.) *Ancient Mind: elements of cognitive archaeology*, 55–75. Cambridge: Cambridge University Press.

Marx, K. 1970 [1864]. *Capital*, Vol. 1. London: Lawrence and Wishart.

Mason, D.J. 2003. Comments on The Declaration of Independence. www.duke.edu/eng169s2/group1/lex3/self-ev.htm. Accessed 7 May 2003.

McBryde, I. 1997. The ambiguities of authenticities. *Conservation and Management of Archaeological Sites*, 2, 93–100.

Mithen, S. 2001. Archaeological theory and theories of cognitive evolution record. In I. Hodder (ed.) *Archaeological Theory Today*, 98–121. Cambridge: Polity Press.

Murra, J.V. 1989. Cloth and its function in the Inka state. In A.B. Weiner and J. Schneider (eds.) *Cloth and Human Experience*, 275–302. Washington, DC: Smithsonian Institute Press.

Nash, J. 1979. *We Eat the Mines and the Mines Eat Us: dependency and exploitation in Bolivian tin mines*. New York: Columbia University Press.

Platt, T. 1983. Conciencia Andina y Conciencia Proletaria: Qhuyaruna y Ayllu en el Norte de Potosí *HISLA: Revista Latinoamerican de Historia Económica y Social*, 2, 47–73.

Platt, T. 1986. Mirrors and maize: the concept of *yanantin* among the Macha of Bolivia. In J. Murra, N. Wachtel and J. Revel (eds.) *Anthropological History of Andean Polities*, 228–59. Cambridge: Cambridge University Press.

Randall, R. 1982. Qoyllur Rit'i, an Inca fiesta of the Pleides: reflections on time and space in the Andean world. *Boletín del Instituto Francés de Estudios Andinos (Lima)*, 11:1–2, 37–81.

Randall, R. 1987. Communication with the other world: the tale of Isicha Puytu. *Journal of Latin American Lore*, 13:2, 155–81.

Reinhard, J. 1992. Sacred peaks of the Andes. *National Geographic*, 181:3, 84–111.

Reinhard, J. 1996. Peru's ice maidens: frozen in time, 500-year-old mummies promise fresh understanding of the Inca Empire. *National Geographic*, 189:6, 62–81.

Rösing, I. 1991. *Las Almas Nuevas del Mundo Callawaya*. La Paz: Editorial 'los Amigos del Libro'.

Sallnow, M.J. 1987. *Pilgrims of the Andes: regional cults in Cusco*. Washington, DC: Smithsonian Institution Press.

Sallnow, M.J. 1989. Precious metals in the Andean moral economy. In J. Parry and M. Bloch (eds). *Money and the Morality of Exchange*, 209–31. Cambridge: Cambridge University Press.

Schiffer, M.B. 1999. *The Material Life of Human Beings: artefacts, behavior, and communication*. London: Routledge.

Sillar, B. 1996. Playing with God: cultural perception of children, play and miniatures in the Andes. *Archaeological Review from Cambridge*, 13:2, 47–63.

Sillar, B. 2000. *Shaping Culture: making pots and constructing households. An ethnoarchaeological study of pottery production, trade and use in the Andes*. Oxford: BAR International Series 883.

Silverblatt, I. 1987. *Moon, Sun and Witches: gender ideologies and class in Inca and colonial Peru*. Princeton, NJ: Princeton University Press.

Sterner, J. 1989. Who is signalling whom? Ceramic style, ethnicity and taphonomy among the Sirak Bulahay. *Antiquity*, 63, 451–59.

Stobart, H. 1995. *Sounding the Seasons: music ideologies and the poetics of production in an Andean hamlet (Ayllu Macha, Northern Potosí, Bolivia)*. PhD thesis, University of Cambridge.

Stobart, H. 2003. Interlocking realms: knowing music and musical knowing. In H. Stobart and R. Howard-Malverde (eds.) *Knowledge and Learning in the Andes*. Liverpool: University of Liverpool Press.

Swenson, E.R. 2003. Cities of violence: sacrifice, power and urbanization in the Andes. *Journal of Social Archaeology*, 3:2, 256–96.

Tarlow, S. 1999. *Bereavement and Commemoration: an archaeology of mortality*. Oxford: Blackwell.

Titu Kusi Yupanki. 1985 [1570]. *Ynstuçion del Ynga Don Diego de Castro Titu Cussi Yupanqui para el muy ilustre señor el liçençiado Lope Garçia de Castro, governador que fue destos Reynos del piru, tocante a los negoçios que con Su Magestad, en Nombre, por Su Poder a de tratar; la qual es esta que se sigue*, edited by Luis Millones, Lima.

Tylor, E.B. 1913. *Primitive Culture: researches into the development of mythology, philosophy, religion, language, art and custom*. London: Murray (5th edition).

Ucko, P.J. 2000. Enlivening a 'dead' past. *Conservation and Management of Archaeological Sites*, 4, 67–92.

Van den Berg, H. 1989. La celebración de los difunctos entre los campesinos Aymara de Altiplano. *Anthropos*, 84, 155–75.

Van den Berg, H. 1990. *La tierra no da asi nomas: los ritos agrícolas en la religion de los aymara-cristianos*. Yachay Temas Monograficos No. 5, Universidad Catolica Boliviana, Cochabamaba.

Weber, M. 1976 [1904]. *The Protestant Ethic and the Spirit of Capitalism*. London: Allen and Unwin.

Weismantel, M. 1993. Viñachina: making children. Paper presented for the International Conference on Kinship and Gender in the Andes, 6–11 September 1993, St. Andrews, Scotland.

Whitedeer, G.W. 1997. Return of the sacred: spirituality and the scientific imperative. In N. Swidler, K.E. Dongoske, R. Anyon, and A.S. Downer (eds.) *Native Americans and Archaeologists: stepping stones to common ground*, 37–43. Walnut Creek, CA: AltaMira Press.

Zuidema, R.T. 1989. Parentesco y culto a los antepasados en tres comunidades Peruanas: una relacón de Hernández Príncipe de 1622. In *Reyes y guerreros: ensayos de cultura Andina* (collected essays of R.T. Zuidema). Lima: Grandes Estudios Andinos.

CHAPTER 10

BEING IN A SIMULACRUM: ELECTRONIC AGENCY

Mark W. Lake

INTRODUCTION

The goal of this chapter is to provoke colonisation of an intellectual landscape that barely impinges on the horizon of the 'agency in archaeology' debate. Specifically, it aims to demonstrate that archaeologists interested in agency stand to benefit from a dialogue with contemporary Artificial Intelligence (AI). Not only are the interests of contemporary AI more closely aligned with those of the social sciences than is perhaps widely appreciated, but the conceptual clarity required of AI researchers who seek to construct working models may help archaeologists decide what they want from a concept described by Dobres and Robb (2000: 3) as "an ambiguous platitude meaning everything and nothing". This is not to claim that AI necessarily holds a monopoly over all that is useful in the debate about agency in archaeology: indeed, it may be that the limitations of contemporary AI research are its most informative aspects. That said, this chapter is intended to support the claim that it would be negligent to dismiss the relevance of AI on the basis of a fifteen-year-old reading of the discipline, or indeed on the basis of a collection of archaeological borrowings which barely touch upon some of the most important developments over that period.

The theoretical landscape occupied by agency in archaeology can be mapped using various schemata. One is intellectual heritage, distinguishing between, for example, Mithen's (1990) use of optimal foraging theory and Barrett's (1994) appeal to phenomenology. Others are more overtly thematic, for example Dobres' and Robb's (2000: 10) quintet: "intentionality and social reproduction; scale; temporality and social change; material culture; and the politics of archaeological practices." It would be possible to forge links between AI and archaeological interests in agency across all five of these themes, but for reasons of time and space such comprehensive treatment is not attempted here. Instead, this chapter aims to show how contemporary AI either addresses, or is beginning to address, the three key elements in the existing critique of archaeological borrowings from AI: the allegedly limited ability (or perhaps desire) to deal with alternative rationalities, alternative forms of reason, and non-discursive knowledge. The chapter begins with a brief review of multi-agent simulation and its use in archaeology, since this has been the main subject of the critique of AI in archaeology.

ARTIFICIAL INTELLIGENCE IN ARCHAEOLOGY

Archaeologists have drawn on AI techniques for a variety of purposes, ranging from the analysis of use-wear patterns on stone artefacts (Barceló *et al.* 2000) to the construction of multi-agent computer simulations of past societies. It is the latter which concerns us here. The history of computer simulation in archaeology is somewhat chequered (Lake 2001a). The first models ranged in their subject matter from Palaeolithic social systems (Wobst 1974) to Anasazi settlement (Cordell 1972) and mostly treated culture as an adaptive system. The optimism of the early 1970s soon waned as it became apparent that the models were either overly simplistic or required more input data than was available (Doran and Hodson 1975), although a number of systems models continued to be created up until the early 1980s. Following a ten year hiatus, the 1990s saw a revival of interest in computer simulation of past societies, largely as a result of developments outside archaeology. Growing interest in non-linear dynamical systems, popularised under the rubric 'chaos theory', gave rise to a new breed of systems models of social processes that differed from their predecessors in their emphasis on endogenous structural change (e.g. McGlade 1997; van der Leeuw and McGlade 1997). Meanwhile, increasing use of multi-agent simulation in biology and, more recently, sociology inspired a number of agent-based models in archaeology. The latter, with their explicit reference to individual agents, are more closely aligned with the increasing interest in agency.

Multi-agent simulations have their origins in Distributed Artificial Intelligence (DAI), which represents a response to increasing scepticism about the classical AI project. A substantial element of the philosophical critique of classical AI – which began with research on the automatic demonstration of theorems (Newell *et al.* 1957) and has had some notable successes with machines designed to perform very specific tasks, such as chess computers (Goodman and Keene 1997) – focuses on its failure to produce 'intelligent' machines capable of interacting in any significant way with their environment and other machines of their own kind (Dreyfus 1972; Searle 1992). More pragmatically, designers of industrial expert systems realised that the knowledge of a group of workers is greater than the sum of the knowledge possessed by each individual worker (Ferber 1999: 3). Thus, for both philosophical and practical reasons, DAI attempts to create systems whose 'intelligence' results from the interaction between a number of computational entities (Bond and Gasser 1988). These entities are often construed as agents, whether or not they are intended to represent individual human beings. The idea of representing living organisms with computer agents has recently gained further impetus from the nascent field known as Artificial Life (AL). Whereas DAI is primarily concerned with reasoning, AL focuses on behaviour, autonomy and viability (Ferber 1999: 28). AL is potentially of considerable relevance for the 'agency in archaeology' debate, but is not considered in this chapter because the archaeological critique of computer models has mainly focused on what agents think. That said, the discussion of non-discursive knowledge touches on an area of research at the interface between DAI and AL.

The most important way in which multi-agent simulations differ from those based on systems-thinking is that they allow system-wide phenomena to emerge from the actions of individual agents. AI adopts a minimal definition of an agent as "anything that can be viewed as perceiving its environment through sensors and acting upon that environment through actuators" (Russell and Norvig 2003: 32). The agents in archaeological multi-agent simulations are typically intended to represent individual human beings (but see Kohler *et al.* 2000 for an example of the household as agent), at least to the extent that they possess the following properties: a state, which may include energy levels, happiness, etc.; knowledge of their environment, which may be imperfect; one or more goals; and the ability to act in their environment in a way that tends towards satisfying their goals given the available knowledge, skills and resources. Such agents may also be able to communicate with other agents and possibly even reproduce themselves. To date, archaeologists have employed multi-agent simulation to investigate problems ranging from the evolution of cultural learning in early hominids (Lake 2001b, 1995) and the appearance of increased social complexity in Upper Palaeolithic Europe (Doran *et al.* 1994), through hunter-gatherer (Mithen 1990; Lake 2000) and early farming (Reynolds 1986) subsistence, to the settlement patterns of Late Ancestral Pueblo and Anasazi populations of the US southwest (Kohler *et al.* 2000; Dean *et al.* 2000).

Given the importance of agents to contemporary AI it is striking that Dobres' and Robb's ((eds.) 2000) landmark *Agency in Archaeology* addresses neither AI in general nor multi-agent simulation in particular. On the one hand this was predictable, at least to the extent that archaeologists tend to be more comfortable – perhaps as a result of training – with the social sciences than with what are often termed the cognitive sciences (AI, neuroscience, psychology and philosophy of mind). On the other hand, archaeologists' preference for the social sciences only serves to make Dobres' and Robb's omission of AI all the more surprising, since the social sciences have entered into a sustained dialogue with AI. Not only are the social sciences borrowing from AI, as evidenced by *Simulating Societies* (Gilbert and Doran (eds.) 1994), *Artificial Societies* (Gilbert and Conte (eds.) 1995) and *Simulation for the Social Scientist* (Gilbert and Troitzsch 1999), but AI is borrowing from the social sciences, as evidenced by *Simulating Social Phenomena* (Conte *et al.* (eds.) 1997) and *Human Cognition and Social Agent Technology* (Dautenhahn (ed.) 2000). Furthermore, this dialogue is sufficiently established to have generated an internal critique (O'Sullivan and Haklay 2000). Paradoxically, it may be that the nature of the existing archaeological engagement with AI has contributed most to the perception that AI has little to offer the 'agency in archaeology' debate. In particular, many of the limited number of archaeological multi-agent simulation studies have not been *about* agency. This is largely true of the studies by Dean *et al.*, Kohler *et al.* and Lake, all of which invoke agents with certain properties and propensities, but none of which problematise agency in the sense that they do not include substantial discussion of one or more of Dobres' and Robb's five 'difficult issues'. This omission cannot be a complete explanation, however, since some studies have included explicit discussion of one or more of the 'difficult issues', notably Mithen's (1990) *Thoughtful Foragers*, Doran *et al.*'s (1994) account of their work on Upper Palaeolithic social change and, perhaps the most wide-ranging,[1] Kohler's (2000) introduction to *Dynamics in Human and Primate Societies: agent-based modeling of social and spatial processes*. Instead, it seems likely that the real problem is that existing archaeological studies involving multi-agent simulation have not attempted to model alternative rationalities, alternative forms of reason and non-discursive knowledge. This appears to have led to a generalisation that simulation studies cannot model non-Western modes of thought (see, for example, Thomas 1991) even when there is nothing in AI that precludes it.

RATIONALITY AND REASON

Most, if not all, archaeological studies that make use of multi-agent simulation appeal to some form of methodological individualism (Watkins 1952) as an important element in their *raison d'être*. Mithen has been particularly explicit about this, arguing for the importance of individuals in explanation (1989a, 1990) and also for multi-agent simulation as a methodological tool to infer individual actions from archaeological evidence which comprises a palimpsest of such actions (1990, 1988, 1993). The premise that individuals constitute the appropriate analytical unit for archaeological explanation is not in itself especially controversial (but see Clark 1992 and Murray and Walker 1988) and has been widely held across the spectrum of archaeological theory since at least the mid-1980s (for example: Shanks and Tilley 1987a; Earle and Preucel 1987; Shennan 1986; Hodder 1985). What is controversial, however, is the rationality according to which the individuals in multi-agent simulations act. This debate revolves around two questions: what kind of rationality is appropriate (considered in this section) and how much human behaviour is actually rational (considered in the next section)?

To date, the agents in archaeological multi-agent simulations have been ascribed a rationality that is grounded in either evolutionary biology or economics. The former, which is usually the case in studies of hunter-gatherer societies (see Mithen 1990; Lake 2000; Mithen 1989b), is typically quite explicit, drawing on predictions from optimal foraging theory (Winterhalder 1981) or evolutionary psychology. Indeed, Kohler (2000: 5–9) has suggested that evolutionary psychology opens up the possibility of "strong social simulation". The economic rationality found in other simulation models, particularly those dealing with sedentary societies (Kohler *et al.* 2000; Dean *et al.* 2000), is typically less explicit, but usually involves some sort of means-ends reasoning about expected utility. It is this grounding of agent rationality in evolutionary biology or modern economics which has led to the claim that multi-agent simulation necessarily projects modern rationality back into the past. For example, according to Thomas (1991: 1), "The rationality which Mithen seeks to identify on the part of his Mesolithic foragers is a very specific one: it is the instrumental reason of late capitalism". Similarly, Shanks and Tilley, while not specifically addressing multi-agent simulation, express disquiet about recourse to either evolutionary biology or economics, since in their view the former leaves a "plastic, malleable cultural dope incapable of altering the conditions of his or her existence" (Shanks and Tilley 1987b: 56) and the latter "naturalizes what are historically and culturally specific values as universal features of humanity" (Shanks and Tilley 1987a: 188).

More recently, Cowgill has claimed that "The allegedly universal rationality assumed by 'economic man' models is shown by anthropological knowledge to be the very opposite" (Cowgill 2000: 55), while Clark, comparing an approach to agency rooted in evolutionary theory with one rooted in practice theory, complained that "the individuals in optimal foraging models know more than real agents could know. Rational decisions require perfect knowledge of particulars and decision-making rules, which are cultural" (Clark 2000: 108). For the purposes of this chapter, the question is not whether attributing to agents rationalities grounded in evolutionary biology or economics is appropriate, but rather, whether multi-agent simulation in particular and AI in general is limited to these kinds of rationality?

In order to address this question it is necessary to understand how the notion of rationality that is deployed in AI relates to that deployed by the critics – and indeed some of the proponents – of rationalities grounded in economics or evolutionary biology. The textbook view from AI is that "A rational agent is one that does the right thing" (Russell and Norvig 2003: 34); in other words, one "whose actions make sense from the point of view of the information possessed by the agent and its goals (or the task for which it was defined)" (Russell 1999: 13). This (informal) definition may appear trivial, but the important and perhaps surprising consequence is that "What counts in the first instance is what the agent does, not necessarily what it thinks, or even whether it thinks at all" (Russell 1999: 13). Thus the emphasis is first and foremost on what Simon (1976) termed *substantive rationality* – what decision to make – rather than *procedural rationality* – how to make the decision. AI researchers formalise substantive rationality through the *agent function*, which can be conceived as a table that records what action an agent performs as a result of a given percept sequence (a history of everything the agent has ever perceived). Procedural rationality is formalised through the *agent program*, which is the internal mechanism used by the agent to implement the agent function and which, in the case of a cognitive agent, will be some kind of reasoning process. It is worth noting that most of the day-to-day work of the AI community focuses on the design of agent programs (Russell and Norvig 2003).

Those who warn against projecting rationalities grounded in modern economics or evolutionary biology back into the past are not all equally explicit about what they mean by 'rationality'. Cowgill (2000) is unusually explicit. For him, "'rationality' is 'using reasoning as a major factor influencing action'" and he is "careful not to define reasoning and rationality in terms of getting the correct answer" (Cowgill 2000: 55). This puts him directly at odds with the concept of rationality employed in AI, which as noted above, privileges outcome over process. Indeed, reasoning as construed by Cowgill, that is, "a fairly distinct kind of mental activity . . . [which] means things like weighing alternatives, and trying to figure out the likely consequences of doing this or doing that", is not necessarily even required for an agent to be rational in the AI sense. Of course, consideration of such semantic niceties is only relevant here insofar as it helps one translate Cowgill's views on the universality – or otherwise – of particular rationalities into AI terminology. It appears that he is open to three possibilities, which are not mutually exclusive. One is that past agents may have had different rationalities in the sense that their rationalities should be described by different agent functions. This is the sense implied when he suggests that the women in a particular case-study "are probably not being less (or more) rational than capitalist CEOs; they are being rational in regard to different perceived issues, in relation to different contexts, different experiences, and different knowledge" (Cowgill 2000: 55–56). A second possibility, that the rationalities of past agents should be described by different agent programs, is implied in the statement that "we all reason, but what we reason about and *the procedures we use* may differ greatly" (Cowgill 2000: 55, emphasis added). The third possibility, which is less about kinds of rationality and more about the scope of rationality, can be disentangled from Cowgill's claim that the image provided by 'economic man' models of "highly individualistic actors whose *only* important mental processes are reasoning in relation to explicit goals, is, in fact, exceptionally culture-specific and ethnocentric" (original emphasis). Given the centrality of reasoning to Cowgill's notion of rationality, this suggestion that reasoning in relation to specific goals may be less important in other 'cultures' carries with it the logical corollary that rationality may also be less important in those 'cultures', presumably in the sense of being more restricted in scope.

For Clark, rational means "logical means-ends thinking" (Clark 2000: 100), where means-ends thinking involves the "choice of appropriate means to achieve desired ends" (Clark 2000: 95). Unlike Cowgill's notion of rationality, Clark's is compatible with that employed in AI to the extent that it focuses on doing the 'right thing', in other words, on the agent function. It differs, however, in that he insists on logical thinking, which implies a particular agent program or kind of agent program. The issue of agent programs, or how to think, is considered further in the next section. So far as the universality of rationality is concerned, it appears that Clark is only interested in the first of the possibilities raised by Cowgill: that the rationalities of past agents might need to be described by different agent functions. Thus, comparing Boone's (1992) evolutionary ecology model for the origins of hereditary inequality with the practice model he developed with Blake (Clark and Blake 1994), he states that, in contrast with Boone's agents, his "just have different motives; one pursues food and the other fame" (Clark 2000: 101). Indeed it appears that Clark's dislike of evolutionary ecology models has less to do with the rationality which they attribute to past agents and more to do with his belief that such models result in tautologous explanation (see especially the discussion on p. 102).

It has already been noted above that both Shanks and Tilley (1987a) and Thomas (1991) believe that studies grounded in evolutionary ecology (and by implication the majority of simulation studies in archaeology) project present-day values into the past. Unlike Shanks and Tilley, Thomas explicitly addresses the issue of rationality. In an exchange with Mithen (1991) about whether evolutionary ecological approaches to the Mesolithic of northern Europe had rendered it a "cybernetic wasteland" (Thomas 1988: 64), Thomas argues that "The fundamental point is not that it is wrong to argue that human action is rational, but to imagine that there is a single, eternal rationality for it to follow" (Thomas 1991: 16). He does not, however, explain exactly what he means by 'rationality'. On the one hand he places considerable emphasis on reason; that is, on how agents make decisions. For example, he states that "Desires, emotions, *forms of reason* and techniques of self-interpretation are all contingent and historically situated" (Thomas 1991: 17, emphasis added) and further, drawing on Foucault's (1973) analysis of pre-Modern medical thought, he argues that "past forms of scientific discourse are not simply less perfect versions of 20th Century reason . . . [but] distinct systems of thought with *their own architecture and logic*" (Thomas 1991: 18, emphasis added). On the other hand, his view that the nature of past forms of scientific discourse indicates "not merely that we may speak of a 'history of reason', but that a multiplicity of 'forms of rationality' are dispersed through time and space, often overlapping and competing with each other", appears to suggest that he also believes that rationalities can differ in ways other than the forms of reason which they employ.[2] Thus, translating Thomas' views into AI terminology, there can be little doubt that he believes that past agents may have possessed different rationalities in the sense that they should be described by different agent programs, but it is less clear whether he believes that they should also be described by different agent functions.

The question posed at the outset of this discussion of rationality was: does multi-agent simulation in particular and AI in general require the projection of modern rationality back into the past? The answer is not straightforward, partly because contributors to the 'agency in archaeology' debate are not consistent in their usage of the term 'rationality' and partly because it raises difficult questions about the nature of thought and intelligence. It was argued above that archaeologists who are sceptical of the biological and economic rationalities that underpin existing multi-agent simulations variously use the term rationality to refer to one, or the other, or possibly both the agent function (what decisions to make) and the agent program (how to make decisions). Multi-agent simulation and AI more generally simply does not *require* agent functions derived from either modern economic theory or evolutionary biology. It is true that it must be possible to formally state the agent function and it may be that it is easier to do this for economic and biologically grounded rationalities because we have explicitly theorised them. Nevertheless, in principle, there is no reason why multi-agent simulations should necessarily project modern *substantive* rationality back into the past. It is less certain, however, that agent programs are similarly unconstrained in principle. From an archaeological perspective the critical question is whether all possible forms of reasoning that humans have employed, or do employ, can be implemented on the computing devices currently available to us. The obvious response is that this question is unanswerable because philosophers and AI researchers are famously unable to agree about the limitations of machine intelligence (see Russell and Norvig 2003, chapter 26 for a guide to the main arguments). An alternative response, which is perhaps more apposite here, is that we do not in any case know all the forms of reasoning that humans have employed. Indeed, it is notable that those who warn against projecting modern forms of reasoning back into the past do not also provide detailed descriptions of alternative forms which they believe were employed in specific contexts. The simplest explanation for this lacuna is, of course, that it is difficult to make such inferences, but even if that were not the case, it is doubtful whether archaeologists interested in past rationalities currently possess a language adequate for the task of describing them. Consequently, while it must be accepted that multi-agent simulation may impose some (unknown) limits on models of past *procedural* rationalities, an attempt to devise non-modern agent programs would at least provoke much-needed discussion about how to describe alternative forms of reasoning.

UNREASON

Even if, as suggested in the previous section, multi-agent simulation and AI need not result in the projection of modern – at least in the case of substantive – rationalities back into the past, that still does not address Cowgill's apparent belief that the scope of rationality may be more restricted in some 'cultures'. This raises the question: can AI techniques be used to model non-rational thought? Of course, one could argue that this problem only arises because, as discussed earlier, Cowgill employs a process-oriented concept of rationality which equates rationality with certain forms of reasoning: if he accepted the outcome-oriented concept current in AI then behaviours that are not instigated as a result of "weighing alternatives" (Cowgill 2000: 55) could still be accepted as rational so long as they benefit the agent. While logically compelling, this argument effects a sleight of hand to the extent that it answers the question by proposing that it is probably not necessary to model non-rational thought in the circumstances he has in mind. A more generous and interesting response is to accept that Cowgill is concerned with procedural rationality and return to the question, not of what decisions to make, but of how to make them. This question has important implications for two issues that have been raised in the 'agency in archaeology' debate: the emotions (considered here) and non-discursive thought (considered in the next section).

When Thomas (1988: 64) suggested that evolutionary ecological approaches had rendered the Mesolithic of northern Europe a "cybernetic wasteland", Mithen responded by arguing that Thomas' claim was wrong since "Rationality and emotion are intimately linked" (Mithen 1991: 9). Mithen draws on the cognitive and functional theories of emotion proposed by Oatley and Johnson-Laird (1987) and Frijda (Frijda 1987; Frijda and Swagerman 1987) to suggest the nature of that linkage. Both theories propose that emotions form a sort of management system which facilitates switching between multiple plans and goals, a view which finds some support from the study of neuropathologies (Damasio 1995). Thus emotions make rational thought possible by overcoming the problem of what to do in the face of conflicting goals, as well as overcoming the 'insufficiency of reason', that is, the difficulty of taking account of all information and exploring the consequences of possible actions (de Sousa 1987). Given the vital role that these theories accord emotions it is not surprising that Mithen regards emotional life as "quintessentially human": a universal feature of *homo sapiens sapiens* who do not have cognitive pathologies (Mithen 1991: 10).

Thomas' response to Mithen's defence of evolutionary ecological approaches is contradictory. On the one hand he accuses Mithen of believing "the world to be composed of the rational, that which is susceptible to the exercise of reason, and the emotional, the 'irrational'" while on the other hand complaining that Mithen is able "to overcome the 'false opposition' between rationality and emotion" by subsuming the latter under the former (Thomas 1991: 16). Why, one is tempted to ask, should Mithen have attempted to overcome a false opposition in which he apparently believes? More importantly, it is unclear whether Thomas believes that emotions play a role in rational thought. His statement that "the combination of rationality and emotion seems an oddly selective definition of humanity" supports the view that he does not regard them to be separable, in which case the crucial question is whether he would accept the proposal that emotions serve to support rationality if the rationality in question happened not to be grounded in evolutionary biology or economics. A negative answer would lead one to ask whether his suggestion that "Desires, emotions, forms of reason and techniques of self-interpretation are all contingent and historically situated" (Thomas 1991: 17) is intended to extend beyond the specificities of those enterprises to the connections between them? As noted earlier, this chapter does not attempt to adjudicate between claims and counter-claims about which aspects of human behaviour are biologically grounded and which historically, but rather to investigate whether dialogue with AI requires acceptance of biological and economically grounded approaches.

As Doran (2000) notes, the modelling of emotions is an active topic in Artificial Intelligence. This endeavour is grounded in the 'functional view' (Frijda 1995) that emotions "serve a purpose" (Cañamero and van de Velde 2000: 144), which is to aid decision-making, particularly activity selection. This is of course the view summarised by Mithen, so in light of Thomas' concerns, the critical question is whether it rules out modelling emotions that support alternative rationalities, or even emotions that do not support rationality at all. The first point of disjuncture with Mithen is that some recent AI models *explicitly* model emotions, whereas he merely proposes that emotions are *implicitly* included in models of adaptation via rational decision-making (Mithen 1991: 9). Thus, although Mithen argues that in his model of Mesolithic foraging, changes of state between, for example, stalking and killing "are only made possible by emotions acting as a system of internal communication: monitoring the success and failure of sub-goals and the need to adjust behavioural plans" (Mithen 1991: 13), this did not require any extra computer code that could have been discarded in the absence of any reference to emotions (see Chapter 6 of Mithen 1990). In contrast, recent AI models that include emotions typically incorporate computer code whose sole *raison d'être* is the implementation of those emotions. One particularly sophisticated example provides its agents with a 'synthetic physiology', which includes variables necessary for survival (e.g. heart-rate, energy, blood sugar level) and hormones released under different emotional states which modify the amount of the controlled variables, thereby amplifying motives and thus ultimately influencing behaviour (Cañamero 1997). The important point about this difference is that whereas the outcome of the emotional influence on rationality is completely predetermined in Mithen's model, this is not true in Cañamero's model, at least to the extent that the complexity of the interplay between emotions and reason may be sufficient to render it unpredictable in practice. In other words, Cañamero's model holds out the prospect of observing emotionally influenced behaviour that was not expected in a given situation and which therefore had not been *explicitly* imposed by the modeller.

Nevertheless, it may still be objected that Cañamero's synthetic physiology merely provides for the ultimate reduction of emotion to biology, thereby underwriting the rejection of 'history' which Thomas finds unhelpful. Since the physiology of Cañamero's agents is synthetic there is presumably no reason why it could not be altered to reflect an alternative understanding of the effect of particular hormones on decision making. This would still fail, however, to accommodate the social constructivist claim (e.g. Averill 1990) that expressions of emotion are socially prescribed and learned responses to given situations rather than results of particular physiological states. Cañamero and van de Velde (2000: 148) argue that the constructivist nature of emotions is in fact "not in contradiction with the fact of emotions corresponding to internal states, even though they can be defined and elicited by social relations". Accordingly, they describe at length a conceptual design for a multi-agent simulation model which would allow each agent some control over the expression of emotions according to its state, interests and the image it has of the other. In this way they hope to allow emotional states to contribute to the construction of intersubjectivity (Cañamero and van de Velde 2000: 147). Since Cañamero and van de Velde have not implemented the model as a computer program it is difficult to judge whether it is technically feasible and, if so, to what extent the results would have been 'built in'. Even so, it is clear that at least some AI researchers are prepared to entertain a social constructivist view of emotions. Such attempts to formalise the link between physiology and the expression of emotion in a social context can only help tease out what it means to claim that emotions are contingent and historically situated.

NON-DISCURSIVE THOUGHT

The question of *how* decisions are made in AI models connects not only with the issue of emotions, but also with that of non-discursive thought and being-in-the-world. As Hodder (2001: 10) notes, both Barrett and Thomas have responded to a perceived need for archaeologists "to develop a theory of behaviour which goes beyond the models of language and discourse". Barrett has drawn extensively on Giddens' theory of structuration and Bourdieu's writing about practice to explore what it is that should be the proper subject matter of archaeology and how that is implicated in the so-called archaeological 'record'. He takes from Giddens the notion that the social sciences should study "social practices ordered across time and space" (Giddens 1984: 2). This raises important questions about the equation of agency with individuals, a subject where AI may offer useful insights, but which is not discussed further in this chapter. Of more immediate concern here is Barrett's recognition, which owes much to Bourdieu (1977), that social practices are undertaken by agents who have practical knowledge, that is, who know "how to go on" in the world "as it is" without consciously reflecting upon it (Barrett 2001: 151). Such knowledge is literally non-discursive in the sense that it is not and cannot be spoken about.

Although Thomas arrives at the problem of knowledge from a different perspective – one more concerned with the relationship between human beings and nature – he too is led to emphasise the importance of non-discursive thought.

He seeks to replace a "very harsh Cartesianism in which the human body inhabits a geometrical world of mere objects, and all meanings are events which take place in the metaphysical space of the mind" (Thomas 2001: 171) with an understanding that meaning is produced through bodily engagement with the world. To this end he draws indirectly on Gibson's (1986) ecological approach to perception, which posits that entities in the world have intrinsic meaning for animal behaviour – meaning that can be recovered by attending to surfaces. This attention to surfaces is an aspect of being-in-the-world, in which "we negotiate and make sense of our surroundings without having to think about them analytically for much of the time" (Thomas 2001: 172). Thomas is not the only archaeologist to have emphasised the importance of embodiment: Tilley draws on Merleau-Ponty's (1962) phenomenology of perception to argue that the "human body provides the fundamental mediation point between thought and the world" (Tilley 1994: 14).

The idea that much human knowledge is non-discursive and that meaning arises through embodiment cuts to the heart of what is perhaps the most contentious debate in AI: whether all interesting aspects of human cognition can be modelled as though they involve the manipulation of representations of an independently existing world. Classical AI research has centred on thinking and, in particular, thinking construed in terms of reasoning between alternatives using symbolic models of the world. Such research typically assumes that the world is something "quite separate from the agent but passively available for the agent's activity" (Aylett and Barnes 2000: 197). Multi-agent simulation models constructed for archaeological purposes have, to date, adopted the classical framework for implementing environment-agent interaction. What the critics of those models do not discuss, however, is that the classical project has been the subject of a sustained critique from within the wider AI community.[3] Doubts about classical artificial intelligence have been raised on three grounds (but see Russell and Norvig 2003, Chapter 26 for a defence): the alleged insufficiency of monism; that human brains are not explicit, algorithmically driven devices; and that classical AI machines are disembodied. Since critics of the use of AI in archaeology do not resort to the first of these arguments it is not considered further. The other two are directly relevant to the issues of non-discursive knowledge and embodiment.

Writing about the possibility of understanding creativity by building computational models of it, Donald argues that "It is far more useful to view computational science as part of the problem rather than the solution. The problem is understanding how humans can have invented explicit, algorithmically driven machines when our brains do not operate in this way" (Donald 1994: 538). Attempts to build computer models that purport to mimic the operation of the human brain, not just its output, use artificial neural networks. Neural networks were first formalised in the 1940s (McCulloch and Pitts 1943), initially implemented by computer scientists in the early 1960s (e.g. Winograd and Cowan 1963) and then revisited with renewed vigour in the mid-1980s (Rumelhart and McClelland (eds.) 1986) under the banner *connectionism*. Although connectionist models have been built to solve practical problems requiring machine intelligence, connectionism has close links with the neurosciences, where it has been argued from the study of neuropathologies that the resilience of the human brain provides strong evidence that thinking is a distributed phenomenon. Thus connectionists see thoughts arising as emergent properties of neural networks rather than through the manipulation of symbols according to clearly specified rules. Indeed, some connectionists have questioned whether symbols have any explanatory role in detailed models of cognition (Russell and Norvig 2003), although the textbook view is that this question remains unanswered and that classical AI and connectionism are complementary rather than competing (Russell and Norvig 2003).

Connectionism provides ample evidence that the use of AI methods does not necessarily constrain agent cognition to the manipulation of symbols. It is less clear, however, that neural networks actually offer the most appropriate route for creating agents who have non-discursive knowledge. This uncertainty hinges on the *raison d'être* for creating artificial agents. If the purpose is to explain how non-discursive knowledge is immanent in the brain, then connectionism – particularly as it is practised in computational neuroscience – probably does provide the most appropriate conceptual and technological tools. If, on the other hand, the primary interest is to explain how non-discursive knowledge arises out of, and contributes to, an agent's engagement with the world, then connectionism may not have so much to offer because what is really required is a model of actions rather than brain states. Given that those archaeologists who have drawn attention to the importance of practical knowledge have not expressed great interest in brain states, it would probably be better to search elsewhere for a framework for the creation of artificial agents who have practical knowledge. An obvious starting point is the response to the criticisms of Dreyfus (1972) and Searle (1992) that classical AI machines are disembodied; in other words that they fail to interact in any significant way with their environment and other machines of their own kind.

As noted at the beginning of this chapter, the emergence of Distributed Artificial Intelligence (DAI) was a response to the problem of embodiment, at least to the extent that it allows problems to be solved as a result of interaction between a number of computational entities. Most DAI models assume that intelligence proceeds from the manipulation of symbols (Ferber 1999), but since the mid-1980s a number of researchers have taken what Aylett and Barnes (2000: 198) label a "behavioural approach" in which "Agent and environment together form a composite and dynamic system", so that there is a sense in which agent activity is always situated (Suchman 1987). Maris' and te Boekhorst's (1996) experiments with Didabots provide one example of the behavioural approach. Didabots are small autonomous robots that can, in small groups, push approximately half a set of randomly distributed polystyrene cubes into a central heap and line the remainder up against a wall. This outwardly simple task represents a non-trivial challenge to conventional (symbolic) DAI because it would require that the robots have concepts of a heap and a line, and, furthermore, that they be able to communicate about these. Didabots, however, have no such concepts: they accomplish their task simply by adjusting their motion in response to input from four sensors mounted on their chassis. From an archaeological perspective, the significance of Maris' and te Boekhorst's experiments lies in the concrete demonstration that a highly structured distribution of material does not necessarily provide evidence for complex reasoning with symbols. Rather, in this case, the structure arises out of the physical interactions between the Didabots and their world, so much so that one Didabot alone cannot produce the heap and line, even though the Didabots do not communicate in any conventional sense.

While Maris' and te Boekhorst's experiments clearly demonstrate that not all contemporary AI is wedded to the manipulation of symbols, it might nevertheless be objected that Didabots provide rather poor models of human non-discursive knowledge for at least two reasons. The first is that the Didabots do not have social relations with one another. In other words, any patterning that may exist in the encounters between any two Didabots is ultimately referable to the initial spatial distribution of polystyrene cubes and Didabots: it is not the result of Didabots reacting to one another differently according to who they are. Aylett and Barnes (2000) describe an experiment which comes closer to achieving some kind of sociality, at least to the extent that it involves joint attention mediated through action. Two robots, Ginger and Fred, are given the task of carrying a pallet to a docking station marked by a beacon. The beacon 'broadcasts' its location by means of infra-red (which the robots can detect), but the straight-line path to the beacon is blocked by obstacles which they must circumnavigate. Since each robot carries one end of the pallet on its 'head', they must keep apart by a distance that is roughly equal to the length of the pallet. What makes this particularly interesting for present purposes is that the robots are not equipped with a concept of distance, or a co-ordinate system that would allow one of them, on encountering an obstacle, to instruct the other to move in a particular direction, say, right or east. Instead, each robot simply attempts to keep the end of the pallet centred on the top of its 'head' while at the same time avoiding contact with obstacles. According to Aylett and Barnes, this provides feedback "a bit like the sensory feedback two people carrying a table would receive from the pressure of the table" and thus allows Ginger and Fred "to communicate though they have no concept of communication and no exchange of symbolic information takes place" (Aylett and Barnes 2000: 212–13).

The second reason why one might consider that Didabots provide poor models of human non-discursive knowledge concerns the nature and origin of their knowledge; in particular, is it hard-wired, or do they know something about how-to-go-on in the world that they did not know prior to their encounter with the polystyrene cubes? These are difficult questions to answer because they require a clear notion of what non-discursive knowledge is, in the sense of in what is it immanent? In more concrete terms, how would one find out what non-discursive knowledge the Didabots have? Since by definition it is not possible to ask them, the only alternatives are presumably to investigate their electrical wiring or to observe their actions. The Didabots' electrical wiring simply reveals that their wheels turn forward on the side nearest to which they sense the greatest reflected infrared and backward on the other side. It seems unlikely that this would be accepted as non-discursive knowledge since it is not learned, but fixed for the lifetime of the robot. The remaining source of information about the Didabots' non-discursive knowledge is their actions. The problem here is that it is impossible to observe how Didabots go-on in the world as-it-is in any other context (since that would be the world as-it-is-not!). So, either Didabots do not have non-discursive knowledge of the kind envisioned by Barrett, or else non-discursive knowledge is not a property of individual agents, but immanent in the patterning of interaction between agents and the world. Neither are easily discounted. One of the useful things about artifical agents inhabiting artificial (or at least staged) environments is that it is possible to reproduce the world as-it-is. When this was done by Maris and te Boekhorst (1996), the Didabots behaved identically from experiment to experiment: they did not learn to divide the cubes more equally or create the heap and line more quickly. It would, of course, have been astonishing if this were not so, given that their wiring is fixed. Perhaps if the Didabots were adapted in such a way that they could re-wire themselves in response to the outcome of their actions then they would be able to *learn* to move the cubes more quickly and so stake a more convincing claim to non-discursive knowledge? That may be so, but in order for their knowledge to remain non-discursive they would have to learn to do this without using a symbolic representation of their goal. One way that this might come about would be if the Didabots' modified world, the heap and line of cubes, afforded them some positive benefit. This, however, returns us to the notion that non-discursive knowledge is immanent in the patterning of interaction between agents and the world, a view which finds some support from the so-called Santiago Theory of Mind proposed by Maturana and Varela (1980). The most important point to take from this discussion of robotics is not that AI research necessarily has answers to questions posed by social scientists about the relationship between action and knowledge, but that it is engaged with some of those questions and provides a source of both real and thought experiments that may be helpful in thinking about them.

CONCLUSION

The 'agency in archaeology' debate has been conducted as though AI has nothing to say about agents and as though the extended dialogue between AI and the social sciences had never been established. Early in this chapter it was suggested that this lacuna may be at least partially a result of – rather than in spite of – the use of multi-agent simulation in archaeology. Specifically, existing simulation models have been populated with agents possessing rationalities grounded in modern economics or evolutionary biology, who reason by manipulating symbols and whose actions are never the result of non-discursive thought. As a result, it has been all too easy, unwittingly or otherwise, to dismiss multi-agent simulation and AI more generally as irrelevant to the study of a past in which the experience of being human might have been substantially different. The principle claim made in this chapter is that to continue in this vein would be unfortunate, if not willfully negligent, since it would deprive archaeology of access to a rich body of theory and perhaps even a practical methodology of direct relevance to the understanding of agency. Most concretely, it has been argued that it should be possible to construct multi-agent simulations whose agents act according to alternative rationalities. Indeed, the challenge here is not so much one for AI, but for archaeologists to adequately describe the rationalities in which they are interested. Admittedly, the construction of simulation models whose agents' 'reasoning' is not restricted to the manipulation of representations of an independent external world does represent more of a challenge for AI, but, contrary to the impression given by existing archaeological simulations, it is very much an active area of research involving constructive dialogue with the social sciences. Even at minimum, AI provides a useful conceptual framework for the task of teasing apart competing claims about the universality or otherwise of the experience of being human – a task that might otherwise founder on the missing answers to vital questions that were never asked amidst the fog of incompatible terminologies.

While – optimistically – this chapter may persuade those who are particularly interested in rationality, reason and non-discursive knowledge to take a fresh look at contemporary AI, others may feel that it has barely touched upon what they regard as the central aspects of agency. Regrettably all that can be done here is to restate the claim that AI offers insights across the range of Dobres' and Robb's themes in agency. This is particularly true of "scale" and "temporality and social change", which are served by a growing literature on the problem of causality in emergent phenomena (see Ferber 1999, Chapter 16 and Gilbert 1995 for a brief summary in a social science context), but it extends to intersubjectivity (briefly touched upon above) and even the political context (e.g. O'Sullivan and Haklay 2000). Perhaps the most important message is that if archaeologists really wish to explore the possibility that the experience of being human was different in the past, then the most exciting feature of contemporary AI is the question which it now asks, which is less "'What is mind?' or 'What are the necessary and/or sufficient conditions for something to be conscious?'" and more "How many different kinds of minds are there and how do they differ in their architectures and their capabilities?" (Sloman 1999: 41). The same spirit is evident in Artificial Life, which, it has been argued, "can contribute to theoretical biology by locating life-as-we-know-it within the larger picture of life-as-it-could-be" (Langton 1989: 1). It may be time to think seriously about the possibility that AI and AL could contribute to archaeology through the exploration of agency-as-it-may-have-been.

Notes

1   Although admittedly too recent to have influenced Dobres' and Robb's ((eds.) 2000) *Agency in Archaeology*.
2   Alternatively it could be that Thomas is switching between two different usages of the term 'reason': one to refer to a modern Western way of making decisions in particular, and the other to refer to ways of making decisions in general.
3   It is curious in this respect that Julian Thomas cites H. Dreyfus' (1991) commentary of Heidegger's *Being and Time* in his discussion of the nature of lived space (Thomas 2001: 172), but omits the same author's highly influential critique of artificial intelligence (Dreyfus 1972) from his discussion of the limitations of computer modelling (Thomas 1991).

References

Averill, J.R. 1990. A constructivist view of emotion. In R. Plutchik and H. Kellerman (eds.) *Emotion: theory, research and experience, Volume 1*, 305–39. New York: Academic Press.

Aylett, R. and Barnes, D. 2000. Connecting reflection and reaction. In K. Dautenhahn (ed.) *Human Cognition and Social Agent Technology*, 197–223. Amsterdam: John Benjamins Publishing Company.

Barceló, J.A., Vila, A. and Gibaja, J. 2000. An application of neural networks to use-wear analysis: some preliminary results. In K. Lockyear, T.J.T. Sly and V. Mihailescu-Bîrliba (eds.) *CAA96: Computer Applications and Quantitative Methods in Archaeology*, 63–70. Oxford: Archaeopress (BAR International Series 845).

Barrett, J.C. 1994. *Fragments from Antiquity: an archaeology of social life in Britain, 2900–1200 BC*. Oxford: Blackwell.

Barrett, J.C. 2001. Agency, the duality of structure and the problem of the archaeological record. In I. Hodder (ed.) *Archaeological Theory Today*, 141–64. Cambridge: Polity Press.

Bond, A.H. and Gasser, L. 1988. An analysis of problems and research in distributed artificial intelligence. In A.H. Bond and L. Gasser (eds.) *Readings in Distributed Artificial Intelligence*, 3–35. San Mateo, CA: Morgan Kaufman.

Boone, J.L. 1992. Competition, conflict, and development of social hierachies. In E.A. Smith and B. Winterhalder (eds.) *Evolutionary Ecology and Human Behavior*, 301–37. New York: Aldine de Gruyter.

Bourdieu, P. 1977. *Outline of a Theory of Practice*. Cambridge: Cambridge University Press.

Cañamero, D. 1997. Modeling motivations and emotions as a basis for intelligent behaviour. In W.L. Johnson (ed.) *Proceedings of the First International Conference on Autonomous Agents*, 148–55. New York: ACM Press.

Cañamero, D. and van de Velde, W. 2000. Emotionally grounded social interaction. In K. Dautenhahn (ed.) *Human Cognition and Social Agent Technology*, 137–62. Amsterdam: John Benjamins Publishing Company.

Clark, G.A. 1992. A comment on Mithen's ecological interpretation of Palaeolithic art. *Proceedings of the Prehistoric Society*, 58, 107–09.

Clark, J.E. 2000. Towards a better explanation of hereditary inequality: a critical assessment of natural and historic human agents. In M.-A. Dobres and J.E. Robb (eds.) *Agency in Archaeology*, 92–112. London: Routledge.

Clark, J.E. and Blake, M. 1994. The power of prestige: competitive generosity and the emergence of rank societies in lowland Mesoamerica. In E.M. Brumfiel and J.W. Fox (eds.) *Factional Competition and Political Development in the New Word*, 17–30. Cambridge: Cambridge University Press.

Conte, R., Hegselmann, R. and Terna, P. (eds.) 1997. *Simulating Social Phenomena*. Berlin: Springer-Verlag.

Cordell, L.S. 1972. *Settlement Pattern Changes at Wetherill Mesa, Colorado: a test case for computer simulation in archaeology*. PhD thesis, University of California, Santa Barbara.

Cowgill, G.E. 2000. 'Rationality' and contexts in agency theory. In M.-A. Dobres and J.E. Robb (eds.) *Agency in Archaeology*, 51–60. London: Routledge.

Damasio, A.R. 1995. *Descarte's Error: emotion, reason and the human brain*. London: Picador.

Dautenhahn, K. (ed.) 2000. *Human Cognition and Social Agent Technology*. Amsterdam: John Benjamins Publishing Company.

de Sousa, R. 1987. *The Rationality of Emotion*. Cambridge, MA: MIT Press.

Dean, J.S., Gumerman, G.J., Epstein, J.M., Axtell, R.L., Swedlund, A.C., Parker, M.T. and McCarroll, S. 2000. Understanding Anasazi culture change through agent-based modeling. In T.A. Kohler and G.J. Gumerman (eds.) *Dynamics in Human and Primate Societies: agent-based modelling of social and spatial processes*, 179–205. New York: Oxford University Press (Santa Fe Institute Studies in the Sciences of Complexity).

Dobres, M.-A. and Robb, J.E. 2000. Agency in archaeology: paradigm or platitude? In M.-A. Dobres and J.E. Robb (eds.) *Agency in Archaeology*, 3–17. London: Routledge.

Dobres, M.-A. and Robb, J.E. (eds.) 2000. *Agency in Archaeology*. London: Routledge.

Donald, M. 1994. Computation: part of the problem. *Behavioral and Brain Sciences*, 17, 537–38 (Comment on M.A. Boden, Précis of *The Creative Mind: Myths and Mechanisms*).

Doran, J.E. 2000. Trajectories to complexity in artificial societies: Rationality, belief and emotions. In T.A. Kohler and G.J. Gumerman (eds.) *Dynamics in Human and Primate Societies: agent-based modelling of social and spatial processes*, 89–144. New York: Oxford University Press (Santa Fe Institute Studies in the Sciences of Complexity).

Doran, J.E. and Hodson, F.R. 1975. *Mathematics and Computers in Archaeology*. Edinburgh: Edinburgh University Press.

Doran, J.E., Palmer, M., Gilbert, N. and Mellars, P. 1994. The EOS project: modelling Upper Palaeolithic social change. In N. Gilbert and J. Doran (eds.) *Simulating Societies*, 195–221. London: UCL Press.

Dreyfus, H.L. 1972. *What Computers Can't Do: a critique of artificial reason*. New York: Harper and Row.

Dreyfus, H.L. 1991. *Being-in-the-World: a commentary on Heidegger's 'Being and Time', Division 1*. Cambridge, MA: MIT Press.

Earle, T.K. and Preucel, R.W. 1987. Processual archaeology and the radical critique. *Current Anthropology*, 28, 501–38.

Ferber, J. 1999. *Multi-Agent Systems: an introduction to distributed artificial intelligence*. Harlow: Addison-Wesley (English edition).

Foucault, M. 1973. *The Birth of the Clinic: an archaeology of medical perception*. London: Tavistock.

Frijda, N.H. 1987. *The Emotions*. Cambridge: Cambridge University Press.

Frijda, N.H. 1995. Emotions in robots. In H.L. Roitblat and J.-A. Meyer (eds.) *Comparative Approaches to Cognitive Science*, 501–16. Cambridge, MA: MIT Press.

Frijda, N.H. and Swagerman, J. 1987. Can computers feel? Theory and design of an emotional system. *Cognition and Emotions*, 1, 235–57.

Gibson, J.J. 1986. *The Ecological Approach to Perception*. Hillsdale, NJ: Lawrence Erlbaum Associates.

Giddens, A. 1984. *The Constitution of Society: outline of a theory of structuration*. Cambridge: Polity Press.

Gilbert, N. 1995. Emergence in social simulation. In N. Gilbert and R. Conte (eds.) *Artificial Societies: the computer simulation of social life*, 144–56. London: UCL Press.

Gilbert, N. and Conte, R. (eds.) 1995. *Artificial Societies: the computer simulation of social life*. London: UCL Press.

Gilbert, N. and Doran, J. (eds.) 1994. *Simulating Societies: the computer simulation of social phenomena*. London: UCL Press.

Gilbert, N. and Troitzsch, K.G. 1999. *Simulation for the Social Scientist*. Buckingham: Open University Press.

Goodman, D. and Keene, R. 1997. *Man Versus Machine: Kasparov versus Deep Blue*. Cambridge, MA: H3 Publications.

Hodder, I. 1985. Post-processual archaeology. In M. Schiffer (ed.) *Advances in Archaeological Method and Theory*, 8, 1–25. New York: Academic Press.

Hodder, I. 2001. Introduction: a review of contemporary theoretical debates in archaeology. In I. Hodder (ed.) *Archaeological Theory Today*, 1–13. Cambridge: Polity Press.

Kohler, T.A. 2000. Putting social sciences together again: an introduction to the volume. In T.A. Kohler and G.J. Gumerman (eds.) *Dynamics in Human and Primate Societies: agent-based modelling of social and spatial processes*, 1–44. New York: Oxford University Press (Santa Fe Institute Studies in the Sciences of Complexity).

Kohler, T.A., Kresl, J., West, C.V., Carr, E. and Wilshusen, R.H. 2000. Be there then: a modeling approach to settlement determinants and spatial efficiency among Late Ancestral Pueblo populations of the Mesa Verde region, US southwest. In T.A. Kohler and G.J. Gumerman (eds.) *Dynamics in Human and Primate Societies: agent-based modelling of social and spatial processes*, 145–78. New York: Oxford University Press (Santa Fe Institute Studies in the Sciences of Complexity).

Lake, M.W. 1995. *Computer Simulation Modelling of Early Hominid Subsistence Activities*. PhD thesis, University of Cambridge.

Lake, M.W. 2000. MAGICAL computer simulation of Mesolithic foraging. In T.A. Kohler and G.J. Gumerman (eds.) *Dynamics in Human and Primate Societies: agent-based modelling of social and spatial processes*, 107–43. New York: Oxford University Press (Santa Fe Institute Studies in the Sciences of Complexity).

Lake, M.W. 2001a. Numerical modelling in archaeology. In D.R. Brothwell and A.M. Pollard (eds.) *Handbook of Archaeological Sciences*, 723–32. Chichester: John Wiley and Sons.

Lake, M.W. 2001b. The use of pedestrian modelling in archaeology, with an example from the study of cultural learning. *Environment and Planning B: Planning and Design*, 28, 385–403.

Langton, C.G. 1989. Artificial life. In C.G. Langton (ed.) *Artificial Life*, 1–47. Redwood City, CA: Addison-Wesley (Santa Fe Institute Studies in the Sciences of Complexity, No. 6).

Maris, M. and te Boekhorst, I.J.A. 1996. Exploiting physical constraints: heap formation through behavioural error in a group of robots. In *Intelligent Robots and Systems, Proceedings of the 1996 IEEE/RSJ International Conference on Intelligent Robots and Systems (IROS96) Part III*, 1655–61. Osaka.

Maturana, H. and Varela, F. 1980. *Autopoiesis and Cognition*. Dordrecht: D. Reidel.

McCulloch, W.S. and Pitts, W. 1943. A logical calculus of the ideas immanent in nervous activity. *Bulletin of Mathematical Biophysics*, 5, 115–37.

McGlade, J. 1997. The limits of social control: Coherence and chaos in a prestige-goods economy. In S.E. van der Leeuw and J. McGlade (eds.) *Time, Process and Structured Transformation in Archaeology*, 298–330. London: Routledge.

Merleau-Ponty, M. 1962. *Phenomenology of Perception*. London: Routledge and Kegan Paul.

Mithen, S.J. 1988. Simulation as a methodological tool: inferring hunting goals from faunal assemblages. In C.L.N. Ruggles and S.P.Q. Rahtz (eds.) *Computer and Quantitative Methods in Archaeology 1987*, 119–37. Oxford: BAR International Series 393.

Mithen, S.J. 1989a. Evolutionary theory and post-processual archaeology. *Antiquity*, 63, 483–94.

Mithen, S.J. 1989b. Modeling hunter-gatherer decision making: complementing optimal foraging theory. *Human Ecology*, 17, 59–83.

Mithen, S.J. 1990. *Thoughtful Foragers: a study of prehistoric decision making*. Cambridge: Cambridge University Press.

Mithen, S.J. 1991. 'A cybernetic wasteland'? Rationality, emotion and Mesolithic foraging. *Proceedings of the Prehistoric Society*, 57, 9–14.

Mithen, S.J. 1993. Individuals, groups and the Palaeolithic record: a reply to Clark. *Proceedings of the Prehistoric Society*, 59, 393–98.

Murray, T. and Walker, M.J. 1988. Like WHAT? A practical question of analogical inference and archaeological meaningfulness. *Journal of Anthropological Archaeology*, 7, 248–87.

Newell, A., Shaw, J. and Simon, H. 1957. Empirical explorations of the logic theory machine: a case study in heuristics. In F. Feigenbaum and J. Feldmann (eds.) *Computers and Thought*, 109–33. New York: McGraw-Hill.

Oatley, K. and Johnson-Laird, P. 1987. Towards a cognitive theory of emotions. *Cognition and Emotions*, 1, 1–29.

O'Sullivan, D. and Haklay, M. 2000. Agent-based models and individualism: is the world agent-based? *Environment and Planning A*, 32, 1409–25.

Reynolds, R.G. 1986. An adaptive computer model for the evolution of plant collecting and early agriculture in the eastern valley of Oaxaca. In K.V. Flannery (ed.) *Guila Naquitz: Archaic foraging and early agriculture in Oaxaca, Mexico*, 439–507. London: Academic Press.

Rumelhart, D.E. and McClelland, J.L. (eds.) 1986. *Parallel Distributed Processing*. Cambridge, MA: MIT Press.

Russell, S. 1999. Rationality and intelligence. In M. Woolridge and A. Rao (eds.) *Foundations of Rational Agency*, 11–33. Dordrecht: Kluwer Academic Publishers.

Russell, S. and Norvig, P. 2003. *Artificial Intelligence: A Modern Approach*. Upper Saddle River, NJ: Pearson Education (2nd edition).

Searle, J.R. 1992. *The Rediscovery of the Mind*. Cambridge, MA: MIT Press.

Shanks, M. and Tilley, C. 1987a. *Social Theory and Archaeology*. Cambridge: Polity Press.

Shanks, M. and Tilley, C. 1987b. *Re-Constructing Archaeology*. Cambridge: Cambridge University Press.

Shennan, S. 1986. Evolution, adaptation and the study of prehistoric change. In S.E. van der Leeuw and R. Torrence (eds.) *What's New? A closer look at the process of innovation*. London: Unwin Hyman.

Simon, H.A. 1976. From substantive to procedural rationality. In S.J. Latsis (ed.) *Method and Appraisal in Economics*, 129–48. Cambridge: Cambridge University Press.

Sloman, A. 1999. What sort of architecture is required for a human-like agent? In M. Woolridge and A. Rao (eds.) *Foundations of Rational Agency*, 35–52. Dordrecht: Kluwer Academic Publishers.

Suchman, L.A. 1987. *Plans and Situated Actions: the problem of human-machine communication*. Cambridge: Cambridge University Press.

Thomas, J. 1988. Neolithic explanations revisited: the Mesolithic-Neolithic transition in Britain and south Scandinavia. *Proceedings of the Prehistoric Society*, 54, 59–66.

Thomas, J. 1991. The hollow men? A reply to Steven Mithen. *Proceedings of the Prehistoric Society*, 57, 15–20.

Thomas, J. 2001. Archaeologies of place and landscape. In I. Hodder (ed.) *Archaeological Theory Today*, 165–86. Cambridge: Polity Press.

Tilley, C. 1994. *A Phenomenology of Landscape: paths, places and monuments*. Oxford: Berg.

van der Leeuw, S.E. and McGlade, J. 1997. Structural change and bifurcation in urban evolution: a non-linear dynamical perspective. In S.E. van der Leeuw and J. McGlade (eds.) *Time, Process and Structured Transformation in Archaeology*, 331–72. London: Routledge.

Watkins, J.W.N. 1952. Ideal types and historical explanation. *British Journal of the Philosophy of Science*, 3, 22–43.

Winograd, S. and Cowan, J.D. 1963. *Reliable Computation in the Presence of Noise*. Cambridge, MA: MIT Press.

Winterhalder, B. 1981. Optimal foraging strategies and hunter-gatherer research in anthropology: theory and models. In B. Winterhalder and E.A. Smith (eds.) *Hunter-Gatherer Foraging Strategies*, 13–35. Chicago, IL: University of Chicago Press.

Wobst, H.M. 1974. Boundary conditions for Palaeolithic social systems: a simulation approach. *American Antiquity*, 39, 147–78.

CHAPTER 11

AGENCY AND VIEWS BEYOND META-NARRATIVES THAT PRIVATISE ETHICS AND GLOBALISE INDIFFERENCE

Stephanie Koerner

PREFACE

In his influential 1940 essay, 'Theses on the Philosophy of History' (1992 [1940]), Walter Benjamin argued that a 'state of emergency' marked contemporary social life, not in an exceptional sense, but as one of its principal rules. Contemporary lack of attention to the problem was not without precedents, but was nonetheless a radical manifestation of the extraordinary range of ways in which powerful meta-narratives render the barbarity of civility invisible (cf. Elias 1982; Hale 1993). Such insights, Benjamin said, might help us bring about a corresponding 'state of emergency' in relations between academia and human affairs, and a struggle with forms of knowledge and power that threaten the variability of human life-worlds.

Among the challenges facing critics of meta-narratives, Benjamin stressed the phantasmagorical ways in which academia has responded to various crises, thus ignoring the need to question traditional pictures of progress as some sort of boundless, linear and necessary process, with its own paradoxically a-historical modes of operation. Benjamin was particularly critical of responses of 'surprise' and 'amazement' to crises that, according to these pictures, should not be occurring.

In Paul Klee's painting, *Angelus Novum*, Benjamin found an image useful for understanding these 'counter-striving dispositions'. The angel looks out from the canvas towards its past, with its back to the future's conditions of possibility. Wings spread, he looks as though he is being blown away from something that he is fixedly contemplating. This, Benjamin said, is how the angel of meta-narratives ought to be depicted. You and I may experience a variety of events arising from largely uncomprehended conditions. The angel perceives only one *transcendent* catastrophe hurling wreckage in front of him. He may want to make good what has been smashed, but the storm has caught his wings and is propelling him into a future towards which his back is turned. The pile of *immanent* debris grows skyward. Similarly, exponents of images that envisage progress as a smooth linear process respond with 'surprise' to crises that, according to their view, should not be occurring.

The stakes have increased since Benjamin's times. Consider, for instance, the most frequent response to questions about turning points in the trial at

Nuremberg. Eyewitnesses almost invariably recall the presentation of a film of the concentration camps as they had been found by the advancing allied troops. The defence counsel had been invited to see the film the night before. Only a handful showed up. None who saw it in court the next day ever forgot it. A viewer recorded: "The impression we get is of an endless river of white bodies flowing across the screen, bodies, ribs sticking out through the chests, pipe stem legs, skulls, eyeless faces" (Tusa and Tusa 1995: 160). The flickering beam continued for hours, projecting onto the screen worldscapes of tumbling bodies, bodies with holes between the eyes and bodies being shovelled like dirt by giant bulldozers over cliffs into common graves, and bodies that were not bodies at all but charred bone and flesh – an "endless river" – grotesque thin arms reaching towards the sky. For security a light was left on in the defendants' box. Many in the courtroom watched their reactions, and saw how they looked away from the screen. The court artist drew portraits of what Hanna Arendt (1963) would describe as the alarming 'banality of evil'. As the film ended, the room was frozen in stunned silence. At last, the judges rose and left, not even managing to speak the usual formal words of adjournment.

In *Negative Dialectics* (1973 [1963]: 361–63), a book that would become foundational to the 'critique of meta-narratives', Adorno wrote that, after Auschwitz, we can no longer talk with confidence about truth and necessity. Actual events have shattered beliefs about what sorts of abstract metaphysical ideals can be reconciled with experience. The rivers of bodies and smoke rising from crematoria of Auschwitz were not simply a particular take on a problematic world picture. They hinged upon the (embodied and materialised) ways in which the duality of wholly *privatised ethics* and *globalised indifference* was unified in a single order, and directed (under previously unimaginable conditions of power and violence) towards the destruction of variability among life-worlds. The film was (like an apocalypse) at once too early *and* too late: too early, since it was still as inconceivable as it was in plain view, and too late, since we had already entered a state of amnesia as to the scales on which human life-worlds had been transformed (symptomatically, academia saw a remarkably increased emphasis on normative paradigms in the 1940s through to the 1970s). It would be quite some time before we came to grips with the historical implications of Freud's observations on 'historical memory' and 'repetition', or with what is rendered invisible by widespread dualist paradigms for human nature, history and knowledge.

INTRODUCTION

The last decade has seen a remarkable growth of interest among participants in discussions of archaeological theory in concepts of 'agency' (and such related themes as 'material culture' and 'historical memory'). Something of the range of approaches is suggested by the literatures on: (a) 'factionalism and political development' (Brumfiel and Fox (eds.) 1994); 'agency and structure' (e.g. Dobres and Robb (eds.) 2000); (b) 'ethnic' or 'cultural identity' (e.g. Shennan (ed.) 1989; Graves-Brown, Jones and Gamble (eds.) 1996); (c) time and material culture

(Thomas 1996); (d) archaeology's historical relationships to nationalist, imperialist and colonialist political ideologies (e.g. Trigger 1984; Kohl and Fawcett (eds.) 1995; Díaz-Andreu and Champion (eds.) 1996; Schnapp 1996; Atkinson, Banks, and O'Sullivan (eds.) 1997); and (e) 'historical archaeologies' of hitherto 'invisible people and processes', including those of the 'contemporary past' (e.g. Moore and Scott (eds.) 1997; Buchli and Lucas (eds.) 2001; McGuire 2002).

Despite the variability of these literatures, we can identify several questions on which the sharpest disagreements turn, including: 'if agency is important for understanding particular human activities, must it be included in explanations of long-term socio-cultural change?' (cf. Dobres and Robb 2000: 11–12). Some positive responses to this question point to the importance of ethics to archaeology's epistemic conditions of possibility (e.g. Moore 2000; Barrett 2000; Gero 2000; Johnson 2000).

The most influential positions on agency build upon constructs drawn from two bodies of theory. One is associated with the expression, the 'critique of meta-narratives', the other with the terms 'globalisation' and 'multi-culturalism'. Little attention is given to tensions between these bodies of theory; the impact on archaeology of wider academic and public debates arising from these tensions (such as those centring on the supposed dichotomy of 'human rights' and 'cultural identities'); or the bearing that archaeological enquiries into the diversity of past and present day life-worlds may have on these tensions.

This chapter expands upon the above-mentioned topics, and argues for the relevance to these issues of an ontology of the historicity of agency, in which ethics plays a central role.

PART 1: ASPECTS OF THE CRITIQUE OF META-NARRATIVES

The first two sections concern tensions between the meta-narratives critique and conceptions of, and influential paradigms for, globalisation. In the present section, emphasis falls on the implications of dualist paradigms for human nature and history for the status of ethics in contemporary epistemology and ontology. The next section compares sociological, anthropological and philosophical perspectives on globalisation, and considers, in light of these, Anthony Giddens' (1981) very influential model of 'agency and structure'.

Dualist paradigms for human nature and knowledge

Despite the diversity of the works of major contributors to the meta-narratives critique, we can identify some common foci. One is the critique (or deconstruction) of the epistemic bases of dualist paradigms for *human nature* and *knowledge*. At issue are the essentialist categories that underwrite the notion of a transcendental, timeless, and placeless human agent, which has functioned for over two centuries as a supposedly universally valid foundation for understanding all human thought and behaviour. This critique has powerful implications. It illuminates the interdependence of a wide range of dualist categories (subject-object, mind-body, nature-culture, science-values, Western-non-Western) and challenges claims about an a-historical standpoint from which one can make judgements about reason, knowledge, appropriate action, and what is definitive of being human. These categories and claims hinge upon dividing the world between *perceiving* and *extended things*, such as Immanuel Kant's (1955 [1790]) division of the capacities of the human mind for *rational freedom and moral responsibility* from a universe filled with things determined by *causal necessity*.

Historical meta-narratives

It is difficult to overstate the importance to these paradigms for *human nature* and *knowledge* of meta-narratives concerning *history* that are rooted in Enlightenment and Romantic images of the 'coming into consciousness' of the aforementioned divisions. The most influential narratives centre on the 'Scientific Revolution' and the 'Birth of Modernity'. Their critique has complex theoretical, political and ethical implications too. It shows how these narratives standardise the criteria whereby human experience and culture can be said to vary (e.g. Friedman 1992; Miller (ed.) 1995; Wilk 1995; Koerner 2001), and how nationalist, colonialist, and imperialist ideologies (to use Trigger's 1984 terms) exploit these criteria to eclipse discrepant experience and render some human beings 'invisible' to the ethical faculties of their contemporaries (cf. Gaitta 2000; Geertz 2000).

Some features of these narratives are actually of extraordinary antiquity, dating to the earliest horizons of traditions that have been seen as constitutive of the history of Western intellectual culture. These include: (a) dualist structures; (b) notions that human history forms a unilinear trajectory; and (c) essentialist premises concerning the conditions of historical knowledge. All relate to Collingwood's (1956 [1949]) arguments concerning the modes of reasoning that can be expected to result in *universal*, *providential*, *apocalyptic*, and *periodised* narratives.

The paradigms for the expansion of the Roman empire written by Eusebius of Caesaria (*Historia ecclesiastica*, 1973) and Augustine of Hippo (*De civitate Dei*, 1963), in the early 4th and early 5th centuries AD respectively, provide useful examples for illustrating the antiquity of these features. These bishops' accounts differ in several respects, relating to opposing positions on the relationships between Church and Empire. In Eusebius' *Historia ecclesiastica*, the entire history of the world (sacred *and* profane) is portrayed as an evolutionary process guided by Divine Providence: humanity is to be restored to its original 'royal nature' through the evolution, expansion, and transformation of the Roman empire to Christianity. Objecting to the radical implications of such a view, Augustine (1963) emphasised an ontic gap between the origins and evolutionary trajectories of *the City of God 'wandering on the earth' (the Church)* and *the profane worldly city of man (Rome)*. Nonetheless, their works converge on key points. Both Eusebius and Augustine combine principles drawn from Graeco-Roman philosophy and Judeo-Christian apocalyptic teleology (Funkenstein 1986). Both envisage the Roman empire as *the* paradigmatic example for understanding truths about human nature, knowledge, and relations between sacred and profane world history. But Eusebius envisages the empire as the means whereby sacred ideals and human realities *will be joined in a unified order*, while for Augustine the empire reveals the reasons why humans *fail to realise such an order*. This contrast compares interestingly with differences between Enlightenment and Romantic perspectives on science, progress, human nature and history.

The importance of essentialist ontologies to ancient and modern dualist models of the conditions of historical knowledge is difficult to overstate. Such ontologies concern 'being', how the sorts of things that exist came to be, and why these rather than other sorts of things exist. Since antiquity, essentialising approaches have been structured around two opposing poles, with absolute unity and permanence on one side, and dis-unity (pure flux) on the other (McGuire and Tushanska 2001). Questions about change (in particular, historical change) are rendered problematic by this dichotomy. The most influential approach has been that put forward by Aristotle in the *Metaphysics*, which centres on the question: if something can be said to be subject to change, what is the essence of that something? He offered three alternative answers: (1) the unchanging aspect, (2) the changing aspect, and (3) both – that is, the interaction of changing and unchanging aspects. In the views which underwrite the narratives under consideration, the important answer is (1), and the others have to be reducible to it.

Focusing on the *unchanging* essence of things leads to the disregard of questions about how things come into being, and the reduction of ontology's task to classification. It means that ontology is supposed to focus on questions like: what (underlying substance) makes particular items what they are? What distinguishes them from one another? What timeless substances distinguish different categories of entities? It demands that the answers to these questions add up to universally-valid generalisations about the range of categories in terms of which all things existing at all times can be classified (McGuire and Tushanska 2001: 45–47). And it demands *the division of all spatial and temporal scales* into categories that conform with its mode of dichotomising *universals and particulars*.

These modes of reasoning have underwritten the most influential theories about the conditions of historical knowledge (and the epistemic conditions of archaeology). Essentialism permits only a-historical theories of knowledge (such as those structured around a subject-object dichotomy) and modes of historical description and explanation that fit these theories (such as narratives centring on nature-culture, individual-society, and Western-non-Western dichotomies). The terms employed in these narratives have to be valid for all times and places, as well as accounting for their variability. These requirements impose severe restrictions on options for historical representation. Modern options centre on the aforementioned ontic division of all things between *perceiving things* (individual 'minds' and, until quite recently, God) and *extended things* (all the rest, like nature and society). One option treats history as a perceptual experience, which exists in the minds of individual subjects (as cognitive 'content' of 'mental states'). The other treats history as an 'extended thing' that can occur in different forms, such as the social types of band, tribe, chiefdom and state, or cultures of different times and places: Neolithic Britain, Bronze Age Denmark, Medieval France, Renaissance Italy, Modern Europe.

According to Benjamin (1992 [1940]: 252–53), among the requirements of dualist meta-narratives, the notion of homogeneous empty time is particularly significant. The critique of these narratives has shown how crucial this notion is for: (a) the equation of reality with epistemic necessity; (b) dualist paradigms for socio-cultural change; and (c) the division of all spatio-temporal scales between categories that conform to a mode of dichotomising universals and particulars, as just discussed. Through these mechanisms, it underwrites, for instance, (a) the reduction of cultural variability to imaginary measures of evolutionary progress; (b) a number of problematic current core-periphery models of globalisation; and (c) the reduction of human agency to images of "timeless, featureless, interchangeable and atomistic individuals, untethered to time or space" (cf. Gero 2000: 38).

Dualist paradigms for the conditions of archaeological knowledge are based on a notion of a 'record' that depends on these modes of reasoning. Linda Patrik's paper, 'Is there an archaeological record?' (1985) deals with the options they offer. One treats the 'record' as a fossilised imprint of the operations of past social systems, the other treats it as a 'text' that can, through interpretation, reveal the operations of past symbolic systems or mental states. Both depend on the aforementioned notions of time and epistemic necessity, and divisions of spatio-temporal scales of socio-cultural change between categories that fit the universals-particulars dichotomy.

In these notions, in order for something to be epistemically possible (i.e. knowable) it must be somehow presently real, and vice versa. No allowance is made for potentiality, or the possibility that something can be known that is not a current reality. Spatialised notions of time are crucial for the aforementioned conceptions of an archaeological 'record'. In order for the past or future to be epistemically possible, they must actually exist somewhere now. They have to exist as a sort of 'hidden' present. In consequence, past and future function simply as labels given to a supposedly contemporary reality. If we treat this 'hidden' (*transcendent*) reality as though it exists alongside contemporary (*immanent*) reality (say, the archaeological materials collected), we must ignore all temporally-contingent relationships. The past loses its status as past, the present its potentiality, and the future its futurity. Past and future are collapsed into one timeless all embracing *now*, an entity that eclipses the ontic variability of past, present, and future. It is no accident that such ideas also underpin paradigms that centre on the importance of 'empathy' as a methodological tool for gaining insight into the cognition of past individuals (cf. Bell 1994).

The aforementioned options for the conditions of historical knowledge have also underwritten the leading paradigms for social change, including: *subject-centred* (or methodological individualist) explanation, which treats the mind or cognitive content of mental states as the primary source of change, and *system-centred* (idealist and materialist) explanations, which attribute all changes that are singled out as being historically significant to forces that transcend (and explain) the thoughts and actions of individuals. These apparently antithetical paradigms for socio-cultural change converge on key points, including: (a) categories for dividing the spatio-temporal scales on which change occurs, which conform with their modes of dichotomising universals and particulars; and (b) the roles they give to these categories of scale in respect of how they relate human activities to historical processes (as evidenced by treatments of relations between the particular activities of individuals and periodisation of the histories of social systems or cultures). In this light, it should be no surprise that we are unable to give intelligible support to claims that the former (particular activities) could bring about change in the latter (social systems). In order to satisfy dualist requirements for the conditions of historical knowledge, we must ignore all qualities and processes that are deemed unnecessary to their classificatory schemes. This means ignoring, among other things, questions of the contributions that temporally-contingent social relationships make to the diversity of human forms of life.

There are many good examples of the range of narratives that have been structured around the above-outlined requirements. The one that had the most significant impact on the works of Hegel (1975 [1831]), Marx and Engels (1975 [1846]), Morgan (1963 [1877]), Durkheim (1960 [1914]), and Weber (1958 [1904]), as well as numerous other contributors to the current state of theory, is Immanuel Kant's account of the histories of nature and culture. Kant entitled this account an 'Idea of a universal history from a cosmopolitan point of view' (1963 [1784]). Prior to Kant, the relationship between these histories (as well as between human beings' natural and cultural dimensions) was conceptualised as a problem that impeded the scientific (epistemic) status of the human sciences and historiography (Cassirer 1960). Kant's (1963 [1784]) 'universal history' addressed this supposed problem in a new way. It lifted the methodological difficulties of integrating nature and culture to the metaphysical level of an antithesis, and applied the resulting notion of a dialectic to a theory about the unity of nature's and culture's history. Kant's solution to the problem of the scientific status of historical and anthropological knowledge treated (a) culture as a necessary outcome of the history of nature (indeed the means whereby 'nature's hidden plan' would be realised), and (b) the dialectics of nature-culture and subject-object as the causally-necessary forces driving human history (cf. Collingwood 1956 [1949]). Kant situated his narrative between the 'things in themselves' (out there) and the capacities of the mind for 'phenomena'. It described history as proceeding through a unilinear series of stages in the evolution of nature; human capacities for 'reason' and 'moral freedom'; and the phenomena that structure culture. The series begins with nature introducing particles governed by Newtonian principles of Matter and Motion into infinite time-space (cf. Kant 1963 [1784]). It then leads to the emergence of 'primitive' forms of human consciousness and social life, then the 'Copernican Revolution' and rational modes of consciousness, and is supposed to eventuate in the unification of social ideals and realities in an ideal 'civic order' (Kant 1963 [1784]).

The effects of such approaches to culture became apparent in the 1960s, when categories structured around the Western-non-Western dichotomy became the focus of sophisticated anthropological critiques. The critiques advanced by Eric Wolf (1982) and Johannes Fabian (1983) have had impacts throughout the human sciences and humanities. Among other things, these authors show how dualist paradigms deny the coevality of different contemporary ways of life by classifying them in ways that reduce cultural *differences* to *distances* in cultural evolutionary time. Such denial of coevality has had serious consequences, including the rendering of some people invisible to the ethical faculties of members of powerful 'majorities', and the legitimation of the marginalisation and oppression, even unto death, of 'minorities'.

Critiques of meta-narratives have influenced archaeology in many ways. For instance, the recent literature on archaeological methods and theory includes works on the complex historical relations between predominant paradigms for research and 19th and 20th century nationalist, colonialist and imperialist ideologies. There are also now publications that concern 'peoples and processes' that traditional paradigms render invisible. Another theme is the impact of Enlightenment and Romantic philosophies of history. For example, Bruce Trigger (1995) writes the following about opposing 'processualist' and 'post-processualist' paradigms for research:

> European thought has been dominated for over 200 years by a pervasive dichotomy between rationalism, universalism and positivism on the one hand and romanticism, particularism (or 'alterity'), and idealism on the other. The first of the philosophical packages was initially associated with French liberalism, the second with German reaction ... Both ethnic nationalism and post-modernism (which is the essence of post-processualism) are products of the romantic side of the polarity (Trigger 1995: 263).

Despite these concerns with the historicity of dominant research programmes, little attention is given to tensions between such critiques of dualist paradigms and the impact of widespread academic and public discussion of globalisation. Although ethics is now a key theme, emphasis has not fallen on the status of ethics in contemporary epistemology and ontology. This status is tied up with the various epistemic and ontic matters outlined above, and perpetuates the apparent unresolvability of debates over whether human agency must be included in accounts of not only particular events, but also long-term socio-cultural change.

Dualist paradigms for agency and the privatisation of ethics

Two features of modern meta-narratives are particularly relevant: (a) the role they give to the dichotomies nature-culture, subject-object, and individual-society; and (b) their notion of a 'subject', a notion that motivates Hannah Arendt's (1977 [1961]: 147) critique of the "privatisation of ethics". These features underpin the a-historical notion of a human 'self' (subject), which is now a key theme in the archaeological literature on agency and the critical literatures of the human sciences and philosophy in general (e.g. Barnes 2000; Geertz 2000). Some of the terms involved are of considerable antiquity, but the ways in which they have been defined in these meta-narratives lack pre-modern precedents (cf. Blumenberg 1983).

These features did not develop in a vacuum. They are rooted in responses to the need for new social structures and modes of solidarity which developed in the wake of the Thirty Years War (1618–48). Social changes had counterparts in intellectual culture. An example was the notion that one could develop new *social* ideals and institutions on the basis of principles that the emerging physical sciences were using to investigate (and manipulate) *nature*. The key question was that of whether one could model both universally-valid explanations of the physical world and new forms of social organisation (and solidarity) on mathematics and logic (e.g. Hobbes 1962 [1651]; see, for example, Shapin and Schaffer 1985).

In the views of a number of Enlightenment scholars, Descartes' epistemology and Newton's mathematical laws of Matter and Motion suggested that the answer to this question could be yes (Descartes 1984–91; Newton 1934 [1687]). Descartes' (1984–91) epistemology hinged on an ontic distinction between the *rational freedom of moral intellectual decision in the human world* and the *causal necessity of mechanical processes in nature*. One consequence was the radical transformation of traditional notions of the 'subject', with profound implications for the status of ethics in modern epistemology. Louis Dupré (1993: 112–14) explains that throughout most of the history of Western intellectual culture, the 'subject' was an ontic principle that referred to the underlying essence of things (and the ontic foundation of all things was God or an ideal Nature). In Cartesian epistemology, the individual human subject is forced to function as the primary source of all meaning and value (cf. Blumenberg 1983).

The emergence of debates over the extent to which this situation was a *cause for uncertainty* took place in the midst of social, theological, and epistemic crises (Toulmin 1990: 45–88; Dupré 1993: 113–15; Funkenstein 1986: 290–327). During the 16th century, writers such as Disiderus Erasmus, François Rabelais, William Shakespeare, Michel de Montaigne and Francis Bacon had suggested that the self (human agent) was the *source* of all uncertainty (Toulmin 1990: 19–20, 56–57). The approach to uncertainty that Descartes proposed established the foundations of the status of ethics in modern epistemology. It turned issues of moral (as well as social and ontological) uncertainty into an epistemic problem. Specifically, Descartes translated these issues into philosophical '*doubt*', and made doubt the basis of a method for attaining epistemic *certainty* (Toulmin 1990: 45–89; Dupré 1993: 114–16).

But it was not until Kant that modern moral philosophy divided a supposed inner realm of 'mental substance' ontologically from the causal network of the social and physical universe. Kant articulated this separation in terms of the aforementioned image of human nature, history and knowledge. Kant's approach centres on:

(a) A meta-narrative in which supposed nature-culture, individual-society, subject-object antitheses function as explanations of the driving forces in human history.

(b) A 'transcendental metaphysics' in which the individual subject is both envisaged as the source of all meaning and value and reduced to a node through which the 'final cause' of human capacities for 'reason' is to be realised, namely the 'perfect civic constitution' (Kant 1963 [1784]).

(c) The restriction of ethics to the mind's capacity for 'reason' and 'moral freedom' (Kant 1955 [1790]).

Arendt (1977 [1961]: 147) suggests that the withdrawal of moral freedom from the material physical and social order ('out there') to the inward domain of individual mental states may have realised the objective that modern thought had been pursuing from the onset, namely: "the privatization of freedom". Once meaning and value can be envisaged as a function of the supposedly disembodied individual mind, it can be conceptualised as independent of historically contingent social and ethical circumstances. Thus, moral privatisation removes ethics from its traditional status *at the centre of epistemology and ontology*, and reduces social life to inter-individual systems of contractual structures. Here, we may glimpse the bases of the a-historical conceptions of the individual (self) that critics of meta-narratives challenge, and which have become the focus of much cross-disciplinary discussion of agency, material culture, and historical memory.

PART 2: GLOBALISATION AND ASSOCIATED CONCEPTIONS OF AGENCY

Today, few terms occur with greater frequency in the current theoretical literatures of the human sciences and humanities than that of 'globalisation'. This section concerns tensions between the aspects of the meta-narratives critique outlined above and leading paradigms for globalisation, and examines the most influential framework for 'agency and structure' associated with the latter.

Sociological, anthropological and philosophical perspectives on an 'age of globalisation'

The literature on globalisation is vast and reflects sharply contrasting points of view, ranging from transnational economics (where the term originated) to international law, and from national heritage institutions to post-colonial studies and anthropology. Anna Tsing (2002: 454) says: "Click on worldmaking connections. Your screen fills with global flows ... [Indeed,] in the last ten years, ... many commentators imagine a global *era*, a time in which no units or scales count for much except the globe." Despite the variety of sociological and anthropological perspectives, it may be possible to identify some key contrasts, as well as to explore some philosophical issues posed that relate directly to our considerations thus far.

In their introduction to *The Anthropology of Globalization: a reader* (Inda and Rosaldo (eds.) 2002), Jonathan Xavier Inda and Renato Rosaldo note that, in anthropology, the term refers to:

> ... the intensification of global interconnectedness, suggesting a world full of movement and mixture, contact and linkages, and persistent cultural interaction and exchange. It speaks ... to the complex mobilities and interconnections ... of capital, people, commodities, images and ideologies – through which the spaces of the globe are becoming increasingly intertwined (Inda and Rosaldo 2002: 2).

Some of the most controversial debates concern discrepancies between (a) ethnographic studies that investigate globalisation through the "prism of the local" (to borrow Miller's 1995 expression), and (b) core-periphery models, which envisage globalisation as a process of homogenisation, and the "spread of western goods" as evidence of "the absorption of peripheral cultures into a ... mass-mediated global marketplace" (Inda and Rosaldo 2002: 14). At issue is not so much whether certain forms of material culture, which have been classified as 'modern Western', can be found in an increasing number of places, but whether predominant models provide satisfactory accounts of this distribution and the extent to which they obscure "discrepant experiences" (to borrow Said's 1993 term) of the world we live in today.

Spatialised conceptions of time figure essentially to many leading paradigms for globalisation. Notable are models that envisage globalisation as centring on the transformation of time-space *perception* in a world of de-territorialised *extended* things, put forward by David Harvey (1989) and Anthony Giddens (1990). In Harvey's (1989: 141) model, globalisation involves fundamental change in experiences of time and space. 'Time-space compression' is a function of the social, economic, and especially technological processes, which shrink experience of relations between temporal and spatial distances. Time and space are no longer perceived as major constraints on human activities.

By contrast, Giddens' model centres on human perception of 'time-space *distanciation*', which follow from the stretching of human activities across time and space. In this model, social life is torn away from locality, and interaction increasingly centres on relations between absent others apart from face-to-face interaction. The model hinges on a dichotomy of two types of interaction: pre-modern/'traditional' versus modern. The former is characterised by 'face-to-face interaction' in closely bounded local spaces. The latter has resulted in disembedded social relations interlocked by global space-time (Giddens 1990: 22).

The complementarity of these models is difficult to overemphasise. Despite appearances to the contrary, they share several problematic features, including (a) spatialised (and largely mechanical) conceptions of time, and (b) an ontic division of all things between perceiving and extended things. Remarkable too is a conception of human agency consisting of features which date back to Locke's proposal, in *An Essay on Human Understanding* (1975 [1689]), of an atomic psychology and atomic sociology, on the basis of his interpretation of Newtonian laws of Matter and Motion. While the former explains away mind as a mosaic of sensations and ideas linked in the 'mental states' of individual agents, the latter reduces society to a cluster of human atoms attracting and repelling each other (cf. Koyré 1968).

Anthropologists are particularly worried about models which envisage globalisation simply as (a) a Western, (b) a homogenising, and (c) a core-periphery affair. The consequences are alarmingly similar to those which concern Wolf's *Europe and the People Without History* and (1982) and Fabian's *Time and the Other* (1983). In several models of globalisation, an abstract notion of modern Western culture continues to function as the standard for interpreting the variability of all others. Now, though, the 'yardstick' seems to be potential for de-territorialisation – the degree to which they can be separated from territorial moorings and the speed with which they can move across the world, leaving a trail of uniformity behind. De-territorialised culture seems to function as symbolic currency in a multi-cultural 'global village' (cf. Laclau 1990). Patterns of exclusion and appropriation, immigrations and migrations, and the crises giving rise to these are obscured by phantasmagorical efforts to extend the norms of pre-existing meta-narratives (cf. Benjamin (1992 [1940]; Appadurai 1991, 2002 [1996]; Friedman 1992; Latour 1993, 2000; Bhabha 1994; Miller (ed.) 1995; Wilk 1995; Prazniak and Dirlik (eds.) 2001).

One of the questions posed is that of whether models based on metaphysical 'yardsticks' for measuring time-space *compression* and *distanciation*, in a world of isolated perceiving things and deterritorialised extended things, risk rendering invisible patterns of social *exclusion* and *appropriation*. One wonders what happened to arguments such as those of Benjamin and Adorno mentioned at the outset; and why *trauma* and *diaspora* have become key themes in literatures relating to agency, material culture, and historical memory.

These issues are being broached by recent critics of universalising perspectives on globalisation, and of the relations between academia and public affairs, which render invisible the diversity of contemporary life-worlds. Trauma and diaspora are recurrent themes in publications arising from efforts to replace notions of 'human rights' and 'cultural identity' that are rooted in Enlightenment and Romantic pictures of human nature and history (for instance, Wilson (ed.) 1997; Cowan, Dembour and Wilson (eds.) 2001; Prazniak and Dirlik (eds.) 2001), and from attempts to probe the limits of historical representations in order to shed light upon aspects of the contemporary world that are absent from these pictures (cf. Friedlander (ed.) 1992; Bhabha 1994; Wilson 1997a and b). In part 4, we will return to these topics and consider how they relate to archaeological discussions of agency. Here, we examine conceptions of agency that underwrite several leading models of globalisation.

Agency-structure and 'ontological insecurity'

Archaeological interest in new approaches to agency developed in relation to concerns to expand the scope of social (or anthropologically-oriented) archaeology. For instance, in the introduction to the volume *Factional Competition and Political Development* (1994: 3), Brumfiel discusses the potential relevance of "agent-centered practice theory developed in the work of Barth [1966], Giddens [1979], and Ortner [1984]" to both the critique and extension of "the two prevailing approaches to prehistoric social change: cultural ecology and Marxism". One of Brumfiel's (1994: 3) arguments is that an "agent-centered perspective maximizes the amount of data drawn into the analysis and thus permits the most detailed and complete account of specific cases of political continuity and transformation". This view builds upon the premise that "any particular sequence of development is uniquely complex and contingent . . . In the face of such complexity, it is necessary to alternate between a subject-centered and a system-centered analysis" (Brumfiel 1994: 12):

Both cultural ecology and structural Marxism postulate the narrow constraint of human behavior and decision-making within these systems: by stringent consideration of energetic efficiency in cultural ecology and by the limits of structurally-determined consciousness in Marxism ... These same constraints operate equally for all members of society, implying a condition of cultural homogeneity for human groups (Brumfiel 1994: 13).

Brumfiel (1994: 12–13) says that agency-centred approaches offer an alternative to cultural ecology and Marxist paradigms that ignore the importance of human choice in the complexity of historical situations and, thus, in the study of social change. At issue are concerns with 'free will' or the capacity of humans to behave voluntarily. Brumfiel's arguments touch upon the problem that we need at least some notion of intentionality in order to broach questions of how it is possible for people to engage prevailing constraints, and transform the circumstances from which these arise.

There are many differences of opinion on the potential of agent-centred approaches, and on the impacts of their historical rootedness in problematical images of modern capitalism. Wolf (2001: 410), for example, was sceptical about the explosion of the late 20th century popularity of models of "how agents construct themselves in relation to power and interest". He (2001: 410) objected to their being "unduly voluntaristic" and argued for more sophisticated treatments of issues posed by Marx's argument that 'men make their own history, but they do not make it as they please'. Wolf's concerns are shared by some critics in archaeology of a-historical images of "timeless, featureless, interchangeable and atomistic individuals, untethered to time or space" (Gero 2000: 38). Indeed, Joan M. Gero, in her contribution to *Agency in Archaeology* ('Troubled travels in agency and feminism') asks whether recent emphasis on agency-centred approaches is:

... not just another homogenizing, meta-MANeuver to fit nuanced and gendered human experience into pre-determined, categorical masculinist modes of thought ... Once again we confront a concept that is put into service to reduce the infinitely diverse ways in which humans take action ... to a unidimensional mode ... All human action is expressed as a single (suitably vague) dynamic, divorced from context, content and condition, and agents in any single socio-historical moment are made to be roughly equivalent to [the same as] agents in any other (Gero 2000: 38).

The impact of Giddens' framework for 'agency and structure' on current approaches to both agency and globalisation makes it particularly useful to our considerations. An influential version is presented in his contribution ('Agency, institution and time-space analysis') to the volume, *Advances in Social Theory and Methodology: towards an integration of micro- and macro-sociologies* (Knorr-Cetina and Cicourel (eds.) 1981).

Giddens believes that what is needed in order to solve the problems that dualist paradigms create in the human sciences and philosophy is a framework for 'bridging' gaps between micro- and macro-analytic scales. He focuses our attention on how rationalist and empiricist theories of knowledge centring on a subject-object dichotomy divide these scales between 'action theory' and 'institutional analyses'. While action theory centres on the subject (conceived as an omniscient free-willed individual), institutional analysis centres on the object (essentialising an out-thereness that determines human experience and action). Neither view concerns connections between activities and events, which occur on micro-analytic scales, and processes that occur on macro-analytic scales. The resulting 'gap' relates to the apparent unresolvability of the question of whether agency matters not just for studies of particular events, but also for those concerning long-term socio-cultural change (cf. Dobres and Robb 2000: 11–13).

Giddens' (1981) proposed 'bridge' hinges on a model of human behaviour centring on two terms: *capability* and *knowledgability*. The former refers to the capacity of human beings to 'act otherwise' (that is, a distinguishing feature of human behaviour is that it is 'voluntary' or 'chosen'). Knowledgability is the means whereby members of society apprehend its structures and operations. Structures (institutions) are both resources and constraints. They are conditions of possibility for human agency, but since human behaviour is voluntary, structures cannot be said to determine (or *cause*) it directly. Giddens (1981: 172) divides the process into three parts: (a) *structure*, recursively organised rules and resources that have a virtual existence outside of time-space; (b) *system*, reproduced relations between actors or collectivities, and situated in time-space; and (c) *structuration*, conditions governing system reproduction.

Time is an essential component of both Giddens' paradigms for globalisation and for integrating micro- and macro-sociological analyses. Giddens (1981: 173) points to the importance to his approach of Braudel's (1966 [1958]) distinction between the time scale of daily social activities and the *longue durée* of historical time. This suggests something of the reasons why agency does not figure importantly in Giddens' approach to what Braudel (1966 [1958]) called *conjunctures* in the *longue durée*. In both Braudel's and Giddens' approaches, *conjunctures* occur on the time scales of the latter. Both Giddens' and Braudel's approaches to major socio-cultural change (*conjunctures*) hinge upon the division of spatio-temporal scales between categories that conform with their modes of conceptualising contrasts between the *particular* and the *general*. Thus, in light of our considerations of these themes in part 1, *conjunctures* are particular instanciations of the generalities that constitute the *longue durée*. Remarkable also is the importance of the aforementioned dichotomy between ontic *perceiving* and *extended* things to these space-time-history paradigms. *Conjunctures* occur in the *longue durée* of extended things (like geography, social systems, and in the structures of collectively-shared 'mental equipment' [*outillage mental* or *mentalité*]). An excellent example is Braudel's definition of such a structure as:

> ... a reality which can distort the effect of time changing its scope and speed ... [Structures] operate simultaneously as a support and an obstacle. As obstacles, they act as limitations ... 'envelopes' in the mathematical sense from which man and his experiences can never escape (1966 [1958]: 18).

Within this view, the capacity to act voluntarily is a function of perceiving things (individual minds), and 'mental equipment' (such as historical narratives) structures the cognitive content of mental states. However, individuals and their activities function only as (micro-scale) nodes through which such (macro-scale) mental structures and social systems operate.

Some additional light can be thrown on these themes by asking how Giddens envisages the ways in which 'agency and structure' become linked in the first place. In considering this question, as well as the aforementioned themes, it bears stressing that Giddens is not explicitly concerned to offer an ontology of agency and structure (or of capability and knowledgability). Moreover, as Barry Barnes points out, in *Understanding Agency: social theory and responsible action* (2000), much of Giddens' work is not so much concerned with change as with questions of why individuals act routinely and how this relates to patterns of continuity and change in social systems. Barnes (2000: 29) suggests that, "[f]aced with the need to account for the patterned character of social action", Giddens' initial emphasis on the undifferentiated and embodied capacities of agency for change became overshadowed by concerns with "the internal states of a differentiated psyche". In this connection, he gave the notion of an anxiety-engendered individual need for "ontological security" an increasingly important explanatory role. In Giddens' terms:

> ... [a]ctors wants remain rooted in a basic security system, largely unconscious and established in the first years of life ... Ontological security can be taken to depend upon the implicit faith actors have in conventions (codes of signification and frameworks of normative regulation) via which, in the duality of structure, the reproduction of social life is effected. In most circumstances in social life, the sense of ontological security is routinely grounded in mutual knowledge employed such that interaction is 'unproblematic', or can be 'taken for granted' (Giddens 1979: 218–19).

The idea of a need for 'ontological security' is based on a Freudian image of the individual psyche. It does provide an answer to such questions as why individuals with agency act routinely and how they come to function as nodes through which systems operate. But it conflicts with developments in evolutionary psychology and philosophy, which bear upon the ontic preconditions of what Giddens calls 'capability' and 'knowledgability' (for instance, Johnson 1987; Cosmides 1989; Boyer 1990, 2000; Kusch 2002). Also, if we accept this idea, we gain a concept for tying 'agency to structure' in a way that fits the spatio-temporal scale requirements of Braudel's (1966 [1958]) model. But we remain unable to offer intelligible answers to such questions as: why the capacity to act otherwise should be seen as a distinguishing feature of human agency; whether agency should be included in explanations of socio-cultural transformations; or how it is possible for people to engage prevailing constraints, and transform the circumstances from which these arise.

PART 3: ETHICS AND THE ONTOLOGY OF THE HISTORICITY OF AGENCY

This section argues for the relevance to some of the challenges facing critiques of meta-narratives in an 'age of globalisation' (to borrow Prazniak's and Dirlik's expression) of an ontology of the historicity of agency, which gives ethics a central role. For heuristic purposes, I take my departure from two influential responses in archaeology to the meta-narratives critique, namely: (a) arguments against the notion of a human self, which is prior to its embodied and material preconditions (cf. Foucault 1980; Bourdieu 1990; Butler 1993); and (b) concerns to focus attention on discrepant experiences (e.g. Gero 1991; Appadurai 1991, 2002 [1996]; Said 1993; Mattingly (ed.) 1997). I admire much of the epistemic work that has been motivated by objections to traditional notions of a timeless, placeless, disembodied agent. But I worry that, if we come too close to reducing agency to embodied material preconditions, we are unlikely to be able to address issues posed by studies seeking to focus on discrepant experiences.

Fortunately the last decades have seen some relevant developments take place in archaeology, in philosophical approaches to intersubjectivity, and in regard to probing the limitations that dualist paradigms impose on historical representation, which have been expanding the scales on which meta-narratives privatise ethics and globalise indifference. In the case of archaeology, the works of John Barrett (1994, 2000) and Christopher Gosden (1994) provide good examples. Both authors reject essentialist perspectives on the conditions of archaeological knowledge (an archaeological 'record') and related a-historical notions of agency. Barrett's (2000) approach centres on the terms 'structuring conditions' and 'structuring principles'. The former are envisaged as the historically-contingent embodied and materialised conditions of possibility for human agency. These resemble Wittgenstein's (1958) conception of 'language games' as the conditions of possibility for human 'forms of life', but Barrett emphasises embodied and materialised non-discursive fields of practice. Structuring principles are defined as the means whereby human beings inhabit structural conditions: "they are expressed in the agents' abilities to work on those conditions in the reproduction and transformation of their own identities and conditions of existence" (Barrett 2000: 65).

Gosden's approach stresses the 'materiality' and 'mutuality' of human ways of life. In *Social Being and Time* (1994), he writes that:

> ... the term 'materiality' refers to human relations with the world, 'mutuality' looks at human-interrelationships. Materiality and mutuality are linked here for the simple reason that they are inseparable. Full social relations can only be set up though making and using things; full relations with the world only come about through people working together (Gosden 1994: 82).

These approaches have important advantages. They enable us to abandon notions of an archaeological 'record' that hinge upon the conceptions of time, human nature, scales of socio-cultural change, and the conditions of possibility for historical knowledge, which were discussed in part 1. We can abandon conceptions of the past as a fixed reality 'hidden' somewhere behind its fossilised 'record'. Instead of envisaging (to use Benjamin's 1992 [1940] terms) the "site" of historical dynamics as empty, it can be "filled with the presence of the now". Barrett and Gosden stress the historical contingency of the past and of presently available conditions of archaeological knowledge. Causal relations obtain only contingently between successive events, and *all* simultaneous conditions of possibility for human life-worlds are independent of one another since, as conditions, they cannot act on their own.

The relationships that concern Barrett's and Gosden's approaches are not reducible to a dichotomy between mental states, locked into the minds of individual subjects, and a world of objects (including society) 'out there' (Barrett and Koerner 2001). They concern processes of perception and modes of objectification that occur in a wide range of historically-contingent implicit and explicit scales and modes (cf. Miller 1987; Rorty 1989; Bourdieu 1990; Brandom 1994). There is no such thing as a timeless, placeless 'self' that can be understood apart from its embodied and material preconditions. But we do not have to risk reducing thought to practice (cf. Foucault 1980) or abandon notions of human selves and intentionality altogether.

Robert Brandom's work, *Making it Explicit: reasoning, representing and discursive commitment* (1994), indicates why this is the case, and suggests something of the bearing that Barrett's and Gosden's approaches have on the importance of ethics to an ontology of the historicity of agency. Brandom shows that we can replace traditional dualist notions of *representation* by the open-ended concept, *expression*. The latter enables us to replace the opposition between (a) *internal* and *external* representations (on which treatments of history as either a product of *perceiving* things or as an *extended* thing hinge) with (b) a range of *implicit* and *explicit* socially-situated processes of objectification, which carry the materiality and mutuality of human relationships forward over time.

Brandom's work also indicates why replacing traditional notions of representation is necessary if we want to pursue some of the promising implications of notions of 'social agency' *without abandoning the importance of intentionality for understanding processes of individuation*. Ignoring these processes makes it impossible to account for how humans can have discrepant experiences, and even for how they can interact (Arendt 1989 [1958]). Brandom explains:

> Only a creature who can make beliefs explicit – in the sense of claiming and keeping discursive score on claims – can adopt the simple intentional stance and treat another as having beliefs implicit in its intelligent behavior. Just so, only a creature who can make attitudes towards the beliefs of others explicit – in the sense of being able to ascribe scorekeeping attributions – can adopt the explicitly discursive stance and treat others as making their beliefs explicit, and so as having intentionality (Brandom 1994: 639).

The value of these observations extends beyond their advantages for an intelligible approach to human individuation and interaction. They relate to the relevance of an ontology of the historicity of human agency, which gives ethics a central role, to several challenges facing critics of meta-narratives in 'an age of globalisation'. Our treatment of our fellow humans as possessing intentionality is essential to the constitution of ourselves. *We not only make our shared epistemic and ontological commitments (our collectivity) explicit, we make ourselves explicit as social agents by making that collectivity explicit.*

Brandom's arguments relate to questions about how 'structuring principles' articulate with 'structuring conditions' (Barrett 2000) and how 'materiality and mutuality' (Gosden 1994) are linked. They bring into relief the importance of ethics to an ontology of these linkages, which eschews 'invisible hand' meta-narratives centring on dichotomies between individual perceiving things and extended things, and between how concrete embodied human beings *are* and how rational 'mental states' *ought to be*.

Your and my experience informs us that human beings are mutually accountable and mutually susceptible social creatures (Barnes 2000). As Barry Barnes (2000) points out, our interaction is informed by our experience that human beings are creatures that act voluntarily. Focusing on ethics enables us to understand the ways in which human beings freely choose and freely act as mutually accountable and mutually susceptible creatures, and that they do so while affecting and being affected by each other as creatures of this kind. Our interaction as human agents is always situated in contingent ethical relationships (commitments), which make self-understanding possible. Our relationships to the world (ontic, epistemic, social, material, and historical commitments) are created through our ethical relationships to one another as mutually susceptible, mutually accountable, (intentional) beings (Brandom 1994; Barnes 2000; McGuire and Tuchanska 2001). Such a view takes us beyond a-historical dichotomies of *agency* and *structure*, and suggests alternatives to images of agents that reduce human beings to "timeless, featureless, interchangeable and atomistic individuals, untethered to time or space" (Gero 2000: 38). It rejects the very dichotomies of *being* and of *acting*, of the *self* and the acting for *others* in history on which metaphysics hinges.

Focusing on the importance of ethics to an ontology of the history of agency allows us to develop alternatives to pictures of society as a sum of atomic individuals. As Norbert Elias (1991: 12, 17–19) puts it, human communities are very particular sorts of 'wholes'. Such pictures envisage human communities as harmonious unities without "contradictions, tensions, or explosions" (Elias 1991: 12). They either render contradictions invisible or treat them as obstacles to the realisation of norms (cf. Benjamin 1992 [1940]). Openness, changeability and internal tensions characterise the histories of all communities. The 'wholeness' of communities is not a function of interacting atomic entities, consisting of natural and cultural parts (cf. Hobbes 1962 [1651]; Locke 1975 [1689]; Kant 1963 [1784]). Rather, whatever we are treating as the 'wholeness' (or *identity*) of communities may consist of the implicit and explicit fields of thought and practice that constitute the life-worlds of mutually susceptible and mutually accountable ethical agents, who have differing experiences of the world precisely as such beings.

These observations would seem to have bearing upon the concerns that are motivating current discussions of discrepant experiences (e.g. Gero 1991; Appadurai 1991, 2002 [1996]; Said 1993; Mattingly (ed.) 1997). They relate to the question of whether agency must be taken into consideration not only in studies of particular events, but in long-term trajectories of socio-cultural change. Concerns with these kinds of issues motivated Edmund Husserl's (1970 [1936]) emphasis on the importance of ethics for understanding the dynamics of human life-worlds. In *The Crisis of European Science and Transcendental Phenomenology* (1970 [1936]) Husserl challenged the long tradition of philosophies of history structured around such dichotomies as those of subject-object, mind-body, and is-ought. For Husserl, human beings were not atomistic, interchangeable nodes through which social systems or cultural histories operate. A human life-world can be envisaged as a prism of diverse fields of experience, including the inanimate world given in sensation, the vital world that is given to us as embodied living beings, and an ethical dimension in which other human beings are apprehended as centres of meaning and value. These fields are interrelated, and our considerations of the mutual susceptibility and accountability of human beings suggest something of the nature of their interconnections, as well as of what Barrett (2000) refers to as "structuring conditions". In the approach outlined here, ethical fields cannot emerge without the others. However, they are ontically prior to the others and constitutive of historically-significant relations between them.

PART 4: SOME CONCLUDING COMMENTS RELATING TO CHALLENGES FACING CRITIQUES OF META-NARRATIVES IN AN 'AGE OF GLOBALISATION'

In his 'Theses on the Philosophy of History' (1992 [1940]), Walter Benjamin argued for a change in relations between academia and human affairs centring on critiques of historical meta-narratives, which render invisible violence done to the variability of human conditions of possibility. The stakes at issue have changed since Benjamin's times. Increasingly phantasmagorical world-pictures have been created and employed to legitimate the marginalisation, exploitation and oppression even until death of 'minorities'. It has taken a long time for academia to call into question the ways in which apparently unresolvable debates centring on dualist paradigms for human nature, knowledge and history impede our ability to engage the consequences and corollaries of *privatised ethics* and *globalised indifference*.

These concluding comments take their departure from themes mentioned at the outset, such as the question of whether agency should be included in approaches to major historical *conjunctures*. We noted that several positive responses to this question emphasise the importance of ethics to archaeology's epistemic conditions of possibility (e.g. Moore 2000; Barrett 2000; Gero 2000; Johnson 2000). For instance, Henrietta Moore, in a paper entitled 'Ethics and ontology: why agents and agency matter' (2000) presents the following arguments:

> The social engagement archaeologists have with the people they study is through the ethical spaces created by the pre-theoretical assumptions and values that make the discipline and its practice possible. These assumptions might be better termed the very conditions of possibility of archaeology itself. They include, for example, the idea that people in the past had societies and social relations . . . But the past has never just been about the past; it has always been what makes the present able to live with itself. And we could not live with ourselves if our archaeology left no space for individuality, freedom of choice, will, self-determination, creativity, innovation, and resistance. No archaeologist could live with such a view because humans would then have no role, or very little in the making of their own history (Moore 2000: 261).

This emphasis did not develop in a vacuum. It relates to changes in the roles given to ethics in contemporary epistemology and ontology, new relationships between academia and public affairs, and growing awareness of the complexity of the challenges facing critics of meta-narratives in an 'age of globalisation'.

The first two parts of this chapter concerned tensions between the two main bodies of theory informing current discussions of agency: the 'critique of meta-narratives' and discourses on 'globalisation'. Part 3 took its departure from two responses to the meta-narratives critique: (a) arguments against the notion of a human self, which is prior to its embodied and material preconditions, and (b) concerns to focus attention on discrepant experiences. I argued for the relevance to tensions between these responses (and to challenges facing critics of meta-narratives in an 'age of globalisation') of an ontology of the historicity of human agency in which ethics plays a central role. The requirements of the proposed approach suggest that the ethical fields around which human life-worlds are structured cannot emerge without the others (embodied and materialised). But they are prior to the others and constitutive of historically-significant relations between them.

Such a view offers a fresh perspective on how human agency can (a) make a difference, (b) act against external constraints, and (c) transform the social systems from which these constraints arise. It suggests that single discrepant experiences and single ethical acts can 'irradiate' other fields of human experience. They can take on paradigmatic qualities, as evidenced by new practices and modes of material culture, the arts, etc. (such as those being discussed in the current literatures touching upon the question of how human communities constitute their 'identities'). Insofar as these qualities attest the existence of an ethical field, single ethical acts can transform life-worlds. That is, single acts can render explicit experiences of discrepancies between how things are and ought to be *on the very scales on which human meanings and values are generated*. In this view, it may be the structure of human experiences of meanings, values and practice (or what Barrett and Gosden are referring to with the terms 'structuring principles' and 'mutuality and materiality') that constitute historical *conjunctures* and the emergence of new cultural forms and conditions. However, in order to illuminate these processes, we abandon teleological images of a *longue durée*.

It is not possible here to discuss the proposed approach in more detail, or to go step by step over the ways in which it relates to issues examined in parts 1 and 2. Instead I will conclude by suggesting something of what it implies for archaeology's relevance to challenges facing critiques of meta-narratives in an 'age of globalisation'. Emphasis falls on efforts to develop alternatives to traditional modes of envisaging 'human rights' and 'cultural identity' as a dichotomy, and to probe the constraints dualist paradigms impose on our options for historical representation.

Archaeology and critiques of meta-narratives

Images of human 'origins' and other 'origin events' are essential to dualist meta-narratives concerning human nature, knowledge and history (for instance, Ingold 1986; Schnapp 1996; McManus (ed.) 1996; Stone and MacKenzie (eds.) 1990; Rudebeck 2000; Mizoguchi 2002). The consequences are not simply academic. Steven Toulmin puts this eloquently in *Cosmopolis: the hidden agenda of modernity* (1990):

The terms in which we make sense of the past, and the ways in which our view of the past affects our posture in dealing with the future. The beliefs that shape our historical foresight represent (as German philosophers put it) our *Erwartungshorizonten*, or horizons of expectations. Those horizons mark the limits to the field of action in which, at the moment, we see it as possible or feasible to change human affairs, and to decide which of our most cherished practical goals can be realized in fact (Toulmin 1990: 1).

Archaeology is in an ideal position to engage some of the most problematic generalisations about human nature and history. Through its roles in education and numerous other public institutions, archaeology may be in a likewise excellent position to critique pictures of an 'age of globalisation', which eclipse the extraordinary diversity of past and present day human worlds.

Contextualising 'human rights' and 'cultural identity'

There is now an impressive literature suggesting archaeology's importance to new ways of conceptualising 'human rights' and 'cultural identities' (for instance, Wilson (ed.) 1997; Cowan, Dembour and Wilson (eds.) 2001; Prazniak and Dirlik (eds.) 2001). In *Culture and Rights: anthropological perspectives*, Jane Cowan (2001: 3) argues that the variety of today's human rights discourses obliges us to go beyond traditional modes of associating human rights with the Enlightenment, and culture with Romantic political ideology. These result in assumptions that the relation of rights to culture must be one of opposition: rights versus culture, universalism versus relativism (Cowan 2001: 4). Richard Wilson examines the impacts on anthropology of these views in *Human Rights, Culture and Context* (1997a):

> Anthropology has only begun to respond to this expansive transnational legal discourse ... In 1988, the edited volume *Human Rights and Anthropology* [Downing and Kushner (eds.) 1988], demonstrated the overlap between anthropology and indigenous rights advocacy, and in 1994, the American Anthropological Association (AAA) convened on the theme of human rights. Increasingly anthropologists began to ponder the relationship between anthropological debates about culture, identity and state violence and the activities of human rights organizations. However, the number of anthropologists actively researching transnational legal processes is relatively small, and of these the number specializing in human rights law is even smaller (Wilson 1997a: 1).

> At present discussions of the cross-cultural applicability of human rights still revolve around the universalism/relativism debate and the importance of culture ... Two main issues here are: first what concept of human ontology is to be used, and what rights naturally extend from that view of human nature; and second, what significance should be given to the notion of 'culture' in the construction of a normal moral order, and to what degree does global diversity in systems of justice undermine any basis for the universality of human rights (Wilson 1997a: 3).

Despite the range of viewpoints represented in these volumes, they seem to agree that "the ubiquity and the diversity of both rights discourses and rights practices, on the one hand, and their enormous implications for justice and peace on the other, make it more compelling than ever to widen the debate and make it more interdisciplinary" (Cowan 2001: 1). Several authors stress creating new approaches to culture "as an object of rights discourses, as well as to the local and global conditions which compel and constrain such claims and the contexts in which they are articulated" (Cowan 2001: 3). Wilson argues that what is needed "are more detailed studies of human rights according to the actions and intentions of social actors within wider constraints of institutionalized social power" (Wilson 1997a: 3–4).

The situation compares interestingly with views presented in a volume entitled *Places and Politics in an Age of Globalization* (Prazniak and Dirlik (eds.) 2001). The contributors share concerns with the 'oppressive implications' of 'dehistoricised and desocialised essentialist' notions of 'collective identities' (Prazniak and Dirlik (eds.) 2001). But they argue for moving "beyond politically nihilistic preoccupation[s] with essentialism, ... [that] have exhausted their critical power and serve little purpose beyond an involutional elitist narcissism", in order to be able to "rephrase the problem of identity in politically more productive ways" (Prazniak and Dirlik (eds.) 2001: 3).

Jonathan Friedman's (2001) paper centres on some of the difficulties at hand. It begins with observations on the massive increase in the activities of indigenous minorities throughout the world since the 1970s: "[t]heir struggles have become global news, and they have entered numerous global organisations so that they have become an international presence." It is a mistake, however, to treat this as evidence that these people have 'become globalised'. Many are "struggling for control over their conditions of existence, conditions that have been denied to them at the very least ... They have been marginalised in their own territories, boxed and packaged, and sometimes oppressed unto death ... This struggle is not about culture as such, but about social identities which are constituted around cultural and experiential continuities that are only poorly mirrored in western categories, not least, in anthropological categories" (Friedman 2001: 53).

Some recent archaeologies of the recent or 'contemporary' past suggest useful approaches to these cultural and experiential continuities, and especially the embodied, materialised and ethical fields that constitute their conditions of possibility. They also relate to cross-disciplinary efforts to probe the limitations of the dualist options for historical representation.

Probing the limits of options for historical representation structured around the dichotomy of perceiving and extended things

Recurrent themes in the aforementioned volumes, as well as some recent 'archaeologies of the contemporary past' (Funari, Hall and Jones (eds.) 1999; Orser 1996; Schmidt and Patterson (eds.) 1996; Buchli and Lucas (eds.) 2001; McGuire 2002), are those of 'the absent present', and the relevance to the problem of probing the limits of traditional options for historical representation (cf. Friedlander (ed.) 1992; Bhabha 1994; Ratner and Abrams 1997; Wilson 1997b).

Wilson's (1997b) work touches on these themes. Building upon the debate about representation that exists for the Holocaust (cf. LaCapra 1992), he argues for new approaches to relationships "between social research (and particularly anthropology) and human rights reporting, so that the texts of researchers might restore local subjectivities, values and memories", as well as to "the wider global social processes in which violence is embedded" (Wilson 1997b: 157). Wilson's view has bearing on studies of not only the 'absent present', but also the diversity of past human life-worlds (for instance, Benjamin 1992 [1940]; Wolf 1982; Fabian 1983; Prazniak and Dirlik (eds.) 2001; Butler 1993; Bhabha 1994; Buchli and Lucas 2001a).

Some of the most difficult challenges facing critiques of dualist paradigms for human nature (agency), knowledge and history in an 'age of globalisation' are brought into relief by discussions of the 'absent present'. Victor Buchli and Gavin Lucas (2001a: 12) write that as "a theme, it resonates with the growing body of literature on post-modernity and post-colonialism ... The realm of the disenfranchised, the subaltern, while usually outside the realm of discourse, is precariously near and as such it is not an unknown object of discourse but rather a non-object, forming the boundaries of the social and enfranchised". Several authors employ notions of 'nature-cultures' and 'hybrids at the interstices' in order to go beyond paradigms structured around such dichotomies as those of subject-object, mind-body, nature-culture, science-values, Western-non-Western, core-periphery, etc. (cf. Latour 1993; Butler 1993; Bhabha 1994).

These new concepts have advantages for focusing our attention on life-worlds that are rendered invisible or relegated to the margins by predominant meta-narratives. However, it may be useful to explore some of their limitations in light of the long history of associations of realms of *subvisibila* and *supravisabilia* with notions of *chance* and *contingency* (cf. De Certeau 1992; Koerner and Perks 2003). It bears stressing how often these images have occurred in response to discrepant experiences of contemporary ideals. For instance, Joseph Leo Koerner (1998), in an article on the role of contingency in the works of Hieronymous Bosch (d. 1516), notes that medieval Christian theologians "coined the term *contingentia* to express the ontological constitution of the world as it was created out of nothing, is sustained only through divine Will, and shall pass away". Bosch's paintings of subvisible and supravisible realms are brimming with entities that, according to Aristotelian logic and classification, are impossible. For Bosch, Koerner explains, the world that we inhabit is not the necessary source of all meaning and value; "it could just as well not have been, or been otherwise, and it owes its existence to God's unconditional being" (Koerner 1998: 264). Painted under the historical conditions that marked the eve of the Reformation, Bosch's pictures of the world in its constitution as that which could be otherwise, argue for contempt of the worldly order of things.

In this light, efforts to address challenges facing critiques of meta-narratives in an 'age of globalisation' on the basis of 'hybrids at the interstices' may shift focus towards the "disinfranchised, the subaltern" (Buchli and Lucas 2001b: 12). But it remains open to question whether they are leading to constructive alternatives to the tensions outlined in parts 1 and 2. On the other hand, archaeology may in the future be able to unpack notions of 'hybrids', and to render explicit hitherto 'absent presents' on the very scales on which the meanings and values of the 'age of globalisation' are generated. Such efforts are likely to be highly relevant to the probing of the limits of dualist historical representation, and to changes in the status of ethics in contemporary epistemology and ontology.

Acknowledgments

Warm thanks to my dear friend and colleague, Andrew Gardner, for inviting me to take part in the 'Agency Uncovered' workshop, and our continuing discussions and debates. Special appreciation to John Barrett for our ongoing discussions and collaborations. A summary of some of the issues discussed in this paper, in relation to a session at the World Archaeological Congress 2003, appeared in the *World Archaeological Bulletin* 17 (2003), 60–68.

References

Adorno, T. 1973 [1963]. *Negative Dialectics*. London: Routledge and Kegan Paul (Translated by E.B. Ashton).

Appadurai, A. 1991. Global ethnoscapes: notes and queries for a transnational anthropology. In R. Fox (ed.) *Recapturing Anthropology: working in the present*, 191–210. Santa Fe, NM: School of American Research Press.

Appadurai, A. 2002 [1996]. Disjuncture and difference in the global cultural economy. In J.X. Inda and R. Rosaldo (eds.) *The Anthropology of Globalization: a reader*, 46–64. Oxford: Blackwell.

Arendt, H. 1963. *Eichman in Jerusalem: a report on the banality of evil*. London: Faber.

Arendt, H. 1977 [1961]. *Between Past and Present*. New York: Penguin.

Arendt, H. 1989 [1958]. *The Human Condition*. Chicago, IL: University of Chicago Press.

Aristotle (384–322 BC). 1941. *The Basic Works of Aristotle*. Oxford: Oxford University Press (Translated by B. Jowett; Edited by R. McKeon).

Atkinson, J.A., Banks, I. and O'Sullivan, J. (eds.) 1997. *Nationalism and Archaeology*. Glasgow: Cruithne Press.

Augustine, Saint, Bishop of Hippo (354–430 AD). 1963. *The City of God [De civitate Dei]*. Oxford: Oxford University Press.

Barnes, B. 2000. *Understanding Agency: social theory and responsible action*. London: Sage Publications.

Barrett, J. 1994. *Fragments from Antiquity: an archaeology of social life*. Oxford: Basil Blackwell.

Barrett, J. 2000. A thesis on agency. In M.-A. Dobres and J.E. Robb (eds.) *Agency in Archaeology*, 61–68. London: Routledge.

Barrett, J. and Koerner, S. 2001. *Views Beyond Dualist Paradigms for Human Nature, History and Archaeological Knowledge*. A seminar in the Department of Archaeology, University of Gothenburg, Sweden, 9–11 May.

Barth, F. 1966. *Models of Social Organization*. London: Royal Anthropological Institute, Occasional Paper 23.

Bell, J.A. 1994. *Reconstructing Prehistory: scientific method in archaeology*. Philadelphia, PA: Temple University Press.

Benjamin, W. 1992 [1940]. Theses on the philosophy of history. In H. Arendt (ed.) *Illuminations: works of Benjamin*, 245–55. London: Fontana Press.

Bhabha, H. 1994. *The Location of Culture*. London: Routledge.

Blumenberg, H. 1983. *The Legitimation of the Modern Age*. Cambridge, MA: MIT Press (Translated by R.M. Wallace).

Bourdieu, P. 1990. *The Logic of Practice*. London: Polity Press (Translated by R. Nice).

Boyer, P. 1990. *Tradition as Truth and Communication: a cognitive description of traditional discourse*. Cambridge: Cambridge University Press.

Boyer, P. 2000. Human cognition and cultural evolution. In H. Moore (ed.) *Anthropological Theory Today*, 206–32. Cambridge: Polity Press.

Brandom, R. 1994. *Making it Explicit: reasoning, representing and discursive commitment*. Cambridge, MA: Harvard University Press.

Braudel, F. 1966 [1958]. *The Mediterranean and the Mediterranean World in the Age of Philip II*, 2 vols. New York: Harper and Row (Translated by S. Reynolds).

Brumfiel, E.M. 1994. Factional competition and political development in the New World: an introduction. In E.M. Brumfiel and J.W. Fox (eds.) *Factional Competition and Political Development in the New World*, 3–13. Cambridge: Cambridge University Press.

Brumfiel, E.M. and Fox, J.W. (eds.) 1994. *Factional Competition and Political Development in the New World*. Cambridge: Cambridge University Press.

Buchli, V. and Lucas, G. 2001a. Presencing absence. In V. Buchli and G. Lucas (eds.) *Archaeologies of the Contemporary Past*, 171–74. London: Routledge.

Buchli, V. and Lucas, G. 2001b. Introduction. In V. Buchli and G. Lucas (eds.) *Archaeologies of the Contemporary Past*, 3–18. London: Routledge.

Buchli, V. and Lucas, G. (eds.) 2001. *Archaeologies of the Contemporary Past*. London: Routledge.

Butler, J. 1993. *Bodies that Matter*. London: Routledge.

Cassirer, E. 1960. *The Logic of the Humanities*. New Haven, CT: Yale University Press (Translated by C. Smith Howe).

Collingwood, R.G. 1956 [1949]. *The Idea of History*. Oxford: Oxford University Press.

Cosmides, L. 1989. The logic of social exchange: has natural selection shaped how humans reason? *Cognition*, 31, 187–276.

Cowan, J.K. 2001. Introduction. In J.K. Cowan, M.B. Dembour and R.A. Wilson (eds.) *Culture and Rights: anthropological perspectives*, 1–26. Cambridge: Cambridge University Press.

Cowan, J.K., Dembour, M.B. and Wilson, R.A. (eds.) 2001. *Culture and Rights: anthropological perspectives*. Cambridge: Cambridge University Press.

De Certeau, M. 1992. *The Mystic Fable*. Chicago, IL: University of Chicago Press.

Descartes, R. 1984–91. *The Philosophical Writings of Descartes* [CSM]. Cambridge: Cambridge University Press (Translated by J. Cottingham, R. Stoothoff and D. Murdoch).

Díaz-Andreu, M. and Champion, T. (eds.) 1996. *Nationalism and Archaeology in Europe*. Boulder, CO: Westview Press.

Dobres, M.-A. and Robb, J.E. 2000. Agency in archaeology: paradigm or platitude? In M.-A. Dobres and J.E. Robb (eds.) *Agency in Archaeology*, 3–17. London: Routledge.

Dobres, M.-A. and Robb, J.E. (eds.) 2000. *Agency in Archaeology*. London: Routledge.

Downing, T.E. and Kushner, G. (eds.) 1988. *Human Rights and Anthropology*. Cambridge, MA: Cultural Survival Inc.

Dupré, L. 1993. *The Passage to Modernity: an essay in the hermeneutics of nature and culture*. New Haven, CT: Yale University Press.

Durkheim, E. 1960 [1914]. The dualism of human nature and its social conditions. In K.H. Wolff (ed.) *Essays on Sociology and Philosophy*, 325–40. New York: Harper.

Elias, N. 1982. *The Civilizing Process*, 2 vols. Oxford: Blackwell (Translated by E. Jephcott).

Elias, N. 1991. *The Society of Individuals*. Oxford: Basil Blackwell (Edited by M. Schröter and translated by E. Jephcott).

Eusebius of Caesarea (ca. 260–339 AD). 1973. *The Ecclesiastical History of Eusebius Pamphilus*. Cambridge: Cambridge University Press (Translated by K. Lake).

Fabian, J. 1983. *Time and the Other: how anthropology creates its object*. New York: Columbia University Press.

Foucault, M. 1980. *Power/Knowledge: selected interviews and other writings 1972–1977*. New York: Pantheon Books (Edited by C. Gordon; Translated by L. Marshall, J. Mepham and K. Soper).

Friedlander, S. (ed.) 1992. *Probing the Limits of Representation: Nazism and the "Final Solution"*. Cambridge, MA: Harvard University Press.

Friedman, J. 1992. The past in the future: history and the politics of identity. *American Anthropologist*, 94:4, 837–59.

Friedman, J. 2001. Indigenous struggles and the discreet charm of the bourgeoisie. In R. Prazniak and A. Dirlik (eds.) *Politics and Place in an Age of Globalization*, 53–70. Lanham, MD: Rowman and Littlefield Publishers.

Funari, P.P.A., Hall, M. and Jones, S. (eds.) 1999. *Historical Archaeology: back from the edge*. London: Routledge.

Funkenstein, A. 1986. *Theology and the Scientific Imagination: from the Middle Ages to the Seventeenth Century*. Princeton, NJ: Princeton University Press.

Gaitta, R. 2000. *A Common Humanity: thinking about love and truth and justice*. London: Routledge.

Geertz, C. 2000. *Available Light: anthropological reflections on philosophical topics*. Princeton, NJ: Princeton University Press.

Gero, J.M. 1991. Who experienced what in prehistory: a narrative explanation from Queyash. In R.W. Preucel (ed.) *Processual and Post-Processual Archaeologies: alternative ways of knowing the past*, 226–39. Carbondale, IL: Center for Archaeological Investigations of the Southern Illinois University Occasional Paper No. 10.

Gero, J.M. 2000. Troubled travels in agency and feminism. In M.-A. Dobres and J.E. Robb (eds.) *Agency in Archaeology*, 34–39. London: Routledge.

Giddens, A. 1979. *Central Problems in Social Theory*. London: Macmillan.

Giddens, A. 1981. Agency, institution, and time-space analysis. In K. Knorr-Cetina and A.V. Cicourel (eds.) *Advances in Social Theory and Method: toward an integration of micro- and macro-sociologies*, 161–75. London: Routledge and Kegan Paul.

Giddens, A. 1990. *The Consequences of Modernity*. Stanford, CA: Stanford University Press.

Gosden, C. 1994. *Social Being and Time*. Oxford: Basil Blackwell.

Graves-Brown, P., Jones, S. and Gamble, C. (eds.) 1996. *Cultural Identity and Archaeology: The Construction of European Communities*. London: Routledge.

Hale, J.R. 1993. *The Civilization of Europe in the Renaissance*. London: Simon and Schuster.

Harvey, D. 1989. *The Condition of Postmodernity*. Oxford: Blackwell.

Hegel, G.W.F. 1975 [1831]. *Lectures on the Philosophy of History*. Cambridge: Cambridge University Press (Translated by H.B. Nisbet).

Hobbes, T. 1962 [1651]. *Leviathan*. New York: Collier Books.

Husserl, E. 1970 [1936]. *The Crisis of European Science and Transcendental Phenomenology*. Evanston, IL: Northwestern University Press.

Inda, J.X. and Rosaldo, R. 2002. Introduction: a world in motion. In J.X. Inda and R. Rosaldo (eds.) *The Anthropology of Globalization: a reader*, 1–34. Oxford: Blackwell.

Inda, J.X. and Rosaldo, R. (eds.) 2002. *The Anthropology of Globalization: a reader*. Oxford: Blackwell.

Ingold, T. 1986. *Evolution and Social Life*. Cambridge: Cambridge University Press.

Johnson, M. 1987. *The Body in the Mind: the bodily basis of meaning, imagination and reason*. Chicago, IL: University of Chicago Press.

Johnson, M. 2000. Self-made men and the staging of agency. In M.-A. Dobres and J.E. Robb (eds.) *Agency in Archaeology*, 213–31. London: Routledge.

Kant, I. 1963 [1784]. Idea of a universal history from a cosmopolitan point of view. In *On History*. Beck, IN: Bobbs-Merrill (Translated by L. White).

Kant, I. 1955 [1790]. *Critique of the Faculty of Judgement*. London: Henry G. Bohn (Translated by J.H. Bernard).

Knorr-Cetina, K. and Cicourel, A.V. (eds.) 1981. *Advances in Social Theory and Method: toward an integration of micro- and macro-sociologies*. London: Routledge and Kegan Paul.

Koerner, J.L. 1998. Bosch's Contingency. In G. v. Graevenitz, O. Marquard, and M. Christen (eds.) *Poetik und Hermeneutik 17 (Kontingenz)*, 245–84. Munich: Wilhem Fink Verlag.

Koerner, S. 2001. Archaeology, nationalism, and problems posed by science/values, epistemology/ontology dichotomies. *World Archaeology Bulletin*, 14 (Aug/Sept), 57–96.

Koerner, S. and Perks, S. 2003. *Contingency, Necessity and the Invisible Things of the World in 20th Century Physics, Art, and the Critique of Meta-Narratives*. Paper in the panel, "20th Century Physics, International Human Rights Legislation, and Conceptions of Agency" in the Association of Social Anthropologists Decennial Conference, University of Manchester, 14–18 July 2003.

Kohl and Fawcett (eds.) 1995. *Nationalism, Politics and the Practice of Archaeology*. Cambridge: Cambridge University Press.

Koyré, A. 1968. *From the Closed World to the Infinite Universe*. Baltimore, MD: John Hopkins University Press.

Kusch, M. 2002. *Knowledge by Agreement: the programme of communitarian epistemology*. Oxford: Clarendon Press.

LaCapra, D. 1992. Representing the Holocaust: reflections on the historian's debate. In S. Friedlander (ed.) *Probing the Limits of Representation: Nazism and the "Final Solution"*, 108–27. Cambridge, MA: Harvard University Press.

Laclau, E. 1990. *New Reflections on the Revolution of Our Time*. London: Verso.

Latour, B. 1993. *We Have Never Been Modern*. Cambridge, MA: Harvard University Press.

Latour, B. 2000 *Pandora's Hope: essays on the reality of science studies*. Cambridge, MA: Harvard University Press.

Locke, J. 1975 [1689]. *An Essay Concerning Human Understanding*. Oxford: Clarendon Press (Edited by P.H. Nidditch).

Marx, K. and Engels, F. 1975 [1846]. *The German Ideology: Collected Works*, 5 vols. New York: International Publishers.

Mattingly, D.J. (ed.) 1997. *Dialogues in Roman Imperialism: power, discourse, and discrepant experiences*. Portsmouth, RI: JRA Supplementary Series 23.

McGuire, J.E. and Tuchanska, B. 2001. *Science Unfettered: a philosophical study in sociohistorical ontology*. Athens, OH: Ohio University Press.

McGuire, R.H. 2002. *Archaeology as Political Action: digging up the Colorado Coal Field War*. Paper presented at the meeting of the Theoretical Archaeology Group, 21–23 December 2002, Manchester, UK.

McManus, P.M. (ed.) 1996. *Archaeological Displays and the Public: museology and interpretations*. London: Institute of Archaeology, University College London.

Miller, D. 1987. *Material Culture and Mass Consumption*. Oxford: Basil Blackwell.

Miller, D. (ed.) 1995. *Worlds Apart: modernity through the prism of the local*. London: Routledge.

Mizoguchi, K. 2002. *An Archaeological History of Japan, 30,000 BC to AD 700*. Philadelphia, PA: University of Pennsylvania Press.

Morgan, L.H. 1963 [1877]. *Ancient Society*. New York: World Publishing Company.

Moore, H. 2000. Ethics and ontology. In M.-A. Dobres and J.E. Robb (eds.) *Agency in Archaeology*, 259–63. London: Routledge.

Moore, J. and Scott, E. (eds.) 1997. *Invisible People and Processes: writing gender and childhood into European archaeology*. Leicester: Leicester University Press.

Newton, I. 1934 [1687]. *Mathematical Principles of Natural Philosophy*. Berkeley, CA: University of California Press (Translated by A. Motte and F. Cajori).

Orser, Jr., C.E. 1996. *A Historical Archaeology of the Modern World*. London: Plenum Books.

Ortner, S.B. 1984. Theory in anthropology since the sixties. *Comparative Studies in Society and History*, 26, 126–66.

Patrik, L.E. 1985. Is there an archaeological record? In M. Schiffer (ed.) *Archaeological Method and Theory, Volume 3*, 27–62. London: Academic Press.

Prazniak, R. and Dirlik, A. (eds.) 2001. *Politics and Place in an Age of Globalization.* Lanham, MD: Rowman and Littlefield Publishers.

Ratner, S.R. and Abrams, J.S. 1997. *Accountability for Human Rights Atrocities in International Law: beyond the Nuremberg legacy.* Oxford: Oxford University Press.

Rorty, R. 1989. *Contingency, Irony, and Solidarity.* Cambridge: Cambridge University Press.

Rudebeck, E. 2000. *Tilling Nature Harvesting Culture: exploring images of the human being in the transition to farming.* Stockholm: Almqvist and Wiksell International.

Said, E. 1993. *Culture and Imperialism.* London: Chatto and Wardus.

Schmidt, P.R. and Patterson, T.C. (eds.) 1996. *Making Alternative Histories: the practice of archaeology and history in non-western settings.* Santa Fe, NM: School of American Research Press.

Schnapp, A. 1996. *The Discovery of the Past: the origins of archaeology.* London: British Museum Press.

Shapin, S. and Schaffer, S. 1985. *Leviathan and the Vacuum Pump: Hobbes, Boyle and the experimental life,* including a translation of Thomas Hobbes's *Dialogue Physicus de Natura Aeris* by S. Shaffer. Princeton, NJ: Princeton University Press.

Shennan, S. (ed.) 1989. *Archaeological Approaches to Cultural Identity.* London: Unwin Hyman (One World Archaeology 10).

Stone, P.G. and MacKenzie, R. (eds.) 1990. *The Excluded Past: archaeology in education.* London: Unwin Hyman Ltd.

Thomas, J. 1996. *Time, Culture and Identity.* London: Routledge.

Toulmin, S. 1990. *Cosmopolis: the hidden agenda of modernity.* Chicago, IL: University of Chicago Press.

Trigger, B. 1984. Alternative archaeologies: nationalist, colonialist, imperialist. *Man* (NS), 19, 355–70.

Trigger, B. 1995. Romanticism, nationalism, and archaeology. In P.L. Kohl and C. Fawcett (eds.) *Nationalism, Politics and the Practice of Archaeology,* 263–79. Cambridge: Cambridge University Press.

Tsing, A. 2002. The global situation. In J.X. Inda and R. Rosaldo (eds.). *The Anthropology of Globalization: a reader,* 453–86. Oxford: Blackwell.

Tusa, A. and Tusa, J. 1995. *The Nuremberg Trial.* London: Macmillan.

Weber, M. 1958 [1904]. *The Protestant Ethic and the Spirit of Capitalism.* New York: Scribner's Press.

Wilk, R. 1995. Learning to be local in Belize: global systems of common difference. In D. Miller (ed.) *Worlds Apart: modernity through the prism of the local,* 110–33. London: Routledge.

Wilson, R.A. 1997a. Human rights, culture and context: an introduction. In R.A. Wilson (ed.) *Human Rights, Culture and Context: anthropological perspectives,* 1–27. London: Pluto Press.

Wilson, R.A. 1997b. Representing human rights violations: social contexts and subjectivities. In R.A. Wilson (ed.) *Human Rights, Culture and Context: anthropological perspectives,* 135–60. London: Pluto Press.

Wilson, R.A. (ed.) 1997. *Human Rights, Culture and Context: anthropological perspectives.* London: Pluto Press.

Wittgenstein, L. 1958. *Philosophical Investigations.* New York: Macmillan (3rd edition in both English and German, translated by G.E.M. Anscombe).

Wolf, E. 1982. *Europe and the People Without History.* Berkeley, CA: University of California Press.

Wolf, E. 2001. *Pathways of Power: building an anthropology of the modern world.* Berkeley, CA: University of California Press.

COMMENTARY

CHAPTER 12

AGENCY, STRUCTURE AND ARCHAEOLOGICAL PRACTICE

Matthew Johnson

The concept of agency is, as this collection of papers demonstrates, one of the most productive and exciting themes in archaeological thinking today. I want to argue in this discussion that, at heart, the idea of agency is very simple and very strong. This does not mean that, once accepted, the implications of agency for archaeological theory and practice are not very complex; and, perhaps more importantly, it does not mean that the issues agency raises for archaeological interpretation are not extremely difficult for archaeologists to resolve in a coherent or positive manner.

I suggest that this extreme simplicity, and this extreme difficulty, resides in the tension between two propositions. Both propositions are 'true', but each also necessarily comes into conflict with the other.

POTS ARE MADE BY PEOPLE

The archaeological record is made up of, among other things, the direct and indirect results of countless individual actions – the choice whether to zig or zag on ceramic decoration, the angle of retouch on a flint blade, the decision to dig a pit here rather than there. Unless the laws of nature were radically different in the past (that is, if we accept a uniformitarian assumption) then the archaeological record was created, at least in large part, by the actions of individual human beings.

It is worth exploring the limits of this first proposition. The most obvious limit is that archaeologists do not always deal with the detritus of human beings, that is *homo sapiens sapiens*. Where archaeologists examine the archaeological record of early hominids, there is scope for the understanding of different ideas of identity, of agency, and of culture. Giddens' presuppositions of knowledgable social agents operating in a certain way do not necessarily hold, just as they do not necessarily hold for the study of non-human primates. Though it is written from a very different theoretical orientation than my own, I suggest this is why the evolutionary thinking of Palaeolithic archaeologists such as Mithen (1998) is so important to the project of archaeology, not to mention the project of understanding what makes us human. Again, Gravina's observations on 'Neanderthal social relations' in this volume encompass the potential and the difficulties in this area of research.

A second limit to our first proposition is the question of to what extent the archaeological record is the intended consequence of human actions. Most would agree that humans intentionally make pots of a certain form, even if some details are down to 'motor habit variation' or related practices. In the Introduction, Gardner discusses the question of whether different theoretical models over-privilege habitual action; my point here is that to the extent that they do over-privilege habit, the need to extend the bounds of agency is more apparent. However, while the digging of a pit and the deposition of 'rubbish' is an intentional act, the variety of what Schiffer would call n-transforms which succeed it is arguably not so. Again, it is at this margin that we find some of the most productive work in archaeology today, in the understanding of deposits as the result of intentional 'structured deposition' rather than simply rubbish pits, or in fragmentation (Chapman 2000).

A third limit, it might be argued, is one of scale. Pots and stone tools might be created by individual agents but it is difficult to say the same of very large-scale structures, such as pyramids and castles. Again, I suggest that much recent work has focused on this very margin. For example, my own work on castles has stressed how any one structure, however huge, represents a meeting-point of many different agencies, often involved in contestation: the owner, the craftsmen involved at different levels in any building project, the community at large involved in the creation and maintenance of oral tradition surrounding the structure (Johnson 2002: 181). More generally, the concept of heterarchy in particular, so popular in recent Americanist accounts of early state societies, focuses on the way very large-scale social and material structures and transformations articulate with intentions and social strategies of groups and individuals at a much smaller scale (Brumfiel 1992).

The problem of scale occurs in time as well as space: that is, the maintenance of a long-term cultural 'tradition' that is uniform across a community, region or wider area might be argued to be somehow beyond 'agency'. Such an attitude is perhaps unwittingly echoed in much avowedly atheoretical archaeology, when lack of change and/or cultural uniformity is ascribed to an untheorised 'innate conservatism' on the part of craftsmen. However, the thrust of recent thought has been that such cultural traditions do not exist *sui generis*, are themselves statements of identities played out at individual, group and community levels (as explored in Pauketat (ed.) 2001).

To conclude: an exploration of the margins of agency has shown that much recent work has actually expanded the purview of agency theory into new areas: mindless breaking of pots and burying of rubbish have become intentional acts of fragmentation and structured deposition, massive monuments built by monolithic managerial elites in early state societies have become sites for multiple and conflicting agencies, tradition has become a conscious strategy. So it is not merely a truism that pots are made by people; this statement expands and deepens its validity and applicability as archaeological thought progresses.

Agency, then, *in theory*, is absolutely central to our understanding of the archaeological record.

HOWEVER, POTS NEED TO BE CLASSIFIED

In practice, however, our understanding of the archaeological record depends very fundamentally on a series of concepts that bypass or even contradict agency completely. I am thinking here of the ideas that have historically conditioned archaeology, that arguably make us distinctive as a discipline, that were used to bring archaeology together as a discrete and coherent body of knowledge in the 19th century and which continue to be part of the basic vocabulary of archaeological thinking today.

Let us take as an example the division of time into discrete periods and spaces based on the uniformity or similarity (whether real or supposed: Shennan 1978) of material culture within those periods and spaces. Historians of archaeology have traced many times how 19th century evolutionary ideas, in which it was implicitly or explicitly maintained that all societies went through the same stages of development albeit at different rates in different parts of the world, gave way to the culture-historical description of particular cultures in particular times and places. My point here is that both early evolutionary and culture-historical conceptions of the archaeological record were remarkably totalising; they both bypassed agency, and continue to bypass agency, in a quite complete way. In both, social agents really are pawns of wider historical processes, whether of technological or social evolution on the one hand, or Gordon Childe's patchwork quilt of cultures moving around on the other. Similar comments could be made about concepts such as those of assemblage and types; and about many of the basic principles of field recording and classification of sites; and concepts such as that of horizon. Bruce Trigger first pointed out how culture-historical ways of looking at the archaeological record contributed to a view of Native American prehistory as static, unchanging and even stagnant (1980), by implication therefore agency-free.

The problem here is that all these concepts can be shown to be theoretically flawed, but they work – or, more accurately, archaeology has repeatedly found itself unable to write a coherent and plausible account of the past without reference to these concepts. In the early history of archaeology, concepts of period, type, culture and assemblage were necessary organising principles in the task of making some kind of coherent order out of a great jumble of artefacts, most obviously in the case of Thomsen's three age system or Childe's reduction of Eastern European prehistory to order. We might argue over the extent to which it is still necessary to have such organising principles, but the truth is that we cannot now simply do away with them.

Much recent work on agency can be argued to be parasitic upon the very totalising frameworks it is trying to get away from. Gardner's chapter is perhaps the best example of this. It is a subtle, nuanced and convincing account of small-scale actions. However, I doubt that an audience could make any sense of it, or fit Gardner's analysis into a wider archaeological understanding, without at least a schoolchild's knowledge of the 'Decline and Fall of the Roman Empire'. His actors live out their agency within the late Roman fort of Caernarfon, a building that is both a standardised, top-down element of social and material structure and also the focus of an overwhelming archaeological tradition of classification within the culture-historical framework. Similarly, I have tried to stress the importance of local context and the actions of individuals in medieval and postmedieval England, but have always found myself inexorably drawn back to much wider and abstracted models of the feudal/capitalist transition when pressed for a wider explanation of these contexts and actions (see, for example, Johnson 1996: esp. 42–43).

We see this tension in the chapters by Morris and Gravina. Justin Morris' chapter struck me as a very careful and thoughtful discussion of an archaeological dataset; I nevertheless disagreed with its conclusions. He writes that "an understanding of the motivations of individuals seems to be reliant on an archaeological record that differentiates between the specific actions of individuals". His reservations are echoed by Gravina in his comments on the inability of the data to confront questions of agency in Middle Palaeolithic sites. My response is that Morris' production sequence and the detritus it left behind were and are *by definition* the product of agency, as discussed above; if the data apparently lack a sufficiently fine level of resolution to look at individual action, this tells us something about the nature of tradition and of craft practice rather than being an 'obstacle'. But Morris is right in a wider sense, namely that, as I have argued, our existing conceptual apparatus for the understanding of this material directs us towards larger categories and the task of understanding agency is methodologically so complex in this case as to be of great difficulty.

I am struck here by the similarity of 'agency' as an intellectual project to the project of an evolutionary archaeology as advocated by Robert Dunnell and his students (Dunnell 1980; Barton and Clark (eds.) 1997). Dunnell set out an agenda for a fully scientific, evolutionary archaeology. He set off from a strong and tightly argued theoretical position – namely, that sociocultural evolution owed its intellectual ancestry to Spencer rather than Darwin; that a genuinely thorough-going Darwinian approach to the archaeological record had hardly been attempted; and that such an approach was the only way forward for anyone attempting seriously to create a science of archaeology. However, even after several decades of work by Dunnell and his students, convincing and coherent accounts of the past have yet to be created by this school (to the extent that others sympathetic to an evolutionary or ecological position, such as Lake and Shennan in this volume, make little reference to their work). I suggest that this is in part down to the implications of Dunnell's position, which are quite logical but extremely radical: namely, that all conventional archaeological concepts of period, type, etc. have to be jettisoned. And as with agency theory, this wholesale abandonment of the centuries-old traditions of archaeological enquiry proves almost impossible to do in practice.

I am also struck by the similarity of this archaeological conundrum to that of traditional sociology. Sociologists have long acknowledged that the action models of micro-sociology (most classically Goffman) and those of large-scale social theory (Marx, Durkheim, Weber) have never been satisfactorily integrated (most painfully between the different elements of Max Weber's thought). Giddens has claimed to have done this through structuration theory, but it is possible to believe in the value and utility of structuration theory without accepting this larger claim. The first half of Koerner's chapter traces some of this terrain also.

There is, of course, a monumental irony here. Agency theorists have stressed the importance of structure – that while social actors are not pawns or prisoners, they are nevertheless heavily constrained by the mental and material structures of the world they live in, in particular those enduring from the past. Followers of Giddens have further stressed that social actors are aware, but only imperfectly aware, of these structures. I am arguing here that, as practicing archaeologists, while we are not pawns or prisoners, we are heavily constrained by the mental and material structures of the discipline within which we work and which gave us our mental training and intellectual apparatus. We are aware of these structures, though we are probably not as perfectly aware of them as we would like to be. Indeed, if the arguments of Handley and Schadla-Hall hold any validity, we are quite unaware of and powerless before those structures in their political dimension – even if behind those structures lurk a few (unnamed) individuals.

Bill Sillar's chapter offers a particular twist on this observation. Sillar comes very close to attributing active power to the ancestors, saints and deities of the Andean world. Where other archaeologists find themselves constrained by traditions of enquiry that are arguably Eurocentric and were certainly colonialist in their origins, Sillar finds himself constrained by his close engagement through the day-to-day practice of ethnographic method with the Andean world-view. I cannot accept his attribution of agency to these deities, but I have to acknowledge that he might well respond that the archaeologist working within Western traditions is in no better or more authoritative a position from which to make judgements on agency.

I think that the perspective on agency I have tried to outline here – that is, of a pressing theme in archaeological enquiry pulled in one direction by theory and in another by practice and tradition – helps us move beyond some of the divides seen in existing discussion of agency, most obviously between broadly processual and post-processual conceptions of the term. The chapters in this volume continue a debate started in the Dobres and Robb volume (2000). In her concluding discussion to that volume, Elizabeth Brumfiel divided the papers into those who see agency in a cross-cultural way, and those who see it as constructed differently in different historical circumstances (2000: 249–50). My work in that volume was placed firmly in the latter camp, as its central thrust was an empirical examination of how, in historically contingent circumstances, the notion of the autonomous social agent was constructed in the Renaissance.

I was expecting therefore to find plenty to debate in the chapters by Lake and Shennan in this volume; I was both surprised and perplexed to find little in those chapters to specifically disagree with. I suspect that the fissures would appear when the debate moved to discussions of concrete archaeological problems, as the conclusion to Lake's chapter hints. This is what I think happened in the Mithen-Thomas debate, as Lake accurately recounts: the sharpness of the divide was accentuated not merely by a different intellectual ancestry, but also by the disjuncture created by a concretely different way of thinking about the Mesolithic compared to that of the Neolithic, two periods that, as Thomas pointed out at the time, actually do not empirically look very different from each other in many respects. I also suspect that the closer one would get to concrete archaeological case studies, the more the Lake/Shennan view would have to be complemented by a more hermeneutic reading of the particular context in order to provide an account of the archaeological record that is convincing and coherent. In a sense, this is what Peter Jordan does in his chapter – he identifies the utility of ideas of efficiency and adaptive strategy in understanding forager behaviour, but when confronted by the archaeological reality of the Nämforsen carvings goes on to develop a much more hermeneutic perspective.

One way forward in the study of agency, then, may be to forsake extended theorising and instead examine the potential and constraints of specific cases where agency, structure and power intersect. Thus Astrid Lindenlauf looks at the intersection of the individual, the group and ideas of cleanliness and dirt. I learnt from this chapter that, in this specific social context as in others, cultural ideas and metaphors could be deployed and manipulated by different groups and at different levels within a social system, and this suggested to me that one way forward is the empirical examination of different levels of historical process beyond simply agency versus structure.

I would argue then, in conclusion, that many of the ideas and debates over agency are going to be moved forward by two strategies. First, we need to bring into focus existing ways of thinking about the archaeological record, and acknowledge the importance of enduring structures, almost as a form of *habitus*, on our work. Secondly, we need to return to concrete archaeological case studies and ask how, in this or that specific situation, ideas of agency help us produce better, more complete, fuller understandings of the archaeological record. The chapters in this volume do this, and move discussions of agency forward in both theory and practice.

References

Barton, C.M. and Clark, G.A. (eds.) 1997. *Rediscovering Darwin: evolutionary theory in archaeological explanation*. Arlington, VA: American Anthropological Association (Papers of the American Anthropological Association 7).

Brumfiel, E.M. 1992. Distinguished lecture in archaeology: breaking and entering the ecosystem – gender, class and faction steal the show. *American Anthropologist*, 94, 551–67.

Brumfiel, E.M. 2000. On the strategy of choice: agency studies as a research stratagem. In M.-A. Dobres and J.E. Robb (eds.) *Agency in Archaeology*, 249–55. London: Routledge.

Chapman, J.C. 2000. *Fragmentation in Archaeology: pots, places and broken objects in the prehistory of South-Eastern Europe*. London: Routledge.

Dobres, M.-A. and Robb, J.E. (eds.) 2000. *Agency in Archaeology*. London: Routledge.

Dunnell, R.C. 1980. Evolutionary theory and archaeology. In M. Schiffer (ed.) *Advances in Archaeological Method and Theory*, 3, 35–99. New York: Academic Press.

Johnson, M.H. 1996. *An Archaeology of Capitalism*. Oxford: Blackwell.

Johnson, M.H. 2002. *Behind the Castle Gate: From Medieval to Renaissance*. London: Routledge.

Mithen, S. 1998. *The Prehistory of the Mind: a search for the origins of art, religion and science*. London: Phoenix.

Pauketat, T.R. (ed.) 2001. *The Archaeology of Traditions: agency and history before and after Columbus*. Gainesville, FL: University Press of Florida.

Shennan, S. 1978. Archaeological 'cultures': an empirical investigation. In I. Hodder (ed.)
    The Spatial Organisation of Cultures, 113–39. London: Duckworth.
Trigger, B.G. 1980. Archaeology and the image of the American Indian. *American Antiquity*,
    45, 662–76.

Index